MASTERS
and MEN

Cover art by

Jane A. Evans

MASTERS and MEN

*The Human Story in the Mahatma Letters
(a fictionalized account)*

By Virginia Hanson

*This publication made possible
with the assistance of the Kern Foundation*

**The Theosophical Publishing House
Wheaton, Ill. U.S.A.
Madras, India/London, England**

A Quest book. Published by the Theosophical Publishing House, a department of the Theosophical Society in America.

Library of Congress Cataloging in Publication Data

Hanson, Virginia.
    Masters and men.

    Bibliography: p.
    Includes index.
    1. Sinnett, Alfred Percy, 1840-1921—Fiction.
2. Blavatsky, Helene Petrovna Hahn-Hahn, 1831-1891—
Fiction. I. Title.
PZ3.H1998Mas   [PS3515.A53644]   813'.52   79-3665
ISBN 0-8356-0534-5 (pbk.)

Printed in the United States of America

To all those, known and unknown, who have kept alive the torch of the Wisdom down the darkened corridors of time.

Contents

"We are not gods, and even our chiefs—they hope."
                —*The Mahatma Letters to A. P. Sinnett*

Probably no one who takes up this book will be unaware of what the *Mahatma Letters* are. The compilation of letters, addressed almost exclusively to Mr. A. P. Sinnett, prominent Anglo-Indian journalist, carefully preserved by him, and published under the title *The Mahatma Letters to A. P. Sinnett*, constitutes one of the most remarkable volumes in theosophical literature. Unfortunately, with few exceptions, it represents only one side of a unique correspondence, although in any thorough study of the book, one gains many hints of the other, unrecorded, part to which the published letters are in reply.

The story that unfolds as one reads the letters in chronological order (which, regrettably from one point of view, is not the arrangement in the book) is inextricably bound up with the history of the Theosophical Society during the years immediately following the transfer of its headquarters from New York to India. The roots of the story can be traced back to earlier events, but because of the almost inexhaustible wealth of material available, a line must be drawn somewhere. Many details, and even references to individuals, which in strict historical perspective should be included, must be omitted. The aim has been to follow the main thread of the story with some continuity and to preserve those elements which seem to give it the greatest meaning and substance.

This is not a history. Nor is it fiction. It is a story set in a historical framework, dealing with people who actually lived and events which actually took place. Since it *is* a story rather than a literal recitation of events, some fictional devices are inevitable, for the exigencies of storytelling are as demanding and as rigorous in their own way as are those of recording history; every writer of fictionalized history takes some liberties in the name of "literary license." There is, however, no imagined person or event; the facts are there, and it is the storyteller's belief that in no instance has the spirit of those facts been violated. Authentic accounts have been drawn upon, quoted from, and indeed form the basic fabric on which the fictional elements are, one might say, embroidered, but embroidered in colors and designs determined by the nature of the fabric.

A chronological listing of the *Letters* is included in this volume, and it is strongly recommended that this be used in any study of their content. For this listing I owe a debt of gratitude to Mr. George E. Linton, with whom I collaborated in the preparation of *A Readers Guide to the Mahatma Letters*. A new and carefully worked out chronology prepared by Mr. Linton appeared in that book. A few slight alterations have been made in the present listing, but basically it is the same. With his meticulous engineer's approach, Mr. Linton studied the originals of the *Letters* held by irrevocable deed in the British Museum in London.

Their presence in that prestigious institution is in itself of special interest. On the death of Mr. A. P. Sinnett, to whom most of the *Letters* were addressed, they were turned over to his Executrix, Miss Maud Hoffman. She later engaged Mr. Trevor Barker to arrange and edit them for publication. After the book was in print, Mr. Barker was faced with the problem of what to do with the priceless originals. I am obliged to Mrs. Elsie Benjamin, one of the Trustees of the Mahatma Letters Trust in London, for information passed on by Mr. Barker concerning the solution of the dilemma. The time, Mrs. Benjamin writes, was shortly after the publication of the book, *Who Wrote the Mahatma Letters?* by the brothers Hare, which attempted to show that H.P. Blavatsky and not the Mahatmas was the author. "The war came," Mrs. Benjamin continues, "and Trevor wanted to present the letters to the British Museum, so he took them to the Keeper of Rare Manuscripts. Trevor, always leaning over backward to be 150% honest, told the official about the book and suggested that he read it and make up his own mind concerning the genuineness of the Letters before accepting them. Mr. Barker was asked to return in a week. He did so, at which time the Keeper of Rare Manuscripts said enthusiastically, 'Genuine, Mr. Barker, definitely very genuine!'"

It seems unnecessary in these days to belabor the question of the existence of Mahatmas, or "Masters"—those individuals who have progressed so far beyond ordinary humanity as to represent an evolutionary goal of tremendous power and attraction. That they still have human characteristics is made quite clear in the *Letters* themselves, for it is affirmed repeatedly, in effect, that they are men, not gods. Yet it cannot but be apparent that they are also very much more than men in the commonly accepted sense.

In a letter written to a friend on July 1, 1890 and published in *The Theosophist* for September 1951, H. P. Blavatsky commented: "Their knowledge and learning are immense, and their personal holiness of life is still greater—still they are mortal men and none of them 1,000 years old, as imagined by some."

At one time, in conversation with the author Charles Johnston, when the latter asked her about her own Master's age, she replied: "My dear, I cannot tell you exactly, for I do not know. But this I will tell you. I met him first when I was twenty. . . He was at the very prime of manhood then. I am an old woman now, but he has not aged a day. He is still in the prime of manhood. That is all I know. You may draw your own conclusions."

When Mr. Johnston persisted and asked whether the Mahatmas had discovered the elixir of life, she replied seriously: "That is no fable. It is only the veil hiding a real occult process, warding off age and dissolution for periods which would seem fabulous, so I will not mention them. The secret is this: for every man there is a climacteric, when he must draw near to death: if he has squandered his life-powers there is no escape for him; but if he has lived according to the law, he may pass through and so continue in the same body almost indefinitely."

Most of the *Letters* are over the signature of the Mahatma Koot Hoomi, usually signed simply "K.H." A Kashmiri Brahmin by birth, at the time of the correspondence he was a Buddhist. Koot Hoomi is a mystical name which he instructed H.P.B. to use in connection with his correspondence with Mr. Sinnett. It is possible that his real name was Nisi Kanta Chattopadhyaya, as that seems to have been the name by which he was known when he was attending at least one European University. He was fluent in both English and French and was sometimes affectionately spoken of by the Mahatma Morya as "my Frenchified K.H."

At one time, under special circumstances, the Mahatma Morya took over the correspondence temporarily. He too used only his initial as a signature. "He was a Rajput by birth," said H.P.B., "one of the old warrior race of the Indian desert, the finest and handsomest nation in the world." He was "a giant, six feet eight, and splendidly built; a superb type of manly beauty." The Mahatma K.H. referred to him humorously as "my bulky brother." He was not proficient in English and spoke of himself as using words and phrases "lying idle in my friend's brain"—meaning, of course, the brain of the Mahatma K.H.

It is assumed that readers of this book will know something of the general background of the Theosophical Society. The account of how H. P. Blavatsky and Col. Henry Steel Olcott—its principal founders—were brought together for so uncertain an undertaking is told in Chapter I of the First Series of *Old Diary Leaves,* Olcott's delightful memoirs. The interested student can do no better than to read the six volumes of these memoirs for a masterly first-hand account of significant events from the time of that meeting to December of 1905, a little over a year before Col. Olcott died.

The first three years of the Society's existence form no essential part of the story in this book, save perhaps as indicating the character of the founders. They were, says Olcott, "three years of struggles; of obstacles surmounted; of crude plans partly worked out; at literary labours; of desertions of friends; of encounters with adversaries; of the laying of broad foundations for the structure that in time was destined to arise for the gathering of the nations, but the possibility of which was then unsuspected."

The first year of the Society's activities in India was to see the beginning of the correspondence with which this story deals. Most significant was making the acquaintance of Mr. Alfred Percy Sinnett, editor of the Allahabad *Pioneer,* a leading Anglo-Indian newspaper, and another gentleman, Mr. Allan O. Hume, member of the government and a noted ornithologist who maintained an impressive ornithological museum at his home in Simla.

Several historic milestones were reached during that year. Especially important was the establishment of the magazine, *The Theosophist,* to which the Mahatmas themselves, particularly the Mahatma Koot Hoomi, later contributed.

Also notable was the addition to the headquarters staff of Damodar K. Mavalankar, member of a wealthy Indian family who had received an excellent education in English and who went so far as to abandon caste in order to devote himself to the work of the Theosophical Society. He is spoken of as one of the "chief architects" of the Society. Col. Olcott wrote, in *Old Diary Leaves*, of how he had "thrown himself heart and soul into the work with a devotion which could not be surpassed." For a biography of this young man see *Damodar and the Pioneers of the Theosophical Movement* by Sven Eek, Theosophical Publishing House, Adyar, 1965.

Many other individuals play a part in the story. They will walk on the stage, stay for a shorter or longer time, and then disappear, having made their contributions to, or impacts upon, the course of events. As *dramatis personae* they are as interesting and, at times, as strange and bizarre a collection of human beings as one is likely to find in any account, whether fact or fiction. As Col. Olcott himself expressed this idea at the close of his first year in India: "To turn over the leaves of my Diary for 1879, and see how and when our long-tried and often famous colleagues came into the current of our lives, is really like watching the entrances and exits of actors in a play; and most instructive it is to trace back to the causes which brought them into the Society, and the others which in many cases threw them out of it."

Acknowledgements

In sending forth what it is hoped will be a contribution to a greater understanding of a unique and too-neglected book, my deep appreciation is expressed to all those writers who have left such priceless records of the Theosophical Society and of some of its notable members; to Mary Doyle McCain, who awakened my interest in the *Letters* by presenting me with a copy of the volume as a Christmas gift in 1951; to Mr. Wayne Montgomery and Miss Mary Jo Schneider in the library at Olcott, the headquarters of the Theosophical Society in America, for so promptly and courteously supplying me with needed references, often on very short notice; to Mr. Daniel Caldwell of Tucson, Arizona, an indefatigable student of the *Letters,* who has been kind enough to send me valuable items, especially in connection with the chronology but also occasionally shedding light on other facets; to those students at the Krotona School of Theosophy whose sustained interest in the *Letters* during the two years in which we delved into them together proved an ongoing inspiration to me; to Mr. Boris de Zirkoff, compiler and editor of the *H. P. Blavatsky Collected Writings,* who never failed me when I called on him for information; and to Miss Joy Mills, my esteemed colleague and friend, whose encouragement and counsel made it possible for me to complete the work. To many others—friends and acquaintances—who have expressed interest in the project and thus stimulated my often faltering intentions, my appreciation and gratitude go in full measure.

Virginia Hanson

List of Abbreviations

(The following abbreviations are used in Footnotes and References)

Autobiography   *Autobiography of Alfred Percy Sinnett* (unpublished)

CW   *H. P. Blavatsky Collected Writings*, ed. by Boris de Zirkoff; Adyar and Wheaton: Theosophical Publishing House

Damodar   *Damodar and the Pioneers of Theosophical Movement*, by Sven Eek; Adyar: Theosophical Publishing House, 1965

Daylight   *When Daylight Comes*, A Biography of Helena Petrovna Blavatsky, by Howard Murphet; Wheaton: Theosophical Publishing House, 1975

Early Days   *The Early Days of Theosophy in Europe* by A. P. Sinnett; London, Theosophical Publishing House, Ltd., 1922

Guide   *A Readers Guide to the Mahatma Letters* by George E. Linton and Virginia Hanson; Adyar: Theosophical Publishing House, 1972

Guest   *My Guest—H. P. Blavatsky* by Francesca Arundale; Adyar: Theosophical Publishing House, 1932

Hammer   *Hammer on the Mountain*, The Life of Henry Steel Olcott, by Howard Murphet; Wheaton: Theosophical Publishing House, 1972

LBS   *The Letters of H. P. Blavatsky to A. P. Sinnett*, ed. by A. Trevor Barker, London: T. Fisher Unwin, Ltd., 1925; Facsimile Edition, Pasadena: Theosophical University Press, 1973

LMW   *Letters from the Masters of the Wisdom*, First and Second Series, ed. by C. Jinarajadasa; Adyar: Theosophical Publishing House, 1973

ML*   *The Mahatma Letters to A. P. Sinnett*, ed. by A. Trevor Barker; Adyar: Theosophical Publishing House, 1923, 1926, 1962

MTL   *The Mahatmas and Their Letters* by Geoffrey A. Barborka; Adyar: Theosophical Publishing House, 1973

*References in ML are to page numbers, not to the numbers of the *Letters*. Page numbers in different editions are indicated by a separating diagonal line; the number before the diagonal is in the page in the first and second editions; the number following the diagonal is the page in the third edition.

ABBREVIATIONS

ODL   *Old Diary Leaves* by Henry Steel Olcott; 6 vol.; Adyar: Theosophical Publishing House, 1949

OW   *The Occult World* by A. P. Sinnett; London: Theosophical Publishing House. *All references herein are to the 9th edition, published in 1969 and containing later material than found in the original edition of 1881.*

Reminiscences *Reminiscences of H. P. Blavatsky and The Secret Doctrine* by Countess Constance Wachtmeister, Quest Edition; Wheaton: Theosophical Publishing House, 1976

"Report"   *A Report of Observations Made During a Nine-Month Stay at the Headquarters of The Theosophical Society* by Dr. Franz Hartmann; Madras: Graves, Cookson & Co., 1884. (Quotation marks to distinguish this Report from the Report of the Society for Psychical Research.)

SH   *A Short History of The Theosophical Society* by Josephine Ransom; Adyar: Theosophical Publishing House, 1938

Theosophy   *How Theosophy Came to Me* by C. W. Leadbeater; Adyar: Theosophical Publishing House, 1975

Prologue

It is doubtful whether Col. Henry Steel Olcott and Madame Helena Petrovna Blavatsky had more than the most nebulous idea of how to carry out their mission when they set sail from New York for London, en route to India, on December 17, 1878. The principal founders of the Theosophical Society, they had, with William Q. Judge—a third founding member and Counselor for the Society—kept the organization alive when interest in its newness and fascination with what some regarded as its strangeness gradually lost their original intensity. The voyagers meant to see that this waning interest did not bring about the demise of the Society altogether.

Madame Blavatsky had published *Isis Unveiled* (the first impression of which sold out in nine days), had fought with the Spiritualists over the rationale of their phenomena, and—as was to be her wont throughout her life—had made devoted friends and bitter enemies. Because she never bothered to explain her actions—the motivations for which were among her best-kept secrets—she subjected herself to the most vituperative criticism; at the same time she enchanted many with her wit and charm and with the vitality which not only emanated from her but with which she seemed able to infuse those about her.

Col. Olcott had distinguished himself by exposing and helping to eliminate graft in the Army and Navy Departments during the American Civil War and as a result of his subsequent appointment as special investigator into the assassination of President Lincoln. He had further made a name for himself by writing articles for New York newspapers and by a work on scientific agriculture which became a classic in its field; later,

1

as a lawyer, he had become a specialist in Customs, Revenue, and Insurance cases, with a large and lucrative practice. He was leaving all this behind to take up residence in a strange country and devote his considerable abilities to the cause which had become the passion of his life: the dissemination of Theosophy and the promotion of the Theosophical Society.

Through correspondence, the "Theosophical Twins," as they were sometimes called, had formed an alliance with an already established group in India, the Arya Samaj, whose aims and objectives were similar to those of the Theosophical Society. This arrangement, they felt, would immediately give them entree into the Indian community, and they meant to re-establish the headquarters of the Theosophical Society in that ancient country. It was a country dear to Madame Blavatsky from earlier years, and perhaps equally dear to Col. Olcott, since they would be closer to those Mahatmas with whom they had been in touch and whose emissaries they confidently believed themselves to be.

With them on the SS *Canada* were two other members of the Theosophical Society, Miss Rosa Bates, a schoolteacher who hoped to escape from the tedium of trying to force knowledge into unwilling young heads, and Mr. Edward Wimbridge, a designer and architect who had fallen upon difficult times. Both were hoping to improve their circumstances as well as share in what promised to be a rather exciting adventure. Their commitment to Theosophy was tentative.

The departure from New York seemed anything but propitious. Although they boarded the SS *Canada* on December 17, the ship did not get away from the wharf until 2:30 p.m. on the 18th, and then, having lost the tide, had to anchor off Coney Island and cross the Sandy Hook bar only at noon on the 19th.[1] That Madame Blavatsky herself was less than optimistic is attested by an entry she made in the Colonel's diary on the day on which they finally moved out to sea: "Magnificent day. Clear, blue, cloudless, but devilish cold. Fits of fear lasted until 11. The body is difficult to manage." In a letter to her sister written in London on January 14, 1879, with the first leg of their journey completed, she said: "I shall write from Bombay *if I ever reach it.*"[2]

The *Canada* entered the British Channel "in a sea of fog on New Year's Day, 1879."[3] The Colonel felt this was "typical of our unmanifested future." Nevertheless, the time spent in London was not without encouraging results. A British Theosophical Society had been formed, and Olcott presided at the meeting at which the officers were elected. The little group from New York made many friends and managed to stimulate a considerable interest in Theosophy during their stay.

Their hosts on this visit were Dr. and Mrs. Billings, whose home was the rallying center for London Theosophists at that time. The days were "spiced with phenomena by H.P.B." wrote the Colonel.*[4]

It was here, too, on one evening, that H.P.B. tried to explain to the group something of the mystery of her personality—a mystery which remains one, in spite of her attempted explanation and many subsequent efforts made by others to probe the secret. Even Col. Olcott, who knew her so well, commented much later, ". . . to me, her most intimate colleague, she was from the first and continued to the end an insoluble riddle. How much of her waking life was that of a responsible personality, how much that of a body worked by an overshadowing entity, I do not know."[5]

The party of four from America left London for India on January 18, 1879. This voyage too began inauspiciously. The SS *Speke Hall* on which they embarked was dirty and disagreeable; the damp tapestries and carpets in the saloon and cabins smelled abominably; and a dismal and disheartening downpour did little to lighten their spirits. The vessel was so heavily loaded that the deck was almost at the water's level and, in the rough seas through which they later struggled, every wave washed over it. During the worst part of the journey, H.P.B. was pitched against a leg of the dining table and injured a knee. No doubt her comments on that occasion were decisive and colorful. She had, according to Col. Olcott, been "making it lively for the servants and her fellow passengers who, with one or two exceptions, were shocked at her ironclad language, outraged by her religious heterodoxy, and unanimously voted her a nuisance." Nearly everyone succumbed to seasickness, even H.P.B., who had ridiculed others for their weakness of will and then was herself "overtaken by Karma," as the Colonel expressed it.[6]

*For an account of meeting a Master in London and the subsequent phenomenon performed by H.P.B. *see* ODL 2:4-7

Among their fellow passengers was Ross Scott, a young Irishman on his way to India to take up a post as a British civil servant. He was fascinated when he caught a hint of the interests and intentions of the little group of Theosophists; when he was not prostrated with seasickness, and H.P.B. and Olcott were experiencing some surcease from the affliction, he plied them with innumerable questions. Rather wistfully, he hoped for some manifestation of the powers which Col. Olcott indicated H.P.B. possessed, but she did not feel equal to the demands of satisfying him. Nevertheless, he quite won both her heart and those of her colleagues with his almost boyish eagerness, and when it came time for them to part they felt a sense of loss. He promised, however, to call on them before leaving Bombay for his post in the north of India.[7]

The *Speke Hall* finally arrived in Bombay Harbor on February 16, after a tumultuous voyage relieved only by a short but restful stop at Port Said.

"The first thing I did on touching land," wrote Col. Olcott, "was to stoop down and kiss the granite step; my instinctive act of pooja!* For here we were at last on sacred soil: our past forgotten, our perilous and disagreeable sea-voyage gone out of mind; the agony of long deferred hopes replaced by the thrilling joy of presence in the land of the Rishis, the cradle country of religions, the dwelling-place of the Masters..."[8]

*Worship

1

1879

ol. Olcott sat back in his chair, scanning the letter in his hands with lively interest.

'Well, here's something!" he exclaimed. "We've been in India...how long?...a little over a week. And the editor of the *Pioneer* wants to know more about us!"

"It must be an epidemic," came the response from across the table. "But I thought the English were immune."

The arrival in Bombay from America of the principal founders of the Theosophical Society had indeed created a stir among the educated Indians, but the English community had so far held wholly aloof from them.

"I suppose he *is* English?" the voice added on a questioning note.

Two beautiful shapely hands put down knife and fork as their owner momentarily forgot the appetizing breakfast which the Indian servant boy, Babula, had earlier placed before her.

The other two persons at the breakfast table, Miss Rosa Bates and Mr. Edward Wimbridge, listened with tentative interest but without comment.

"Yes, I think so," said the Colonel, glancing at the signature. "Name's Sinnett. A. P. Sinnett. He wants to meet the celebrated Madame Blavatsky."

"Notorious, he probably means," that lady replied. "Or doesn't he know I'm supposed to be a Russian spy?"

Olcott's eyes twinkled.

"He doesn't mention it. Maybe he can help us clear up that canard. I believe the *Pioneer* is an influential newspaper and has the respect of the government." He adjusted his spectacles and went back to the letter. "He says he's willing to publish interesting facts about our mission in India, and he's especially curious about the remarkable things you've been doing."

"Well, *I'm* not remarkable," said Madame Blavatsky flatly, as she resumed her interrupted breakfast. "And if he thinks I'm going to introduce him to my Boss,* he's mistaken."

After a few moments, during which the Colonel read on silently, she raised a pair of unusually penetrating and compelling eyes.

"What else does he say?"

An amused smile spread over Olcott's typically American face.

"I thought you'd come again."

"Flapdoodle!"

"All right, Mulligan," agreed Olcott good-naturedly, using the nickname with which he had endowed her during their New York days.[1] "I couldn't resist a little teasing. But this is in earnest, I'm sure, and it's the most encouraging thing that has happened since we arrived. Mr. Sinnett says he's more interested in occult matters than most journalists are. When he was in London he had opportunities to investigate some remarkable phenomena, but he never got to the bottom of them and feels that the conditions under which they took place weren't very satisfactory. He's never been fully convinced, but he continues to feel there may be something to all these manifestations. If we ever come up country, he hopes to meet us."

"Up country?"

"Allahabad. That's where the *Pioneer* is published. I must say, he seems friendly—more so than most of the newspaper people have been."

"They haven't been very sympathetic," put in Mr. Wimbridge. His position in the household was somewhat anomalous, but from New York days he had lent a measure of support and loyalty to the two persons who had befriended him. Neither he nor Rosa Bates, whom he had met at a gathering of Theosophists, had been in affluent circumstances when it was decided that they were to accompany the Colonel and Madame Blavatsky to India, and while they were by no means secure now, their immediate future seemed provided for.

Miss Bates pressed her lips together and nodded doubtfully. She was not entirely happy with her situation, feeling that her status as a schoolteacher had been lowered by taking up the

---

*An affectionate and wholly respectful term with which H.P.B. often designated the Mahatma Morya.

duties of housekeeper in the new establishment. Nor did she feel especially kindly toward Col. Olcott; she knew that he had been persuaded over his own objections to bring her along on the voyage. It happened that both she and Wimbridge were English, although they had lived in America for several years, and Madame Blavatsky had argued that this would weigh heavily with the Anglo-Indian authorities. This had to some extent modified the Colonel's reluctance, but Miss Bates was aware that he continued to have reservations about her.*

"Well," said Olcott with his usual cheerful positiveness, "We'll no doubt find opportunity to meet Mr. Sinnett. I think it would be useful for us to make a tour of some of the major cities, and we can include Allahabad. In the meantime, I'll answer this letter and express our appreciation."

Babula appeared with a pot of fresh coffee, H.P.B.'s favorite beverage,[2] his face alight with eagerness to please. He had no cause for worry; his employers were delighted with him. They had discovered that, in addition to his unfailing ability to anticipate their needs, he was an unusual person in his own right who spoke five languages, including French and English. An interested member of the Society had found him for them when they had moved to their present quarters in a reputable section of Bombay, and already he seemed devoted to them. Although they did not then know it, he was to remain with them, a devoted servant, for many years to come.[3]

"Thank you, Babula," said H.P.B., as he filled her cup to the brim. "But no more food, if you please."

She warmed the boy's heart with her winning smile and met the Colonel's raised eyebrows with the wry comment: "I mean to stay at 156 pounds for a while at least."

He grinned his approval, remembering the weeks preceding their departure from New York, when she had taken off almost ninety pounds by a strange little ritual of drinking a small glass of plain water after each meal, first holding one palm over it and looking at it mesmerically. He could never explain

---

*See ODL 2:109-10. It is clear from Col. Olcott's comments that these reservations were justified. Miss Bates proved to be something of a troublemaker and always seemed to manage to involve Wimbridge in the consequences. Eventually, both of them parted company with H.P.B. and Olcott. Mr. Wimbridge was a designer and architect and Olcott helped him start a business in Bombay in which he prospered. Miss Bates also obtained suitable employment elsewhere. See also *Damodar*, 579.

to himself the rationale of the process, and she did not enlighten him, but it had been effective. He was to add later that she stayed at this weight "until long after we reached India, when the obesity reappeared and persisted, aggravated with dropsy, until her death."[4]

The conversation became desultory as plans for the morning's activities began to intrude into the thoughts of the group. Finally, H.P.B. rose from the table and the others followed.

H.P.B. and the Colonel repaired to their sitting room to discuss a reply to Mr. Sinnett's letter. Miss Bates went about her housekeeping duties, and Mr. Wimbridge retired to his room to design an invitation for use should his two benefactors decide to hold a gathering which had been tentatively discussed.

The founders were barely settled before Babula announced a visitor and ushered into the room a young man with a pleasant Irish face and an engaging smile.

"Ross Scott!" exclaimed H.P.B. delightedly, both hands immediately outstretched in welcome.*

The young man came to her at once and grasped her hands warmly before turning to greet the Colonel with equal friendliness.

"It is good to see you, Scott," said Olcott heartily. "I thought you might still be recovering from that beastly voyage."

Scott chuckled. "I can laugh at that now, but there was a time when I wondered if I would ever laugh again. But do you know," he added seriously, "it was worth it. If I hadn't been on that ship I wouldn't have met you and Madame Blavatsky and had my eyes opened to things I had never even thought about."

"Come, sit down," said H.P.B., indicating the sofa beside her. "I wondered whether you might have already gone north to your post."

"No—I've had quite a few things to do," he explained as he seated himself. "But I promised I wouldn't go without stopping by to say hello and farewell. Besides," a friendly grin

---

*Ross Scott's visit actually took place at the home of Hurrychund Chintamon on the first evening after the arrival of the travelers in Bombay. It is transposed to this place in the story for convenience. Although somewhat fictionalized here, the incident itself is historical. (*See* ODL 2:16-17)

lighted up his face, "surely you wouldn't let me go so far away without giving me one single proof of all these psychical powers you and Col. Olcott discussed on shipboard. You wouldn't show me a single marvel then."

"I was too miserable—and so was everyone else," replied H.P.B. Now she smiled warmly. "What would you like me to do?"

"Yes," put in the Colonel, "let Scott suggest something himself. Then he'll know you aren't cozening him."

"I'd never think her guilty of that," the young man protested. "Let me think a moment." He ran his hand through his thick mop of reddish hair. "It should be something different from the phenomena you told me about on shipboard."

He glanced about the room until his eye fell on the handkerchief which H.P.B. held in her hand.

"I have it!" he said. "May I borrow your handkerchief, please?"

She surrendered it to him and he called attention to her name embroidered in one corner.

"Make that name disappear and another name take its place," he challenged.

"Very well," she agreed calmly. "What name would you like?"

Again he paused to think. Then his eyes lighted with mischief.

"Hurrychund's."

"Hurrychund!" exclaimed Olcott in consternation.

H.P.B. smiled. "Well, why not?" she asked.

Among the persons who had met the travelers on their arrival in Bombay was Hurrychund Chintamon, with whom they had carried on some correspondence while still in New York, and to whom they had sent some six hundred rupees ("not then a vanishing silver disc but a substantially valuable token")[5] as membership fees in the Arya Samaj, the Indian movement devoted to the revival of the pure Vedic religion with which it was planned the Theosophical Society would unite.* Hurry-

---

*The connection with Arya Samaj, never firmly established, was later to be severed when the head of that movement, Swami Dayanand Sarasvati, suddenly turned against the Theosophists and engaged in bitter vituperation. From that time until the present, there has been no alliance with another organization and the Theosophical Society has maintained its own organizational integrity.

chund invited them to stay in his house. This was small but, according to Olcott, "being predisposed to find everything charming, we felt perfectly contented."[6] A reception was held in their honor, and Hurrychund seemed not to be able to do enough for them.

A few days later, however, Hurrychund rendered his accounts.

"Our supposed hospitable entertainer put in an enormous bill for rent, food, attendance, repairs to the house, even the hire of three hundred chairs used at our reception, and the cost of a cablegram he had sent us, bidding us hasten our coming!" the Colonel wrote later. The total, he added, made his eyes stare; at such a rate they would soon be without funds to carry on. It was finally discovered that the money earlier sent to Hurrychund for the Arya Samaj "had got no further than his hand." Col. Olcott commented: "I shall never forget the scene when H.P.B., at a meeting of the Arya Samaj, let loose at him the bolts of her scorn and forced him to promise restitution. The money was returned but our dealings with the man came to a sudden stop."[7]

Very soon after their disillusionment with Hurrychund, they had moved to their present temporary headquarters while they looked for a more suitable location.

"I suppose, why not, indeed," said Olcott now, somewhat ruefully. "Although he is a painful memory. That's up to you, Mulligan."

She nodded and turned to Scott.

"You hold the embroidered corner," she directed, "and give me the opposite one."

They sat thus for a few minutes, the handkerchief between them, while Olcott watched with the greatest interest. He had never seen H.P.B. perform this particular phenomenon and he wondered whether she could do it.

"You may look now," she said finally.

Scott did so and his eyes widened in surprise. There in his hand, in the corner of the linen square where her name had been, Hurrychund's name now appeared in precisely the same kind of embroidery. He had felt nothing.

Even the Colonel was impressed, although he teased her by saying he had seen her do far more remarkable things. But Ross Scott was excited.

"You did it! You really did it!" He held the handkerchief up before him and examined it with delight. "I didn't really doubt you could, but—"

"Yes I know—'but'," she answered with a chuckle. "You may keep it. I have no use for it now."

He was silent for a moment, gazing at the handkerchief in his hand. Suddenly he raised his head, a startled expression in his eyes.

"Do you know," he said wonderingly, "I feel like a fish that has just discovered what water is!"

A delighted gurgle of laughter from H.P.B. greeted this remark. The gurgle turned into a clear, rollicking cascade, a kind of childlike abandonment to mirth that struck the young man as the most joyous sound he had ever heard.* In it he felt the spirit of all the happy "little people" of his native Ireland; his heart warmed to her.

"Thank you for that," he said, half earnestly and half laughing himself. "I'll never forget it. But tell me," he turned to Olcott. "how have you been getting on?"

"It's early days yet," said the Colonel. "We had an encouraging letter this morning from a prominent newspaper editor—Mr. A. P. Sinnett of the Allahabad *Pioneer*. It's the first indication of any interest on the part of the Anglo-Indian people. A number of fine Indians have been warm in their reception of us."

"I'm glad to hear that. And why not? And how are your companions? Did they survive the *Speke Hall?*"

In answer, Olcott summoned Babula to ask Miss Bates and Mr. Wimbridge to come in. They greeted the young man cordially—Miss Bates with some reserve, as she did not consider herself suitably attired to receive visitors. Scott quickly overcame her slight embarrassment with his enthusiastic friendliness and they all chatted happily until the visitor decided it was time for him to be on his way.

"I wish I weren't going so far," he said rather wistfully. "God knows when I'll see you again."

"We shall meet again," H.P.B. assured him.

He smiled delightedly. "If you say so, I'm satisfied."

Before he left, Scott gave Col. Olcott his application for membership in the Theosophical Society and pressed into the

---

*See ODL 1:417 for a description of H.P.B.'s laughter by a Hartford, Connecticut reporter.

Colonel's hand an extra five pound note as a contribution to the treasury.

"That's what I call a practical expression of appreciation!" said Olcott, as he heard Babula close the door on Scott's departure. "That was a clever stunt, incidentally."

"It wasn't a stunt," replied H.P.B. shortly. "I had to do something for him. He would have thought all that talk on shipboard was flapdoodle! Besides, I'm fond of him. I'd like to help him."

"I'm sure of it."

Olcott knew that anyone had but to touch her generous and compassionate heart and she would upset the world to help him, never counting the cost to herself or to others with whom she might be associated. However, he too liked Ross Scott and wished him well.

"Maybe we should see that Ross and Mr. Sinnett meet," suggested H.P.B. "He might help to bolster our respectability."

"Ah yes...Mr. Sinnett. Thanks for reminding me. I must answer his letter."

He seated himself at the desk. Pausing now and then to discuss a sentence or an idea with H.P.B. he finally drafted what he considered a suitable reply.

"Thus began," he was to write later, "a most valuable connection and gratifying friendship. Not another Anglo-Indian editor was disposed to be kind to us, or to be just in his discussion of our views and ideals. Mr. Sinnett alone was our true friend and conscientious critic; but he was a powerful ally, since he controlled the most influential newspaper in India, and more than any other journalist, possessed the confidence and respect of the chief officers of the Government."[8]

Through an active correspondence which followed, Col. Olcott and H.P.B. became acquainted with both Mr. and Mrs. Sinnett, and the journey to Allahabad took place in December.

"Mrs. Sinnett's reception of us was most charming," wrote the Colonel, "and before she had spoken a dozen sentences we knew that we had won a friend beyond price."[9]

The friendship with Patience Sinnett was indeed a true one and endured through all vicissitudes.

The visit in Allahabad lasted for the better part of two weeks. It was notable not only for the fact that the Sinnetts joined the Theosophical Society, but also because Olcott and

H.P.B. made the acquaintance of others who were to play some part in the future of the Society in India—Mr. A. O. Hume and his wife "Moggy" from Simla, and Mrs. Alice Gordon, wife of Lieutenant-Colonel W. Gordon of Calcutta. Mrs. Hume was obviously not in good health and seemed nervous and somewhat ill at ease, but Mrs. Gordon was, Col. Olcott wrote in his diary, "in the prime of her beauty and sparkling with intelligence."[10]

This visit, however, was in the nature of a prelude to one which took place the following year in Simla, at that time the summer capital of India, where the Sinnetts had a summer home and Mr. Hume maintained his impressive ornithological museum in "Rothney Castle," his large house on Jakko Hill. It was at Simla that the events took place which eventually resulted in the correspondence between Mr. Sinnett and the revered Mahatma K. H.

2

imla was brilliant and beautiful on that morning in early September of 1880, when the "Theosophical Twins" awoke to their first view of India's thriving summer capital. Refreshing sleep had done much to restore their spirits which had been sorely tried by problems just before leaving Bombay and by the long and difficult journey from that city, and they were able to look forward eagerly to whatever the day might bring.

The invitation to visit the Sinnetts at their home in Simla had arrived at the Bombay headquarters during a domestic crisis brought on by bitter animosity between Miss Rosa Bates and a relative newcomer, Mme. Emma Coulomb. "I should like to have swept them both out with a broom," wrote Col. Olcott, "and it would have been an excellent thing if we had, as things turned out."[1] The basis of the quarrel was trivial but it had blossomed into full blown hostility which eventually separated the household into two factions.

Mme. Coulomb and her husband, Alexis Coulomb, had arrived in a destitute condition at the door of the Theosophical headquarters in March of 1880. Years earlier, in Egypt, as Miss Emma Cutting, the French woman had performed a favor for H.P.B., and the obligation was sacred; they were taken in and given employment about the place. The woman had, in fact, preceded their appearance in Bombay by a letter written from Egypt several months previously in which she told a pitiful tale of financial reverses suffered by her husband and said that she would like to come to Bombay and find work for the two of them.[2] H.P.B. had written her to come, little knowing what tragic consequences were eventually to follow on this step; nor was she to know until much later that Mme. Coulomb had been discharged from a position as a French governess for showing pornographic pictures to her charges, that she had obtained money from several persons under false pretenses, that her husband—following her advice in certain transactions—had failed in business, had become a fraudulent bankrupt, and had stolen 25,000 francs.[3]

Awareness of these facts at the time, had she been guided by them, might have saved H.P.B. the crushing disgrace which ultimately overtook her. She had not, as a matter of fact, trusted the Coulombs from the beginning. She had a presentiment that they would prove treacherous. But when she approached her Master, the Mahatma Morya, concerning the advisability of keeping two such "enemies" in the house, his reply to her was: "So long as there are three men worthy of our Lord's blessing in the Theosophical Society, it cannot be destroyed... They are homeless and hungry; shelter and feed them, if you would not become participant in her karma."[4]

The domestic conflict which had divided the Theosophical household had apparently been resolved by the departure of Miss Bates and Mr. Wimbridge and, much relieved, H.P.B. and the Colonel had boarded the evening mail train on August 27 with some feeling of optimism.

There was, however, one problem which they could not leave behind and which had followed them everywhere for some time. This was the absurd suspicion on the part of the government that they had political intentions and that H.P.B. was a Russian spy; the resulting surveillance—crudely carried out and insultingly obvious—to which they were subjected was a source of real distress to them, although they attempted to treat it lightly. No doubt, they agreed, they had been followed as they boarded the train, and any one of their fellow passengers might be assigned the duty of keeping them under observation.*

A further difficulty awaited them in the course of their journey. At Meerut they met with Swami Dayanand, leader of the Arya Samaj, the Indian movement allied with the Theosophical Society. The Swami had been growing more and more contentious and had written a scornful and bitter letter to Col. Olcott. They found him very much changed, and several days were spent in fruitless and seemingly interminable debate

---

*This ridiculous situation, too complex to be described in detail here, is related in every volume having to do with the history of the Theosophical Society. But see especially OW, 9th ed. pp. x-xiii, with respect to some scurrilous articles about the founders in current magazines.

over their increasingly divergent views. This was the beginning of the rift which ultimately resulted in the agreement that each of the Societies should go on its own way and neither would be held responsible for the other.[5]

Leaving Meerut in the late afternoon of August 30, the Theosophists traveled first to Ambala, where they had to wait until almost midnight before undertaking the next phase of their journey—an all-night drive with some Indian friends up a mountain road in a dakgharry, an oblong, wooden-bodied conveyance resembling a big palanquin on wheels. They had a further five-hour wait at a place called Kalka, following which they finished the journey to Simla in a tonga, a two-wheeled spring cart with seats for four persons, including the driver. They reached Simla at about sunset and were met at the entrance to the city by servants of the Sinnetts with jampans, chairs with long poles, carried by porters, and much more comfortable than the two vehicles in which they had covered the distance from Meerut. "We were soon," the Colonel related, "under the hospitable roof of our good friends the Sinnetts, where a hearty welcome awaited us."[6]

The Sinnetts' home, they discovered on the following morning, was situated on a hill and commanded a magnificent view. In the distance the forest-clad mountains lifted their peaks into a cloudless azure dome; the five rivers in the surrounding area were like silver ribbons threaded through masses of green velvet; and in closer perspective were "the residences of the majority of those high Anglo-Indian officials who conduct the government of this giant empire."[7]

When they had finished breakfast, four-year-old Denny Sinnett was brought down from the nursery to meet them. He was a frail looking child of rather grave demeanor, but his smile, when it flashed forth—as it did when H.P.B. took his hands and smiled into his eyes—was the kind that twisted strange tendrils about her heart, and—always tender toward vulnerable and defenseless creatures—it was captured forever. His manners were exquisite and quaintly mature, and his bow on leaving them to return to the nursery was shy and endearing.

"A charming boy!" said the Colonel, mentally comparing the refinement of training which this English boy was receiving with the somewhat erratic practices of childrearing in his own country and wondering which was ultimately more desirable from the standpoint of the individual's evolution—for Col. Olcott looked at everything through philosophical spectacles.

"Thank you," said Mrs. Sinnett, her adoring eyes on her son's small figure as he ascended the stairs with his Nanny, his hand placed trustingly in hers. "I'm not sure the Indian climate is right for him. He is not strong."

H.P.B. said nothing. She was momentarily visited with a sad prescience: failure surrounded the boy like a gray mist; his childhood's promise would never be fulfilled, nor would he ever reach full maturity. Later, she was to find some comfort in the fact that the Mahatma K.H. took note of him and even provided a lock of his own hair to be worn about the child's neck as a protection for his health.[8]

Patience Sinnett excused herself to give the servants their instructions for the day, and Mr. Sinnett invited their guests onto the veranda, which commanded such a spectacular view of the surrounding area. He pointed out Jakko Hill, on which the Hume residence was situated, and called attention to the tiny figures moving about in the streets far below them, evidence that the city was awakening to the bustle of the day's activity.

The civilities thus taken care of, Mr. Sinnett proceeded tactfully to a subject which he obviously considered important.

"I hope, my dear friends," he said genially, "You will consider this visit wholly in the light of a holiday. Forget all the problems that have been vexing you and just relax and enjoy yourselves. I have always felt that an occasional brief respite from one's heaviest responsibilities can be a very refreshing experience."

The Colonel murmured his agreement and H.P.B. said enthusiastically:

"That should be easy in these charming surroundings and with such hospitality as we have found here."

Sinnett nodded his appreciation.

"Thank you. If I may, I should like to suggest also that, for a time, you set aside any discussion of the Theosophical Society and even its ideas—stimulating and provocative as these are—and especially that you cease to worry over all this nonsensical government spying on you. In the next few weeks, you will meet a great many people who will be in a position to do you much good. It would be well to cultivate their friendship and not give them too much to absorb all at once."

The Colonel glanced aside at H.P.B. Obviously the words carried a warning. But he felt uneasy. H.P.B. was not one to "cultivate" anyone or anything, being completely disposed to be herself in every circumstance and at every moment. How would she take this rather veiled suggestion that she curb her strong impulses and conform to the somewhat rigid code of behavior which ruled in the circles in which the Sinnetts moved? Her face revealed no resistance, however; it was, in fact, rather blandly happy at the moment.

"You are perfectly right, Mr. Sinnett," she replied. "Don't you agree, Moloney?"

This nickname was her countermeasure to his "Mulligan" for her, both growing out of a comic song which he had often been pressed into singing for informal groups during their New York days.[9]

He nodded gravely. "I believe it is of the utmost importance."

He felt little optimism, however, that she would be able to conform to any such restrictions, and he proved to be right. "Of course she promised," he wrote, in reporting Mr. Sinnett's suggestion, "and, equally of course, forgot all about it when the first visitor called."[10]

That visitor chanced to be Mrs. Gordon, whom they had met the previous year in Allahabad, and they were delighted to see her again.

"...and after her," the Colonel recorded, "came a succession of the most important Government officials, whom Sinnett brought to the house to meet H.P.B. From my diary I see that she began doing phenomena at once."[11]

This was certainly not what Sinnett had intended but, during the busy social activities which followed, it had the—perhaps to him—surprising result of making rather a social success out of H.P.B. "...no dinner to which we were invited was considered complete without an exhibition of H.P.B.'s table-rapping and fairy-bell ringing," wrote Olcott. "She even made them sound on and within the heads of the gravest official personages."[12] While perhaps not compatible with the maintenance of official dignity, this fact in itself would no doubt have carried a special challenge for H.P.B.

There was no way of knowing what course the history of the Theosophical Society would have taken had H.P.B. followed Mr. Sinnett's advice, but the fact remains that she did not, so that speculation on that aspect would be totally fruitless.

During this time also, Olcott took occasion to discuss with some leading government dignitaries the misunderstanding concerning H.P.B.'s and his own purpose in being in India. As a result, he arranged with the Secretary to Government in the Foreign Department for an exchange of letters, with copies of his own credentials from President Hayes of the United States and his Secretary of State.*

The days passed swiftly and in the most enjoyable—not to say astonishing—fashion. H.P.B. performed some amazing phenomena—far surpassing the mere ringing of bells, table-rapping, and even the scattering of flowers.†

Even Mr. Sinnett seemed to forget his previous misgivings and became absorbed in all that was taking place. And Col. Olcott—always an enthusiast where the promotion of his beloved Society was concerned—committed an indiscretion which was to have sobering effects later on. This might have passed harmlessly but for one of those twists of fate which seem so often to turn the course of events in other than the intended direction. He had grown a little impatient with Mr. Sinnett for not publishing accounts of the events at Simla in the *Pioneer* and felt that the Theosophical Society members, at least, ought to know about them. Before he and H.P.B. left the Sinnetts' home for an extension of their journey into the north of India, he wrote an article which he entitled, "A Day with Madame Blavatsky,"‡ in which he described some of the startling phenomena which she had performed. He sent this to Damodar Mavalankar, who had been left in charge of their Bombay headquarters during their absence, to be reproduced and circulated among the local members of the Society. In the article, he mentioned the names of several prominent British

---

*For Col. Olcott's account of this move and its results see ODL 2:229-31 and 245-8.

†There is not space to detail these phenomena here, but the reader is referred to Sinnett's book, *The Occult World*, for a full account. This book, in fact, is a must for anyone interested in the origin of the *Mahatma Letters*.

‡See *Damodar*, pp. 156-9, for text of this article.

officials who had been present on some of these occasions. Unfortunately, a Bombay newspaper, the *Times of India*, somehow got hold of a copy of the article and published it, along with a scathing commentary. The individuals named by Olcott were, not surprisingly, extremely unhappy and embarrassed. Damodar wrote a protest which the *Times* refused to publish, and the whole thing boomeranged on H.P.B.

Mr. Sinnett's comments on this development were typically reserved: " . . . some mistakes were made which have retarded the establishment of the Theosophical Society, so far as India is concerned, on the dignified footing that it ought to occupy."[13] Further on, he added: "On the whole. . . Madame Blavatsky became a celebrity in India, her relations with European society were intensified. She made many friends, and secured some ardent converts to a belief in the reality of occult powers; but she became the innocent object of bitter animosity on the part of some other acquaintances who, unable to assimilate what they saw in her presence, took up an attitude of disbelief, which deepened into positive enmity as the whole subject became enveloped in a cloud of more or less excited controversy."[14]

All these unhappy consequences, however, took place some little time after the Simla visit, which lengthened into almost two months. Mr. Sinnett himself became convinced not only of H.P.B.'s good faith, but also of the genuineness of the phenomena which she was performing—for which she herself took no credit but, in response to questionings by the witnesses, attributed to the Adepts or Masters with whom she was always in close communication. He came to feel that ". . . wherever Madame Blavatsky is, there the Brothers, wherever they may be, can and constantly do produce phenomena of the most overwhelming sort, with the production of which she herself has little or nothing to do."[15]

Nevertheless, he realized that it would not be impossible for a thoroughgoing skeptic to throw suspicion on these seeming miracles, and he became more and more eager to have some phenomenon produced which "would leave no room for even the imputation of trickery."[16] Perhaps if he could get in touch with one of the "Brothers" he could present his suggestions convincingly.

The opportunity to mention this to H.P.B. came a morning or so later during a breakfast table discussion of the affairs of the Theosophical Society. He had been rather good-humoredly criticizing H.P.B. for what he considered indiscretion in the management of her phenomena and the unfavorable repercussions this was sure to have on the Society itself. She had taken it all in good part and her rejoinders had carried her usual keenness and wit.

"But see here," he said, finally launching into his proposition. "I'm sure if I could get in touch with the Brothers themselves I would find that they had a great deal more practical commonsense than has been evident in some of the phenomena we've been seeing."[17]

"So you think so?" she asked, smiling, and added ironically, "Of course, you're familiar with all their rules!"

"No, of course not. That's absurd. But I'd like to present my views to them and see what kind of response I get. Do you think, if I addressed a letter to them, I would have an answer?"

She looked doubtful but intrigued.

"It may be possible, but I cannot promise. You know their Chiefs weren't altogether in favor of their efforts to launch the Theosophical Society. They might not be permitted to go as far as you are suggesting."

"It would be to their advantage," he countered.

She gave him a startled glance and then turned thoughtful.

"They do need help in what they are attempting to do. I know that one of them, particularly, has been trying to effect some small reform in the rigidity of their rules in order to bring the Wisdom teachings to Europeans."[18] She was silent for a moment, then appeared to come to a decision. "I will see what I can do, Mr. Sinnett. I should very much like to have your request granted."

He expressed his thanks as best he could, reminding himself that while he must not be overconfident, his plan could not but benefit the Society. He considered that Madame Blavatsky was not temperamentally suited for the presentation of metaphysical ideas in a form that would be acceptable to men of science. And as for Olcott—well, the American probably never would have sufficient standing in the European scientific community for his ideas to carry much weight. . . . [19]

He was, however, so elated at H.P.B.'s willingness to serve as intermediary that, immediately after breakfast he went to his desk and wrote a letter which he addressed to "an Unknown Brother." In it he suggested a test which he felt sure would be absolutely foolproof and which could not fail to convince the most confirmed skeptic. This was the production, in the presence of the group at Simla, of the London *Times* of the same day's date and, simultaneously, the delivery in London of that day's edition of the *Pioneer* published at Allahabad.[20]

With such a piece of evidence in his hand, he argued to himself with great satisfaction, he could undertake to convert everyone in Simla.[21]

3

The First Letter

Unexpectedly finding Madame Blavatsky alone on the veranda one afternoon as he came in somewhat early for tea, Sinnett paused in the doorway, reluctant to disturb her. His first impulse had been to inquire concerning the fate of the letter he had written and which she had transmitted for him, but now he hesitated. She was sitting very still, her eyes fixed in the distance, and there was about her that listening attitude which he had come to associate with some imminent announcement concerning a member of the Brotherhood. He was about to retreat when she became aware of him.

"Mr. Sinnett!" she exclaimed. "I am so glad you came in just now. For I am able to tell you that your letter has been received and you will have a reply."

As the significance of this announcement struck him, Sinnett was probably in as great danger of losing his dignity as he had ever been. He felt quite overwhelmed and deeply sobered. Yet he was so elated that he had difficulty in restraining an enthusiastic exclamation. He controlled the impulse, however, and said:

"Indeed that is splendid, Madame Blavatsky!" Then, with an unexpected upwelling of impatience, "Do you have any idea when..."

Smiling, she shook her head.

"No, but I do not think it will be long."

It occurred to him suddenly to wonder whether he had made his suggestion as strong or as convincing as he might have done. Reinforcing ideas flooded his mind and he determined to get them on paper and, if possible, persuade her to forward them. He said nothing at the moment, however, being uncertain whether she would be willing to do this and feeling that perhaps it would be wiser to write the letter and present it to her. At worst, she could only refuse.

23

His wife and Col. Olcott, who had been chatting in the library, appeared, followed by a servant with the tea tray, and the group fell into animated conversation—concerned, as most conversations were these days, with the startling events which had been taking place.

Mrs. Sinnett turned to the Colonel with a happy smile.

"Col. Olcott has just been telling me that he has had good news today," she said.

"Yes," agreed Olcott, taking a letter from his pocket, "something I've been waiting for. You'll be pleased, H.P.B."

He had finally received, from H. M. Durand, Secretary of the Government of India, a letter stating that the surveillance to which they had been subjected since their arrival in India had been withdrawn, and that this action was taken "in consequence of the interest expressed in you by President Hayes of the United States and the Secretary of State of his Government. . ."[1]

This brought relief to everyone, and Mrs. Sinnett pleased them further by commenting that it passed her comprehension how anyone could suspect political motives on the part of two persons so completely dedicated to a mission of such high purpose as the Theosophical Society.

"But," Olcott added with a wide grin, "Mr. Durand is careful to assure me that this action is not to be taken as expressing an opinion on the part of the government in regard to the Theosophical Society."

"It is not to be made too easy—ever!" said H.P.B. with finality, and although they all smiled, they realized she had stated a sober fact. Privately, Sinnett felt that the way might have been a little smoother if the two from America had proceeded more carefully and a bit more adroitly, but he was too much of a gentleman to point this out to them.

When he could do so gracefully, he excused himself and went to his study where he composed a second letter to the Mahatma, presenting his original arguments in greater and, he hoped, more convincing detail. Satisfied that he had done the best he could, he managed that evening to pass the letter on to H.P.B. with the request that she send it after the other one. Somewhat to his surprise she did not demur, although she gave him an oddly quizzical glance.

During the next day or so he had to guard against watching her too, hopefully. He did not quite know what to expect, although she had assured him the reply would not come by regular post. When it did arrive, it was in a very simple manner: he found it lying on his writing table. He had no idea how it got there. He was certain that H.P.B. herself had not been in the room; in fact, she had not to his knowledge been absent from the group throughout the day.

The letter was written from Toling Monastery, some little distance across the border in Tibet. He was amazed at its bulk; it covered both sides of six sheets of paper.*

He had a momentary wish that he could somehow read the whole thing at once, but he forced his eagerness under control and made himself begin at the beginning.

"Esteemed Brother and Friend."

The opening sentence almost deprived him of breath:

"Precisely because the test of the London newspaper would close the mouths of the skeptics—it is unthinkable."

For a moment he could not read on; the shock was too great. This was the last thing he had expected. His idea had seemed perfect—an opportunity to be eagerly seized upon by the Mahatmas to remove all doubt of their existence and their powers. It could not have occurred to him that this was not their aim. But suddenly he wanted to know why.

His correspondent made much of the matter of skepticism. "...the only salvation of the genuine proficients in occult science lies in the skepticism of the public: the charlatans and the jugglers are the natural shields of the 'adepts.' The public safety is only ensured by our keeping secret the terrible weapons which might be used against it..."†[2]

This was a point of view which Sinnett was not ready to accept. He had occasionally met with a rather close-mouthed attitude on the part of Indians whom he suspected of knowing something of the ancient tradition and it had always slightly irritated him. Surely that tradition was not so precious—or so dangerous—that it could not be entrusted to an educated European such as himself.

He turned again to the letter. There was another reason for the rejection of his proposal. This was one of consideration for

---

*For a detailed commentary on this letter, with elaboration of many points, see MTL Ch. 8, beginning on p. 123.

†Other references in the *Letters* emphasize the necessity for skepticism at this stage of evolution. *See* ML 227, 284.

both himself and H.P.B. The Mahatma pointed out that the results of such a phenomenon would be disastrous: science would be unable to account for it and, therefore, totally unwilling to accept it. The masses would think it a miracle not only for the one who had opened the door (Sinnett himself) but also for H.P.B., who would be placed in a position leading to notoriety and consequent villification and slander.*

"What, then," Sinnett read, "could be expected by those who would offer the world an innovation which, owing to human ignorance, if credited, would surely be attributed to those dark agencies that two-thirds of humanity still believe in?"[3] In fact, his correspondent pointed out, the delivery of the *Pioneer* in London on the day of its publication, which had been a part of Sinnett's proposal, would actually endanger his life.

". . . so long as science has anything to learn," the letter went on, "and a shadow of religious dogmatism lingers in the hearts of the multitudes, the world's prejudices have to be conquered step by step, not at a rush."[4]

This was followed by a knowledgeable discussion of historical events bearing on the comments just made, as well as on the individuals involved in them. Sinnett was deeply impressed with the writer's erudition, for again and again he found references which set him raking his own memory to identify, and he considered himself better read than the average Englishman of his class.

But, it seemed as he read on, the arguments were not yet all in.

"So far for science—as much as we know of it," said the Mahatma. "As for human nature in general, it is the same now as it was a million of years ago: Prejudice based upon selfishness; a general unwillingness to give up an established order of things for new modes of life and thought—and occult study requires all that and much more—pride and stubborn resistance to truth if it but upsets their previous notions of things—such are the characteristics of your age. . . What then would be the results of the most astounding phenomena, supposing we consented to have them produced? However successful, danger would be growing proportionately with

---

*In MTL, p. 129, Geoffrey Barborka mentions Saint Germain and Cagliostro as examples of two persons who suffered for these reasons. Readers will no doubt think of others.

success. No choice would soon remain but to go on, ever *crescendo,* or to fall in this endless struggle with prejudice and ignorance killed by your own weapons. Test after test would be required and would have to be furnished; every subsequent phenomenon expected to be more marvellous than the preceding one."[5]

This, Sinnett had to admit, might possibly be true. He was not given to profound self-examination and analysis, but he realized that the thirst for more and more elaborate phenomena was something from which he himself was not wholly free. The difference, he told himself, was that he was convinced and wanted to convince others. In spite of what the Mahatma had said about skepticism, he wanted to abolish it. Had not he himself once been skeptical? And he had not been tempted to use his new knowledge for evil ends. Why should not efforts be made to convince other skeptics?

He wanted to talk over this aspect with Hume, who knew of his first letter and also that he had been told to expect a reply. Hume had his drawbacks, Sinnett reflected, chief among which was an inability to envision any situation in which he himself did not occupy first place. Still, he was a man of superior intelligence, and if it was impossible for him to conceive that he could be wrong in any of his opinions, this attitude had at least the virtue of providing him with seemingly unshakable arguments.

Sinnett noted the Mahatma's comment that he would not be able to answer the second letter "without taking the advice of those who generally deal with the European mystics. Moreover, the present letter must satisfy you on many points you have better defined in your last; but it will no doubt disappoint you as well."[6]

Toward the end of the letter, the Mahatma suggested that Sinnett "notify the public" of several well-documented phenomena which had taken place at Simla during the visit of Madame Blavatsky "and let them digest these." Sinnett had already published an account of the mysterious recovery of a lost brooch by Mrs. Hume—an account certified by nine witnesses, including himself and Patience.[7] But this, the Mahatma said, "isolated as it is...becomes less than worthless." He asked pardon for offering what looked like advice but added, "It imposed upon you the sacred duty to instruct the public and prepare them for future possibilities by gradually opening their eyes to the truth...One witness of well-known character outweighs the evidence of ten strangers; and if there is anyone in India who is respected for his trustworthiness it is—the Editor of the *Pioneer*."

The letter ended on an encouraging note: "Try—and first work upon the material you have and then we will be the first to help you to get further evidence."

Sinnett had to admit that he was both elated and disappointed over the letter. Having suffered almost an agony of anticipation, envisioning the glorious fulfillment of his ingenious plan, he now felt strangely deflated. He was willing to admit the validity of some of the Mahatma's arguments; at the same time he was not wholly convinced. In addition, there were a few aspects which puzzled him. It would be interesting to hear what Madame Blavatsky might have to say about them.

He had only time to show the letter to Patience but no time to discuss it with her before dinner was announced.

He deliberately refrained from mentioning the letter at the table, for he wanted a more undistracted occasion in which to touch upon his various questions. Later, as the group gathered in the drawing room for after-dinner coffee—their number augmented by A. O. Hume, who had dropped in to find out whether Sinnett had received a reply to his letter—Sinnett asked H.P.B. whether she would be willing to enlighten him on certain points. She readily agreed, subject to her ability to do so. He wondered whether she knew that the letter had arrived, for she had given no indication of such awareness, saying only, as she settled into a chair and lifted her cup and saucer with one beautifully modeled hand, the other being raised slightly in a gesture of interrogation:

"So you have read the letter?"

Momentarily fascinated by the grace with which her gesture was made, the thought crossed his mind: "She is an aristocrat to her fingertips! If only I could always remember that!"

Aloud, he said, "Yes, and I am extremely grateful to you for your good offices. A few things puzzle me."

"Only a few?" she asked with a smile. "I'm often puzzled over more than a few things the Masters do. But never mind—I'll help if I can."

He was leafing over the sheets in his hands.

"First," he said, "I wonder about the letter itself—its appearance. The ink seems to be embedded in the paper in a strange way. There seems to be more than one type of writing, and the signature is different from all the rest of it. It is signed, incidentally, 'Koot Hoomi Lal Singh.'"

"Yes," she answered thoughtfully, "the blessed Koot Hoomi."

He looked up from the letter, touched in spite of himself by the reverence in her voice.

She added with an enigmatic smile, "No doubt, if the correspondence continues, he will drop the 'Lal Singh.'"*

"Oh?" he spoke on an inquiring note, but she did not seem inclined to elaborate.

He continued: "It looks as though some corrections or alterations have been made here and there. This all strikes me as curious."

"Perhaps so," she agreed. "The explanation is both simple and complicated." She paused momentarily. "How can I explain it? You see, the Mahatmas' time is always overfilled. They have much more responsibility on their shoulders than small groups such as we are—even as the Theosophical Society is for that matter, although it is *their* Society. Such a letter as this would be dictated to a chela—or perhaps more than one chela, since you say the calligraphy varies. The ink appears to be embedded in the paper because it *is* so embedded. The words are precipitated, not written."†

Everyone in the room looked at her in astonishment and expectancy.

"What can that mean, Madame?" inquired Hume.

"It is less time-consuming than writing—so far as the Master himself is concerned," she went on, "although it may not seem so from a description of the process. It is done through a chela who is magnetically linked with the Mahatma.

---

*"Lal Singh" appears as part of the Mahatma's signature on the earlier letters. Much later, the Mahatma K.H. indicated that "Lal Singh" was "invented as half a *nom de plume* by Djual Khul." (ML 361/358). This would lead to the supposition that Djual Khul, who was a high chela, was the one to whom this letter was dictated.

†In a subsequent letter, the Mahatma K.H. mentioned: ". . . bear in mind, that these my letters are not written but *impressed* or precipitated and then all mistakes corrected." (ML 19)

The Mahatma makes a clear mind picture of the words—an actual mind picture of the shapes of the letters—and sends them into the chela's mind, driving them into the paper and using the chela's magnetic force to do the actual printing. The materials—red or blue or black—in which the precipitation is done, are collected from the astral light. The Mahatma guides the whole thing by his own tremendous magnetic force and his powerful will.''

All the faces about her now registered bewilderment, and Sinnett asked:

"I don't understand your reference to the astral light. How does the Mahatma draw things from it?''

"One would have to be clairvoyant to understand fully,'' she said patiently. "However, since all things dissolve into the astral light, the will of the magician can call them forth again.''* She looked at Sinnett tentatively. "Do you mind if I see the letter?''

"Certainly not,'' he replied and handed it to her.

She glanced briefly at the pages and handed it back.

"Much of this is in *his*—the Master Koot Hoomi's—writing. I say 'writing' because he has obviously formed the letters in his mind as he would write them. The t's have long crossings, and the m's have small horizontal lines over them. These things are characteristic of his handwriting. † Also you must know,'' she added, "the Master Koot Hoomi is fluent in English.''

"From this letter he could not be anything else,'' Sinnett observed with a smile. "He said something about school in England. Here,'' he read from the letter, *"Roma ante Romulum fuit*—is an axiom taught to us in your English schools.'''[8]

"He attended several universities in Europe,'' said H.P.B.‡

---

*Cf. comments in a conversation between H.P.B. and Charles Johnston, CW VIII, 397-8.

†In the same letter in which he explained that his letters were precipitated, the Mahatma mentioned: "You ought to adopt my old-fashioned habit of 'little lines' over the 'm's'. Those bars are useful. . . ." (ML 19)

‡Of special interest in connection with the tradition of the Mahatma K.H.'s European education are some speculations by Mary K. Neff in an article entitled "Young Madame Blavatsky Meets Her Master" published in

"He is obviously well educated, especially in science and the classics."

"Tell me," put in Hume, "this matter of precipitation—does the Mahatma go over what the chela has done to make sure it is correct?"

"Yes, of course. That explains the alterations mentioned by Mr. Sinnett. Naturally the process is greatly simplified if the chela knows English. Occasionally a chela may write a whole letter, or precipitate it if he is able, without actual dictation from a Mahatma, although he does not do this without the Mahatma's permission or order, and he always knows what the Mahatma wants said."*

"I should think," Hume continued, "this would lead to a great many errors."

"It could," she agreed, "although the Mahatmas are usually careful to see that their meaning is not distorted. Also, if you have ever had any experience with thought transference, you will know that the person who receives the thought, or the

The Theosophist for November 1943. In it, after dealing with the well-known story of the meeting, in London, between H.P.B. and the Mahatma Morya in 1850, when the Mahatma was one of a delegation sent to London by His Highness, the Rajah of Nepal, Miss Neff comments that the names of those making up the delegation were published in the London *Times* for March 2, 1850. Among these names were two which she felt convinced were assumed for the occasion by the Mahatma Morya and his protege, the young K.H., since it was well known that when members of the Order traveled in the outer world they did so incognito. Her arguments in support of this conclusion are less significant here than is her suggestion that the Master K.H. was being escorted to England to begin his education. Miss Neff points out that a notable number of prominent Theosophists had always maintained that this Master attended Dublin University and that, while there, he wrote *The Dream of Raven*, which appeared in the Dublin University Magazine in four issues and was later reprinted in a book to which G.R.S. Mead wrote a preface. Miss Neff adds that the Mahatma K.H. was back in London in the early 1860s, and there is a tradition that he attended Oxford University. In one of the *Letters* he speaks of visiting a certain group in London "about half a dozen times" (ML 210/207). In the 1870s he was in Germany as revealed in connection with one of the later letters (*see* reference to Fechner, ML 44, and in the Alphabetical Notes of the Guide). *See also* ML p. 285, in which the Mahatma refers to a Gaudaemus, or student revelry in Germany, during which a ferrotype of him was taken by an itinerant photographer.

*In a letter from the Mahatma K.H. received in August 1882, we find the words: "Very often our very letters—unless something very important and secret—are written in our handwritings by our chelas."

mental picture, often colors it with his own thought, puts it in his own words and phrases, and in other ways alters it in some way. This may be true when the transference is entirely genuine. The precipitated letters sometimes show that this has happened. This is another reason for some of the corrections one may see in letters—although if the meaning isn't distorted the statements may be left to stand as they are."†

"There is another statement here that intrigues me greatly," said Sinnett. "Well—the whole letter intrigues me greatly—but the Mahatma says that he 'listened attentively' to a conversation we had at Hume's recently. How do you explain that?"

"I think you will have to take that just as it stands," she replied smiling. "Obviously, he listened. He is, of course, quite able to do that."

"He says, Hume," Sinnett turned to his friend, "that your 'arguments are perfect from the standpoint of exoteric wisdom' but that 'When the time comes and he is allowed to have a full glimpse into the world of *esoterism*, with its laws based upon mathematically correct calculations of the future— the necessary results of the causes which we are always at liberty to create and shape at our will but are as unable to control their consequences which thus become our masters—then only will both of you understand why to the uninitiated our acts must seem often unwise, if not actually foolish.' Well—I wouldn't presume to judge that, I think."

"At this point, I suppose," said Hume, giving the impression that he was merely reserving his opinion. "Madame Blavatsky," he added, "I have a mind to address a letter to the Mahatma myself. Could I depend on your good offices to see that it reaches him?"

She looked at him meditatively for a long moment.

"Yes, I will do the best I can," she said.

"I must confess," said Sinnett, "I'm disappointed that the Mahatma doesn't see fit to adopt my suggestion. And I don't quite see the reason for protecting the skeptics."

"Oh, but Percy!" explained Patience in her soft, musical voice; with Olcott she had been a silent listener to the conversation. "I don't believe he means to *protect* the skeptics. He is merely pointing out that skepticism is a fact in our times—in

†Cf. Conversation between H.P.B. and Charles Johnston, CW VIII, 397.

all times, so far as that is concerned—and that it serves as a natural protection against misuse of the knowledge. If you don't believe a thing is possible, you don't try to do anything about it. At least, that is the way I interpret his words. Am I wrong?" She turned to H.P.B.

"No, my dear, you are quite right. Knowledge in the hands of those who would use it for evil ends is perhaps the world's greatest danger. It is to some extent the skeptics who preserve us from that."

"Besides," went on Patience," the Master says that we have already had more phenomena than most people would see in several years. The letter has so much in it. Percy, please read that passage about 'deific powers' and the superficial interest of people in such things."

Obligingly he found the reference: "He mentions that the success of any such venture as I suggested would depend 'entirely on those deepest and most mysterious questions which can stir the human mind—the *deific* powers in man and the possibilities contained in nature.' He doesn't seem to think that many people are concerned with these factors."

Col. Olcott spoke for the first time, and with his usual practical optimism.

"That is the job for the Theosophical Society," he said, "to wake up the world to the truth of these profound subjects, and to gird that truth with the moral stamina and the ethical commitment that must always accompany it if it is to benefit the world."

Hume glanced at the Colonel with a rather pitying expression and commented:

"Waking up the world is a pretty big order. What is needed is someone who can present these ideas to intelligent and educated Europeans." His tone clearly implied that he did not think Olcott and Madame Blavatsky were the ones to do this.

The Colonel looked slightly embarrassed but replied stoutly: "It will come, Mr. Hume. In time it is bound to come."

"And bring much pain in the process," said H.P.B. "Old patterns can't be broken without suffering. I wish it were not so."

"I, too, dear Madame Blavatsky." Patience put out her hand to touch H.P.B.'s arm. "We somehow want everyone to be happy and comfortable, don't we? But when we are comfortable, we don't do much about ourselves."

H.P.B. gave her a winning and compassionate smile.

"I'm not sure you need to do much about yourself," she said gently. "Well, Mr. Sinnett, do you feel satisfied with your first letter?"

"Satisfied?" He pondered silently for a moment. "I'm not sure that's the word. I admit I am disappointed—but I am intrigued also. And I want to answer it. Am I permitted, Madame?"

"By all means," she assured him. "I shall be happy to serve as your post office as long as I am able."

"You will let me see the letter sometime, I assume, Sinnett?" This from Hume, who had shared in the experiences of the past few weeks and had his own reasons for wanting to pursue the matter.

"Certainly. I had intended to do so. When you have read it, we must discuss it further."

"And decide upon a course of action," said Hume, almost taking the matter out of Sinnett's hands.

"I think I must remind you of something," said H.P.B. quickly. "You remember the Master suggested that you might often think his actions foolish. It is sometimes very difficult to bridge the gulf between our world and theirs. You may not always understand his actions—but please remember, too, that he is bound by rules that have governed the Brotherhood for millennia and which will sometimes prevent him from giving you all the facts about anything he does. I hope you will keep this in mind if the correspondence continues."

Noticing the rather scornful expression which spread over Hume's features, Patience again hastened into the breach.

"I hope we can all remember that we have everything to learn in these matters. Now who will have more coffee?"

No one expressed interest and the conversation turned to other matters.

When Hume took his leave he had with him the Mahatma's letter to Sinnett, which he promised to return on the following day. His departure seemed to release a certain tension in the group, and they resumed an easy discussion of some of the things the Master had said.

"I found so much of it reassuring," said Patience, "in spite of—or perhaps because of—the Master's realistic and truthful attitude. And I'm more pleased than I can say, Percy, that he recognizes your integrity."

"As editor of the *Pioneer*," he reminded her, smiling.

"As a person," she insisted. "The fact of your being editor of the *Pioneer* is incidental. Dear Madame," she turned to H.P.B., "We do thank you for your kindness. How shall we ever make you know how profoundly grateful we are to you for introducing us to this knowledge—and for making it possible for Percy to hear directly from a Master."

"You are not troubled with skepticism, I see," H.P.B. said teasingly.

"No—not about this. I don't think I ever shall be. It all seems so very natural—so right."

Sinnett reflected that if he was not yet capable of this total acceptance, he at least was now convinced of the existence of the Brotherhood. His reservations lay in the question of how much he would be able to agree with their point of view.

4

The Pillow Dak*

Sinnett grew increasingly uneasy as the day wore on and Hume had not appeared with the Mahatma's letter, which he had promised to return on the day following its arrival. He left the office early, not wanting to waste a moment of having the letter in his own possession again, but when he reached home there had been no sign of his friend.

"I shouldn't worry, dear," said Patience softly. "You know Allan will take his own time."

Hume's "own time" did not arrive until well after tea, when his carriage drew up in front of Sinnett's residence and he came toward the house with his usual deliberation and dignity. Sinnett ushered him into the study.

"I was beginning to wonder," he said, unable entirely to conceal his irritation. "I wanted to answer the letter..."

"I am sure you did. But I needed to give the matter some thought."

While not naturally disposed to be impressed by anything coming out of India, Hume had been greatly intrigued by the happenings of recent weeks; in spite of his inborn pride and sense of superiority, he was fascinated by the possibility that there might be somewhere a repository of ultimate wisdom, with beings who guarded its precincts. What would it be like, he had asked himself, to be able to absorb and disseminate that wisdom in a manner to astonish and impress the West? Particularly if that involved, as he suspected it did, a deeper knowledge of nature than had ever been revealed by the discoveries of science. What a triumph that would be! But he felt that Koot Hoomi Lal Singh had not been entirely fair in his evaluation of western possibilities and understanding.

---

*dak: an Indian term generally meaning delivery of any sort, mainly referring to the postal service.

"Koot Hoomi's wrong about the European character," he said now, as he seated himself and accepted the cigar which Sinnett offered him. "The educated European must be approached in a certain way—and it will take someone thoroughly familiar with his nature to do it." His manner clearly implied: "And I am the one."

"Yes, I agree," said Sinnett. "But this Brother doesn't seem wholly unfamiliar with the West. You remember Madame Blavatsky said he was educated in European universities. He certainly knows western history."

"But not necessarily with the right interpretation," objected Hume. "At least not in every instance."

Sinnett poured whiskey and soda for both of them before replying. He picked up the letter from the desk where Hume had placed it. He was still not impressed with its appearance. He would never have permitted a letter to leave his desk with smudges and writeovers in it. Remembering Madame's explanation—as well as her statement of how busy the Brothers were—he reminded himself that he was lucky to have any reply at all. He must try to remember that the Mahatma was not English. Besides, what really mattered was the content, not how the letter looked.

"Nevertheless, Hume, it is a powerful letter," he said finally, "and I'm rather shaken by it. I've got to know more. I'll answer this and see whether the Brother will continue the correspondence and share some of all this knowledge. He rather implies that he might, since he says to work on what I have and then he will be willing to give further evidence. That, at least, is encouraging."

"As you know, I plan to write him also," said Hume. "Like you, I've got to know more. I'm not satisfied, Sinnett."

"Is one ever satisfied in matters of this kind, I wonder? Well, we'll pursue it. We've already discussed with the President and H.P.B. the possibility of forming a branch of the Society in Simla. Perhaps we could organize a separate Society, entirely independent of them. I like Olcott well enough, but he's a bit of a bumbler. And Madame is as unpredictable as a cyclone—and I confess sometimes about as trying, no matter how fascinating she can be at other times. Besides, organization isn't her forte."

Hume laughed. "Well said! But your idea is a good one. I take it what you are suggesting is something rather different from a regular branch attached to the main Society. It would certainly give us greater freedom. If we could get this Brother to deal directly with us, we wouldn't be dependent on Madame Blavatsky for the correspondence—or even, perhaps, direct intercourse—and we could set up our own rules without reference to the Colonel."

"Yes," agreed Sinnett thoughtfully. "I think it is a good idea. I'll suggest it."

Hume remained for a short time longer as they discussed the possibilities of this tentative plan. It was fairly well outlined in Sinnett's mind by the time his friend took his leave, and he decided to write his letter before retiring, while the ideas were still fresh in his mind.

If some member of the Brotherhood, he wrote, would take the proposed new body under his patronage and give it guidance, keeping in free and direct communication with its leaders, affording them direct proof that he really possessed that superior knowledge of the forces of nature and the attributes of the human soul which would inspire them with proper confidence in his leadership, a great deal more might be accomplished than if they tried to operate within the restrictions imposed by the President and with the constant threat of interference from him.

What they had in mind, Sinnett pointed out, was the establishment of a group for the special study of occultism, putting aside for the moment the objectives of the Theosophical Society itself. The European mind, the Mahatma should realize, was less hopelessly intractable than he had represented it to be.[1] Sinnett added, although he wasn't sure at this point how heavily it weighed in the situation, that hitherto he had not found sufficient reason to give up the mode of life to which he was accustomed.*[2]

In his own mind, he hoped such a measure would not be required; it would mean not only a radical and uncomfortable change for him, but also inconvenience and perhaps embarrassment for his family and friends.

When he saw Hume again, the latter told him that he had written his letter to the Mahatma and that Madame Blavatsky had agreeably passed it on. Apparently far from unwilling to change his mode of life, Hume had offered to give up every-

See ML page 8 for these statements of Sinnett's quoted by the Mahatma.

thing and go into seclusion if only he could be trained in occultism so that he could return to the world and demonstrate it; he had no doubt of his ability to transform the thinking of the West, and especially of the scientific world, since there were few branches of science with which he was not more or less familiar. He mentioned certain conditions under which he would be willing to make this sacrifice. And he too urged the formation of a separate group for the study of occultism, completely divorced from the Theosophical Society and answerable only to the Brother who might consent to guide and instruct them.

Sinnett thought Hume's suggestion a little more sweeping than anything to which he was yet ready to commit himself and he wondered whether, after all, his friend would be willing to go so far in the event the Brother should accept his proposition.

As before, he waited for several days before he received a reply to his own letter. Apparently the Mahatma had left Toling Monastery but it was not clear where he was at the time of composing his second letter.[3] Sinnett was later to learn that he was somewhere in the Kashmir Valley on his way to consult with the Mahachohan about Hume's offer.[4]

The opening sentence of this second letter was only slightly less startling than that of the first; and it was equally unequivocal:

"We shall be at cross purposes in our correspondence until it has been made entirely plain that occult science has its own methods of research as fixed and arbitrary as the methods of its antithesis, physical science, are in their way."

Clearly, thought Sinnett, as he re-read these words, he was going to be taken to task. Where had he been wrong?

The letter went on:

". . . he who would cross the boundary of the unseen world can no more prescribe how he will proceed than the traveler who tries to penetrate to the inner subterranean recesses of L'Hassa, the blessed, could show the way to his guide. The mysteries never were, never can be, put within the reach of the general public, not, at least, until that longed for day when our religious philosophy becomes universal."

The letter pointed out that there had never been more than a few who had managed to conquer the secrets of nature. "The adept is the rare efflorescence of a generation of enquirers; and to become one, he must obey the inward impulse of his soul irrespective of the prudential considerations of worldly science or sagacity."

The Mahatma mentioned that he had received Mr. Hume's letter, adding that he would have to write to each of them separately, since their motives and aspirations were of diametrically opposite character, and hence "...leading to different results." For, "The first and chief consideration in determining us to accept or reject your offer lies in the inner motive which propels you to seek our instructions."

The Master then proceeded to outline Mr. Sinnett's motivations.

"They are (1) The desire to receive positive and unimpeachable proofs that there really are forces in nature of which science knows nothing; (2) The hope to appropriate them some day—the sooner the better, for you do not like to wait—so as to enable yourself (a) to demonstrate their existence to a few chosen western minds; (b) to contemplate future life as an objective reality built upon the rock of Knowledge—not of faith; and (c) to finally learn—most important this, among all your motives, perhaps, though the most occult and best guarded—the whole truth about our Lodges and ourselves..."

These motives, the Mahatma then assured him, were from the standpoint of the Brotherhood, selfish. "You must be aware," he said, "that the chief object of the T.S. is not so much to gratify individual aspirations as to serve our fellow men." He reminded the Englishman, "...you have ever discussed but to put down the idea of universal Brotherhood, questioned its usefulness, and advised to remodel the T.S. on the principle of a college for the study of occultism. This, my respected and esteemed friend and Brother—will never do!"

Sinnett's emotions, on reaching this point in the letter, were in a turmoil. To be told that he was selfish, when he had never for a moment doubted his own highmindedness, and even, to a certain extent, his condescension in offering to serve as a means of disseminating the occult knowledge to others, was painfully deflating. Inwardly, however, he recognized a quality of utter truthfulness in the Mahatma's words which he could not but respect. A passing flash of resentment changed to sudden—although momentary—insight into his correspondent's point of view, and his aspirations were touched for the first time with a breath of humility.

He read on, to find that the Mahatma was next analyzing the "terms" which he had, without realizing any presumptuousness, imposed if he was to undertake the study "for the public good." This analysis did little to restore his complacency.

But perhaps the most devastating part of the letter brought home to him sharply that he had been unfair to the two friends who had introduced him to the occult philosophy—and to one of whom he owed the very fact that he was now reading a letter from a Brother—in proposing to exclude them from any subsequent association of a similar nature. With superb skill, the Mahatma made him see the situation in reverse and face the fact of his lack of generosity and appreciation.

He was assured that neither Madame Blavatsky nor Col. Olcott had any inclination to interfere with the management of a branch in Simla (tentatively named the Anglo-Indian Branch) but that ". . . the new society, if formed at all, must (though bearing a distinctive title of its own) be, in fact, a Branch of the Parent body as is the British Theosophical Society in London, and contribute to its vitality and usefulness by promoting its leading idea of a Universal Brotherhood, and in other practicable ways."

The letter called attention to Sinnett's own comments that some of the recent phenomena had been unimpeachable and his conviction that, if his suggestion were to be adopted, "good test phenomena could be multiplied *ad infinitum.*"

"So they can," the Mahatma agreed, "in any place where our magnetic and other conditions are constantly offered, and where we do not have to act with and through an enfeebled female body in which, as we might say, a vital cyclone is raging much of the time." (My idea, exactly, thought Sinnett, as he read this.) The Master added quite frankly, "But imperfect as may be our visible agent—and often most unsatisfactory and imperfect she is—yet she is the best available at present. . ."

The letter concluded with the assurance that the Mahatma was ready to continue with the correspondence if Mr. Sinnett would accept the conditions which had been outlined.

Once with his guests again, Sinnett found it not entirely easy to maintain the quite charitable feelings toward them which he had experienced as he had read the Mahatma's comments about them. He could not wholly avoid noticing what he considered a certain gaucherie on the part of Olcott, and his ambivalent attitude toward H.P.B. persisted in spite of his determination to be tolerant of her idiosyncrasies. He had to remind himself that it was always more difficult to do than to know what to do.

The Humes were their guests for dinner that evening. They were accompanied this time by their daughter Marie Jane—usually called simply Minnie—who had just returned from a prolonged visit with a friend. She had to be welcomed, and introductions had to be made all around. She was not an unattractive young woman, although her expression was discontented and she made no effort whatever to ingratiate herself with these new acquaintances. In fact, had they been quite frank about her attitude, they would have considered that she looked down her nose at them. However, H.P.B., who was in her most charming mood, seemed interested in her and soon drew her into somewhat reluctant conversation.

Discussion at the dinner table, as usual, reverted to the subject of the Mahatmas[5] and Sinnett commented that in spite of the Mahatma Koot Hoomi's splendid mastery of English and the vigor of his style, there was often a turn of phrase or an expression that an Englishman would not have used. For example, the form of address: "Esteemed Brother and Friend" in the first letter, or "Much Esteemed Sir and Brother" in the second.

"What should he have said?" asked Mrs. Hume.

"Well, Moggie, an Englishman would probably have said simply, 'My dear Brother,'" he explained. "There is a curious fact—he apparently isn't always located in one place—a Lodge, for example. He seems to have left Toling Monastery by the time he wrote the second letter, but I'm not sure where he was, for he did not specify. What I am most concerned about is how the correspondence is to continue once Madame Blavatsky leaves us."

He looked at her expectantly, for all knew that she and the Colonel planned to depart soon for the completion of their tour through some of the northern cities of India.

She smiled reassuringly.

"I cannot say," she admitted. "But I should not worry if I were you. If he means it to continue, it will be managed."

She turned the conversation then on a point of the spelling used by the Mahatma. This eventually led to other subjects and Sinnett had still not found an opportunity to share privately with Hume the contents of his second letter when the family left for their own home.

On that night and the following day a strange series of events took place which enormously encouraged Sinnett.[6] Sometime during the night he awakened suddenly, aware of the presence in his room of one whom he knew instantly to be the Mahatma Koot Hoomi (whose physical body was in a Kashmir valley at the time). The awareness lasted only a moment and he was again asleep. That is, his body was asleep; he himself was conscious in the adjacent dressing room where he saw another of the Brothers—afterward identified by Col. Olcott as the Master Serapis. This too was a fleeting impression before he was again quite unconscious in his bed.

The next morning the recollection was still quite clear, so he was not entirely surprised to find on the hall table a note from the Mahatma which contained the words:

"In dream and *visions* at least, when rightly interpreted, there can hardly be an 'element of doubt.' . . . I hope to prove to you my presence near you last night by something I took away with me. Your lady will receive it back on the Hill." The note was signed, as the two previous letters had been, by his correspondent's name.[7]

Obviously the Mahatma knew that they were planning a picnic with a few guests on a nearby hill for that day. Something of interest must surely be going to happen there.

He had no opportunity during the morning to tell H.P.B. about the note or of his experience in the night, nor did he think he would do so. He would wait and see what happened. He was aware that she remained in the drawing room with his wife the entire morning, grumbling a bit that she had been ordered to go there and stay but with no idea why. In fact, she was not out of Patience Sinnett's presence during the whole time before they departed for the picnic, she and that lady going on ahead in jampans.

Sinnett had, however, written a few lines of thanks to the Mahatma for confirmation of his appearance during the night and, just as Madame Blavatsky was leaving, he gave this note to her and asked whether she would be kind enough to forward it. She took it quite willingly and was still holding it in her hand when she passed out of his sight. How she dispatched it he had no idea, but it was gone by the time they assembled for the picnic.

During their lunch, however, he observed her suddenly adopt the listening attitude which by now had become familiar and he felt certain that something interesting was going to take place.

"The Master Koot Hoomi is asking where you would like to find the object he is sending you," said H.P.B., a question in her eyes.

For a moment everyone was silent. Then Mr. Sinnett pointed to a pillow against which one of the ladies present was leaning and said, "Inside that cushion." He had no idea why he made this selection; it was the first thing that came into his mind.

But immediately Patience exclaimed: "Oh, let it be inside my pillow!"

He realized that this was perhaps even better, since it was a pillow from their drawing room and his wife had been sitting against it the entire morning; he knew it could not have been tampered with.

"Very well," he agreed.

H.P.B. had said nothing whatever since announcing the Mahatma's question and she now ascertained by her own methods that this would be satisfactory.

"Put the pillow under your rug, my dear," she said to Patience.

The latter obeyed, and the pillow remained there for perhaps a minute or so. Then H.P.B. indicated that it could be removed.

Opening the pillow proved to be no easy matter. It had been sewn securely all around without a break anywhere. Using his penknife, Sinnett cut the stitches one by one, until he had opened one entire side. Then it was discovered that the feathers were stuffed in still another case, also securely sewn. This too was finally opened, and Patience began searching among the feathers.

"Oh, here is something!" she cried excitedly, and produced a sheet of paper folded in a triangular shape. It was addressed on the back:

> A.P. Sinnett Es.
> c/o Mrs. Sinnett

She read it aloud:

"My 'Dear Brother,'

"This brooch No. 2*—is placed in this very strange place simply to show you how very easily a real phenomenon is produced and how still easier it is to suspect its genuineness. Make of it what you like even to classing me with confederates.

"The difficulty you spoke of last night with respect to the interchange of our letters I will try to remove. One of our pupils will shortly visit Lahore and the N.W.P.† and an address will be sent to you which you can always use; unless, indeed, you really would prefer corresponding through—pillows. Please to remark that the present is not dated from a 'Lodge' but from a Kashmir valley.

"Yours, more than ever

Koot Hoomi Lal Singh"

It was quite apparent from the last paragraph of the Mahatma's note, as well as from the form of address which he had used—adopting Sinnett's own statement of how an Englishman would have begun a letter—that he had been aware of the dinner table conversation on the previous evening.

Sinnett had thought, when the letter was first discovered, that it might be a reply to his own note of thanks written before starting out for the picnic; he was a little disappointed that this was not the case, but he forgot his momentary chagrin when Patience, searching further through the feathers, brought out a brooch.

"Why, it's mine!" she said in amazement. "Where in the world did it come from? I've had it for years. I always leave it on my dressing table when I'm not wearing it, but I didn't notice this morning that it wasn't there."

Sinnett took it from her and examined it.

"It is indeed your brooch," he said, "but something has been added."

He gave it back to her and she saw on the back the initials, "K.H."

"Oh, how wonderful! How really wonderful!"

---

*Brooch No. 1 concerned a previous phenomenon performed by H.P.B. and involved a brooch belonging to Mrs. Hume. (OW 68)

†Northwest Provinces.

The others crowded around to look. She felt a sudden reluctance to have it handled and quietly pinned it at her throat.

"It is priceless now," she said.

Before leaving the scene of the picnic, Sinnett wrote another note of thanks to the Mahatma and gave it to H.P.B. This time he went on ahead with his wife and so, again, he had no idea how his communication was transmitted.

The incident was not closed, however. When Sinnett unfolded his napkin at the dinner table that evening, another note fell out of it. Without salutation, this missive began abruptly:

"A few words more: why should you have felt disappointed at not receiving a direct reply to your last note? It was received in my room about half a minute after the currents* for the production of the pillow-*dak* had been set ready and in full play. And—unless I had assured you that a man of your disposition need have little fear of being 'fooled'—there was no necessity for an answer. One favour I will certainly ask of you, and that is, that now that you—the only party to whom anything was ever promised—are satisfied, you should endeavour to disabuse the mind of the amorous Major† and show to him his great folly and injustice.

"Yours faithfully,

Koot Hoomi Lal Singh."

Sinnett commented on this letter in his book, *The Occult World:* "It seemed to bring one in imagination one step nearer a realization of the state of the facts to hear 'the currents,' employed to accomplish what would have been a miracle for all the science of Europe, spoken of thus familiarly." It was,

---

*Geoffrey A. Barborka points out in his book MTL p. 193, that the reference to the "currents" in connection with the production of a phenomenon gives a clue to the means whereby an object may be transmitted over distances. Also, H.P.B., in a conversation with her niece's husband, the author Charles Johnston (CW VIII, p. 398) explained that clairvoyance was necessary "in order to see and guide the currents." The current, she indicated, was a "great magnetic force, a current of will."

†Major Philip D. Henderson, who was present at one of H.P.B.'s most noted phenomena (the cup and saucer incident; *see* OW 58) joined the Theosophical Society on that day, his membership certificate being phenomenally produced on the spot. However, the next day he became suspicious and resigned from the Society. Not satisfied with this, he engaged in active and bitter criticism of H.P.B. and was among those responsible for much of her subsequent unhappiness.

nevertheless, he said, for those present, "as hard a fact as the room in which we sat."[8] Yet they knew, too, that "an impenetrable wall, built up of its own prejudice and obstinacy, of its learned ignorance and polished dullness, was established around the minds of scientific men in the West, as a body, across which we should never be able to carry our facts and our experience."[9]

These three letters, and the incidents connected with them, removed all doubt in Sinnett's mind of the reality of the Mahatmas and their powers. Although he was occasionally to be skeptical and to question details, and although it was a matter of bitter regret to him that he was never permitted to meet his correspondent in person and even had to face the cessation of the letters, he retained his belief in the Mahatmas as long as he lived.

5

An Important Telegram

The evidence provided by the pillow incident seemed to Sinnett so irrefutable that he wrote a short note to the Mahatma asking whether he wished the story to be published in *The Pioneer.* He received an affirmative reply: "It certainly would be the best thing to do, and I personally would feel sincerely thankful to you on account of our much ill-used friend. You are at liberty to mention my first name if it will in the least help you."[1]

The "much ill-used friend" was, of course, H.P.B. The storm of vituperation evoked by Olcott's article "A Day with Madame Blavatsky" had not yet broken, although it was soon to do so. But the previously published story of the brooch phenomenon with the signatures of the nine witnesses had attracted the attention of the Anglo-Indian press, where it resulted in severe ridicule and criticism of those who had been bold enough to attest to its genuineness, although inevitably H.P.B. bore the brunt of it. Sinnett termed this "imbecile criticism" and commented that ". . . in no case did it modify in the smallest degree the conviction which their signatures attested at the time, that the incident related was a perfectly conclusive proof of the reality of occult power."[2]

He sent the story of the pillow incident to *The Pioneer* at once, and it appeared in the November 7, 1880 issue. Rather surprisingly, it provoked little comment, and Sinnett observed that "the people who flooded the Press with their simple comments on the brooch phenomenon, never cared to discuss 'the pillow incident.'"[3]

H.P.B. and Col. Olcott left Simla on October 21, en route for Amritsar, the next stop on their extended tour. The Sinnetts closed their summer residence and returned to their home in Allahabad on October 24. However, just before leaving Simla, Sinnett wrote again to the Mahatma. In this letter he included a resume of the article he had sent to *The Pioneer* in accordance with the Mahatma's permission.* He dispatched the letter by registered post to H.P.B. at the address in Amritsar which she had given him, hoping that since it had not yet been possible to make other arrangements for the transmittal of correspondence, she would see that it reached its destination. It was to result in a convincing piece of evidence, particularly in refuting one of the charges which had been leveled against H.P.B.—that she herself wrote the letters purporting to come from the Masters.[4]

Sinnett's letter reached H.P.B. on October 27, the time being fixed by the postal register at 2:00 p.m. She sent it on immediately to the Mahatma K.H. by her usual means. He was on board a train, in what is now Pakistan, en route to Amritsar to see her. He received the letter at 2:05 p.m. near Rawalpindi.[5] At the next station, which was Jhelum, he got off the train, went into the telegraph office, and wrote out a telegram of acknowledgement and thanks to Sinnett. This was dated and filed by the telegraph agent, the time shown as 16:25 (25 minutes past 4:00 p.m.) 27-10-80.†

The Mahatma returned to H.P.B. the envelope in which Sinnett's letter was enclosed and instructed her to send it back to Sinnett when he received it, he had no idea what he was supposed to do with it, but fortunately he did not throw it away. Later, when, at the instruction of the Mahatma and through the agency of a friend in the telegraph office, he obtained from Jhelum the original handwritten copy of the telegram, he saw the connection. Transmittal of the letter from Amritsar over more than two hundred miles to the Mahatma on a train near Rawalpindi in five minutes was evidence enough that it could not have been sent by ordinary means. The registration stamp on the envelope and the time and date of the telegram confirmed this fact beyond all doubt.[6] Further, the telegram in the Mahatma's own handwriting directly

---

*It is not specifically stated that Sinnett sent this information to the Mahatma. However, it is deduced from the latter's reply, dated October 29, in which some comments quite obviously refer to this matter. The article was not published until November 7, but the Mahatma knew its contents in advance, and he implies in this letter that this information came from Sinnett. *See* ML 13.

†The original telegram, which was in the Mahatma's own handwriting, is on file in the British Museum with the *Letters* from the Mahatmas. *See* facsimile MTL 212-13.

refuted the charges that H.P.B. was herself the author of the communications allegedly coming from him.

The Master's reply to Sinnett's letter was dated October 29 at Amrita Saras (the "Fount of Immortality"), the Golden Temple of the Sikhs in Amritsar.†[7]

As Sinnett opened this letter, Patience was busy with some sewing and he asked her if she would like him to read it aloud.

"Oh, please do! I am always eager to know what the Master has to say."

She dropped her sewing into her lap and looked at her husband with affectionate speculation. She wondered whether he realized that a subtle change had been taking place in his attitude. This was due, she felt sure, to the influence of this novel correspondence in which he was engaged. She knew that he was not given overmuch to self-questioning, but she was aware also that he had been shaken to the core by the events of the past few weeks. He still considered the English a superior race, she knew, and, as the Master had once reminded him, he had never learned "even to tolerate, let alone love or respect" the natives of India. There had been no overt action or comment to indicate any profound modification of this attitude, but she had not missed certain small indications that he was gaining some insight into himself and that he was developing a genuine regard and even affection for the Mahatma.

Both were touched and amused at the same time when the Master explained his unprecedented action in coming to Amritsar. The *Times* of India had just published Olcott's article "A Day with Madame Blavatsky" with an accompanying scurrilous commentary, and the resulting attacks on H.P.B. seemed to come from every side. She had sent him a desperate cry for help.

When he received this message, he said, he was returning from a visit with the Mahachohan, where he had gone to confer about Hume's letter. He was crossing over Karakorum Pass on his way to Ladakh, musing about developments in connection with the Theosophical Society, when he saw an avalanche which brought sharply to his mind how often small beginnings

---

†This temple is described by Col. Olcott in ODL 2:250-51. *See also* ODL 2:255 in which he mentions visiting there on a second occasion and seeing the Mahatma.

can gather tremendous momentum. Further reflection was prevented when "A familiar voice...shouted along the currents, 'Olcott has raised the very devil again! The English-men are going crazy. Koot Hoomi, come quicker and help me!'"

"She forgot in her excitement, that she was speaking English," the Mahatma wrote, and added: "I must say that the 'Old Lady's telegrams do strike one like stones from a catapult.* ...Argument through space with one who was in cold despair and in a state of moral chaos was useless," the Master continued. So he decided to "emerge from the seclusion of many years and spend time with her to comfort her as well as I could."

The disastrous publication of Olcott's article in the *Times* might have been avoided, the Master went on to say, if Sinnett had anticipated it by giving the details of the Simla phenomena in *The Pioneer*, "a much more appropriate place, and where they would have been handled to better advantage— that document would not have been worth anyone's while to purloin for the *Times of India*, and therefore no *names* would have appeared."

Olcott was, no doubt, "out of tune with the feelings of the English people of both classes," the letter commented, "but nevertheless more in tune *with us* than either. Him we can trust under *all* circumstances, and his faithful service is pledged to us come well, come ill. My dear Brother, my voice is the echo of impartial justice. Where can we find an equal devotion? He is one who never questions but obeys; who may make innumerable mistakes out of excessive zeal but never is unwilling to repair his fault even at the cost of the greatest self-humiliation; who esteems the sacrifice of comfort and even life something to be cheerfully risked whenever necessary; who will eat any food, or even do without; sleep on any bed, work in any place, fraternize with any outcast, endure any privation for the cause."[8]

Patience, who had put down her sewing again as her husband read this paragraph, spoke now with genuine feeling.

---

*H.P.B. was often spoken of by the Mahatmas as "the Old Lady"—a term of affection rather than of disrespect, and not indicating her age, since she was just over fifty years of age at this time. "Upasika" (female disciple) was another of their names for her, used often in the *Letters* and the name by which Damodar almost invariably designated her.

"What a superb tribute to that good man! And every word of it true, I'm sure."

Aloud, Sinnett agreed; privately he made the silent reservation that while he admired the Colonel's dedication and rock-like integrity, he could not but deplore the lack of polish in his manner. He wondered why the Mahatmas had not chosen more suitable individuals, such as Hume and himself, for example, as their agents in presenting Theosophy to the Western world. He had to admit that H.P.B.'s cultural background was impeccable and it was impossible not to feel some affection for her, but she could, in one moment's loss of temper, destroy all the good impressions she might already have made.

Although he had intended to make a longer stay in Amritsar, the Master said, on the day he was writing he had decided to leave, finding that he could not "endure for any length of time the stifling magnetism even of my own countrymen.*
. . . I turn my face homeward tomorrow."

Mr. Hume's proposition had been "duly and carefully considered," the Mahatma said. The letter had been answered and permission had been granted by the Mahachohan for correspondence with the two Englishmen. This was gratifying and encouraging and, even as he read, a part of Sinnett's mind was busy planning what he would say in his next letter to the Master.

The letter suggested that he draft a memorandum on the constitution and management of the Anglo-Indian Branch and submit it for consideration. "If our Chiefs agree to it . . . then you will at once be chartered."† But they must first see a plan.
". . . the new Society shall not be allowed to disconnect itself with the Parent Body, though you are at liberty to manage your affairs in your own way without fearing the slightest interference from its President so long as you do not violate the general Rules."[9]

---

*Attention is called to the book itself and to the Mahatma's mention in this paragraph of an English-speaking Vakil (Indian lawyer) declaiming against Theosophy and yog vidya. Within little more than a month, Hume was to accuse the Mahatmas themselves of being responsible for the vakils' ignorance because of the "impenetrable veil of secrecy" by which they surrounded themselves and the "enormous difficulties" imposed by them in "the communication of their spiritual knowledge." ML 99

†According to this letter, charters for new branches of the Theosophical Society had to be approved by the Mahatmas and bear their signatures. ML 14

Another matter with which the letter dealt had to do with efforts to find a substitute for H.P.B. in communicating with the Englishmen. Her health was precarious and it was desirable to ease the burden on her if possible. To this end, the Mahatma K.H. had suggested to her that she select one of his pupils who could go to Sinnett as the bearer of a note from him. She chose a young man, Rattan Chan Bary, a member of the Arya Samaj,[10] "as pure as purity itself," who was, however, as it turned out, "not fit for a drawing room." H.P.B. asked him "in guarded and very delicate terms to change his dress and turban before starting for Allahabad, for although she did not give him this reason, they were very dirty and slovenly." He had consented to undertake the mission, but later wrote her a curious refusal: "Madam," he said, "you who preach the highest standards of morality, of truthfulness, etc., you would have me play the part of an imposter. You ask me to *change my clothes* at the risk of giving a false idea of my personality..." He listed a few other objections, all based on his conviction that the mission would be under false pretenses!

"Here is an illustration of the difficulties under which we have to labour," wrote the Master. "Powerless to send to you a neophyte before you have pledged yourself to us—we have to either keep back or despatch to you one who at best would shock if not inspire you at once with disgust! The letter would have been given him by my own hand; he had but to promise to hold his tongue upon matters he knows nothing about and could give but a false idea of, and to make himself look cleaner. Prejudice and dead letter again!" In a postscript he added, "I will not cease trying."*

The Sinnetts could not help chuckling over this story, although they were concerned for the Master's efforts and regretted the burden on H.P.B.

Patience was warm in her acceptance of the letter and commented, as she had done at other times, on the remarkable pains the Mahatma took to make the situation clear and, when necessary, to explain his own position unequivocally.

Although disappointed in some aspects, Sinnett himself felt encouraged. Never dissembling, the letter was friendly, and he

---

*This postscript is found on page 454/477 as Letter No. 126, chronologically #6. It is on a separate sheet of paper and apparently became detached before the *Letters* were published.

could detect no hint of unfairness in it. He had to admit to his own impatience for more rapid progress, but Patience thought they had already moved as fast as they could.

"Just think of all that has happened since H.P.B. and the Colonel arrived in Simla," she said. "I think our whole lives have been changed. I wonder what Allan will think of this letter."

"I'll send it to him, of course," her husband commented. "Perhaps he'll let us see the one he receives from the Mahatma."

The next morning, Sinnett dispatched the letter to Hume, saying that he would appreciate an expression of the latter's views. Hume returned it promptly, rather sharply criticizing the Brotherhood for not being willing to assign some member of their Order to deal directly with the proposed new branch of the Society without reference to the present officials. He enclosed his own letter from the Mahatma, saying that since it emphasized the necessity of limiting their association to the present arrangement, he deemed it shortsighted. Also, it seemed to him that the Brotherhood did not sufficiently realize the importance of his own offer. He was not sure they were aware of the conditions under which educated Europeans should be approached. He was beginning to lose patience with their secretiveness and what seemed to him their endless hedgings to avoid committing themselves. He hoped Sinnett would go ahead with drafting a plan for the organization of the new branch, after which they would arrange to meet and go over the whole thing with the aim of perfecting it to the greatest extent.

The letter to Hume was a very long one.* After thanking the Englishman on behalf of "the whole section of our fraternity" for his offer and suggestions, the Mahatma pointed out that "with the readiness, but not the right, to meet your advances more than half-way, we are forced to say that the idea entertained by Mr. Sinnett and yourself is impracticable in part. It

---

*Although one of the most important letters to be received from the Mahatma, it is not in the published volume of *The Mahatma Letters*. A copy made by Mrs. Sinnett is included with the originals of the *Letters* to Mr. Sinnett now in the British Museum. It is quoted with a few omissions of personal matters in OW (9th ed.) p.110 et seq. It was published in *The Theosophist* for February 1959. It may be of interest that Annie Besant used a passage from it as the opening of her book, *Karma*.

is, in a word, impossible for myself or any Brother, or even an advanced neophyte, to be especially assigned and set apart as the guiding spirit or chief of the Anglo-Indian Branch... we do not refuse to correspond with, and otherwise help, you in various ways. But what we do refuse is to take any other responsibility upon ourselves than this periodical correspondence and assistance with our advice and, as occasion favours, such tangible, possibly visible proofs, as would satisfy you of our presence and interest. To 'guide' you we will not consent."

Several questions which Hume had posed in a somewhat critical manner were answered forthrightly, but the Mahatma did not move from the position stated.

The same mail brought Sinnett a letter from H.P.B. This came from Lahore, the next stop on the northern tour.[11] The Mahatma K.H. had added a postscript.† It was obvious that H.P.B. was very upset.

Although Sinnett did not know this at the time, she had been seriously ill with Punjab fever. Col. Olcott had left her for a side trip to Multan to deliver a lecture and, when he returned, he found "the faithful boy Babula" frantically trying to take care of her. The Colonel sat up with her all night, but she would not let him send for a doctor. The following morning, however, she was so much worse that a physician was summoned, but the crisis passed on the next day and she was pronounced out of danger. After another good night "she gave unmistakable proofs of her convalescence by buying an hundred rupees' worth of shawls, embroideries, and other things from one of these Indian pedlars called boxwallahs."[12] On the day following, however, she had a relapse, which may have been due to two factors: a disagreeable letter from Hume and an item in the *Bombay Gazette* containing several innuendoes about her and the Russian spy accusation. However, she finally rallied again "and consoled herself with more purchases!"[13]

The letter to Sinnett was written while H.P.B. was recuperating. She told him that she had written a statement in re-

---

†There are numerous instances of messages from the Mahatma being inserted in or removed from letters while in transit, which may have been the case with this postscript. H.P.B. comments in one of her letters to Mr. Sinnett that the Mahatma K.H. "is a better hand at this 'than a Russian official in the Secret Police Department.'" (LBS 9)

pudiation of the "stupid and vile insinuation" in the *Gazette* and had sent it to him with the request that he publish it in *The Pioneer*. Much to her chagrin, this letter had been lost and the Mahatma K.H. had tried to convince her that it would be far better to let Mr. Sinnett himself write a few editorial comments on the matter. Now, still ill and in greatly weakened condition, she accused the Mahatma of playing a trick on her and disposing of her first letter, saying that she did not "hold this as friendly on his part."

"If I am so useless and foolish, why don't they annihilate me?" she asked, and closed with the discouraged comment, "Oh, I have had enough of this old carcase."

In his postscript to this diatribe, the Mahatma asked Sinnett's indulgence "until this dangerous nervous crisis is passed. It was brought on by a series of unmerited insults... and can be cured only by rest and peace of mind... I am sorry to say that I can now only act thro' her upon very rare occasions and under the greatest precautions. Mr. Hume's letter to her, a letter full of suspicion and benevolent insult, proved one drop too much. Her punjab fever...is no worse in itself than many a European has passed through; while I may tell you now that the crisis is over—her reason as well as her life was in peril on Saturday night. As for myself you must always believe me your true and sincere friend."

Sinnett was rather saddened by this communication, and when he shared it with Patience he commented, unconsciously using the name for H.P.B. which the Mahatma had used in his long letter:

"I'm sorry that Hume wrote such a letter to the Old Lady. He didn't tell me he was going to do that. Not that he is answerable to me, of course, but this certainly hasn't helped matters."

His wife's sympathetic heart was touched, and tears stood in her eyes as she looked up from the letter.

"Madame Blavatsky *is* an excitable person, I know," she said, "but why should Allan go out of his way to hurt her? I don't understand him sometimes. I don't believe she has ever done a deliberately malicious thing in her whole life."

"I agree. But being malicious is one thing and reacting so violently that she stirs up additional trouble for herself is another. One could certainly wish she had better self-control."

"Perhaps so, dear. But how compassionate and understanding the Master is. He doesn't seem to take any offense at all from her accusation that he has tricked her."

Her husband smiled. "No, I think he wouldn't. Sometimes I think he doesn't care what anyone thinks about him."

"Well, I shall be glad to see the dear soul again," said Patience, her eyes on H.P.B.'s letter. "When they stop on their way back to Bombay we must try to see that she has some rest and make her as happy as possible."

H.P.B. and Olcott arrived in Allahabad on December 1st; the Colonel went to Benares on the 3rd, and Madame Blavatsky joined him there on the 11th.* Both returned to Allahabad on the 20th and remained until the 28th.[14]

Meanwhile, on November 19, Sinnett replied to the Mahatma's long letter of October 29 and enclosed in it a letter to H.P.B., not knowing of her illness. He received a short note from the Mahatma[15] saying he had taken Sinnett's letter out of the post on the way to H.P.B. and had allowed the letter to her to go on to its destination. He asked Sinnett to be patient, since he wished to be careful and explicit in answering and was completely occupied at the moment. He asked Sinnett to "try to believe more than you do in the 'old lady.' She does rave betimes, but she *is* truthful and does the best she can for you."

Even the Mahatma's next letter was not the expected reply to the letter of November 19 but rather some comments on a communication which the Master had received from Hume. Sinnett knew that Hume had replied to his long letter from the Master; he had not seen that reply, but he knew in a general way what it contained.† However, shortly thereafter, Hume had written another letter to the Mahatma filled with quite arrogant criticism of the latter's remarks to Sinnett in the letter which had been shared with him. He had sent this second letter to Sinnett asking him to read and seal it carefully before sending it on or giving it to Madame Blavatsky for transmission if she had arrived at Allahabad. Sinnett regretted the tenor of this letter and debated whether he should forward it, although he felt that his friend had made a few good points.

---

*For an account of events in Benares, now known as Varanasi, *see* ODL 2:265-85.

†This letter, of course, is not available, but in the Master's reply to it, which is included in ML (207/205) several comments from it are quoted.

But he did as he had been asked, gumming and sealing the letter securely in a stout envelope. The Colonel and H.P.B. having just arrrived, he gave it to her to transmit.

That evening, on returning home to dinner. he found that the letter had not only been sent but had been returned.[16] He examined the envelope carefully. It bore the words: "Read and returned with thanks and a few commentaries. Please open." But the seal which he himself had placed on it was still intact; he was certain of this. He obeyed the instruction to open it and found inside Mr. Hume's letter to the Mahatma and the latter's reply in numbered comments. The reply, however, was not addressed to Hume, but to Sinnett himself.[17]

Sinnett was greatly puzzled by this fact, as well as by the contents of the letter. It seemed of quite a different tenor from other letters from the Mahatma, almost as though the latter had reacted to Hume's comments with a certain amount of personal pique. Although Sinnett judged that he had ample cause to be annoyed at Hume's arrogance, he found it impossible to accept this as an explanation. It was not until some time later that he began to suspect that it might have been meant as a test for Hume and, perhaps to some extent, for himself as well. Writing at a later date, the Mahatma said, ". . . no one comes in contact with us, no one shows a desire to know more about us, but has to submit to being tested and put by us on probation."[18] Elsewhere he commented that in such tests, the aspirant was "assailed entirely on the psychological side of his nature" and that "the rule is inflexible; no one escapes."[19]

The thought of being tested was not a comfortable one. He and Hume had discussed this matter and both found it repugnant. Sinnett learned to accept it without ever being completely reconciled to it. Hume never accepted it. At this point he was beginning to be severely critical of every statement made by the Mahatma which did not agree with his own ideas. He was, however, becoming valuable to the Society in quite another way. He wrote often, and brilliantly, for *The Theosophist*, beginning a series which he entitled "Fragments of Occult Wisdom."* And he authored a number of other works including *Hints on Esoteric Philosophy*.

---

*Eventually he was to abandon this undertaking and Sinnett continued with the series. The "Fragments" formed the basis for Sinnett's second book, *Esoteric Buddhism*, published in 1883.

When H.P.B. and the Colonel returned to Allahabad from their side trip to Benares, the "Old Lady" was in agony with an attack of *dengue* in her left arm, "that terrible 'broken bone' fever which gives more suffering than the persuasive instruments by which the paternal Inquisition promoted orthodoxy."[20] She was quite ill for several days, but was well attended by an Allahabad physician and, by December 24, when the branch of the Theosophical Society in that city held a ceremony to initiate some new members, she had sufficiently recovered that "some of her melodious astral bells were rung, to the surprise and delight of the persons present."[21]

The "Theosophical Twins" left Allahabad on the 28th of December and arrived in Bombay on the 30th, where they went at once to their new headquarters which had been selected by members during their absence. This was a bungalow called the "Crow's Nest" on the rocky slope of Beach Candy. It had been engaged at a low rental because it had the reputation of being haunted! But save for one incident— quickly disposed of by Col. Olcott—they were never troubled.[22] They were delighted with their new quarters, in which they remained until removal in December of 1882 to their permanent headquarters at Adyar, near Madras.

6

The Occult World

It was early in 1881. The Sinnetts were leaving India for a trip to England. Two months had elapsed since the visit of H.P.B. and Col. Olcott in Allahabad, and these had brought a number of letters from the Mahatma K.H. Sinnett felt he now had enough material to write the book which had been forming itself in his mind for some time. The Mahatma had given him permission to use his letters, "having full confidence in your tact and judgment as to what should be presented and how it should be presented."[1] The journey would provide the time for writing, and he was certain that, once in England, he would have no difficulty in finding a publisher.

Other factors too entered into the decision. The owner of *The Pioneer,* who had been tolerant of if not enthusiastic about his interest in Theosophy and occultism, had sold the paper to *Messrs. Rattigan and Walker, proprietors of the Civil and Military Gazette* (dubbed by H.P.B., the "C. & M. Sewer"[2]), and his relations with the new owners were somewhat less than happy, they having no sympathy at all for his private interests. A holiday was due him, and it might be a good idea to remove himself temporarily from their attention. The new branch of the Society at Simla was well on the way to realization; Damodar, now a chela* of the Mahatma K.H. and indispensable worker at the headquarters of the Theosophical Society, had, at the Master's request, submitted some suggestions in that connection—all useful except the rather staggering idea that the admission fee should be increased from ten rupees to two or three hundred rupees, "to keep out the curiosity seekers."[3] This suggestion the Master not unexpectedly characterized as "too exaggerated."[4] But plans were progressing and, all in all, it seemed a good time for the

*Disciple

trip which Patience had long been hoping for; and the change would be good for Denny.

True, the relatively smooth waters of the headquarters life had been ruffled a bit of late by a falling out between H.P.B. and Olcott. But that situation seemed to have improved. It had been arranged by the Mahatma that Olcott was to go to Ceylon† for some extensive work there, and he had made engagements accordingly. H.P.B. had at first expressed her approval. Now she wanted him to stay and help her get out the next issue of *The Theosophist.* He refused to cancel the engagements and she proceeded to shut herself up in her room, from which she sent him formal notes of one kind or another. In one of these she informed him that he could go to Timbuctoo for all she cared![5] She had finally emerged from her self-imposed seclusion and had been visited by the Master, who explained the situation to her. She and the Colonel later had a long and serious talk about the future of the Theosophical Society. One point on which there was total agreement was that more emphasis should be placed upon the principle of brotherhood and less upon occultism as such.[6]

Sinnett himself was still more interested in occultism than in brotherhood—a concept which he had not yet quite grasped. However, he had been concerned about the "Old Lady" and had mentioned the fact in a letter to the Mahatma. He was greatly relieved when, on March 1, as the ship on which he and his family were sailing put in at Galle in Ceylon to take on passengers there, he received a reassuring letter in reply. This letter, interestingly enough, had been sent through Olcott, who was still in Bombay. Enclosed in it was the covering note which the Mahatma had sent to the Colonel himself, telling him to forward the letter to Sinnett without letting H.P.B. know anything about it and instructing him to let her strictly alone for a few days until the storm subsided.[7]

In the letter to Sinnett, the Mahatma commented that he was writing "to quiet the anxiety I see lurking within your mind, and which has even a more definite form than you have expressed" and promising that he would use his best endeavors "to calm our highly sensitive—not always sensible—

†Later, Sinnett was to learn from the Mahatma K.H. that the Colonel's tour in Ceylon (now known as Sri Lanka) was in the nature of an exile, as he was "compromised more than you imagine by his Simla indiscretions." This referred to his article "A Day With Madame Blavatsky." (ML 39)

old friend. . ." Most satisfying of all was the Master's encouragement to "return with a good book in your hand and a good plan in your head."[8]

The rest of the journey was uneventful. Patience and Denny seemed to be benefiting greatly from the rest and sea air, and Sinnett himself, as he had anticipated, found time to complete his book. Entitled *The Occult World*, it contained not only accounts of many phenomena performed by H.P.B. but also excerpts from the letters of the Mahatma K.H. and related commentaries.

Sinnett received only one letter from the Mahatma during his stay in England.* It came soon after his arrival and was sent to him in care of his friend J. Herbert Stack.

The letter was written from Terich-Mir, at an elevation of 25,425 feet, the terminating point of the Hindu Kush Mountains lying mainly in Afghanistan. The Mahatma referred to the location as "the abode of eternal snow and purity" from which, he said, he was sending greetings to "the abodes of vice"—presumably the outer world and specifically Europe. It was at Terich Mir, the Master said, that he expected to spend *his* "summer vacation," a light touch at which he was extremely proficient. Sinnett knew from numerous letters that "vacations" were not in the Mahatma's schedule and that he traveled almost constantly in the interests of the Brotherhood.

"Your future book is a little jewel," the Master wrote.

This comment greatly intrigued Sinnett, for the book was not yet in print, and how could the Master have seen it except by occult means? Perhaps, mused the Englishman, he had watched it being written on board ship.

"In the wild jungle of Spiritualistic literature," the letter continued, "it shall undoubtedly prove a Redeemer. . . It is at this sort of springs that Spiritualists ought to be compelled to slake their thirst for phenomena and mystic knowledge instead

---

*This is ML 31, p. 240/237. The envelope in which this letter was enclosed is included with the letter in the British Museum. It bears a French postage stamp with the usual cancellation, and the writing on the envelope is quite different from the familiar script of the Mahatma K.H., as well as from that of the accompanying letter. Geoffrey A. Barborka, in his book MTL (p. 84) suggests that the Mahatma may have transmitted the letter to an adept member of the Fraternity somewhere in France, who then put it in an envelope, addressed and stamped it, and sent it by regular post to Sinnett. Another possible explanation is that it may have been sent through a chela living in France.

of being left to swallow the idiotic gush they find in the *Banner of Light* and others."†

Of course, Sinnett told himself, some Spiritualists would reject and villify the book, but the Mahatma's approval was sufficient for him. "You have proved faithful and true and have done your best," the letter said. "If your efforts will teach the world but one single letter from the alphabet of Truth...your reward will not miss you."

As he so often did, the Mahatma added a postscript. This informed Sinnett that the "Old Lady" was very ill and "one of us will have to 'fix her' as our worthy Mr. Olcott says, or it will fare bad with her."‡

Sinnett had read this letter at once, while he was still at his friend's office, for he could not wait until he reached the lodgings which he and Patience had taken for their stay in London. When he finally arrived there, Patience was writing in the diary which she had kept almost since the day of their marriage.* As was his practice, he gave her the Mahatma's letter to read. She perused it carefully and, at the end, looked up with shining eyes.

"The book *will* be a success, Percy. I'm sure of it! And how wonderfully the Master encourages you! But poor dear Madame Blavatsky! How does she carry on in such precarious health? I feel almost as though we had deserted her."

"I fear she will be even more deserted, with Olcott away in Ceylon for months on end, which I understand he plans to be. But you mustn't let this blight your holiday, Patty. Come, what have you written in your diary today?"

She shared her latest entry with him and they fell to talking about their own affairs and the friends whom they expected to see while they were in London.

Indeed, the time in that city passed quickly and pleasantly enough. In addition to working with his publisher on bringing out *The Occult World*, Sinnett had one or two missions to

†Publications of the Spiritualist movement.

‡Accounts of H.P.B.'s life contain several references to near-miraculous cures when her health was in a critical state.

*Unfortunately, this diary, which ran into 31 volumes, has been lost, and years of search have failed to locate it. The volumes were apparently "turned over to Maud Hoffman, Sinnett's executrix, but there ends the trail." (*Damodar* 273)

carry out for the Mahatma K.H. One of these was to get in touch with Dr. George Wyld, the President of the British Theosophical Society.

This visit was not particularly successful. Dr. Wyld was a homeopathic physician who, according to the Master K.H. had some rather "original" ideas about the Brotherhood.[9] H.P.B. characterized him as "a bigoted ass" and Sinnett was not far from sharing her opinion, as he found that any attempt to make even a dent in the gentleman's hardbound ideas was quite fruitless. He could not feel very optimistic about the immediate future of the London Society under the doctor's leadership, but he did his best to clarify for him the nature of the Mahatmas as he himself understood them. Dr. Wyld was courteous but apparently unconvinced.

Other contacts were more rewarding. Some time earlier, at the suggestion of the Mahatma K.H., he had entered into correspondence with James Lindsay, the Earl of Crawford and Balcarres, who had made a distinguished name for himself in the field of astronomy. Lord Crawford was a member of the Theosophical Society and served on its governing body, the General Council. The Master spoke of him as "an excellent gentleman imprisoned by the world" and wished that it were possible to do more for him under the circumstances.[10]

Lindsay received Sinnett in his library, which brought the latter close to envy. It was one of the largest libraries in England and contained a vast number of volumes on subjects in which Sinnett was profoundly interested. He had shared with the Mahatma his correspondence with the English nobleman, who deeply aspired to contact with the Master,[11] but, as they discussed the matter and the affairs of the Society in both England and India, it became apparent that there was no way in which Lord Crawford could give more time to spiritual development or to the affairs of the Theosophical Society. Nevertheless, the courtesy and friendliness which made the visit so pleasant left Sinnett with the conviction that the Earl in no way blamed the Mahatma for his lack of progress.

Sinnett called also on William Crooks (later Sir William), the physicist who had discovered what he called "radiant matter" ("one of the grandest discoveries in science" the Master had said[12]) and Prof. Arthur Wallace, a prominent naturalist and author of the book *Miracles of Modern Spiritualism*. Prof. Wallace was, as a matter of fact, more interested in spiritualism than in Theosophy, but he was acquainted with H.P.B. and Col. Olcott and was one of the group which had met them in 1879 when they stopped in London en route from New York to India. The Master had mentioned him in the letter just received and assured Sinnett that his new book would be more useful than the work written by Wallace. Nevertheless, Sinnett was impressed by Prof. Wallace, for he himself still had a half-acknowledged interest in spiritualism, in spite of comments by the Mahatma expressly denying its validity as commonly understood.

His contacts with three English spiritualists, Mr. Charles C. Massey, Mrs. Anna Kingsford, and Mr. Stainton Moses were, he felt, especially rewarding and stimulating.

Massey was a London barrister who had gone to the United States in the late summer of 1875 expressly to verify the accuracy of Olcott's articles in the New York *Daily Graphic* recounting the strange spiritualistic phenomena taking place at the Eddy homestead in Vermont.* He remained until October 13 and was one of those present when the Preamble and By-Laws of the soon-to-be-born Theosophical Society were drafted. Although he had to leave that meeting to board ship for his return to England and was not present at the actual inauguration of the Society on November 17, he was considered one of the founding members.[13] A warm friendship developed between him and the Colonel, and Sinnett had heard only favorable comments about him. Massey was still an active member of the Theosophical Society and was also well known in spiritualist circles. Sinnett found himself liking this fellow-Englishman wholeheartedly.

Mrs. Kingsford, a strict vegetarian and anti-vivisectionist, was a member of the London Theosophical Society and was giving a series of lectures before that group in which she emphasized the Hermetic approach to Christianity and metaphysics. These lectures were later to be brought together and, with the help of another member, Mrs. Kingsford's uncle, Edward Maitland, made into a book which was published in December of 1881 under the title, *The Perfect Way*. Sinnett left England before the conclusion of the series, but he was deeply impressed by the tremendous scope of Mrs. Kingsford's

*For the account of the first meeting between Olcott and H.P.B. at the Eddy farm, *see* ODL 1, Chapter 1.

intellectual knowledge and by the force and brilliance with which she delivered the lectures.[14] As a matter of fact, he was to review the book in the June 1882 issue of *The Theosophist* in a fine piece of writing which drew from the Mahatma K.H. the laudatory comment: "Your review of the *Perfect Way* is more perfect than its author's conception. I thank you, my friend, for your good services."[15]

This development, however, was in the future, as was the fact that some passages from his review were to play a part in a series of communications which brought a further period of suffering and distress to H.P.B. Also in the future, and quite unsuspected by either Sinnett or Mrs. Kingsford at the time, was their ultimate rivalry for the position of President of the British Theosophical Society. They met now as friends and engaged in long and stimulating conversations.

Stainton Moses, a teacher of classics and English at University College in London, was frequently a third participant in these discussions. One of the leaders of the spiritualist movement in England, Moses wrote brilliant articles for its publications under the pen name of M. A. Oxon. Like Wallace, he was more interested in spiritualism than in Theosophy; he had—almost inadvertently—become a medium himself. Sinnett had not previously met him but knew him also through Col. Olcott, who had corresponded with him as early as the New York days of the Theosophical Society and who thought highly of him. The Colonel had once explained that Moses had gone into the investigation of mediumistic phenomena with the sole aim of satisfying himself whether or not they were real, but very shortly had found himself—not too willingly—becoming involved in happenings of a most extraordinary nature, so that soon all the scientific and philosophical ideas that he had absorbed at Oxford were "scattered to the four winds, and he had to accept new theories of matter and force, of man and nature."[16] He regarded as his "spirit guide" an entity whom he called "Imperator," who later became the subject of considerable comment in the letters from the Mahatma.

Sinnett found his conversations with Moses and Mrs. Kingsford so stimulating that, afterward, he often had great difficulty in sleeping. Almost without realizing it, and largely as a result of enthusiastic suggestions from Moses, he began to see the three of them—and particularly himself and Mrs.

Kingsford—as parts of a large design for promoting the occult philosophy and demonstrating it to the world. The Master was to call attention to this "dream (". . . shall we call it a vision?") and to indicate that they were not yet ready for such an undertaking. "It is because we are playing a risky game," he wrote, "and the stakes are human souls that I ask you to possess yours in patience.[17]

Not at the time anticipating this restriction, Sinnett's mood as he embarked again for India would have been one of profound optimism had it not been for his concern at having to leave Patience behind in England. She was expecting another confinement and it was decided that she and Denny should remain with her mother until after this event. Unhappily, the child was stillborn on July 14, and Patience herself did not immediately recover.[18] The Sinnett family was not to be reunited until January of 1882.

In Sinnett's luggage as he departed for India, were a hundred copies of *The Occult World*, which had come off the press during his last week in England. It was an impressive little volume written, he was sure, with honesty and conviction. He arrived in Bombay on July 4 and went immediately to the headquarters of the Theosophical Society, where he was to stay for a few days, and where he was warmly welcomed by H.P.B. and Damodar. He presented each of them with a copy of his new book and left an additional volume for Olcott. Their congratulations were enthusiastic, and H.P.B. said somewhat wistfully:

"It is a shame that Olcott isn't here to greet you and see your book. He would be so pleased and so interested in all that you have been doing."

"How is the Colonel?" he asked, wondering whether H.P.B. had recovered from her pique against him.

"Well, you know him," replied H.P.B., "and you know he isn't sitting around waiting for Samadhi to strike him."

"Oh," put in Damodar in his intense manner, "you should hear of all the things he has been doing. He has been establishing Buddhist schools, lecturing all over Ceylon, and has even written a Buddhist catechism which has been translated into Sinhalese. That was so badly needed, he says, as he found the ignorance of Buddhism very shocking. He has even been working with a committee to establish a Sinhalese Buddhist Fund, and has just been invited to inaugurate a new branch of the Theosophical Society at Tinnevelly."

"That," said H.P.B. generously, "is a special achievement because it will bring Buddhists and Hindus together. I hope it will help to promote the Brotherhood that we agreed to emphasize more than we have done in the past."

"Splendid!" agreed Sinnett, although this element in the Society's program was still of least interest to him. He recognized, however, that even though the Colonel had been sent to Ceylon more or less to remove him from India for a time, he would never for a moment be idle and would inevitably turn it all to good account.

Before leaving England, Sinnett had written a letter to the Mahatma K.H., and he now felt a little disappointed that no reply was awaiting him. He was to receive that reply on the following morning in a rather startling manner.

After breakfast, he and H.P.B. had retired to his room in the headquarters building, hoping for an uninterrupted discussion about the work in both India and England. They were sitting on different sides of a large table, with H.P.B. on Sinnett's left. Suddenly, at his right hand, a thick letter fell "out of nothing" onto the table. It was, he said in writing of the incident, "a deeply interesting letter, partly concerned with private matters and replies to questions of mine, and partly with some large, though as yet shadowy, revelations of occult philosophy, the first sketch of this that I had received."[19] He added that this was the only phenomenon accorded him during his stay in Bombay, as "the higher authorities of the occult world . . . had by this time put very much more stringent prohibition upon such manifestations than had been in operation the previous summer at Simla."[20]

The letter from the Mahatma began encouragingly: "Welcome good friend and brilliant author, welcome back! Your letter at hand, and I am happy to see your personal experience with the 'Elect' of London proved so successful." Then, with his characteristic light touch, "But I foresee that more than ever now you will become an incarnate note of interrogation."[21]

The letter covered many subjects and discussed a number of persons: Hume, Massey, Mrs. Kingsford, and others. Several pages were devoted to Stainton Moses, the strange experiences of his life and the identity of "Imperator." There were comments on occult doctrines concerning Planetary Spirits, cycles, cause and effect, and a reference to "countless kosmical* influences which distort and deflect all efforts to achieve definite purpose," which Sinnett found rather devastating.

Near the end, the letter discussed the attacks already being made on Sinnett's book, *The Occult World,* and predicted that, although these attacks were aimed at the author himself ("who is far from being beloved by his colleagues in India"), they would also "graze the old lady, reviving in the Indian press last year's outcry." Nevertheless, the Master assured him, "when the first hum and dingdong of adverse criticism is hushed, thoughtful men will read and ponder over the book...." The men of science had but to reap where generations of Adepts had sown, he added. "It is our mission to plunge and bring the pearls of Truth to the surface; theirs— to clean and set them in scientific jewels... And we will go on in that periodical work of ours; we will not allow ourselves to be baffled in our philanthropic attempts until that day when the foundations of a new continent of thought are so firmly built that no amount of opposition and ignorant malice... will be found to prevail.[22]

Near the end of the letter, the Master quoted a short poem which he attributed to Tennyson. This puzzled Sinnett for some time, as it was not in any of the familiar published works of that poet.† He asked the Mahatma about it but the latter

---

*The early literature of Theosophy used "kosmos" to designate the totality of the universe and "cosmos" to indicate the world, which might mean only the Earth or planet. (Glossary)

†Sinnett was something of an expert on Tennyson. From childhood he had memorized the latter's poems and was probably as familiar with them as was anyone living at the time. Through many of his later years, he believed himself to be in direct communication with "the Individuality whom, in his last life, we called 'Tennyson' and learned from him that in previous existences he had been the Roman poet Virgil, author of *The Aeneid,* and the English bard Edmund Spenser." In 1920, the year before Sinnett died, the Theosophical Publishing House, London, published a small volume by him entitled *Tennyson: An Occultist,* in which he argued convincingly that the poet could enter at will into a state of higher consciousness, that he was steeped in the Ancient Wisdom and, indeed, that his poems repeatedly reflected these facts for those who had understanding. The statement in quotation marks is from that book.

could not identify it. "Some stray lines picked up in the astral light, or in somebody's brain and remembered," he wrote. "I never forget what I once see or read."† Some time later Sinnett found the poem in the 1830 edition of *Poems Chiefly Lyrical* by Tennyson. It was entitled "The Mystics" and was written before Tennyson was twenty years of age. It was omitted in later editions of the poet's works.

Sinnett pondered long over the Master's letter. It was so rich in content and so rewarding after the weeks without communication, that he readily overlooked the request that he and his London colleagues delay their ambitious plans to astound the world with their presentations of occult knowledge. In fact, these seemed to him now slightly childish and even presumptuous. He wished that Patience were with him so he could share the letter with her.‡

---

†This fact may, indeed, have had some bearing on the disruptive "Kiddle Incident" which grew out of Sinnett's new book and which will be described later in these pages.

‡An editorial note following this letter in the published volume indicates that six lines of the original had been deleted from its closing paragraphs. This is not explained, but one is reminded of the opening paragraph in which the Master tells Sinnett that if his questions are "found premature by the powers that be, instead of receiving my answers in their pristine purity you may find them transformed into yards of drivel." It is possible also that the "powers that be" occasionally found it advisable to delete parts of the letters—probably while they were in transit—as such gaps are not infrequent. As a matter of fact, in a short note received from the Mahatma a few days later, while Sinnett was still in Bombay, thanking him for some gifts he had brought back with him from England, the Mahatma commented (apparently in reply to a question from Sinnett about the missing lines in the long letter): "The blanks are provoking and 'tantalizing' but we cannot go against the inevitable." (ML No. 121, p. 452/445) Thus he seemed to imply that they were beyond his control.

7

The Simla Eclectic Theosophical Society

In the short note received by Sinnett while he was still in Bombay, thanking him for gifts brought from England, the Mahatma K.H. urged him to go to Simla,[1] where the inauguration of the Simla Eclectic Theosophical Society (originally conceived as the Anglo-Indian Branch of the Theosophical Society) was to take place. H.P.B. had been invited to visit the Humes and be present at the event, and Sinnett planned to meet her there. They were in agreement that they should both have a voice in the preliminary steps of founding the new organization.

Sinnett left Bombay for his home in Allahabad before mid-July, feeling that he should get some of his affairs in order before taking another leave of absence. True, he could carry on his editorial work by correspondence from Simla, but the strain in his relations with his employers had not lessened, and he felt that some consultation with them might ease the tension. He had no thought of abandoning his interest in Theosophy and occultism; indeed this would have been impossible, for by this time it had become ingrained. Nevertheless, some effort to make his point of view better understood might be of value.*

As it turned out, the discussions left something to be desired on both sides in terms of satisfaction, but it was agreed to carry on for the time being with the arrangement existing at the time the new proprietors took over the newspaper and, at Sinnett's insistence, his request to remain in Simla for some weeks was approved. After all, he and his family went there every summer in any case. This year, with Patience in

*Nowhere is it stated that consultations with the proprietors of *The Pioneer* actually took place, but it is inconceivable that the interested parties on both sides could have been so arbitrary as never to have sought resolution of their differences through talking them over together.

England, he would not open their summer home but would stay with the Humes as they had suggested.

H.P.B. was already in Simla when Sinnett left Allahabad for that city in early August. As he passed through Amballa, he received another lengthy letter from the Mahatma, who was "just home" as he said, after some lengthy travels; he confessed to being "tired" after more than nine days in the saddle. In spite of this, he undertook to answer a number of Sinnett's questions, although he said humorously that, like a deity described in one of the Upanishads, these questions "loved to be many and to multiply."[2]

Sinnett had received from England, and had sent on to the Mahatma, several reviews of *The Occult World* which had appeared in spiritualistic journals. One of these contained some comments by John King, a well-known seance entity of the time.* The Master commented, "I do feel a little wrathful at the sacreligious utterances of J.K.... The Hobilghan† to whom I showed the passage laughed till the tears streamed down his old cheeks. I wish I could. When the 'Old Lady' reads it there will be a cedar or two damaged at Simla." (A comment which brought a wry smile to Sinnett's face.)

The letter dealt with many other topics. The Master took occasion to ask Sinnett to impress upon his friends in London "some wholesome truths that they are but too apt to forget, even when they have been told them over and over again. The Occult Science is not one in which secrets can be communicated of a sudden, by a written or even verbal communication. If so, all the 'Brothers' would have to do would be to publish a *Hand-book* of the art which might be taught in schools as grammar is. It is the common mistake of people that we willingly wrap ourselves and our powers in mystery—that we wish to keep our knowledge to ourselves, and of our own will refuse—'wantonly and deliberately'‡ to communicate it. The truth is that till the neophyte attains to that condition necessary for that degree of illumination in which, and for which, he is entitled and fitted, most *if not all* of the secrets are

---

*See H.P.B.'s account of John King in *H.P.B. Speaks*, 1:83; see also ODL 1:10-12.

† A term with various ranges of meaning but designating at least a superior Adept. (Glossary) Sometimes spelled Khobilghan.

‡Obviously one of Hume's accusations.

incommunicable. The receptivity must be equal to the desire to instruct. The illumination *must come from within.*"[3]

Further comments dealt with the rigorous requirements of occultism, after which the Mahatma said: "...if all this was more generally known to candidates for initiation, I feel certain they would be both more thankful and more patient, as well as less inclined to be irritated at what they consider our reticence and vacillations."[4]

More and more the Englishman was realizing that the path upon which he had entered was not at all an easy one, and while he would not permit himself to doubt his capacity to meet its requirements, he could not help being sobered by the Master's comments. He smiled, however, when he read the reply to his request for a portrait; he had felt this was a reasonable request in view of the fact that his way of life made it possible for the Master to visit him personally.

"Never had but one taken in my whole life," the Mahatma wrote, "a poor ferrotype produced in the days of the 'Gaudeamus'* by a traveling female artist, and from whose hands I had to rescue it. The ferrotype is there, but the image itself has vanished; the nose peeled off and one of the eyes gone. No other to offer. I dare not promise for I never break my word. Yet—I may try—someday to get you one."†

Again the Mahatma added a line following his signature. In part it concerned his immediate plans but, more significant for Sinnett, it carried a request: "I have a favour to ask of you: try and make friends with Ross Scott. *I need him.*[5]

This request became comprehensible when, upon arriving at Simla, Sinnett found Ross Scott among the guests assembled at "Rothney Castle." He had not previously met the young man, and while he thought him a bit "course-fibered",[6] the smile with which Scott greeted everyone was quite irresistible. Further, he was intelligent and apparently sincere. Sinnett supposed he had some potential which the Master wished to develop and perhaps to test.

---

*Merry-making of college students, a reference to the days when he attended a university in Europe. *See* Fechner, G.T., in *Guide,* 230-231.

†For Sinnett's account of how he later came to see two profile portraits of the Mahatma K.H. (although neither was given to him (personally) *see* OW (9th ed.) 176-180.

This assumption proved to be correct, but Sinnett could never have foreseen the strange manner in which the testing came about.

Sometime earlier, Scott had sustained an injury to one leg, and this still troubled him. H.P.B. repeatedly importuned the Masters to cure him, and they promised they would do so if he passed the sixth-month probation on which they proposed to place him. She was told to find him a suitable wife and that Minnie Hume would "do first rate for him...If he proves faithful and true, and the influence of his wife leaves him unshaken in his beliefs and true to his old friends, then we will attend to his leg."[7]

In relating the Masters' decision to Sinnett, H.P.B. commented: "I had a little visit with Miss Hume at your home last summer. I don't know whether she is right for Ross. I didn't find anything particularly lovable about her. But I have no choice in the matter."

The Mahatmas in the role of matchmakers seemed to Sinnett very curious and he expressed some skepticism concerning their motives.

"Well, I'm upset over the whole thing," H.P.B. confessed. "I don't see anything good that can come of it. Master K.H. asked me whether I would be willing to sacrifice Scott's friendship—and I can assure you it is a genuine friendship which I treasure—if I could thus secure his happiness and see his leg cured. I don't know why the sacrifice of his friendship should be involved, but I couldn't refuse. He's young and full of life and I'd like to see him happy.[8] Besides," she added, shaking her head slightly, "the Brothers always have their reasons. I don't always understand them and sometimes they make me angry, but though I often kick against their decisions, in the end I know I must obey them."

"They sometimes seem to me a little cruel," he said rather tentatively; although H.P.B. herself might criticize the Mahatmas, she was usually quick to leap to their defense when such criticism came from others. But now she only looked thoughtful.

"I know," she agreed, "but I remind myself that they don't do anything without a good reason. I don't have their wisdom so I can't always interpret their motives, but I know they are never ultimately unkind. Never have I known anyone kinder or more tender than K.H.[9] He could never be cruel. I'm sure he could have progressed much faster than he has if it were not for his really divine pity for the world which makes him willing to stay closer to the rest of us."[10]

"That may be true," said Sinnett dubiously, "but all this probation and testing is repugnant to me. I feel surrounded by meshes of tests and probations wrapped in invisible threads[11] and I don't like it."

"Then why don't you disentangle yourself?" she asked with a flash of anger. "You can break the threads if you want to, you know, but I can tell you that you would also break the thread that connects you with K.H. That's all I can say."[12]

But it was not all she could say, for she went on volubly:

"I can tell you that K.H. himself may be said to be on probation—but his is a far higher and more difficult one than yours. I can tell you, too, that he is doing everything he can to help the Simla Eclectic get started in the right way, but you make his task far more difficult and even his personal position dangerous by criticizing him. For, believe me, he has always to work with the threat of the Mahachohan's disapproval hanging over his head. Do you think he is doing all this for himself?"[13]

"Pray calm yourself, my dear friend," Sinnett urged, seeing that H.P.B.'s emotions were surfacing rapidly. "I don't demean K.H. I don't pretend to understand him, but I know he is in a far more exalted position than I am, and if I disagree with him now and then, it is probably because my view is limited. I have every reason to revere and feel affection for him." He patted her gently on the shoulder.

"Well, that's good," she said, somewhat mollified, "but it still doesn't solve the problem of Ross Scott."

He considered this for a moment. From what he had observed, he believed the two young people would not be averse to the suggested marriage. Minnie probably wanted a husband, and Scott undoubtedly liked her and felt slightly flattered at the prospect of a connection with such an influential man as A.O. Hume. At any rate, since it seemed to be what the Mahatmas intended and was, after all, none of his affair, there was no point in raising objections. He had no difficulty in making friends with the young man but he failed at this point to see in what way this could be useful to the Master.

Ross Scott and Minnie Hume were married on December 8 and went to Bombay on their honeymoon. They spent much of their time at the headquarters of the Theosophical Society, and while Scott himself still seemed sincere in his aspirations, it was apparent that his wife was jealous of everyone and everything that engaged his interest.[14] It saddened H.P.B. to see the foreshadowings of the destruction of the friendship about which the Mahatma had warned her. The young couple left Bombay on January 12, 1882, and within a few months H.P.B. was to write to Sinnett that Ross Scott had become suspicious of her and their friendship was now completely destroyed. The new Mrs. Scott had achieved her aim.

"She owes her husband *to the Brothers and me*," wrote H.P.B., "and what more natural than that she should traduce both the 'Brothers' and myself! She is afraid in her petty jealousy lest they or I should retain our hold upon her husband ...M. defined and foretold the situation four months since... *Six months probabion was allowed to Scott.* Only *six months* ...and now behold the fruit!...I do not know how much or in what Scott suspects me. Suffice *that he does.* Suffice that a drop of gall has fallen into the pure waters of our mutual friendship (forgive the stupidly poetic metaphor) to poison them forever. I feel a sincere sorrow for the poor young man; for now—THEY WILL NOT CURE HIS LEG *as they would otherwise* had he remained true to the cause not for one year, but for six months! He will repent, mark my word!"[15]

Such developments were to impress Sinnett repeatedly with the precariousness of probation, although they also helped him to understand better why the Mahatmas considered it necessary.

But these events were still in the future when the group gathered on Jakko Hill to work out the final details for the establishment of the new theosophical branch. This took place on August 21. A. O. Hume was elected President, Mr. Sinnett Vice-President, and Ross Scott Secretary. The stated objects were only two:

1. To support and countenance the Theosophical movement by demonstrating to the native community that many Europeans respect, sympathize, and are desirous of promoting it...

2. To obtain through the assistance of the Adept Brothers
of the First Section of the Parent Society a knowledge of
the psychological truths which they have experimentally
ascertained, and thus acquire a means of successfully
combating the materialism of the present age. The Society shall only admit as members persons already
Fellows of the Theosophical Society.[16]

Apparently the Mahatma K.H. felt some concern that the
members of the new Society might forget the discretion necessary in dealing with the public and that this might have repercussions which would almost certainly draw the disfavor of the
Mahachohan. In his next letter to Sinnett he commented:
"There should be a constant pressure brought to bear upon the
members of the S.E.S. to keep their tongues and enthusiasm at
bay. Notwithstanding the purity of motives, the Chohan
might one day consider but the results, and these may
threaten to become too disastrous for him to overlook. . . there
is an increasing concern in the public mind in regard to your
Society and you may soon be called upon to define your
position more clearly."[17]

Sinnett resolved that he would do his best to impress upon
the members the necessity to proceed slowly and to build
secure foundations, rather than to rear a shaky structure
based on unproven phenomena and unprovable claims. He
didn't know quite what he was going to do with Hume, who
seemed impervious to any hint that his judgment was not
perfect or that his intelligence might be even slightly inferior
to that of the Mahatmas, particularly when it came to knowing
what the public needed. Sinnett realized that he himself had
been unreasonable in repeatedly importuning the Mahatma for
some personal contact with him, and he made a new resolve in
this respect when he read: "My dear friend, you must not feel
surprised if I tell you that I really feel weary and disheartened
at the prospect I have before me. I am afraid you will never
have the patience to wait for the day when I am permitted to
satisfy you." A line at the end suggested one factor which
might have had bearing on the Mahatma's inability to visit
him: "The brandy atmosphere in the house *is* dreadful."[18]

A further statement in the letter startled Sinnett and left
him feeling momentarily as though some powerful hand had
suddenly moved the earth from beneath his feet.

"Very soon," the Master wrote, "I will have to leave you to yourselves for a period of three months."[19]

What could this mean? And what would he himself do when the Mahatma had moved beyond communication of any kind?

He went at once to H.P.B. with his dilemma.

"The Master K.H. is going on a retreat," she said in answer to his question. "Beyond that I can tell you nothing."

He had to be satisfied with this, but he received the distinct impression that it would be a crucial period in the Mahatma's life; he was surprised at his own concern and at an unexpected longing to do something to lessen the strain and the hazard for the Master. Then he shrugged his shoulders. It was something far beyond his ken and no concern of his.

A sudden crisis involving H.P.B. shortly thereafter effectively put other things out of his mind. Her health was never good, and she seemed particularly excitable and nervous of late, especially whenever he passed on to her a message for the Mahatma. He had no way of knowing until much later that, in a letter from Hume to Olcott,[20] his countryman had accused her, together with the Mahatma K.H., of "so muddling and misunderstanding" a letter which he and Sinnett had written jointly that the reply was "wholly inapplicable to the circumstances." It happened that H.P.B. had never seen the letter, as the Mahatma Morya later explained when he tried to make Sinnett understand the circumstances. "I, having neither inclination nor right to look into and mix myself in an affair concerning but the Chohan and K.H." he wrote, "never paid the slightest attention to it." However, when H.P.B. learned of it, she became very upset, and the Mahatma M. rather took her to task, telling her that unless she learned to control herself better, he would put a stop to the letters altogether; that she had better "depart for Ceylon"* rather than "make a fool of herself."[21]

"These words were said to her," the Mahatma Morya continued, "not because I had anything to do with your or any letter, nor in consequence of any letter sent, but because I happened to see the aura all around the new Eclectic and herself, black and pregnant with future mischief, and I sent her to say so."[22]

---

*Perhaps an oblique reference to Olcott's "exile" in Ceylon.

This was not, however, what H.P.B. said when she came bursting into Sinnett's room immediately after receiving the message from her Master. Her face was flushed and her hands were trembling visibly.

"What is it?" she shouted. "What have you been doing or saying to K.H. that Morya should be so angry and should tell me to prepare to go and settle our headquarters at Ceylon?"[23]

Completely taken aback, Sinnett was not as diplomatic as he might otherwise have been and answered her sharply. She flung herself from the room, the tears beginning to run down her cheeks.

Sinnett was not aware that a part of her purpose in his room was to deliver an offer from the Mahatma K.H., made through her own Master, Morya. Had he known and accepted this, the Mahatma K.H. told him in a subsequent letter, he would have had "for an hour or more, the real *baitchooly*† to converse with, instead of the psychological cripple you generally have to deal with now."[24]

Unknowing what lay behind the incident, Sinnett reported it to Hume in what was not the most sympathetic manner, and Hume proceeded to complicate the situation not only by refusing to speak to H.P.B. for several days, but even by ignoring her as though she were not present. When Sinnett finally chided him for this, he denied that he had been discourteous.[25]

"And I don't care a twopence whether my feelings are pleasing to the 'Master' as you call him," said Hume. "I still love the dear old woman.[26] She's no call to get so upset over nothing."

"I hardly think it was 'nothing,'" Sinnett replied quietly. "Although I confess that I haven't been too tolerant over the situation myself."

He was to be convinced that neither of them had been fair to H.P.B. when a short letter from the Mahatma explained something of the psychological handicap under which H.P.B. labored.[27] It was, the Mahatma said, "intimately connected with her occult training in Tibet and due to her being sent out alone into the world to gradually prepare the way for others." After nearly a century of fruitless search, the Master wrote, "our chiefs had to avail themselves of the only opportunity to

†The genuine article; in American colloquism, "the real McCoy."

send out a European *body* upon European soil to serve as a connecting link between that country and our own."

He explained further that no such messenger could be sent out from the "precincts of *Bod-Las*"* without leaving behind some part of himself to serve as a "necessary connecting link—the wire of transmission" and "as the safest warranter that certain things will never be divulged. She is no exception to the rule."†

The letter closed with the words: "I took the trouble to 'ascertain the spirit and meaning' with which everything in Mr. Sinnett's room was said and done; and though having no right to 'condemn' you—since you were ignorant of the true state of things—I cannot otherwise but strongly disapprove of that which, however much polished outwardly, would have been even under quite ordinary circumstances, CRUELTY still."[28]

"I think we owe the Old Lady an apology," Sinnett said thoughtfully, as he folded the letter and returned it to its envelope. Hume agreed, although he confessed that he had often wondered about H.P.B.'s "so-called training" in Tibet and whether it was true that she had spent seven years there.‡

"I don't think it can be denied that she was there," Sinnett replied. "It seems to me that she simply isn't a whole person as we think of normal personalities. If she left something of herself behind in Tibet, and for the reasons the Mahatma cites,

---

*Divine rulers.

†For further descriptions of H.P.B.'s psychological experiences and her complex personality see *Personal Memoirs* by Neff, especially Chapters 33 and 39; ODL; *Reminiscences: Daylight*, especially Chapter 7; *H.P.B. the Mystery* by dePurucker, particularly the early chapters.

‡The August 2, 1884 issue of *Light*, a Spiritualist journal published in England, carried an article by Arthur Lillie entitled "Koot Hoomi Unveiled" in which the author said, among other things, that he had never heard of an initiation lasting for seven years. H.P.B. replied to this article in the August 9, 1884 issue. Her reply is found in CW Vol. VI, pp. 269-80. In it she said: "I will tell him (Arthur Lillie) also that I have lived at different periods in 'Little Tibet' as in Great Tibet, and that these combined periods form more than seven years. Yet, I have never stated either verbally or over my signature that I had passed seven consecutive years in a convent. What I have said, and repeat now, is that I have stopped in Lamaistic convents; that I have visited Tsi-gadze, the Tashi-Lunpo territory and its neighborhood, and that I have been further in, and in such places of Tibet as have never been visited by any other European, and that he can never hope to visit." Biographers of H.P.B. have been unable to find any single block of seven years during which she could have been in Tibet. Another possible explanation has been offered (*See* next fn.).

then it must have been at a tremendous sacrifice, and I for one respect her for it. I think we should be tolerant and try harder to understand her."

"I don't see how we can expect to understand her," Hume said, with a touch of impatience. "Even Olcott doesn't understand her. He insists she isn't a medium in the usual sense. The ordinary medium is controlled by some entity or entities, but H.P.B. controls *them* and makes them do *her* will. Except for the 'Brothers' of course. But if Olcott doesn't understand her, knowing her so well, how can the rest of us expect to?"

"So far as Olcott is concerned," Sinnett commented, "I'm sure of two things, at least. He is absolutely honest, and he is absolutely loyal to his 'chum' as he calls her, even if he doesn't understand her. If he tells the truth about her, it's because he could never bring himself to do anything else. But it would never be with malice or vindictiveness."[29]

"Agreed," said Hume. "The old boy may be a bit crude, but I wouldn't question his integrity."

"He told me once," Sinnett offered, "that he sometimes wondered what happened to her psychologically in the Mentana crisis, when she was so badly wounded and left for dead in a ditch."

Hume looked at him sharply. "I've never heard the whole of that."

"She told Patience the story once. As I recall, she dressed in men's clothing and fought in Garibaldi's army. That was in 1867. One arm was broken by a sabre stroke, and she got musket shots in the shoulder and in one leg. Everyone thought she was dead, and she was left lying by the road when the army moved on. I'm not sure how she was found, but she was still living and was nursed back to health in Italy somewhere."

"What was Olcott's idea about it?"

"Oh, he has—or had—some notion that the proper *jiva** might have been killed out in the battle and that perhaps,

---

*Living entity. Some students conjecture that the person known as H.P. Blavatsky actually did die at Mentana and that her body was taken over by a high Initiate. It has been further suggested that it may have been this Initiate who had actually spent more than seven years in Tibet. This would explain why Olcott felt there were times when the body was artificially animated. (ODL 2:vi-viii) It is speculated that perhaps she herself was not sure at all times what her true identity was. At one time, writing to her sister, Mme. Jelihovsky, she commented: "Several times a day I

when her body wasn't occupied by the Mahatmas, she might be just a kind of artificially animated body. It seems far-fetched. He doesn't know the explanation, but he says she is a 'perpetual psychic mystery.'"[30]

"She is that without a doubt."

"I recall that in the first letter I had from the Mahatma K.H. after I returned from England," Sinnett said thoughtfully, "he mentioned that he wasn't at liberty to say who Imperator is—that's Stainton Moses's control, you know—any more than he, Imperator, would be to say who K.H. is, or perhaps even who H.P.B. is.[31] I've puzzled over that statement."

"I must say I'm not very sympathetic with this attitude of being so secret about everything," said Hume. "And I don't propose to make my apology too abject. As a matter of fact, I'm not sure why we should apologize. But let's get it over with."

It was not difficult. By the time they approached H.P.B. she had regained her composure and the loving, merry quality which so endeared her to her friends. She assured them that the incident was forgotten and that, so long as her health permitted, she would be happy to serve in the transmission of correspondence as she had done in the past.

Within six months, however, Hume was to write an extremely sarcastic letter to her. She sent the letter to Sinnett, and the Mahatma M. interposed some marginal comments while it was in transit. In the letter Hume maintained: "Now I know all about the Brothers' supposed explanation that you are a psychological cripple," and the Mahatma M. added: "He is mistaken, he does not." Hume followed his comment with arguments about which "principle" she could have left in Tibet and concluded that the explanation was unsatisfactory and therefore its having been offered threw suspicion on the whole thing. Here the Mahatma Morya inserted: "Very clever. But suppose it is neither *one of the seven* particularly, but all?

feel that besides me there is someone else, quite separable from me, present in my body. I never lose the consciousness of my personality; what I feel is as if I were keeping silent and the other one—the lodger who is in me—were speaking with my tongue." (*Personal Memoirs of H.P. Blavatsky*, by Mary K. Neff, p. 241) She could not, then, as some maintain, have been a case of schizophrenia (split-personality) since her consciousness as H.P. Blavatsky was never surrendered but merely kept silent while the "other" spoke through her.

Every one of them a 'cripple' and forbidden the exercise of its full powers? And suppose such is the wise law of a far fore-seeing power?"[32]

I must say, thought Sinnett, as he put the letter with his collection of other letters from H.P.B., it seems to me Hume can't bear to think that anybody knows more than he does.

Sinnett himself was not wholly guiltless of this attitude, although his affection and respect for the Mahatma K.H. somewhat tempered his views. While he was still in Simla, however, another communiction from the Mahatma gave him cause for serious thought. This was a report of comments by the Mahachohan on the meaning and work of the Theosophical Society.*[33] Concerned with the apparently irreconcilable divergence of views between himself and the two Englishmen, the Mahatma had consulted his "Chief" and now sent on the results of that consultation with a short note: "An abridged version of the view of the Chohan on the T.S. from his own words as given last night."[34]

The letter was rather long and laid much stress upon the need for brotherhood, benevolence, and philanthropy. Both Englishmen had been, and continued to be, more interested in phenomena and the intellectual aspects of the teachings than in the furtherance of these virtues. After all, they maintained, they were familiar with the Western world; Christianity had tried for almost two thousand years to bring about the brotherhood of man without any conspicuous success. What was needed now, they felt, was something to impress the materialistic scientists and the skeptics with the fact that the existence of Adepts and their knowledge was worth serious consideration. Both men had continued to importune the Mahatma in this vein.

But the Mahachohan did not share their conviction. "Better perish the T.S. with both its hapless founders," he said, "than that we should permit it to become no better than an academy of magic, a hall of occultism. That we the devoted followers of that spirit incarnate of absolute self-sacrifice, of philanthropy, divine kindness, as of all the highest virtues attainable on this earth of sorrow, the man of men, Guatama Buddha, should ever allow the T.S. to represent the *embodiment of selfishness,*

---

*This letter has been called "practically a charter for the work and development of the Theosophical Society throughout the ages." LMW 1:108

the refuge of the few with no thought in them for the many, is a strange idea, my brothers."

"We shall never make them understand," said Hume irritably, when he read the letter. "If we're so hemmed in and restricted in developing the Society's purposes, it will never have the prestige it should have."

"Yet, to be fair," Sinnett reminded him, "the Mahachohan says we have to 'popularize a knowledge of theosophy.'"

"Yes, but you notice he ties that in with the statement that it is the 'self-sacrificing pursuit of the best means to lead on the right path our neighbour...' and so on. I don't deny that, but I disagree with his ideas of what constitutes the 'best means.' They can't seem to see that if the intellectual leaders of the West could be convinced, all the 'neighbors' would follow—and all this without any exaggerated claims of a 'benevolent intermingling of the high and low' and so on."

In spite of his loyalty to the Master, Sinnett could not help being influenced by Hume's strong views. He had never been able to bring himself to regard the Indian natives as other than inferior to the Europeans and it was impossible to root out this attitude entirely.

"Nevertheless," he managed to counter, "I think we have got to pay attention to that aspect if we expect the Master to stay in touch with us and continue to teach us."

"He hasn't taught us much so far," complained Hume, "but if he means what he says, he'll continue to teach us under any circumstances."

"I'm not so sure of that," was Sinnett's thoughtful response.

8

F or myself," wrote Sinnett in the second edition of *The Occult World,* "the most interesting fact connected with my Simla experience of 1881 was this: During the period in question I got into relations with one other of the Brothers, besides Koot Hoomi. It came to pass that in the progress of his own development it was necessary for Koot Hoomi to retire for a period of three months into absolute seclusion."[1]

This was the "retreat" mentioned by H.P.B. when Sinnett questioned her concerning the Master's statement that he would be leaving his correspondents to themselves for a period of three months. Sinnett received a short letter from him, written just before he left on what he termed his "long, *very* long journey" in which he said that he was trying to get his "Brother M." to maintain the contact with the two Englishmen and the Simla Eclectic Society, although "I am really afraid Mr. Hume and he would never agree together." For himself, he assured Sinnett, he had not been in the least offended by Hume's comments. "I never could be," he said. "It is not anything contained in his observations that annoyed me, but the persistence with which he was following out a line of argument that I knew was pregnant with future mischief." He added: "Please assure Mr. Hume of my personal sympathy and respect for him and give him my most friendly regards."[2]

The Mahatma Morya was finally persuaded to take over the correspondence, "reluctantly at first,"[3] and in spite of the fact that "his only hatred in life is for writing."[4]

"The change which came over the character of our correspondence when our new Master took us in hand was very remarkable," recorded Sinnett. "Every letter that emanated from Koot Hoomi had continued to bear the impress of his gently mellifluous style. He would write half a page at any time rather than run the least risk of letting a brief or careless phrase hurt anybody's feelings. His handwriting, too, was always very legible and regular. Our new master treated us very differently: he declared himself almost unacquainted with our language, and wrote a very rugged hand which it was sometimes difficult to decipher. He did not beat about the bush with us at all. If we wrote out an essay on some occult ideas we had picked up, and sent it to him asking if it was right, it would sometimes come back with a heavy red line scored through it and 'No' written on the margin. On one occasion one of us had written, 'Can you clear my conceptions about so and so?' The annotation found in the margin when the paper was returned was 'How can I clear what you haven't got?' and so on. But with all this we made progress under M----and by degrees the correspondence, which began on his side with brief notes scrawled in the roughest manner on bits of coarse Tibetan paper, expanded into considerable letters sometimes. And it must be understood that while his rough and abrupt ways formed an amusing contrast with the tender gentleness of Koot Hoomi, there was nothing in these to impede the growth of our attachment to him as we began to feel ourselves tolerated by him as pupils a little more willingly than at first. Some of my readers, I am sure, will realize what I mean by 'attachment' in this case. I use a colourless word deliberately to avoid a parade of feelings which might not be generally understood, but I can assure them that in the course of prolonged relations—even though merely of the epistolary kind—with a personage who, though a man like the rest of us as regards his natural place in creation, is elevated so above ordinary men as to possess some attributes commonly considered divine, feelings are engendered which are too deep to be lightly or easily described."[5]

The first letter received from the Mahatma M. expressed thanks for the "tobacco-machine" which Sinnett had brought back from England as a gift for him.* "Our frenchified and pelingized Pandit† tells me the little short thing has to be *cooloted*—whatever he may mean by this," the Mahatma

---

*According to H.P.B., the Mahatma M. smoked a water pipe called a "hookah." (*Guide* 73)

†A light reference to the Mahatma K.H., who spoke French fluently and was more familiar with the Western (pelingized) ways than was the Mahatma M.

wrote, "and so I will proceed to do so. The pipe is short and my nose long, so we will agree very well together I hope."[6]

Before leaving on his retreat, the Mahatma K.H. had urged Sinnett to attend the seventh anniversary celebration of the Theosophical Society, which was to take place in Bombay in January 1882.[7] The Mahatma M., in this first short letter, added his urging in the matter. "Could you but go to Bombay to the Anniversary," he wrote, "you would confer upon K.H. and myself a great obligation and a lasting one—but that you know best."‡

The same letter contained a warning about the "peling Sahib" (Hume). "He is as dangerous as a friend as an enemy, very, very bad as both I know him best."

The Mahatma's way of expressing himself brought a smile to Sinnett's face and he commented to himself that this would be one letter that he would not share with the other Englishman. But the closing words softened the smile and touched him with a certain warmth: "Anyhow," the Master wrote, "you Sinnett Sahib reconciled me to a good many things you are true and true I will be."

Sinnett felt a tingle of anticipation. This correspondence was going to be of quite a different nature from his correspondence with the Mahatma K.H. The brusqueness had an astringent quality which was no less intriguing than the literary grace which he had admired and enjoyed in the other Master's letters.

There followed a series of short notes mostly concerned with whether or not a letter dictated by the Mahatma K.H. to Damodar before he left on his retreat—and somewhat garbled by that young chela—should be shown to Hume, as it was

---

‡This meeting took place on January 12, 1882. It was a delayed celebration, as the founding date of the Theosophical Society was November 17. However, in his Annual Report, Olcott explained that it was impossible to hold the meeting on that date, as he was in Ceylon and did not return until December 19, 1881. It was therefore held on the first convenient date thereafter. (SH 165) In making their requests both Mahatmas had referred to some potentially dangerous elements threatening the welfare of the Society, and it was true that some "blackguard handbills" (ODL2:331) had been circulated, charging H.P.B. and Olcott with running the Society for personal profit. They were completely exonerated when Damodar read the Treasurer's report. As it happened, Sinnett went to Bombay in January 1882 to meet Patience and Denny, who arrived there from England on January 6. From several comments in the *Letters*, it would appear that he did not remain for the anniversary meeting. However, in ODL 2:332 in reporting the gathering, Olcott commented that "Mr. Sinnett was present and spoke."

feared he would misunderstand some of the statements and, as the Mahatma M. said, accuse K.H. of "ignorance." "I would not have even the desert wind listen to a word said at low breath against him who now sleeps,"[8] wrote the Mahatma M. —a comment which impressed Sinnett with the unique and beautiful relationship which existed between him and the younger Master. In a longer letter[9] which followed this series of notes, the Mahatma M. quoted his "Brother's" request that he "watch over my work" during his absence, and added: "What is there I would not have promised him at that hour! At a certain spot not to be mentioned to outsiders, there is a chasm spanned by a frail bridge of woven grasses and with a raging torrent beneath. The bravest member of your Alpine clubs would scarcely dare to venture the passage, for it hangs like a spider's web and *seems* to be rotten and impassable. Yet it is not; and he who dares the trial and succeeds—as he will if it is right that he should be permitted—comes into a gorge of surpassing beauty of scenery—to one of *our* places and to some of *our* people, of which there is no note or minute among European geographers. At a stone's throw from the old Lamasery stands the old tower, within whose bosom have gestated generations of Bodhisatwas.* It is there, where now rests your lifeless friend—my brother, the light of my soul, to whom I made a faithful promise to watch during his absence over *his* work."[10]

Much of the long letter concerned Hume and constituted one of the frankest and most devastating—and at the same time most objective—evaluations of that gentleman's character to be found in the *Letters*. This was the more notable as the Mahatma evidently intended it to be shown to Hume.

"Mr. Hume thinks and speaks of me in a way which need only be noticed so far as it affects the frame of mind in which he proposes to apply to me for philosophical instruction," wrote the Mahatma. "For his respect I care as little as he for my displeasure. But passing over his superficial disagreeableness, I recognize fully his goodness of motive, his abilities, his potential usefulness . . . he will find me ready to help, but not to flatter nor to dispute."[11]

---

*See "Master K.H.'s Retreat and the Tower of The Bodhisattwas" by C.N. Drinkwater, *The Theosophist*, August 1978.

Sinnett thought this letter rather better written than the other communications from this Mahatma had been; he assumed that the latter had taken special pains with it, or perhaps had received some help in writing it, since obviously he considered it of importance for the future of the work.

A little further on in the letter, the Mahatma commented: "I am not a fine scholar, Sahibs, like my blessed brother,"[12] and he quoted a rather sad comment by K.H. concerning his difficulties of communication with the Englishmen: "A few days before leaving us, Koot'hoomi said to me as follows: 'I feel tired and weary of these never ending disputations. The more I try to explain to both of them the circumstances that control us and that interpose between us so many obstacles to free intercourse, the less they understand me! Under the most favourable aspects this correspondence must always be unsatisfactory, even exasperatingly so, at times; for nothing short of personal interviews...would satisfy them fully. It is as though we were hallooing to each other across an impassable ravine, and only one of us seeing his interlocutor. In point of fact, there is nowhere in physical nature a mountain abyss so hopelessly impassable and obstructive to the traveler as that spiritual one which keeps them back from me.'"[13]

Of Hume, specifically, the Mahatma added: "He prides himself in the thought that he never had 'a spirit of veneration' for anything but his own abstract ideals. We are perfectly aware of it. Nor could he possibly have any veneration for anyone or anything, as all the veneration his nature is capable of is— *concentrated upon* himself."[14]

But, in contrast to these strictures, the Mahatma commented: "A more honest, sincere, or a kinder man never breathed on the Himalayas. I know actions of his of which his own family and lady are utterly ignorant—so noble, so kind and grand, that even his own pride remains blind to their full worth...but I am forced to tell him the truth: and while that side of his character has all my admiration, his pride will never win my approbation—for which once more, Mr. Hume will not care twopence, but that matters very little indeed...Nor can he be brought to confess that anyone in the world can know better than himself anything that HE has studied and formed his opinion thereupon."[15]

There was more—much more—of this characterization. The Mahatma then reminded Sinnett that he was answering *all* his letters. The Englishman had again been trying to point out to the Mahatma the value of phenomena in convincing the world of the existence of the Brotherhood, and the Mahatma commented: "...where you are and will be ever wrong, my dear sir, it is in entertaining the idea that phenomena can ever become 'a powerful engine' to shake the foundations of erroneous beliefs in the Western mind...I wish I could impress upon your minds the deep conviction that we do not wish Mr. Hume or you to prove conclusively to the public that we really exist. Please realize the fact that so long as men doubt there will be curiosity and enquiry, and that enquiry stimulates reflection, which begets effort; but let our secret be once thoroughly vulgarized and not only will sceptical society derive no great good but our privacy would be constantly endangered and have to be continually guarded at an unreasonable cost of power."[16]

The Master's closing paragraph again brought a wry smile to Sinnett's face:

"Let us drop it. I close the longest letter I have ever written in my life; but as I do it for K.H.—I am satisfied. Though Mr. Hume may not think it, the 'mask of the adept' is kept at _____ _____* not at Simla, and I try to keep up to it, however poor I may be as a writer and a correspondent."

Sinnett was somewhat hesitant to show this letter to Hume, but realizing that the Master evidently expected him to do so, he tendered it to his friend on an occasion when the latter seemed in a relatively receptive mood. Apparently it failed, as other communications had failed, to pierce the wall of the pride which the Mahatma had so deplored. Hume was profoundly irritated and exploded irascibly.

"I think we are wasting our time and energies trying to understand these so-called 'Brothers'!" he said sharply. "And if they exist at all, they are wasting *their* time. They don't seem to grasp the fact that we are better acquainted with the world than they are. If they weren't so possessive about their ideas and would permit us to expound them freely—and with proofs—think what we could do! But no! They don't care whether the world knows they exist! They don't even want the world to know about them! Well, our patience isn't inexhaustible!"

*It is not known to what these blanks refer, but it is assumed they designate a secret "headquarters" of the Brotherhood.

He tossed the letter aside contemptuously. Sinnett picked it up and returned it to the envelope.

"I suppose it is difficult for us to understand that they are absolutely impersonal," he responded. "Besides, I think he is right about having to guard their privacy. I understand they aren't permitted to use power uselessly—or even for self-protection. I admit this Mahatma is rather blunt, but I have an idea that our correspondence with him is going to be extremely interesting."

Hume shrugged indifferently.

"Perhaps so," he said. "I've about finished my 'Stray Feathers'† index and I could do one of the 'Fragments'‡ for *The Theosophist*, but if he wants me to do that, he'll have to send me something to go on."[17]

"I don't think he'll do that unless we ask him some more questions. He seems willing enough to answer those, but he doesn't like to write well enough to expound the philosophy gratuitously. Anyhow, as you know, I must be getting back to Allahabad. I've already seriously jeopardized my job."

"How? You've been quite regular in sending in your editorials."

"But Rattigan hasn't published very many of them. He isn't disposed to look favourably on most of the things I write these days. Besides," he added rather anxiously, "I *have* been away quite a long time."

It was not, however, until almost the first of November that Sinnett returned to Allahabad. Quite as he expected, he received a rather cool reception at the hands of his employer and managed only partially to redeem himself by maintaining a strict silence for a time on all matters having to do with the Theosophical Society or occultism.

H.P.B. left Simla at about the same time for a tour of some cities in northern India. Several letters were received from her during the next few weeks. The first came from Saharanpur, where she met Ross Scott, who was to accompany her on her further travels.[18] His marriage to Minnie Hume was to take place in a few weeks, and he was excited and grateful to H.P.B.

---

†*Stray Feathers* was a quarterly ornithological magazine published by Hume. He was apparently compiling a catalog of the exhibits in his museum.

‡"Fragments of Occult Truth," a series of articles begun by Hume and taken over by Sinnett when Hume abandoned the task.

for her part in bringing it about. She answered his expressions of appreciation quite graciously but with some inward misgivings, since she knew the venture was a precarious one, and her good opinion of Miss Hume was not without qualifications.*

H.P.B.'s letter contained nothing of startling moment save that she commented, "I did not hear or see or smell the Boss† for three days. He must have prigged your letter though, for I see he knows what you do. How many times did you write to him?"

Sinnett had, as a matter of fact, been plying the Mahatma with questions recently, and Hume had directed a number of penetrating inquiries to him. The Master had answered the latter's questions in some detail, and Sinnett had copied off some of the answers but had procrastinated about getting them into his notebook. A further letter from H.P.B.[19] listed several instructions for Sinnett from the Mahatma, among which was a direction to make a true copy of the answers given Hume ("M.'s notes on Cosmogony with the Tibetan words")‡ and to see that H.P.B. also had a copy, since it was not known how much or how accurately Hume might elaborate on them if he used them in his writing. They actually amounted to a tabulation of such of the ultimate principles of the universe as the Mahatma M. was prepared at that time to set forth.

Sinnett decided that he had better get the Master's words into his notebook if he wanted to preserve them just as they were without any meddling by Hume. He would never have believed, when he and the other Englishman had first become interested in Theosophy and had been put in touch with the Mahatmas, that his friend would be the source of so much difficulty, in spite of the fact that when he took his pen in hand to write on occult subjects, he could be supremely convincing. Sometimes Sinnett was inclined to agree with him that he could do a better job of expounding occultism than even the Masters could. But that seemed to be no reason for the sarcastic attitude he so often assumed. However, he reflected

---

See Chapter 7 for the results of the marriage of Ross Scott and Minnie Hume.

†Mahatma Morya.

‡These answers are found as "Cosmological Notes" in LBS Appendix II, p. 376.

honestly, neither of them was characteristically disposed to patience.

A further instruction for Sinnett from the Mahatma was that he should "make a special duty to prevent his little son being made to eat meat—not even fowls, and to write to Mrs. Sinnett. Once the Mother has placed the child under K.H.'s protection, let her see nothing pollutes his nature."*

H.P.B. wrote again from Dehra Dun, her next stop after leaving Saharanpur.[20] She had seen the Mahatma M., she said, and he had dictated to her an answer to a letter from Sinnett which she had found waiting for her. This largely concerned some of the members of the Society in Allahabad, about whom Sinnett had asked advice. But she added a paragraph of her own and enclosed for him a letter which she had received from her uncle, assistant Minister of the Interior in the Russian Government, attesting to her identity and saying that "Prince Dondohof"† would be sending an official document for the same purpose.

Sinnett himself had received a similar letter from H.P.B.'s uncle which he hoped would be useful in quieting the rumors, kept alive by H.P.B.'s enemies, that she was a Russian spy.

A second letter from Dehra Dun was mainly taken up with Society matters and with descriptions of some of the people whom she had met.[21] Of special interest to Sinnett was an item near the end: "The poor *Disinherited*‡ is *very* sick. He fell down a cud and nearly broke both his legs. Had it not been for another chela with him who had time and the presence of mind of doing what was needed to *arrest him in his fall* he would have broken himself to pieces down an abyss of 2,800 feet. M.

---

*Almost a year later, when Mrs. Sinnett was concerned that she might have carried the germs of disease with her from the Humes, where she had been visiting, and where Mrs. Hume was suffering from tuberculosis, and thus run the risk of infecting Denny, the Mahatma K.H. sent her a lock of his hair to place around the child's neck. "Unable as I am to carry into your homestead the full magnetism of my physical person I do the next best thing by sending you a lock of hair as a vehicle for the transmission of my aura in a concentrated condition." (ML 451/443)

†Prince Alexander Mahaylovich Dondukov-Korsakov (1820-1883), a friend for many years of H.P.B. and her family. (CW VI: 432)

‡Djual Khul, called the "Disinherited" or "Benjamin" presumably from the Biblical story of the disinherited brother and because he had been disinherited by his family when he became a chela of the Mahatma K.H. It is understood that he later became an Adept. (*Guide* 228)

says it is a fiendish 'Red Cap'* who did it; who caught the boy off his guard for an instant and positively took advantage of it in a wink . . . one more proof that even a chela and one of the 1st degree can be off his guard sometimes . . ."†

H.P.B. added an appendage to her letter: "Ross Scott sends his love. I wish you heard Mrs. Collector Church swear!"[22] She had earlier described Mrs. Church, a woman whom she had met at Dehra Dun and whom she here endowed with her husband's title of "Collector," as one who used language that "made the root of my hair turn red and burn with shame."[23]

"Her language must indeed be lurid if it shocks the Old Lady!" Sinnett thought, as he placed the letter in the box where he kept his correspondence with H.P.B. The letter was not dated and he neglected, as he often did, to note the date of its receipt.‡

Several letters came directly from the Mahatma M. also about this time. The *Civil and Military Gazette* had renewed its attacks on Olcott and H.P.B., and efforts were being made by other entrenched interests to discredit and disgrace them. Sinnett had written the Mahatma to ask whether he could do anything directly to help the Society through this renewed crisis. To this the Master replied, "No: neither yourself nor the Lord Sang-yias Himself—so long as the equivocal position of the Founders is not perfectly and undeniably proved due to fiendish malice and a systematic intrigue—could help it on."[24] A little further on he added: "Watch the papers—all except two or three; the 'dear old lady' ridiculed when not positively libelled, Olcott attacked by all the hell-hounds of the press and missions. A pamphlet headed 'Theosophy' printed and

---

*Member of a Tibetan sect, at that time regarded as dugpas, or sorcerers. *(Glossary)*

†In a letter written much later by the Mahatma K.H., he commented: "In our mountains here, the Dugpas lay, at dangerous points, paths frequented by our Chelas, bits of old rag and other articles best calculated to attract the attention of the unwary, which have been impregnated with their evil magnetism. If one be stepped upon a tremendous psychic shock may be communicated to the wayfarer, so that he may lose his footing and fall down the precipice before he can recover himself." (ML 369/363)

‡This habitual oversight on Sinnett's part in connection with both LBS and ML, has complicated the matter of determining the sequence of the letters and has resulted in some misdating. The reader is therefore urged to follow the chronological listing in the Appendix in any systematic study of the *Letters.*

circulated by the Christians at Tinnevelly October 23rd on the days of O's arrival there."#

The Mahatma continued in his letter: "If your Rattigan is not quite a scoundrel, one of his papers¶ having thrown and throwing daily dishonor upon an innocent woman, he would be the first to suggest you the idea of translating and publishing her uncle's letters (to you and herself) in the *Pioneer;* with a few words in a leader, to say that a still more substantial official proof is shortly expected from the Prince D. which will settle the vexed question of her identity for ever at rest."[25]

But Rattigan made no such suggestion, and several subtle hints thrown out by Sinnett himself were ignored in stony silence. There seemed no other course than simply to carry on as best he could, taking positive action as seemed indicated and letting the chips fall where they might.

His active correspondence with the Mahatma M. was a great encouragement to him, particularly since the latter had forthrightly declared his dislike for writing. Most of the letters concerned various situations in the Theosophical Society, of which Sinnett was by this time Vice-President. He understood with deepened respect that the Mahatma was willing to undertake the onerous task of carrying on the correspondence because he was concerned that his Brother K.H. should not feel utterly discouraged and disheartened over lack of progress when he returned from his retreat.

#Olcott himself was to relate the circumstances of this attempt to discredit the Society and its founders. He recorded that when he arrived at Tinnevelly, where he had been invited to inaugurate a new branch of the Theosophical Society in the course of his work in Ceylon, he was met by an enthusiastic crowd of some 2,000. All the town notables were dressed in gala costume, and the huge elephants from the Temple had "their mighty brows painted with caste marks" and were "made to raise their trunks and salute us with a roar." There were presentations and salutations and all the paraphernalia of a great public demonstration, all to show the popularity of the Colonel and the Theosophical Society. Olcott overused his voice and, the next morning, awoke with a sore throat. However, he says, "I soon had something else to divert me from my physical disabilities." He received a copy of the pamphlet mentioned by the Mahatma M., which contained reprints of two "meanly slanderous articles against us, from a London and a New York paper." Not to be defeated by such underhanded tactics, however, Olcott met the attack with his usual resourcefulness. Before delivering the lecture for which he was scheduled that afternoon at the Hindu College, he called attention to the pamphlet and "denounced its authors in suitable terms." The blow recoiled upon the heads of the would-be assassins and our popularity was doubled. (ODL 2:310-12)

¶*The C & M Gazette.*

In one letter received toward the end of the year (1881), the Mahatma commented that "The Members would have plenty to do were they to pursue reality with half the fervour they do *mirage*... men who join the Society with the one selfish object of reaching power making occult science their only or even chief aim may as well not join it—they are doomed to disappointment as much as those who commit the mistake of letting them believe that the Society is nothing else. It is just because they preach too much 'the Brothers' and too little if at all *Brotherhood* that they fail. ...It is he alone who has the love of humanity at heart, who is capable of grasping thoroughly the idea of a regenerating practical Brotherhood who is entitled to the possession of our secrets."[26]

A postscript to another letter received in December stated that "the Disinherited" was "on his legs again,"[27] a fact which pleased Sinnett, for he knew that the Mahatma K.H. would be concerned about his chela and undoubtedly would need him when he returned. This letter suggested an action which might be taken to vindicate H.P.B. of some of the charges being made against her, although the Mahatma spoke positively against anything undertaken in a spirit of revenge. "But we have defense and she has a right to it," he said.[28] He suggested that Sinnett draft a circular letter for the signatures of H.P.B. and Olcott for subsequent distribution to all the newspapers. This letter would demand retraction of certain statements published, particularly in *The Statesman,* and threaten suit for libel if such retraction was not made. "This alone will prove sufficient to frighten the traducer for it will reveal him before the public as a 'slanderer' and show to himself that he was in the wrong box." Apparently Sinnett followed this advice and the letter was circularized.

In the meantime, however, H.P.B. wrote what the Mahatma termed a "foolish, childish, and silly letter" to the Bombay *Gazette.* "I have overlooked it," the Master wrote, "But you must not so labour under the impression that it will *undo* all the good yours has done. There are a few sensitive persons on whose nerves it will jar, but the rest will never appreciate its true spirit; nor is it in any way libellous—only vulgar and foolish. I will force her to stop." That H.P.B. suffered acutely the Master recognized but he said he was unable to help her for the causes could not be undone.

"Do not blame the poor woman, blame me," he said. "She is but a 'shell' at times and I often careless in watching her."[29]

Col. Olcott had arrived from Ceylon on December 19, and Sinnett felt that undoubtedly he would be of considerable help in the campaign to combat H.P.B.'s slanderers. His work in Ceylon had been extremely successful. He wrote Sinnett that he was "joyously welcomed by the Headquarters group" and that matters had gone on in their usual way during his absence.[30]

The circular letters had some effect; the charges against H.P.B. and the Theosophical Society appeared less frequently, and the year ended on a reasonably hopeful note. For Sinnett, it was rather a lonely time, but Patience and Denny were on the ocean somewhere en route to India, and he looked forward to their arrival with eager anticipation. In the meantime, he had so much to think about in connection with his correspondence with the Mahatma M. that his loneliness never really oppressed him. He had sent to the Master a series of questions on cosmology; these were to some extent inspired by the "cosmological notes" received by Hume but probed deeply into the concepts which had been set forth.* He felt that they were learning a great deal of the profound philosophy of the Brotherhood.

*Answers to these questions came in January 1882 and are found on pp. 70-78 of the *Letters*, headed "Cosmological Notes and Queries and M.'s Replies."

9

Return from Retreat

"The Master has awaked and bids me write."

These words in the handwriting of the chela Djual Khul greeted Sinnett as he opened the envelope of the first letter received in January of 1882.[1] Somehow, he had anticipated the message; not only had three months elapsed since the beginning of the Mahatma K.H.'s retreat, but the envelope itself, with the address in a strange script, had alerted him to the fact that there was something different inside. His heart had leaped at the sight of it, and he felt a tingling in his fingers as he opened it. He hadn't realized how much he had missed communication with K.H., and now the hope that it was about to be resumed gave him a strangely sweet comfort.

His hope was not to be fulfilled immediately, however, as the next words of Djual Khul's indicated: "To his great regret for certain reasons He will not be able until a fixed period has passed to expose Himself to the thought currents inflowing so strongly from beyond the Himavat."

Sinnett hoped that his eagerness, which he found the greatest difficulty in controlling, would not become a part of the "thought currents" which might further delay the reopening of the correspondence.

The letter continued: "I am to tell you that He is 'quite as friendly to you as heretofore and well satisfied with both your good intentions and even their execution so far as it lay in your power. You have proved your affection and sincerity by your zeal...One year has wrought great change in your heart... you shall hear from me *direct* at the earliest practicable opportunity, for we are not ungrateful and even Nirvana cannot obliterate GOOD.'"

A note from D.K. himself appeared in the next paragraph: "I am personally permitted at the same time to thank you very warmly for the genuine sympathy which you felt for me at the time when a slight accident due to my forgetfulness laid me on my bed of sickness.* . . . I can assure you that I, though but a humble chela as yet, felt your good wishes flowing to me as the convalescent in the cold mountains feels from the gentle breeze that blows upon him from the plains below."

Sinnett knew that this chela spoke and wrote English fluently, and he thought he detected in the last sentence a touch of his Master's felicitous style.

An announcement which followed was received by the Englishman with something less than pleasure.

"I am also to tell you," wrote Djual Khul, "that in a certain Mr. Bennett of America who will shortly arrive at Bombay, you may recognize one who, in spite of his national provincialism, that you so detest, and his too infidelistic bias, is one of our agents (unknown to himself) to carry out the scheme for the enfranchisement of Western thought from superstitious creeds."

Sinnet's somewhat negative reaction to this news proved to be prophetic. He was in Bombay, where he had gone to meet Patience and Denny, when Bennett arrived on January 10. He was otherwise occupied at the time and was not among those who welcomed the American but met him soon afterward and was repelled by his slovenly dress, his uncouth mannerisms, and his generally unprepossessing appearance. Bennett himself did not seem to be entirely at ease in the presence of the meticulously groomed and rather aloof Englishman and so did nothing to redeem himself in the latter's eyes.

The Mahatma M., in one of several letters yet to be received from him before the Master K.H. resumed the correspondence, reproved Sinnett for his attitude:

"You saw only that Bennett had unwashed hands, uncleaned nails and used coarse language and had—to you—a generally unsavoury aspect. But if *that* sort of thing is your criterion of moral excellence or potential power, how many adepts or wonder-producing *lamas* would pass your muster? That is part of your blindness. . . Few men have suffered—and unjustly suffered—as he has; and as few have a more kind, unselfish and truthful a heart. . . B----- is an honest man and of a sincere heart, besides being one of tremendous moral courage

---

*The result of his fall mentioned in Chapter 8.

and a martyr to boot. Such our K.H. loves... There's a moral smell as well as a physical one good friend.''[2]

Sinnett found it impossible to like Bennett but, remembering M.'s comment, he managed not to protest when the American was received into the fellowship of the Theosophical Society. This action was taken after some reluctance even on the part of Col. Olcott, who nevertheless admitted that the situation taught "a lesson too much needed by us all!"

D. M. Bennett was a Freethinker and the editor of that group's organ, *The Truthseeker*. He was, said Olcott, "a very interesting and sincere person who had suffered a year's imprisonment for his bitter—often coarse—attacks on Christian dogmatism."[3] A sham case had been manufactured against him by an unscrupulous detective of a Christian society in New York, and "he was prosecuted and sent to prison. He was made to serve out his whole term of one year, despite the fact that a petition, signed by 100,000 persons, was sent to President Hayes on his behalf. When he was discharged, a tremendous audience welcomed him enthusiastically at the most fashionable public hall in New York, and a fund was subscribed to pay his expenses on a world-round tour of observation of the practical working of Christianity in all lands."

The Colonel learned, in conversation with Bennett, that he and his wife had been members of the Shaker Society for a number of years. "His religious yet eclectic mind had revolted against the narrowness and intolerance of the Shakers and of Christian sectarianism in general; he and the gentle Shakeress in question decided to marry and make a home of their own, and they left the Shaker community."[4]

Bennett had thereafter become a confirmed skeptic and devoted his life to vigorous free-thought propaganda.

"There was," wrote Olcott, "a candor and friendliness about the man which made us sympathize at once." He was not blind to the fact that Bennett made a rather unfavorable impression on first acquaintance but he liked and admired the man. Bennett read Sinnett's book, *The Occult World*, and was greatly impressed. Shortly thereafter he applied for membership in the Society. Then occurred the series of events which resulted in the "much-needed lesson" mentioned by Olcott.

Simultaneously with Bennett's arrival, "A blatant theological Boanerges* named Cook—Joseph Cook (also from America), the *Reverend* Joseph Cook, to be exact—a burly man who seemed to believe in the Trinity—with himself as the Third Person—happened at Bombay on a lecturing tour."[5] Cook was "boomed" by the Anglo-Indian public. "Their journals did their best for him, and used the story of Mr. Bennett's martyrdom as a trump card, denouncing him as a corruptor of public morals and a jailbird whom decent people should avoid. The Christ-like Joseph opened the ball at his first lecture at the town hall, and committed the blind folly of equally denouncing us, Theosophists, as adventurers, in the hearing of a large audience of Hindus and Parsis, who loved and knew us after two whole years of intercourse. The clue thus given to the hostile Press caused them to attack and revile Mr. Bennett to such an extent that I hesitated to take him into membership, for fear that it might plunge us into another public wrangle, and thus interfere with our aim of peacefully settling down to our proper business of Theosophical study and propaganda. It was an instinct of worldly prudence, certainly not chivalric altruism, and I was punished for it, for, on expressing my views to H.P.B., she was overshadowed by a Master who told me my duty and reproached me for my faulty judgment. I was bidden to remember how far from perfect I had been when they accepted my offer of service at New York, how imperfect I was still, and not venture to sit as a judge over my fellow-man . . . I was sarcastically told to look through the whole list of our members and point out a single one without faults. That was enough; I returned to Mr. Bennett, gave him the Application blank to sign, and H.P.B. and I became his sponsors."[6]

Col. Olcott then "turned upon our reverend slanderer† and defied him to meet me in public on a given date and make good his false charges against us."

Some "shifty replies" were received from Cook, giving as an excuse for not accepting the invitation to debate that he had to go to Poona, where he was engaged to lecture. Another member of the Theosophical Society, Captain A. Banon, who was in Bombay at the time, sent him a challenge to meet at

†"Son of thunder," a name given by Jesus to James and John. (Mark 3:17)

*Joseph Cook

Poona, stating to him that "if he again evaded us, he—the Captain—should post him as a liar and a coward." Olcott, H.P.B., and Captain Banon went to Poona on the scheduled date, but found that "Mr. Cook had fled to the other side of India without fulfilling his engagement with the Poona public!" So much for the Reverend Mr. Cook.[7]

Mr. Bennett was duly admitted to membership in the Society and eventually left India to resume his world-wide tour. Col. Olcott wrote that "The record of his observations was embodied in an interesting work entitled *A Free-thinker's Journey around the World*" and that some of his "shrewd and sarcastic notes on Palestine were especially striking."[8]

The events involving Bennett and Cook, however, had not yet taken place when Sinnett received the letter from Djual Khul which alerted him to the fact that he might expect to resume his correspondence with K.H. in the relatively near future. In that letter, Djual Khul assured Sinnett that the Mahatma wanted him to know that he should not feel "such an exaggerated delicacy about taking out the work left undone by Mr. Hume's hands." This was a reference to the series of articles entitled "Fragments of Occult Truth" begun by Hume but abandoned by him when the Mahatmas failed to please him by following his advice. "That gentleman," said Djual Khul, "chooses to do but what suits his personal fancy without any regard whatever to the feelings of other people. His present work also*—a pyramid of intellectual energy misspent —his objections and reasons are all calculated but to exonerate himself only." Further on in the letter, D.K. commented: "As to our revered M.: he desires me to assure you that the secret of Mr. Hume's professed love for Humanity lies in, and is based upon, the chance presence in that word of the first syllable; as for 'mankind'—he has no sympathy for it."[9]

The Master K.H., said Djual Khul, begged him to proceed with his metaphysical studies and "not to be giving up the task in despair whenever you meet with incomprehensible ideas in M. Sahib's notes..."

The Mahatma M.'s answers to Sinnett's questions on cosmology had not yet been received, but he assumed this

---

*The maintenance of his ornithological museum, the publication of *Stray Feathers*, and the elaborate catalog or "index" on which he had been working.

admonition meant that they might soon be forthcoming. In this he was correct, for they arrived shortly after he and his family returned to Allahabad. He labeled them "Cosmological Notes and Queries and M.'s Replies"[10] and laid them aside temporarily until he could find time to give them serious study.

The homecoming was a happy one for all of them. The servants had cleaned and polished until the whole place shone, for one and all they adored Mrs. Sinnett and Denny, and they expressed their welcome not only in these preparations but also in their bobbings and grinnings and gigglings as Patience greeted them and thanked them in Hindi for carrying on so splendidly in her absence. Even Denny, whose vigor had been somewhat restored by the months in England, was excited and ran through the whole house identifying familiar objects and exclaiming with delight over the gifts which his father had placed as a surprise for him in the nursery. Sinnett himself felt a sense of well being that his family was once more united and that he would now have the benefit of his wife's wise counsel in the many situations which were certain to arise. Almost her first undertaking was to read the letters that had been received during her absence. She was deeply impressed with all that had come from the Mahatma M. and quite overjoyed to know that her husband would soon be in touch with the Master K.H. again.

When Sinnett finally came to grips with the Mahatma M.'s answers to his questions, he understood K.H.'s concern that he should not "despair." They were by far the most complicated explanations he had yet received, but he realized with gratification that they could furnish material for several "Fragments" and, he hoped, eventually for another book.*

At the end of his "Notes" M. commented: "Our beloved K.H. is on his way to the goal—the highest of all beyond as on this sphere." And in his closing paragraph he thanked Sinnett "for all you have done for our two friends.† *It is a debt of gratitude we owe you.*"

---

*The "Cosmological Notes" from the Mahatma M., together with a long series of Question & Answer letters which passed between Sinnett and the Mahatma K.H. during the remainder of 1882 formed the basis not only for the "Fragments" articles but also for Sinnett's second book, *Esoteric Buddhism*, published in 1883.

†Olcott and H.P.B.

Several additional letters were received from the Mahatma M. during the succeeding weeks. These dealt with questions asked or with matters on which the Master evidently felt he could assist the Englishman. In one of them he observed: "You ought to come to some agreement as to the terms used when discussing cyclic evolutions. Our terms are untranslatable."[11] The Master K.H. had earlier mentioned the need for developing a nomenclature which would be acceptable to both the Brothers and the Englishmen, and Sinnett resolved that, so far as lay within his power, he would set himself to the task.

It was February before he heard directly from the Mahatma K.H.[12] Since receiving Djual Khul's letter he had not been entirely successful in curbing his eagerness for that event to take place, and it was apparent that the Master was aware of this. The opening sentence of the letter, however, caused a stinging behind Sinnett's eyelids and brought an unexpected and almost embarrassing lump to his throat.

"My Brother—" the Master began, "I have been on a long journey after supreme knowledge. I took a long time to rest."

Chagrin at his own inner lack of restraint made Sinnett accept the gentle rebuke in the second paragraph of the letter with completely good grace:

". . . this is my first moment of leisure. I offer it to you, whose inner Self reconciles me to the outer man who but too often forgets that a great man is he who is strongest in the exercise of patience."

The Englishman excused himself so far as he could: "Perhaps he doesn't fully understand the position of a person at my end of such correspondence." But this thought was immediately dissipated by the Master's reference to conditions in the world and among people in general and the moving entreaty, "Will you not try—for the sake of shortening the distance between us—to disentangle yourself from the net of life and death in which they are all caught. . ."

". . . it is more difficult than before to exchange letters with you," the Mahatma added, "though my regard for you has sensibly increased, instead of being lessened—as you feared—and will not diminish unless—but as the consequence of your own acts. That you will try to avoid raising any such obstacle, I know well."

Certainly not deliberately, Sinnett mentally assured the Mahatma. But he is right, he thought, that "man is the victim of his surroundings while he lives in the atmosphere of society." He recalled Lord Crawford, whose intense aspirations were so effectually blocked by his overwhelming obligations to the world in which he lived. Was it necessary to become a hermit? to throw one's responsibilities to the four winds and concentrate only on one's own development? Something in this idea repelled him. That, he told himself, would be escape. Perhaps one had to achieve a certain attitude which involved taking care of one's obligations and letting them go at the same time. Mentally he shrugged his shoulders. This was a paradox which he felt incapable of resolving.

A second gentle rebuke was to confront him a little further on in the letter. " . . . what you do not know is the great harm produced by your own unconscious indiscretions. Shall I give you an instance? Remember the wrath produced on Stainton Moses by your too imprudent letter quoting *ad libitum* and with a freedom pregnant with the most disastrous results from my letter to you about him . . ."

Sinnett did remember. He *had* passed on to Moses some of the Mahatma's comments about him in the first letter received following his return from England. What had moved him to do this, he did not know, except that he longed to convince the mediumistic Englishman of his errors and bring him to a correct understanding of the nature of the guide "Imperator" and of occultism in general. But perhaps again he had been overeager.

The Master went on in his letter to say that Stainton Moses had now estranged himself from the Society and had "determined in his heart the utter annihilation of the British Branch." A psychic society was being founded, the Mahatma reminded him, and Moses had "succeeded in bringing over to it Wyld, Massey and others."*

This fact had within it the seed of the destruction of the Theosophical Society in London, Sinnett was assured. " . . . the evil may yet be averted," the Master said, although Sinnett's must be the hand to place the first stone in the bridge to a successful future for the Theosophical Society.† "How will you do it?

---

*Undoubtedly the Society for Psychical Research, which later played so heavy a part in the crucifixion of H.P.B.

†Sinnett's help with the London Lodge, beginning in 1883, did do much to strengthen it.

How can you do it?" the Master asked. And then: "I can come nearer to you, but you must draw me by a purified heart and a gradually developing will. Like the needle the adept follows his attractions."[13]

Then came a note of mixed comfort and challenge:

". . . I read your heart and detect in it a shade of sadness, not to say disappointment, that hovers there. . . I write you therefore with some effort to bid you keep a cheerful frame of mind. Your strivings, perplexities, and forebodings are equally noticed, good and faithful friend. In the imperishable RECORD of the Masters *you have written them all*. . . you have stepped within the circle of our work, you have crossed the mystic line which separates your world from ours, and now whether you perservere or not; whether we become later on, in your sight, still more living *real* entities or vanish out of your mind like so many dream fictions. . . you are virtually OURS . . . you cannot avoid meeting us in *Real Existence*. Yes, verily good friend, your *Karma* is ours, for you imprinted it daily and hourly upon the pages of that book where the minutest particulars of the individuals stepping inside our circle are preserved. . . In thought and deed by day, in soul-struggles by nights, you have been writing the story of your desires and your spiritual development. This everyone does who approaches us with any earnestness of desire to become our co-worker, he himself 'precipitates' the written entries by the identical process used by us when we write inside your closed letters and uncut pages of books and pamphlets in transit. I tell you this for your private information and it must not figure in the next pamphlet from Simla."

Here Sinnett smiled rather grimly. This *was* for his information alone and he would not pass it on to the "Altruist of Rothney Castle" as the Mahatma K.H. had once designated Hume.[14] In this he would not be guilty of the indiscretion which the Master so deplored.

Then came a few "mellifluous" passages such as had always delighted Sinnett; for, as he often reminded himself, the grace of expression never seemed to alter in any way the stern reality of what was being said.

"If you hear seldom from me, never feel disappointed, Brother, but say—'It was *my* fault.' Nature has linked all parts of her Empire together by subtle threads of magnetic sympathy, and there is a mutual correlation even between a star and a man; thought runs swifter than the electric fluid, and your thought *will find me* if projected by a pure impulse, as mine will find, has found, and often impressed your mind. We may move in cycles of activity divided—not entirely separated from each other. Like the light in the sombre valley seen by the mountaineer from its peaks, every bright thought in your mind, my Brother, will sparkle and attract the attention of your distant friend and correspondent. If thus we discover our natural Allies in the *Shadow*-world—your world and ours outside the precincts—and it is our law to approach every such an one if even there be but the feeblest glimmer of the true 'Tathagata' light within him—then how far easier for you to attract us. Understand this and the admission into the Society of persons often distasteful to you will no longer amaze you. 'They that be whole need not the physician, but they that be sick'—is an axiom, whoever may have spoken it.''[15]

The Master then closed his remarkable and profoundly moving letter with the admonition not to doubt—"for this complexion of doubt unnerves and pushes back one's progress"—but with a warning of one cloud which "does hover over your path." This was Hume. "He whom you made your confidant—I advised you to become but his co-worker, not to divulge things to him that you should have kept locked within your bosom—is under a baneful influence and may become your enemy. You do right to try to rescue him from it, for it bodes ill to him, to you and to the Society. His greater mind fumed by vanity and charmed by pipings of a weaker but more cunning one, is for the time under a spell of fascination."

Sinnett supposed that the "weaker and more cunning" mind might be Hume's new secretary, Edmund Fern, who seemed to be something of a psychic and who had the ability to ingratiate himself easily with others. That Hume would some day begin to find fault with this young man Sinnett did not doubt.

The closing words of the Master's letter were to remain in the Englishman's memory for a very long time:

"The cause will never be ruined though albeit the Sisyphus' rock may crush a good many toes. Farewell again, my friend— for longer or shorter, as you may determine. I am called to duty. Yours faithfully, K.H.''

Sinnett read and re-read and pondered this letter before he placed it with the other communications from the Mahatma K.H. It held a unique message and a unique charge, and with each rereading his resolve to meet that charge became deeper and at the same time more luminous with gratitude and devotion.

10

A "Strictly Private" Letter

On the 17th of February, 1882, Col. Olcott left Bombay for
a tour of northern India.[1] With him was Bhavani Rao,* a
chela who had been spending some time at the headquarters of
the Theosophical Society. They were due to arrive in Allahabad, en route from Cawnpore to Calcutta, early in March. Their
visit was to provide further evidence that H.P.B. was not
writing the letters purporting to come from the Mahatmas, as
her enemies still found occasion to suggest.

Sinnett himself looked forward to their arrival with some anticipation. He had met Bhavani Rao in Bombay earlier in the
year, when he had gone there to meet his family, and had
learned that the chela had been one of a group, which included
Ross Scott and Damodar, to whom the Mahatma M. had
appeared briefly a few days earlier.[2] This had been possible,
Sinnett recorded, because of "the constant presence of
Madame Blavatsky and one or two other persons of highly
sympathetic magnetism, the purity of life of all habitually
resident there, and the constant influence poured in by the
Brothers themselves."[3] He himself had hoped for a similar
manifestation but had been disappointed. Now, he thought
that perhaps the magnetism of the two visitors might establish the conditions necessary for some phenomena. He had,
in fact, been alerted to this possibility by a sentence in a long
letter received before their arrival from the Mahatma K.H.:
"Bhavani Shanker is with O., and he is stronger and fitter in
many a way more than Damodar or even our mutual 'female'
friend."[4]

Several unusual incidents did, in fact, take place while
Olcott and Bhavani Rao were in Allahabad. One of these was
the instantaneous transportation from the Society head-

*Sometimes called Bhavani Shankar; see *Guide* pp. 219-20.

quarters in Bombay to Allahabad (a distance of some eight hundred miles) of a fragment of a plaster bas-relief, the rest of the object remaining in Bombay. This was a startling phenomenon requiring rather complicated measures to authenticate.†

Of special interest to Sinnett, however, was a note received from the Mahatma K.H. through Bhavani Rao. He had given the chela a letter to the Mahatma, hoping it would be possible for him to deliver it. The following morning, Bhavani presented him with a note from the Master which he had found under his pillow on awakening.[5]

The note was a short one, in the course of which the Master said, "To force phenomena in the presence of difficulties magnetic and other is forbidden as strictly as for a bank cashier to disburse money which is only entrusted to him. Even to do this much for you so far from the headquarters would be impossible but for the magnetism O. and B.R. have brought with them—and I could do no more."

Obviously, thought Sinnett, Bhavani Rao was not proving as strong as the Master seemed to have hoped.

Not realizing the force of those final words—"I could do no more"—and more impressed by an earlier passage in the letter —"It is easy for us to give phenomenal proofs when we have necessary conditions"—Sinnett wrote next day suggesting one or two things which he thought might be done to take advantage of the conditions presented by the introduction into his house of available magnetism different from that of H.P.B., who had been so much—however absurdly—suspected of imposing on him.

He gave this note to Bhavani on the evening of the 13th of March, and on the morning of the 14th, he received a few words from K.H. saying simply that what he had proposed was impossible and that he would write more fully through Bombay.[6]

"When in due course I so heard from him," Sinnett wrote in a later edition of *The Occult World*, "I learned that the limited facilities of the moment had been exhausted, and that my suggestions could not be complied with; but the importance of the explanations...turns on the fact that I did, after all,

†This and other happenings at the time are related in detail in OW 163-68, 9th ed.

exchange letters with Koot Hoomi at an interval of a few hours, at a time when Madame Blavatsky was at the other side of India."[7]

Much to his—and his wife's—surprise, Patience received a short note from the Master while their visitors were with them.[8] K.H. had always shown the deepest respect for Mrs. Sinnett and, on this occasion, he sent her a lock of his hair. She still suffered from recurring attacks of weakness following her illness as a result of her confinement while in England, and the gift was evidently intended as an amulet. "Wear the hair enclosed in a cotton tape (and if preferred in a metal armlet)" the Master wrote, "a little lower than your *left* armpit below the left shoulder. Follow advice that will be given you by Henry Olcott. It is good and we shall not object."

A strange admonition followed: "Harbour not ill-feelings even against an enemy and one who has wronged you; for hatred acts like an antidote and may damage the effect of even this hair."*

"How very kind and thoughtful the Master is!" exclaimed Patience. "I'm sure this will help me, not only physically, but perhaps in my understanding. I sometimes have the feeling, Percy, that we have become involved in something too big for us—like the old cliche about having a tiger by the tail."

She smiled as she said this so he supposed her worry was not too great.

"Nonsense," he replied. "Why should you feel that way?"

"I'm sure it is foolish," she admitted. "But sometimes I do feel overwhelmed. I think it is partly because it all seems too good to be true."

"But it is true, Patty. And I personally am very grateful to K.H. for his thoughtfulness. You know I'm concerned that you should be restored to full health again."

"Yes, I know, dear, and I am stronger every day, I think."

He patted her on the shoulder.

"I am glad for that," he said gently.

---

*It may seem strange to think of as gentle a person as Mrs. Sinnett harboring ill feelings or hatred toward anyone. Speculation might tempt one to identify the object of such feelings, if they did exist, as Mr. A. O. Hume, who did indeed create distress among those who held the Masters in deep respect and reverence and who found it difficult to understand their long-suffering attitude toward him. This is, however, entirely speculation. It is not known what advice Olcott gave to Mrs. Sinnett.

In the earlier long letter from the Mahatma K.H., in which he had mentioned the forthcoming visit of Olcott and Bhavani, he had discussed some of the material planned for the next issue of *The Theosophist*. Among the items mentioned was an article entitled "The Elixir of Life" by Mirza Moorad Ali Beg, which, "in its haziness," the Master said, "may remind you of a man who, stealthily approaching one, gives him a hit upon his back, and then runs away."[9]

On the evening before their guests' departure, as they settled down for coffee following their dinner, Sinnett remembered the Mahatma's mention of this article and asked Olcott whether he knew the author.

"Indeed I do," replied Olcott, "and to my sorrow."

"Oh?" said Sinnett, raising his eyebrows slightly, "In what way?"

"He came to our headquarters for help," Olcott explained. "Such a strange, wild creature! He was in a state of mental and moral conflict such as I have never seen in any other human being. He was under the sway of evil influences that were 'dragging him hither and thither' as he expressed it. We couldn't but pity him, but somehow he gave one a sense of horror also."

"How so?" persisted Sinnett, mindful of the Mahatma's comment about this author.

"Well, it's a tragic story," said Olcott. "Understand, he is a brilliant young man, well read, and with a fine mind, but he looked more like an actor made up for a part than anything else. He was dressed like a Muslim, except that he wore his hair—which was long and a very light brown—tied in a kind of Grecian knot at the back of his head, like a woman. But he wasn't effeminate, in spite of this—and his very fair skin and rather impressive blue eyes. He had suffered a great deal during the previous few years and I tried to help him, although all the time I was torn between compassion and a kind of abhorrence of his story. He had brought it all on himself, you see."

Olcott sipped his coffee thoughtfully, while the others in the room waited expectantly. He debated in his mind just how much of the tragic tale to reveal, especially since Patience was a member of his audience and he was aware of her kind heart and sensitivity. Finally he went on:

"He had got himself involved with some evil entities that he had summoned to help him get a certain virtuous lady in his power. He had sat in a closed room for forty days, pursuing a practice under the instruction of his 'guru' which he was told to continue until he could actually see the lady's face as if it were alive. When her lips moved as if to speak, he was informed, she would have been completely fascinated and would come to him of her own accord. Unfortunately, it all turned out as he had been told, and the woman was ruined. But also unfortunately—tragically—Mitford—that's his real name, you know—Mitford couldn't rid himself of the evil powers he had invoked and whose assistance in his nefarious plan he had accepted. He simply hadn't the moral strength to dominate them. They wouldn't let him alone."

A smothered exclamation from Patience made him turn to her sympathetically.

"I'm sorry, Mrs. Sinnett. It isn't a pretty story, I know."

"But what happened to the poor creature?" she asked. "Is he still at headquarters?"

"No, he left there," answered Olcott, "and quite a relief it was to us at the moment, although we were aghast at what happened later. He was one of the most distressful persons to be with that I have ever known—nervous and excitable and unable to fix his attention on anything for more than a few moments. The sad part of it was that he saw the higher possibilities of man's nature—otherwise he wouldn't have written what is really a valuable article—but he simply couldn't reach them. He asked to join the Society, but I was reluctant to approve that because of his instability. But you know how H.P.B. is—always springing to the defense of anyone who is down. She said she would be responsible for him, and she kept insisting, so finally I relented. But I must tell you how he repaid her generosity."

"It might have been expected," put in Bhavani Rao.

"Yes, I suppose so, for he was unpredictable. But I'm sure none of us ever dreamed he would be guilty of such an action. One day when H.P.B. was with him at Wadhwan station, he suddenly snatched a sword from a sepoy who was standing nearby and tried to kill her. Of course the sepoy was able to overcome him, but he kept shouting that she and all her Mahatmas were devils and she deserved to die! In short, he went quite mad. He has always seemed to me a most telling example of the danger of dabbling with occult powers while the animal passions are still rampant."*

"I agree, it is a sad tale," said Sinnett, more intrigued than ever at the Mahatma's request that he pay special attention to the man's article. "K.H. mentioned another contribution scheduled for the next *Theosophist*—a protest, I gather, from William Oxley over the review of his book, *The Philosophy of the Spirit*, which appeared in the journal last December, I believe."

"Ah, yes," said the Colonel. "Oxley did send in something on that, I think."

"The review was apparently by Djual Khul," Sinnett added, "and K.H. says it ought never to have been permitted to see the light of day."[10]

"I wonder why," said Olcott.

"Well, apparently it had quite a few errors in it."

Sinnett remembered suddenly that the Master had closed the letter by reminding him that it was "strictly private"— undoubtedly to prevent a repetition of the indiscretion of which he had been guilty in connection with Stainton Moses. He was still sensitive—although without resentment—over the rebuke and decided it might be best to change the subject. He was saved from having to think of a timely topic when Denny and his nanny came into the room so that the small boy could say goodnight to the group. He did this with his quaint, oddly grown-up grace and sweetness, and when he had disappeared the earlier subject seemed to have been forgotten.

As a matter of fact, Sinnett was still intrigued by what the Master had written about Oxley. He had met the English spiritualist briefly in London the previous year but had not become well-acquainted with him. He remembered that Oxley had mentioned his interest in the Mahatmas and expressed his

---

*The story of Mirza Moorad Ali Beg is told in ODL 2:289-91. Olcott added that he had been doing rather well for some time and, had he only been content to stay with them for a while, he might have retrieved much of his lost spirituality. ". . . but after giving his promise to do so, he obeyed an irresistible impulse and rushed back to Wadhwan and to destruction. His mind did not recover its equilibrium; he turned Roman Catholic, then recanted to Islam, and finally died." He was English by birth, although born in India. His real name was Godolphin Mitford; he was a member of a well-known writing family of England. The article, "The Elixir of Life," was to become rather famous. It is mentioned elsewhere in the *Letters*, with some hints that it may have been written under special inspiration. (See *Guide*, p. 230)

intention to write to K.H.—a decision whose wisdom Sinnett questioned but was in no position to deny. There had, in fact, been no opportunity to pursue the subject, as their short discussion had taken place just before the opening of a meeting and he had not seen the author again.

The guests departed on the following morning, Bhavani Rao to return to Bombay and Olcott to go on to his next stop at Behar.[11] In spite of some frustrations, Sinnett had enjoyed their visit and felt an unusual kindliness toward the American, who had proved a considerate guest.

"I missed H.P.B." said Patience, as they settled back into their ordinary routines. "But Col. Olcott is a lovable gentleman, isn't he?"

Her husband's response to this was a tentative grunt which she chose to regard as assent.

"I'd love to see Madame again," she said now, appealingly. "I wonder if she would come if we invited her."

Sinnett frowned slightly.

"I can't contemplate it with much pleasure," he said, "but I'll be writing to her in a day or so and I'll suggest it if you like."

"Oh please do. She has such a vast store of knowledge, and so long as nothing happens to upset her, she is such delightful company. You know I always enjoy her."

Sinnett did invite H.P.B. in a letter which was perhaps not altogether enthusiastic. He received a refusal in reply. She thought the Sinnetts had had enough of her, she said, and she would rather give them "the momentary annoyance of a refusal than the prolonged annoyance of a visit." Besides, she said, she felt they were better friends with several hundred miles between them![12]

"...do you really think you know ME, my dear Mr. Sinnett?" she asked. "Do you believe that because you have fathomed—as you think—my physical crust and brain; that shrewd analyst of human nature though you be—you have ever penetrated even beneath the first cuticles of my *Real Self?*... for whatever there is inside...it is *not what you think* it is...I (the inner real 'I') am in prison and cannot show myself as I am with all the desire I may have to."

In a further comment, H.P.B. showed that she gauged well the character of Sinnett's regard for her:

" . . . you *do not hate me;* you only feel a friendly, indulgent, a kind of *benevolent* contempt for H.P.B. You are right there, so far as *you know her*—the one who is ready to fall into pieces. Perchance you may find out yet your mistake concerning the other—the well hidden party."

In her closing paragraph she asked him not to be angry with her, and she added a postscript: "My sincere love to Mrs. Sinnett and a kiss to dear little Dennie."

"All this mystery about who H.P.B. really is!" Sinnett exclaimed impatiently as he gave the letter to Patience to read. "She makes too much of it!"

"Does she, really?" asked Patience, giving him a curious glance. "Perhaps all of us are something different inside, so far as that goes. I sometimes feel that I myself must be different from the woman you know."

He relented and said gently: "Well, my dear, I'm quite satisfied with the woman I know."

"Oh, thank you, sir," she said, with her luminous smile. "Now I am set up for the day. But I am sorry Madame Blavatsky isn't coming."

Reviewing the Master's long letter again before the next one arrived, Sinnett was relieved that he had restrained himself from discoursing on its contents to Olcott. The "Manchester Seer" (the Mahatma's name for Oxley) had apparently made good his statement that he was going to write to K.H., for he had done so, detailing some of his spiritualistic experiences. The Mahatma commented:

" . . . having received no reply to his summons to K.H., he criticizes—mildly so far—the utterances of that 'Internal Power'—for which new title I feel rather obliged to him. At the sight of the gentle rebuke, our blunderbus Editor (H.P.B.) failed not to explode. Nor would she be soothed, until Djwal-Khul,* with whom the famous review was concocted . . . was authorized, under the safe *nom-de-plume* of 'Reviewer' to answer (by correcting some of his blunders) the Seer, in a few innocent footnotes."[13]

Some approving comments followed: "Yet, I must say, that of the present English 'prophets,' W. Oxley is *the only one* who has an inkling of the truth; hence the only one calculated to effectually help our movement. The man runs constantly in and

---

*The name is spelled in several different ways.

out of the straight road, deviating from it every time he thinks he perceives a new path; but finding himself in a cul-de-sac as invariably returns to the right direction. I must admit there is much sound philosophy here and there in what he says."

It was, however, Oxley who later moved the Master K.H. to take an unprecedented action. He wrote for *The Theosophist* what H.P.B. called "an interminable article"[14] and which she intended not to publish until she was ordered by the Mahatma K.H. to do so. In the article he claimed that the Mahatma Koot Hoomi had thrice visited him "by astral form" and that, in conversation with him, the Master had given him "certain explanations in reference to astral bodies in general, and the incompetency of his own *Mayava-rupa* to preserve its consciousness simultaneously with the body "at both ends of the line!" Djual Khul issued a statement at the Mahatma's direction saying that "Whomsoever Mr. Oxley may have seen and conversed with . . . it was not with Koot Hoomi;" that the Master had never approached Oxley "astrally or otherwise" nor had any conversation with him; and since such claims might lead many Theosophists into error, Koot Hoomi found it necessary to state that "Henceforth any medium or seer who will feel disposed to claim either to have been visited by, or to have held conversation with (him) will have to substantiate the claim by prefixing his or her statement with THREE SECRET WORDS, which he . . . will divulge to and leave in the safe keeping of Mr. A.O. Hume and Mr. A.P. Sinnett . . . As long as they do not find these three *words* correctly repeated . . . the claim shall be regarded as gratuitous assumption and no notice will be taken of it. . . . The above declaration and statement to be appended as a footnote in Mr. Oxley's published statement."[15]

These three "secret words" were given in a postscript to another letter to Sinnett. They were "Kin-t-an," "Na-lan-da," and "Dha'ra'ni."[16]

These events had not yet transpired when the Mahatma wrote the letter to which Sinnett was giving such serious study. In that letter, he followed his comment about the "sound philosophy" of Oxley's writing by asking:

"Why is it, that every one of those 'Seers' believes himself the Alpha and Omega of Truth? . . . You have heard and read about a good many Seers, in the past and present centuries, such as Swedenborg, Boehme, and others. Not one among the number but (is) thoroughly *honest, sincere,* and as well-educated as (several persons he had previously mentioned); aye, even learned. Each of them in addition to these qualities has or had an + ("Imperator"; guide) of his own, a 'Guardian' and a *Revelator*—under whatever mystery and 'mystic name' —whose mission it is—or has been—to spin out to his spiritual ward a new system embracing all the details of the world of Spirit. Tell me, my friend, do you know of two who agree? And why, since truth is one, and putting entirely aside the question of discrepancies in details—we do not find them agreeing even upon the most vital problems—those that have either '*to be* or *not* to be'—and of which there can no *two* solutions.[17]

"Well," thought Sinnett, "I suppose the Mahatmas do agree on ultimate principles, but they don't always agree on methods of applying them."

For the Master K.H. had written: "Morya...wanted me to acquaint you with the totality of the subtle bodies and their collective aggregate, as well as with the distributive aggregate of the *sheaths.* I believe it is premature...What I blame him for, is that he allowed you to begin from the wrong end—the most difficult unless one has thoroughly mastered the preparatory ground."[18]

The Mahatma referred to a manuscript which Sinnett had sent to the Mahatma M. some time earlier asking for his comments. K. H. now assured his correspondent that he had read this manuscript, and "more than once I detected on the white margin the shadow of your face, with its earnest, inquiring gaze in the eyes; your thought having projected your image on the spot you had on your mind, and which you longed to receive back *filled*—'thirsting' as you say—for more notes and information." He promised that if M. did not take care of the matter soon, he himself would do so, for "...to write for you is no ungrateful task, as you make the best use of the little you may pick up here and there." Then he added: "...you will find that it was never the intention of the Occultists really to conceal what they have been writing from the earnest determined students, but rather to lock up their information for safety-sake, in a secure safe-box, the key to which is— intuition. The degree of diligence and zeal with which the hidden meaning is sought by the student is generally the test —how far he is entitled to the possession of the so buried treasure."[19]

Sinnett considered that there was nothing wrong with his diligence and zeal, but there was, he knew, a wall somewhere beyond which he had been unable to go. Exasperatingly, he felt that the wall had no real substance but was rather—to him as yet—a nebulous and impenetrable cloud where his mind got lost. Intellectually, he understood the teachings which the Mahatmas had been giving in their long, explanatory answers to his questions and those of Hume, but he did not yet have that key of intuition which would unlock the meaning for which he hungered. Perhaps, some day, he thought hopefully, the cloud would disperse and he would pierce through to the real light beyond.

In due time, Sinnett received from the Mahatma the letter "thro' Bombay" promised in the short note which came while Olcott and Bhavani Rao were at Allahabad.

"You seemed annoyed," the Master said, "disappointed when reading the words, 'Impossible: no power here, will write through Bombay,' Those eight words will have cost me eight days recuperative work—in the state I am in at present. But you know not what I mean; you are absolved."[20]

Then, referring to Sinnett's hope that some phenomena would be performed through the power of the visitors' presence, the Mahatma said: "It is not *physical* phenomena that will ever bring conviction to the hearts of the unbelievers in the 'Brotherhood' but rather phenomena of *intellectuality*, philosophy, and logic, if I may so express it. . . . Do you not realize that were it not for your exceptional intellect and the help to be derived therefrom the Chohan would have long ago closed every door of communication between us?"[21]

Since the Englishman's only real fear was that some action of his might result in cutting off his correspondence with the Master, he told himself that he would have to be satisfied with the situation as it was—at least for the time being.

11

The Vega Visitation

In Howrah, a suburb of Calcutta, Col. and Mrs. Gordon were hosts to William Eglinton, a popular young medium from England. Eglinton had heard of Madame Blavatsky and the "Brothers" and had determined to go to India and find out for himself whether she was reliable and the Brothers real beings, or whether the whole thing was a hoax. He had stayed at first with a wealthy English merchant, J. G. Meugens, but when the latter returned to England and the Gordons invited Eglinton to their home, he accepted with pleasure; since they were Theosophists he felt that, with them, he would have an opportunity to learn more about Madame Blavatsky and those mysterious beings from whom she alleged her knowledge came. Because his own "guides" appeared to know nothing about the Mahatmas and had not informed him of their existence, Eglinton maintained that they were a fiction, that Madame Blavatsky was simply a medium who pretended to be something more, and that the phenomena occurring in connection with her were due solely to the agency of spirits.[1]

However, Eglinton saw nothing of either H.P.B. or Col. Olcott during all the time he was in India, and he was not to meet them until two years later when they were in London.* Hume became interested in him and considered inviting him to Simla; and, indeed, it seemed that the Masters themselves had some thought of bringing him there for training, since they were still trying to find someone who could act for them in place of H.P.B.[2] However, this did not work out and Eglinton remained in Calcutta while he was in India.

---

*In LBS, p. 3 (Letter #2) a reference is made to Eglinton and the events which are to be recorded in this chapter. In Mary K. Neff's personal copy of this volume she has inserted a marginal note to the effect that the reason Eglinton was not approached officially by the Theosophical Society was to save him from the suspicion attached by some to the Society and H.P.B.

One day Mrs. Gordon received a letter from H.P.B. in which she said that Eglinton's "guides" had been made to realize the existence of the Masters. When Mrs. Gordon questioned the young medium about this, he denied any knowledge of it.

Two or three evenings later, a seance was held in the Gordon's home and, to Mrs. Gordon's amusement, one of Eglinton's guides referred to the "Illustrious"—a name used occasionally for the Mahatma Morya but quite unknown to Eglinton. While the young man himself was in trance, Mrs. Gordon learned from his guides that he would soon return to England and that, after his departure, some striking phenomenon involving him would be performed. They said the "Brothers" had consented to this.

When Eglinton returned to his normal state, he was told of all this and given H.P.B.'s letter to read.

"He was not at all elated at having a belief in the 'Brothers' forced on him," wrote Mrs. Gordon, in her account of the incident,[3] "their alleged superiority to *mediums* being rather a sore point between us! However, he had no alternative but to accept them, as a communication was given by his chief 'guide,'* in direct writing to the same effect."

Very shortly after this seance, Eglinton received news from England which he felt made it necessary for him to return there at once. He sailed on March 15, 1882, saying that he expected to return to India in a few months.†

---

*Eglinton's chief guide was named "Ernest."

†He was not to realize this expectation. Some danger (the nature of which is not revealed but which is referred to in the *Letters* 452/445 and 247/244) threatened him on the very day of his departure. Some time later, after Eglinton had reached home, Sinnett received a postcard from the Mahatma K.H. saying that E. could not return to India until he was thoroughly protected against a recurrence of this danger. "If Mr. Hume is anxious to save him," wrote K.H., "let him for want of something better offer him the place of his private secretary... If you or Mr. Hume is really anxious to see me—or rather my *astral* Self—there's a chance for you. H.P.B. is too old and not passive enough. Besides she has done too many services to be forced into it. With Mr. Eglinton, and he willing, the thing would become easy... In a year more it will be too late." (ML 452/445) Curiously, this card bears the dateline "London, April 27" and is addressed to Mr. A.P. Sinnett, Editor Pioneer, Allahabad." There is no explanation of this dateline, but perhaps it may be speculated that the message was transmitted through Eglinton as a trial of his abilities and the possibility of his use for this purpose if he returned to India. This is indicated in LBS, p. 361, in a letter from Eglinton to Sinnett, with an added note by K.H.: "This—to prove that living men *can* appear—thro such EXCELLENT mediums, in London, even tho' themselves in Tzi-gadze, Tibet." (*See also* ML #17, 118/115 (5))

On the night of March 22, soon after the S.S. *Vega* on which Eglinton had sailed left Ceylon, a startling event occurred: the Mahatma K.H. appeared to him in person.

In the meantime, the Master had informed Sinnett in a letter that this was going to happen. He was writing, he said, because he felt that Sinnett might feel "involuntary envy" over the situation. "For reasons that you will appreciate, though at first you will be inclined to consider (in regard to yourself) unjust, I am determined to do that for once which hitherto I have never done; namely, to *personate myself* under *another form* and, perhaps—character. Therefore, you need not grudge Eglinton the pleasure of seeing me personally, to talk with me, and—be 'dumbfounded' by me, and with the results of my visit to him, on board 'The Vega.' This will be done between the 21st and 22nd of this month and, when you read this letter, will be a 'vision of the past'! ...As he will see someone quite different from the real K.H., though *it will still be K.H.*—you need not feel like one wronged by your trans-Himalayan friend. Another reason is to save the poor fellow from the suspicion of boasting; the third and *chiefest* though neither least nor last, is that theosophy and its adherents have to be vindicated at last. Eglinton is going home; and were he upon his return to know *nothing* of the Brothers, there would be a sore day of trial for poor old H.P.B. and H.S.O. Mr. Hume twitted us for not appearing to Eglinton. ...For reasons which he may or may not be able to appreciate—but that *you* will—we could not or rather *would* not do so as long as E. was in India. No less had we very good reasons to forbid H.P.B. to either correspond with him, or take too much notice of him in the *Theosophist.* But now that he is gone, and will be on the 22nd hundreds of miles away at sea; and that no suspicion of fraud can be brought against either of them, the time for the *experiment* has come. He thinks of putting *her* to the test—he will be tested himself."

The Master asked Sinnett to inform Mr. Hume of the situation. "Tell him," he said, "that there are persons—*enemies*—who are anxious to catch the 'old lady' at cheating, to entrap her, so to say, and that for that very reason I am determined to settle the question and have it once for ever at rest. Say to him that, profiting by his suggestion and advice I—K.H., will appear to Eglinton in *propria persona* as *in actu* at sea, between the 21 and 22 of this month; and that, if successful in bringing the rebel who denies the 'Brothers' to his senses, Mrs. Gordon and consort will be notified of the fact immediately. . . . We have waited on purpose to produce our experiment until his departure, and now—WE MEAN TO ACT."[4]

The Mahatma added a postscript: "Till the 25th of March, Mr. Sinnett is expected to keep his lips closed as they will be in death. . . Not a *soul* but Mrs. S., your good lady, must know one word of this letter. This I expect of your friendship, and now put it to test. To Mr. Hume—you may write just now so that the letter might be received by him on the 24th, in the afternoon. . ."

Sinnett wrote the note to Hume, as the Master requested, but he did not bother to frame his words with too much care. He found he could not be entirely objective about the situation. In spite of the fairness of the Master's explanation, he felt at first a little offended. What claim could Eglinton possibly have on the Mahatma that could earn him such unprecedented recognition? None whatever!

When he said this to Patience, she reminded him that no one had a claim of this kind on the Master; that indeed the Master had told him several times that, although he cherished the greatest friendship for Sinnett, he could not come into the atmosphere created by the meat-eating and alcohol which Sinnett was not yet ready to forego.

"Besides," she reminded him, "he says he is going to 'personate' himself under another form, and that Mr. Eglinton will 'see somebody quite different from the real K.H.'"

"Yes, but he also says it will 'still be K.H.' He's right that they 'expound mysteries by mysteries.' I know Hume was a bit sarcastic because the Mahatmas hadn't appeared to Eglinton.[5] But I wonder why they were so anxious for Eglinton to know of their existence when they've said several times they don't care to convince the skeptics!"

Patience's delightful chuckle greeted this remark.

"Eglinton isn't just any 'skeptic.' The Master gave you his reason. I do believe you are just looking for something to feel hurt about, Percy! He says plainly enough that it was all because of H.P.B. that they let Eglinton alone when he was here but couldn't have him going back to England feeling that they were her creations. Oh, do be reasonable!"

He smiled somewhat ruefully and said he would try. He did not know until some time later that the Mahatma himself paid a price for the venture.

"...to satisfy Mr. Hume—at least in one direction—I got myself into a *scrape* with the Chohan," the Master wrote in July. "...he was far from satisfied that I should have allowed Eglinton to believe it was *myself*. He had permitted this proof of the power of *living men* to be given to the Spiritualists through a medium of theirs, but had left the programme and its details to ourselves, hence his displeasure at some trifling consequences. I tell you, my dear friend, that I am far less free to do as I like than you are in the matter of the *Pioneer*."[6]

In the meantime there were further developments in connection with the Master's appearance on board the *Vega*. Col. Olcott, who had been visiting in another city, stopped in at Howrah to see the Gordons. There, both he and Mrs. Gordon received telegrams from H.P.B. saying that K.H. had seen Eglinton; a still later telegram asked the Gordons to set a time when the three of them (Olcott, Col. Gordon and Mrs. Gordon) could be together. They decided on nine o'clock on the evening of March 24th.

Accordingly, that night, they sat in the well-lighted room in which Eglinton had stayed during his visit.

Suddenly Olcott saw, outside the open window, the Mahatmas M. and K.H. One of them pointed into the room, over Mrs. Gordon's head, and a letter dropped from the ceiling. The Mahatmas then vanished.

Mrs. Gordon related what happened next:*

I now turned and picked up what had fallen on me, and found a letter in Mr. Eglinton's handwriting, dated on the *Vega* the 24th; a message from Madame Blavatsky dated at Bombay the 24th, written on the backs of three of her visiting cards; also a larger card, such as Mr. Eglinton had a packet of, and used at his seances. On this latter card was the, to us, well-known handwriting of K.H., and a few words in the handwriting of the other 'Brother' who was with him outside the window, and who is Colonel Olcott's chief. All these cards and the letter were threaded together with a piece of blue sewing silk. We opened the letter carefully by

---

*More detailed accounts of these occurrences appear in several places: OW 169-74; *Damodar* 185-91; *Hints on Esoteric Theosophy* (Hume) No. 1, 155-58, 1909 ed.

slitting it up one side, as we saw that someone had made on the flap in pencil three Latin crosses, and so we kept them intact for identification. The letter is as follows:

S.S. *Vega*, Friday, 24th March, 1882

"My dear Mrs. Gordon—At last your hour of triumph has come! After the many battles we have had at the breakfast-table regarding K.H.'s existence, and my stubborn scepticism as to the wonderful powers possessed by the 'Brothers,' I have been forced to a *complete belief* in their being living distinct persons, and just in proportion to my scepticism will be my *firm unalterable* opinion respecting them. I am not allowed to tell you all I know, but K.H. *appeared* to me in person two days ago, and what he told me dumbfounded me. Perhaps Madame B. will already have communicated the fact of K.H.'s appearance to you. The 'Illustrious' is uncertain whether this can be taken to Madame or not, but he will try, notwithstanding the many difficulties in the way. If he does not I shall post it when I arrive at port. . . . you are requested by K.H. to keep this letter a profound secret until you hear from him through Madame. A storm of opposition is certain to be raised, and she has had so much to bear that it is hard she should have more."

Then follow some remarks about his health and the trouble which was taking him home, and the letter ends.

In her note on the three visiting cards Madame Blavatsky says: "Headquarters, March 24th. These cards and contents to certify to my doubters that the attached letter addressed to Mrs. Gordon by Mr. Eglinton was just brought to me from the *Vega*, with another letter from himself to me. K.H. tells me that he saw Mr. Eglinton and had a talk with him, long and convincing enough to make him a believer in the 'Brothers' as actual living beings, for the rest of his natural life. Mr. Eglinton writes to me: 'The letter which I enclose is going to be taken to Mrs. G. through your influence. You will receive it wherever you are, and will forward it to her in ordinary course. You will learn with satisfaction of my complete conversion to a belief in the "Brothers," and I have no doubt K.H. has already told you how he appeared to me two nights ago, etc., etc.' K.H. *told me all.* He does not, however, want me to forward the letter in 'ordinary course,' as it would defeat the object, but commands me to write this and send it off without delay, so that it would reach you all at Howrah tonight, the 24th. I do so...H.P. Blavatsky."

On the card taken from Eglinton's packet was the following message in the handwriting of K.H.: "William Eglinton thought the manifestation could only be produced through H.P.B. as a 'medium', and that the power would become exhausted at Bombay. We decided otherwise. Let this be a proof to all that the spirit of *living men* has as much potentiality in it (and often more) as a disembodied *soul.* He was anxious to *test her,* he often doubted; two nights ago he had the required proof and will doubt no more. But he is a good young man, bright, honest, and true as gold when once convinced...This card was taken from his stock today. Let it be an additional proof of his wonderful mediumship. K.H."

Mrs. Gordon added a postscript to the effect that since the above statement was written, a paper had been received from Bombay signed by seven witnesses who had seen the letter arrive there from the *Vega.*[7]

When Sinnett learned of all the happenings and circumstances following upon the Mahatma's appearance on board the *Vega,* he managed to put aside his umbrage and rejoice with his theosophical friends at the success of the undertaking. He had never lost his interest in spiritualism, despite the fact that the Mahatma K.H. termed it "the most insane and fatal of superstitions."[8] Sinnett maintained that it was not the manifestations of spiritualism which the Mahatma denied, but rather the interpretation given by spiritualists to those manifestations.

"...the phenomena and the experiences of spiritualism are facts," he wrote, "and nothing can be incompatible with facts. But Theosophy brings on the scene new interpretations of those facts, it is true, and sometimes these prove very unwelcome to spiritualists long habituated to their own interpretation. Hence, such spiritualists are now and then disposed to resist the new teaching altogether, and hold out against a belief that there can be anywhere in existence men entitled to advance it. ...Let spiritualists once realize that the Brothers do exist, and what sort of people they are, and a great step will have been accomplished. It is only by prolonged intercourse with the Brothers that a conviction grows up in the mind that, as regards spiritual science, they *cannot* be in error...So I cannot but hope that the coruscations of phenomena connected with the origin and adventures of the letter written on board the *Vega* may have flashed out of darkness to some good purpose, showing the spiritualistic world quite plainly that the great Brother to whom this work is dedicated (the Mahatma K.H.) is, at all events, a living man, with faculties and powers of that entirely abnormal kind which spiritualists have hitherto conceived to inhere merely in beings belonging to a superior scheme of existence."[9]

Sinnett remembered several comments made by the Mahatmas about spiritualism and mediumship. On one occasion, writing of those who had passed out of physical existence but remained for a time, for whatever cause, "within the earth's attraction," the Master K.H. wrote: "Woe to those whose *Trishna**   will attract them to mediums, and woe to the latter, who tempt them with such an easy *Upadana*.† For in grasping them, and satisfying their thirst for life, the medium helps to develop in them—is in fact the cause of—a new set of *Skandhas*‡, a new body, with far worse passions and tendencies than was the one they lost. All the future of this new body will be determined thus, not only by the *Karma* of demerit of the previous set or group but also by that of the new set of the future being. Were the medium and Spiritualists but to know, as I said, that with every new 'angel guide' they welcome with rapture, they entice the latter into an *Upadana* which will be productive of a series of untold evils for the new Ego that will be born under its nefarious shadow, and that with every seance —especially for materialization—they multiply the causes for misery, causes that will make the unfortunate Ego fail in his spiritual birth, or be reborn into a worse existence than ever— they would, perhaps, be less lavishing (of) their hospitality . . . now you may understand why we oppose so strongly Spiritualism and mediumship."#[10]

*Thirst for earthly existence.

†Usually translated as clinging to or grasping for earthly existence.

‡Attributes of personality which carry over into future existences.

#Since the Mahatmas had shown so much interest in Eglinton and had even contemplated the possibility of his usefulness in replacing H.P.B. for the transmission of letters, it may perhaps be assumed that, as he was basically an honest and decent person with the peculiar sensitivity necessary for mediumship, they had in mind training him to eliminate from his nature all those negative and passive elements which made him so successful a medium and to develop in him the strong and positive qualities of character which would enable him instead to become an intermediary.

Eglinton returned to England still a medium but thoroughly convinced of the actual existence of the Mahatmas and of their unusual powers. He wrote to Sinnett: "I am certain if I were in any other position than that of a medium gaining his living by his gifts, the Bros. would be enabled to manifest with great clearness and certainty."†[11]

Sinnett had hopes that, even though Eglinton had returned to England, the Mahatmas might eventually be able to work through him, for it seemed certain that H.P.B. would one day be totally unable to function in the transmission of the letters and he found the prospect of their cessation difficult to contemplate. A month or so later, writing of Eglinton, the Master K.H. commented that he would try his best to make him "a vegetarian and a teetotaler." "In good hands E. will do an immense good to the T.S. in India," K.H. said, "but for this he has [to go through] a training of purification. M. had to prepare him for six weeks before his departure, otherwise it would have been impossible for me to project into his atmosphere even the *reflection* of my 'double.' I told you already, my good friend, that what he saw was *not* me."[12]

Later, in the same letter, after pointing out some of the formidable difficulties faced by Eglinton himself in maintaining his stand of believing in the Brothers, the Mahatma said, "We must allow the natural course of events to develop . . . It would never do to *force* events, as it would be only making 'martyrs.'" Once more he asked Sinnett to have patience.[13]

Eglinton, the Mahatma said in another letter, "is a strong medium, and were it not for an inherent good nature and other good qualities, strongly counteracted by vanity, sloth, selfish-

†Years later, C.W. Leadbeater, a young English cleric interested in spiritualistic phenomena, became acquainted with Eglinton. On one occasion, when he was visiting the medium, the latter's "control," Ernest, "put in an appearance." Ernest spoke of the Masters "with the most profound reverence and said that he had on various occasions had the privilege of seeing Them." Leadbeater at once asked whether Ernest was prepared to "take charge of any message or letter for Them" and the guide said that he would willingly do so and "would deliver it when opportunity offered." It was never delivered. In relating these circumstances, Leadbeater commented: ". . . in connection with this I had later a good example of the unreliability of all such communications. Some considerable time afterwards some spiritualist wrote in *Light* explaining that there could not possibly be such persons as Masters, because Ernest had positively told him that there were not. I wrote to the same newspaper to say that I had it on precisely the same valueless authority that there *were* Masters, and that Ernest knew Them well. In each case Ernest had evidently reflected the thought of the questioner, as such entities so often do." (*How Theosophy Came to me*, C.W. Leadbeater, 24-29).

ness, greediness for money and, with other qualities of modern civilization, a total absence of will, he would make a superb *Dugpa*, yet as I said he is a 'good fellow' every inch of him; *naturally* truthful; under control the reverse. I would if I could save him from such a life of infamy."‡

It must be recorded that Eglinton never became of use to the Mahatmas. His fame as a medium, however, spread throughout the world, and many prominent members of the Society for Psychical Research attended his seances. He attempted other ventures, however, and when he died on March 10, 1933, he was editor of the magazine *The New Age* and a director of a firm of British Exporters.[14]

‡The first part of this quotation is found on page 122/119 at the end of ML-18. The words "such a life of infamy" occur at the beginning of ML-95, p. 429/423, which is actually a continuation of ML-18. Obviously the pages of the letter became separated.

12

Another Failure

The summer of 1882 was notable for the rich supply of occult teachings received by Sinnett and Hume and for the failure of yet another brilliant prospect for a successor to H.P.B.

The Sinnetts had, as usual, gone to Simla for a few months, and there the two Englishmen spent many hours poring over the explanations given by the Mahatma K.H. in answer to their many questions.* Hume had undergone what was apparently at least a temporary "conversion"[1] in his attitude toward the Mahatmas, and while his overweening pride never seemed to be tempered, he fully matched his friend in his eagerness to learn the technicalities of the esoteric philosophy.

The greatest difficulty in such communication, the Mahatma K.H. reminded them more than once, was that of language. "Our terms are untranslatable," he wrote on one occasion.[2] On another, he commented, "I will draw your attention to the tremendous difficulty of finding appropriate terms in English which would convey to the educated European mind even an approximately correct notion about the various subjects we will have to treat upon."[3] And, again, "Our mystic terms in their clumsy retranslation from the Sanskrit to English are as confusing to us as they are to you—especially to 'M'. Unless in writing to you one of us takes his pen *as an adept* and uses it from the first word to the last, he is quite as liable to 'slips' as any man."[4]

At one time it looked as though the Englishmen would have some special instruction from T. Subba Row, an exceptionally brilliant young Advaiti Brahman, who was being urged by H.P.B. to undertake this task. He was reluctant to do so, since

---

*It is recommended that the student consult the chronology (Appendix) to identify the letters received during this period. Glossaries and reference texts, including the *Guide*, will be helpful in understanding the explanations given by the Mahatmas.

he was basically opposed to sharing the Eastern teachings with Westerners. Finally, however, the Mahatma M., who was his Chief, ordered him to help "to a certain extent in lifting up a portion of the first veil of mystery."

Subba Row wrote to Sinnett, setting forth the conditions under which he would give this help.[5] Some of these seemed reasonable to the Englishmen; others seemed restrictive, especially one which committed them to future actions in accordance with directions which would be given.

"I need hardly tell you," Subba Row added, "that the Mahatmas can hardly be expected to undertake the work of personal instruction and supervision in the case of beginners like you, however sincere and earnest you may be in your belief in their existence and the reality of their science and in your endeavors to investigate the mysteries of that science. When you know more about them and the peculiar life they lead, I am sure you will not be inclined to blame them for not affording to you *personally* the instruction you are so anxious to receive from them."[6]

"Beginners, are we!" snorted Hume, when he read this letter. He had dropped in at the Sinnett residence to discover, if he could, the latest developments in the correspondence with the Mahatmas. Hume himself had received several letters, one or two of which he thought he might show to his friend, but he was aware that most of the communications were addressed to the latter, who usually shared them.

"Well, I suppose we are, in their view," Sinnett replied.

"If we are, it isn't our fault! It's like pulling teeth to get information out of these people. Questions! Questions! Ask questions! Why don't they set forth the philosophy in some sort of systematic way? Then we would know where we are and what we are attempting." He tossed the letter onto the table beside him.

A servant set brandy and glasses before them and Sinnett paused to pour generous portions for both of them..

"I suppose it really isn't that simple," he replied, finally. "I'm told that is the method of instruction in the East—the pupil asks questions and the teacher answers. Perhaps the idea is that you show how much you know by the questions you ask. Anyhow, we might as well try to change the direction of the earth's rotation as to go against such an established custom." He picked up the letter and ran his eyes over the page. "What do you think of these so-called 'conditions' under which Subba Row would be willing to instruct us?"

"Nonsense!" said Hume shortly, sipping his brandy appreciatively. "How can they expect us, situated as we are in the English community, to become ascetics? Further, how can we be expected to commit ourselves to future actions of which we now know nothing? Well—they had their chance! I offered myself as a chela several times, you remember, but got nothing but rejections."[7]

Sinnett held up his glass to catch the light through the liquid.

"I've been told by the Master K.H. several times," he said, "that I can't expect any closer contact with him so long as I don't—well, give up this sort of thing, for instance." He indicated the brandy. "And he himself recognizes that all these testings and probations are distasteful to us."[8]

"They're completely incompatible with any Western code of honor," Hume replied. "They seem to me very underhanded."

"But if we agree to these conditions we'll have to put up with them. Remember that. It's a question of how far we want to go. I believe Subba Row is supposed to do more than simply answer our questions. Koot Hoomi seems quite willing to continue that practice, and you must admit he has been generous with his answers recently. We've gained a lot of information. But it seems the Mahatma Morya has in mind developing powers in us in true chela fashion—and, as might be expected—Koot Hoomi doesn't approve of it.[9] Anyhow, we've got to meet these conditions before it will even be considered."

Hume moved restlessly.

"Ridiculous!" he said. "We've managed pretty well in our own way so far."

Sinnett forebore to remind him that he had just been complaining that the whole situation was unsatisfactory.

"Perhaps," he suggested, "we can agree to enough to persuade this prickly gentleman that we would be satisfactory subjects for instruction. We might even be able to point out a few things to him."

"A great deal, I should think," responded Hume. "See what you can do, anyhow. I'll leave it to you."

Sinnett wrote to Subba Row, giving a "qualified assent"[10] to the conditions imposed by the Brahman, who then found it necessary to "consult the Brothers for their opinion and orders."

Subsequently Subba Row wrote to Sinnett:

"I am sorry to inform you that anything like practical instruction in the ritual of Occult Science is impossible under the conditions you impose. So far as my knowledge goes, no student of Occult Philosophy has ever succeeded in developing his psychic powers without leading the life prescribed for such students; and it is not within the power of the teacher to make an exception in the case of any student. The rules laid down by the ancient teachers of Occult Science are inflexible and it is not left to the discretion of any teacher whether to enforce them or not to enforce them according to the nature of the existing circumstances. If you find it impracticable to change the present mode of your life, you cannot but wait for practical instruction until you are in a position to make such sacrifices as Occult Science demands...You will be taking a very low view of Occult Science if you were to suppose that the mere acquirement of psychic powers is the highest and the only desirable result of occult training. The mere acquisition of wonder-working powers can never secure immortality for the student of Occult Science unless he has learnt the means of shifting gradually his sense of individuality from his corruptible material body to the incorruptible and eternal Non-Being represented by his seventh principle."

He added that he would be willing to give the two Englishmen "theoretical instruction in the Philosophy of the Ancient Brahmanical religion and Esoteric Buddhism."[11]

The Master K.H. later wrote to Sinnett strongly advising him not to undertake a task beyond his strength and means. "...*for once pledged,*" he said, "were you to break your promise it would cut you off for years, if not for ever, from any further progress. I said from the first to Rishi 'M' that his intention was kind but the project *wild.* How can you in your position undertake any such labour? Occultism is not to be trifled with. It demands *all* or nothing. I read your letter to S.R. sent by him to Morya and I see you do not understand the first principles of chela training. Poor Subba Row is 'in a fix' ...On the one hand he has the indomitable H.P.B., who plagues Morya's life to *reward* you, and M. himself who would if he could gratify your aspirations; on the other he encounters the unpassable Chinese wall of rules and *Law.* Believe me,

good friend, learn what you can under the circumstances...
the *philosophy* of the phenomena and our doctrines on
Cosmogony,inner man, etc...."*

It is impossible to determine how much of the philosophy
which later found its way into the published writings of the
two Englishmen came from the strictly "theoretical instruction" given by Subba Row, if indeed such instruction ever
really developed. The arrangement originally contemplated by
the Mahatma M. was apparently abandoned, but the Master
K.H. wrote long explanations to both Sinnett and Hume in
answer to the many questions posed by them. Among these
explanatory letters was one particularly which resulted in
some objections and further questions from them, since
neither of them was especially pleased with it; the whole
concept was foreign to their habitual way of thinking. This was
the so-called "Devachan Letter" in which the states of consciousness of Egos between incarnations, as well as the
conditions and actions which led to these states, were
described.†[12]

An interesting postscript to this letter, which had nothing
to do with the philosophy set forth in it, rather apologized for
the "blotched, patchy and mended appearance" of several of
the Master's recent communications, saying this was due to
the fact that his leisure had "come in snatches, by constant
interruptions" and that his writing had been done "in odd

---

*This message is found in part on page 460/453 and in part on p. 376/369. Two
kinds of paper were used in writing the letter, which may have been the
reason why the sheets became separated. The first part ends with the words
"...do not understand the first principles of..." and the second part
begins with the words "chela training."

†This letter is one of the relatively few in which both questions and answers
are given. It covers 17½ pages of the book and is too technical to quote
from here. The student interested in the subject is urged to study the letter,
as well as a further letter received in February of 1883 (ML-25, p. 191/188)
dealing with some questions and objections raised in response to the first
letter. The two Englishmen, especially Hume, had complained that some of
the Mahatma's explanations were filled with contradictions. The Mahatma
asked them to send a list of these. Sinnett finally got around to compiling
such a list. He had sent it to the Master sometime earlier but did not receive
it back with the latter's comments until September 1882. These are found in
ML-20A and 20B, 178/175 and 180/177. Letter 20B is notable for its information on adeptship. "An adept—the highest as the lowest—is one *only
during the exercise of his occult powers.*" (180/177) This is followed by comments on *when* these powers may be used, what happens when they are used,
and how errors creep in when they are *not* used. The letter is particularly
valuable in emphasizing the human side of the Mahatmas.

places here and there, with such materials as I could pick up."
But for the rule which forbade the use of any occult power
"until every ordinary means had been tried and failed," he
said, he might have produced "a lovely precipitation," but "I
console myself for the miserable appearance of my letters with
the thought that perhaps you may not value them the less for
these marks of my personal subjection to the way-side annoyances which you English so ingeniously reduce to a minimum
with your appliances of sorts.‡ As your lady once kindly remarked, they take away most effectually the flavour of miracle
and make us human beings, more thinkable entities—a wise
reflection for which I thank her."#[13]

He then commented that H.P.B. was "in despair "because
the Chohan had refused M. permission to let her come to see
him, and "M. cooly made her unpack her trunks."[14]

Probably it was this letter to which H.P.B. had reference
when she herself wrote to Sinnett around the end of June 1882.
She began by saying, "As K.H. just kindly flopped on my nose
a whole *Iliad* to your address, you will not care much to read
my letter." Anyhow, she had nothing good to say, she added.
Her plans were "burst." Because of her continued ill health she
was in a depressed state of mind and had gained the permission of her Master to go for a short visit with him. She was all
packed and ready to leave when the "Old One"—as she designated the Chohan—refused permission because of unsettled
conditions between England and Egypt.* Olcott had again

‡Many of the original letters in the British Museum show corrections and,
as the Master says here, "blotched, patchy, and mended appearance." This
is explained by the fact that frequently they were dictated to chelas, who
then penned or precipitated them, following which "all mistakes (were)
corrected." (ML 19)

#An indication that the Mahatma was often aware of what was going on
in the Sinnett household. Numerous references in the *Letters* bear witness
to the humanity of the Masters, as well as to their ability to rise above
human limitations when the occasion demands.

*Obviously, this did not refer to military operations in India or Tibet, for,
in his postscript, the Master K.H. said, "The Egyptian operations of your
blessed countrymen involved such local consequences to the body of occultists still remaining there (in Egypt) and to what they are guarding, that
two of our adepts are already there. . . three more on their way." He explained that he had been offered the "agreeable privilege of becoming an
eye-witness to the human butchery, but—declined with thanks." (ML 116/
112) In a subsequent letter from H.P.B. she indicated that K.H.'s superiors
were unhappy with his refusal to take part in the matter. (LBS 27)

sailed for Ceylon, and Damodar had been "packed up to Poona for a month, his foolish austerities and hard work having broken down his physical constitution."[15] H.P.B. was feeling neglected and alone, and even resentful toward the Chohan and others of the superior adepts (who must have had a voice in the decision to prevent her making the journey) whom she termed "heartless dried up big-bugs, and I must call them that if they had to pulverize me for this."[16]

Sinnett couldn't help sympathizing with the "Old Lady" although he reflected that, when caught up in one of her emotional storms, she seemed to forget the respect and reverence in which, intrinsically, she held all members of the Brotherhood. She had even been known now and then to berate her own Master, the "Illustrious," but Sinnett felt sure that, faced with the necessity, she would cheerfully have died for him. She was a mystery, he had to admit—a continual enigma who, to say the least, contributed variety and interest to the lives of all who knew her, even if sometimes she was a bit overpowering. In spite of his frequent annoyances with her, he felt deeply grateful to her for the services which she continued to perform as an agent for the transmission of correspondence with the Master. He wondered whether a suitable substitute would ever be found. Apparently Eglinton had proved of no real use.

Some weeks earlier, a young India-born Englishman named Edmund W. Fern had entered Hume's employ as a secretary. He joined the Simla Eclectic Theosophical Society and was elected its Secretary. He had some clairvoyance and a certain sensitivity which drew the interest of the Mahatma M., who accepted him on probation. The members of the Simla group were all interested in him, for in spite of the fact that he had some peculiar traits, including a tendency to boastfulness, he had a certain insouciance which to some extent mitigated his arrogance and made him rather likable.

The Mahatma K.H. pointed out in a letter concerning Fern: "The option of receiving him or not as a regular chela—remains with the Chohan. M. has simply to have him tested, tempted and examined by all and every means, so as to have his real nature drawn out. This is a rule with us as inexorable as it is disgusting in your Western sight, and I could not prevent it even if I would. It is not enough to know thoroughly what the chela is capable of doing or not doing at the time and under the circumstances during the period of probation. We have to know of what he may become capable under different and every kind of opportunities."[17]

Sinnett knew that Hume was inclined to be jealous[18] of Fern's status; as a matter of fact, Hume had betrayed this shortly after he engaged the young man.

"I can't understand what everyone sees in him, and I wonder why I took him on," he complained. "He *is* intelligent, I have to admit, but in a sort of crafty way. What the Mahatma M. sees in him—if he really sees anything and Fern isn't inventing the whole thing—is more than I can comprehend. I don't think I am being egotistical when I say that it is incredible to me that he should be accepted on probation when I have been rejected several times.[19] What do these Orientals see in *him,* I wonder!"

Sinnett had some sympathy with his friend's complaint. Fern certainly was beginning to be a bit insufferable, claiming to be a seer,[20] fabricating stories to suit what was an apparently increasingly inflated idea of his own importance and, in his own way, even trying to test the Masters to satisfy himself whether they were "myths or frauds."[21]

Eventually, Hume lost patience with Fern entirely and wrote a long letter to the Mahatma K.H. listing some of the young man's offenses, accusing the Mahatmas of "utterly spoiling" him, and further asserting that Fern had "thoroughly humbugged Morya."

The Master might never have answered what was, in essence, an insulting letter had it not been that the Chohan ordered him to do so.[22] Fern was not his chela and he barely knew the young man,[23] nor would he interfere with M.'s ways of training, "however distasteful" these might be to him personally.[24] However, he wrote a long reply to Hume in which he told the latter some rather unpleasant facts about himself; at the same time, and in all fairness, he gave Hume his due for the work he had done for the Theosophical Society and for "humanity at large."[25] However, since he felt himself unable to judge the precise limits of the Western ideas of politeness, he sent the letter to Sinnett to read and determine whether it should be passed on to his friend.

"I am in a most disagreeable position," wrote K.H., in a short accompanying note,[26] "placed as I am between the risk of betraying a friend and—your *code* of honour . . . I hope I may place an entire confidence in your personal friendship and *of course* honour...Do not be frightened for indeed the whole thing is more ludicrous than dangerous. Yet there is a danger of losing Hume."* He would not, he said, send him Hume's letter to read, since that was labeled "private and confidential" but he wished Sinnett to read his reply and determine whether it should "either be sent or destroyed." He promised to write more fully on the following day.

The letter to Hume was indeed frank and, for the Mahatma K.H., extremely blunt in places.[27] In all probability it never reached Hume,† but it is of interest to the student for its lucid descriptions of the requirements of chelaship and for the clear distinction which it makes between Eastern and Western methods of training.

The promised additional letter[28] reached Sinnett on the day following receipt of the letter to Hume.‡ It was headed "Strictly private and confidential" and was, the Master said, "a tolling of *jeremiads,* a doleful story of discomfiture, which may or may not make you laugh as it does that bulky brother of mine#—but which makes me feel like the poet who could not sleep aright,

> For his soul kept up too much light
> Under his eyelids for the night.

"I hear you uttering under your breath: 'Now what in the world *does* he mean?'" the Master added. "Patience, my best Anglo-Indian friend, patience; and when you have heard of the disreputable conduct of my wicked, more than ever laughing Brother, you will plainly see why I come to regret that instead of tasting in Europe of the fruit of the Tree of Knowledge of Good and Evil¶—I have not remained in Asia, in all *sancta*

---

*In another letter to Sinnett, the Mahatma K.H. said: "...notwithstanding his faults, Mr. Hume is *absolutely* necessary, so far, to the T.S. I grow sometimes very irritated at his petty feelings and spirit of vindictiveness; yet withal, I have to put up with his weaknesses." (ML 296/292)

†The original is with the letters to Sinnett now held in the British Museum.

‡It would seem that the letter to Hume—and probably this letter to Sinnett—were not sent through H.P.B., for the Mahatma began by saying that his letter to Hume had been registered for him "somewhere in Central P. (Province) by a happy, *free* friend."

#The Mahatma M.

¶Reference to the Mahatma K.H.'s education in Europe.

simplicitas of ignorance of your ways and manners, for then—I would be now grinning too."[29]

After explaining that very often their letters—unless dealing with something important or secret—were written in their handwritings by chelas,[30] the Mahatma commented, "Thus , last year, some of my letters to you were precipitated, and when sweet and easy precipitation was stopped†—well, I had but to compose my mind, assume an easy position, and—think, and my faithful 'Disinherited'‡ had but to copy my thoughts, making only occasionally a blunder...this year, for reasons which we need not mention, I have to do my own work—the whole of it, and I have a hard time of it sometimes and get impatient over it. As Jean Paul Richter says somewhere, the most painful part of our bodily pain is that which is bodiless or immaterial, namely, our impatience and the delusion that it will last forever...Having one day permitted myself to act as though I were labouring under such a delusion, in the innocence of my unsophisticated soul, I trusted the sacredness of my correspondence into the hands of that *alter ego* of mine, the wicked and "imperious chap,'# your 'Illustrious,' who took undue advantage of my confidence in him and—placed me in the position I am now in! The wretch laughs since yesterday, and to confess the truth I feel inclined to do the same."

The Master then explained that he was willing to put up with Hume because of his value to the Theosophical Society, but that the "Illustrious" was "not precisely of that opinion. Mr. Hume's pride and self-opinion—he argues—wish, as our saying goes—that all mankind had only two bent knees, to make puja¶ to him; and he, M., is not going to humour him. He will do nothing, of course, to harm or even to vex him purposely; on the contrary, he means to always protect him as he has done until now;§ but he will not lift his little finger to disabuse him."

†Apparently simultaneously with his involvement in the Simla Eclectic Theosophical Society, which it seems did not have the unqualified approval of the Chohan.

‡Djual Khul

#Hume's description of the Mahatma M. (ML 235/232)

¶Worship

§In K.H.'s long letter to Hume (sent to Sinnett (228/225) he described several instances in which the Mahatma M. had protected Hume from attacks, both physical and with respect to his reputation.

The Master said that he had recently written a number of letters to Hume** and,[31] wishing to keep all the Simla phenomena quite separate from anything that was happening at the headquarters of the Society in Bombay (which was perennially under suspicion because of H.P.B.'s enemies) he had taken steps to have them delivered without involving H.P.B. He had given one to M. for delivery by one of his chelas to the Hume residence. Another was "thrown on his (Hume's) table by Djual Khul . . . a pucka phenomenon and Hume has no need to complain." Several others were delivered in various ways, but "however ordinary the means by which the letters reached him, they could not but be phenomenal in reaching India from Tibet. But this does not seem to be taken into consideration by him."

The circumstance which precipitated the Master's "jeremiads" involved Edmund Fern. The Master K.H. commented that he blamed M. for permitting this and exonerated Fern, "who could not help it . . . The boy was led to become guilty of a deliberate deception rather through Hume's constant insults, suspicious attitude, and deliberate slights at meals, and during the hours of work, than from any motives in consequence of his loose notions of morals."[32]

Fern, it seemed, was living in the Hume residence and was therefore a rather constant abrasive to his employer. The latter made no effort to hide his irritation, and Fern, who was beginning to think of himself as specially chosen, found just as constant reasons to resent the slights and faultfinding which invariably characterized Hume's attitude toward him.

One morning early, before the family was about, a chela of K.H.'s came to the house with a letter for Hume. He gave it to Fern with the injunction that it must be delivered to the addressee immediately.

Fern took the letter, a bit annoyed at having to play messenger. As he closed the door on the chela, he heard sounds from above stairs which indicated that the family was about to assemble for breakfast. Not wishing to be found with the letter in his hand, he hurried to the breakfast room and threw it on the table. Then a brilliant idea struck him. Why not give his haughty employer something to think about? He had just time

---

**Only a few of the Mahatma's letters to Hume appear in the published volume; the others undoubtedly remained in Mr. Hume's possession.

to place the letter in the folds of Hume's napkin and take his place behind his chair.

The family seated themselves in their usual morning silence and Hume took up his napkin and shook it. The letter, of course, fell to the floor. Moggy exclaimed in a kind of superstitious fear.

"Mercy on us! What was that?"

Hume felt no fear, only some surprise and a surge of satisfaction. He was about to lean over and pick up the letter when his habitual suspicion of his secretary asserted itself. He turned to the young man and asked, with a disagreeableness which he could not keep out of his voice:

"Did you put that letter there, Fern?"

The young man was frightened but breathed an inner sigh of relief. "Now I am saved," he thought. "I can swear I never put the letter *there,* on the floor where it lies. He never asked me if I put it in his napkin!"

"No sir," he said aloud. "I did not put it there."

He had a sudden vision of the Mahatma M. and a feeling of intense satisfaction and relief that he had, as he felt, not been guilty of a direct lie. The fact of self-deception never entered his mind. Rather, self-congratulation was his major emotion, for getting the better of his employer was something on which he often brooded for long moments at a time. Now the opportunity had simply been given to him gratis!

All this was described in the Master's letter to Sinnett.[33]

"Truly your friend (Hume) was taken in but once," the Master said, "and I would pay any price if I could but *recall* the event and replace my letter with somebody else's message. M. tells me he gives me *carte blanche* to tell anything I like to *you,* but he will not have me say a word to Hume; nor would he ever forgive you—he says, were you to interfere between the punishment of Hume's pride and—fate. Fern is not really to be blamed for thinking that so long as the result is accomplished the details are of no account, since he was brought up in such a school, and he has the welfare of the Cause at heart, whereas, with Hume—it is really *bona fide* selfishness, egotism—the chief and only motive power. 'Egotistic philanthropist' paints his portrait at full length."

The Master K.H. then related a few other instances of Fern's conceit and duplicity and said that he had finally aroused his "too indifferent Brother from his apathy" and the latter had sent a telegram to Fern.*[34] The Mahatma K.H. said that he himself had strictly forbidden his letters or anything connected with his affairs to be given to Fern under any circumstances. He then suggested to Sinnett that he think very carefully before passing on to Hume the long letter which he had sent for Sinnett's perusal. "Better keep it as means for future emergency to prove to him that at least I am one who will not permit even my enemies to be won over by *unfair means.*"

"But above all, good and faithful friend," the Master said, "do not allow yourself to misconceive the real position of our Great Brotherhood. Dark and tortuous as may seem to your Western mind the paths trodden, the ways by which our candidates are brought to the great Light—you will be the first to approve of them when you know *all*...Fern is the queerest psychological subject I have ever met. The pearl is inside, and truly profoundly hidden by the unattractive oyster-shell.[35] We cannot break it at once; nor can we afford to lose such subjects ...While *protecting yourself*—protect him from Hume."[36]

Again there was the inevitable postscript. The first two paragraphs were in the handwriting of the Mahatma K.H. and complimented Sinnett on the excellence of two articles he had recently written. The last paragraph was in the script of the Mahatma M.: "I pray you, kind sir, to lock the foolish letter sent on yesterday to Hume-Sahib into your trunk and leave it there to roost until in demand. I tell you it will create *mischief* and no better. K.H. is too sensitive by far—he is becoming, in your Western Society, a regular Miss." This was signed with the letter "M."

Fern's fate was not a happy one. He ultimately failed his probation; later he was dismissed from the Theosophical Society.

On November 27, 1882, Col. Olcott, at the headquarters of the Theosophical Society, wrote in his diary: "A Brother showed himself in the lower terrace to a number of delegates. M. orders me to expel Fern. Reasons not given. What's up?"†

On December 6, Fern himself came to see Olcott and explained certain matters which the Colonel saw necessitated the

---

*This may have been Fern's first warning of the Master M.'s displeasure.

†This page of Olcott's Diary is in the archives at the International Headquarters of the Theosophical Society; not in the published volumes.

expulsion. The reasons were not psychical, but were purely on the material plane, dealing with business transactions.[37]

Perhaps Fern's action in seeking out the President of the Society was inspired by a letter received from the Mahatma M.—an almost classical bit of irony—which closed with the words: "...do not think of me any the worse if I close this letter with *sending* you a SECOND WARNING."*[38]

Thus another seeming possibility for relieving H.P.B. from her duties as an occult post-office proved a disappointment.

---

*The editor of the two volumes, *Letters from the Masters of the Wisdom*, C. Jinarajadasa, comments in introducing this letter that the two Mahatmas had quite different temperaments. "Both show a keen sense of humour," he says, "but while that of the Master K.H. is more akin to the French notion of wit, that of the Master M. is far more allied to what the Greek tragedians mean by 'irony.' Irony excludes ridicule completely. It contrasts, with great dispassion, facts as they are with what they are supposed to be. Those who can appreciate the Master's 'irony' find great inspiration in the glimpses gained of things seen from His angle of vision." Perhaps Fern had claimed to receive other letters from the Mahatma M., for the Mahatma K.H. wrote to Sinnett: "With the exception of the telegram, M. never wrote Fern but one letter, the five or six other letters in his handwriting emanating from the *Dugpa* who has charge of Fern." (ML 294/289)

13

The "H. X." Letter

In the late summer of 1882, Mr. Hume caused a regrettable disturbance in the Theosophical Society. This marked the beginning of the end of his association with the Mahatmas although, incredibly to many who knew him, they still attempted to work with him for some time to come. His "conversion" had apparently been short-lived, for a series of letters and articles in *The Theosophist* brought to the surface a vindictive resentment, subtly clothed in the graceful prose in which he had such facility.

The series of incidents began with the publication, in the June 1882 issue of the journal, of a letter from a member who signed himself "Caledonian Theosophist." This was probably a man by the name of Davidson, or Davison, a scientific ornithologist who at one time worked for Hume in connection with his bird hobby, serving in the capacity of a private secretary. He later left Hume's employ in disgust and returned to England.[1] The letter was headed "Seeming Discrepancies" and called attention to what the writer believed were contradictions or discrepancies between what was said in one of the "Fragments of Occult Truth" and what H.P.B. had written earlier in *Isis Unveiled,* the first book to come from her pen. Davidson's letter was accompanied by a long "Editor's Note" in which the points at issue were explained in some detail and which concluded with the words: "But there never was, nor can there be, any radical discrepancy between the teachings in 'Isis' and those of this later period, as both proceed from one and the same source—the ADEPT BROTHERS."

In London, C.C. Massey read this exchange between Davidson and H.P.B. and wrote a letter to the *Banner of Light,* a British Spiritualist publication, taking issue with some of the points made by H.P.B. in her editor's note. This was published in the July 8, 1882 issue of that journal. This issue is not available, but Massey's comments were quoted in the August 1882 issue of *The Theosophist*, along with H.P.B.'s answer to *him* in another editor's note. Mr. Massey's letter brought in an added element: the same issue of *The Theosophist* in which Davidson's letter was published carried Sinnett's review of *The Perfect Way*, the book written by Anna Kingsford and Edward Maitland based on the series of talks which had so impressed Sinnett when he was in London the previous year.* Calling attention to H.P.B.'s statement that there could be no discrepancies such as Davidson had claimed, Mr. Massey quoted from Sinnett's review and then from *Isis*. He claimed there *was* a discrepancy and attempted to show that this concerned the subject of reincarnation.

In her reply to Massey,[2] H.P.B. said that, when writing *Isis*, she had not been permitted to enter into details, but she had now been told to do so and was obeying the command, although, she said, "We feel more inclined to hang our diminished head in sincere sorrow and exclaim: *Et tu Brute!* than to quote old truisms. Only where that (even) 'seeming discrepancy' is to be found between the two passages—except by those who are entirely ignorant of the occult doctrine—will be certainly a mystery to every Eastern Occultist who reads the above and who studies at the same school as the reviewer of 'The Perfect Way.' Nevertheless the letter is chosen as the weapon to break our head with." She gave a clear explanation of the seven principles of man and pointed out how they naturally formed a triad and a quarternary "or, as some have it, a 'Compound Trinity' sub-divided into a triad and two duads...." In *Isis*, she said, the reference was "to the *personality*... a compound of imponderable elements composed of the 5th and 4th principles. The former as an emanation of the One Absolute is indestructible; the latter as an elementary compound is finite and doomed sooner or later to destruction with the exception of the more spiritualized portions of the 5th principle (the *Manas* or mind) which are assimilated by the 6th principle when it follows the 7th to its 'gestation state' to be reborn or not reborn as the case may be, in the *Arupa Loka* (the Formless World)." The remainder of her editor's note is an elaboration and elucidation of these statements.

---

*This was the review which the Mahatma said was "more perfect than the authors' conception." (ML 430/424)

Mr. Hume then took up the cudgels in a letter to *The Theosophist.* He began by saying that *Isis* "teemed with errors and misconceptions," that it "never had been and never will be unveiled to any outsiders," and all that could be said was that there were "a few rents in the veil." He added that the whole work was "essentially destructive in character." He went on to criticize the Mahatmas severely for the manner in which they gave the teachings—or, in his view, had *not* given them—saying that their methods were so repulsive to him that he had "more than once" been on the point of closing his connection with them altogether.

He said further uncomplimentary things about the Mahatmas and then proceeded to set Mr. Massey right (as he thought) on the matter which had puzzled him. He signed the letter "H.X."

This letter appeared in *The Theosophist* for September 1882, with another editor's note by H.P.B. which was followed by a further letter headed "A PROTEST" signed by eleven chelas. The protest opened with the words:

"We, the undersigned, the 'Accepted' and 'Probationary' Hindu *Chelas* of the Himalayan Brothers, their disciples in India and Northern Cashmere, respectfully claim our right to protest against the tone used in the above article and the bold criticism of H.X.—a lay chela."*

H.P.B. did not want to publish the H.X. letter but was told by the Mahatma to do so, the original command having come from the Mahachohan himself.[3] She wrote Sinnett an anguished letter in which she said: "...I *positively* and emphatically decline to receive such letters. He (Hume) may or may not remain in the Society—it's the Brothers' business. He may or may not do it and me, under the pretext of philanthropy, all the injury he can think of, but he will not do it *through* me, nor will he take me as his mouthpiece to repeat to K.H. messages which are the most impudent ones in the world ...Why the dickens does he not write all this to K.H. himself? ...I would have thrown the article into the fire, not for what it contains of *me*, or against *Isis*...but what it says of the Brothers, when he calls them 'selfish Asiatics,' blames and criticizes them, warns the public against them, etc....but K.H.

---

*The complete story of the H. X. Letter, with the full text of all the communications involved, is included as Appendix D in the *Guide*.

sent word with Morya that he wanted it absolutely published and I have of course but to shut up."[4]

There was more in the same vein. A bit later on she commented: "The Brothers have had enough of Europeans by this time, I guess. You *alone* have never insulted, never quarreled with them, disgusted as you may often feel at the state of things. For even I, a half *Asiatic* and with none of your niceties and English pruderie and fidgetiness, even I felt disheartened more than once at the crumbling of my *ideals.* But that was long ago; years since; and since then *I* learned to know them better, and if they lost in my *fiction,* they won the more in my real reverential respect. I do not judge them any more on appearances as you do. I know there are many things in their reality which do not agree with our European sense or notions of right—as Hume says in his article, but then, my dear Mr. Sinnett, they have a hundred times more of that which you will *never* get or have in Europe; nor have they any of our horrible voices and small faults."[5]

Referring again to Hume, she said, "I knew he was too haughty to bear with our Brothers. He offering himself as a chela and you innocently believing in *his* conversion! Fiddlesticks! A Jupiter offering himself as a goat-herd to the God Hermes, to teach the latter manners! . . . The T.S. is not going to die with us, and we all are but diggers at its foundations."

And then a tribute to K.H.: "He (Hume) calling K.H., the grandest, noblest, purest of men—selfish! A truer and better than whom never existed outside the walls of their low asrum;* one who, young as he is might have become Chohan and perfect Boddhisatwa long ago, were it not for his really divine pity for the world."

When the H.X. letter was published in *The Theosophist,* H.P.B. closed her editorial note with the words: "Had it not been for the express orders received from the Brothers we should have never consented to publish such a—to say the least—ungenerous document. Perchance it may do good in one direction; it gives the key, we think, to the true reason why our Brothers feel so reluctant to show favors even to the most intellectual among the European 'would-be' mystics."

Perhaps as a result of all this (at any rate, in sequence) Hume wrote a letter to the Mahatma K.H. in which he said

*Ashram

that he could no longer rely solely on him, as the manner in which he taught was "so slow and unsatisfactory that it would not be right" for him not to look elsewhere.[6] He had, as a matter of fact, taken up with another teacher, the "Swami from Almora," a man who seems to have made considerable pretensions but of whom the Mahatma K.H. spoke as having "no powers whatever."[7] He had written some articles for *The Theosophist* under the pen name of "Paramahansa Swami." These were published in the September 1882, February 1883, and March 1883 issues and called forth severe criticism from Subba Row. The "good old Swami," as Hume called him, was in effect an enemy of the Mahatmas and, according to H.P.B.,[8] had once threatened to "expose them as Dugpas." He died not long after Hume took up with him.[9]

In the course of all this, Sinnett received a letter from the Mahatma K.H. in which he pointed out, "I had no right to suppress the 'offensive article'...for several reasons. Having allowed our name to be connected with the T.S. and ourselves dragged into publicity, we have to suffer (the verb a simple figure of speech if you please)...as Olcott would put it, 'the penalty of our greatness.' We must permit the expression of every opinion whether benevolent or malevolent; to feel ourselves picked to pieces—one day; 'preached' on the following, worshipped on the next; and—trampled down to the mud on the fourth. Reason No. 2—the Chohan has ordained it."[10]

With reference to the alleged discrepancy, the Master commented: "In *reality* there is no contradiction between the passage in *Isis* and our later teaching; to anyone who never heard of the *seven* principles—constantly referred to in *Isis* as a trinity, without any more explanation—there certainly appeared to be as good a contradiction as could be. 'You will write so and so, give *so far*, and no more'—she was constantly told by us when writing her book. It was at the very beginning of a new cycle, in days when neither Christians nor Spiritualists ever thought of, let alone mentioned more than two principles in man—*body and Soul*, which they called Spirit ...[Since there were] endless polemics and objections to the effect that *there could not be in man two souls*, we thought it premature to give the public more than they could possibly assimilate, and before they had digested the 'two souls'; and thus the further sub-division of the trinity into 7 principles was left unmentioned in *Isis*."[11]

Of Hume, the Master said: "...is it possible that you should not have perceived that he will never allow *even an adept* to know more or better than himself; that his was a *false* humility; that he is an actor, who enacts a part for his own benefit, regardless of the pleasure or displeasure of his audience, though when the latter is manifested to the slightest degree, he turns around, concealing admirably his rage, and hisses and spits *internally* ...Every time I prove him wrong ...the record he keeps against me swells, and he comes out with some new accusation."[12]

Hume, it will be remembered, was President of the Simla Eclectic Theosophical Society. In this letter, the Master K.H. commented, "If he desires to retain his official position in the Eclectic, help him to do so. If not, I beg you most urgently to accept the position of President yourself. But I leave all this to your tact and discretion. Let him know that the *Protest* of the Chelas is no work of ours, but the result of a positive order emanating from the Chohan. The *Protest* was received at the Headquarters two hours before the postman brought the famous article [the H.X. Letter] and telegrams were received from several chelas in India on the same day.[13]

Very shortly after the furor over the H.X. Letter, Hume did resign as head of the Simla Eclectic Society; he sent several communications to the Mahatma K.H., one of which concerned his resignation. The Master replied in an entirely courteous letter,*[14] accepting Hume's statement that he preferred to be "simply a zealous tho' independent theosophist, a simple member of the Society," with whose objects—however faulty the system—he sympathized "from the bottom of my heart."[15] K.H. observed, however: "I cannot leave unnoticed the remark that your want of progress has been due to the fact that you were not allowed to come to us and be taught personally. No more than yourself was Mr. Sinnett accorded any such privilege. Yet he seems to understand perfectly well whatever he is taught, and even the few hazy points upon subjects of an extremely abstruse nature will be very soon cleared for him. Nor have we ever had 'one word of unpleasantness' between us—not even between him and M .. whose bluntness in speaking out his mind is often great."

*This letter will repay reading in its entirety; it is too long to be fully quoted here. *See* LMW 1:66-74.

The Mahatma pointed out further that, as President of the Simla Eclectic Society, Hume had done nothing whatever for the branch, "however great the services—in connection with literary worth—rendered by Mr. A. O. Hume." He had done a great deal, the Master said, in acquiring a comprehension of the philosophy, but "no attempt was ever made to organize your Branch on a firm foundation, nor even regular meetings held; on the plea that you were not allowed to know *all*, you gave your fellows *nothing*."

The letter closed with a generous offer: "Whenever you need me, and when you have done your study with the 'Swami'— then I will be again at your service."

All the distress resulting from these unfortunate complications was too much for H.P.B., and again she became seriously ill; for a time even her life was in danger. When she revived sufficiently she wrote to Sinnett that Hume was not delicate enough to comprehend that K.H. would to the last be kind and polite.

"He is beginning to be *off his head*," she said. "He bamboozles himself into the insane belief that he is fast becoming an adept, and he *sees sights* and believes in them as revelations." She added that she had wanted to write to Hume to tell him what she thought of him, but the Master prevailed upon her not to do so. However, feeling "suffocated" she got up from her bed and wrote a note expressing her opinion of him. "To this K.H. did not object," she wrote, but said that as Hume was necessary to them for some purposes yet "he would send him *an antidote* to soothe his anger against me. The antidote went to Hume in the shape of a telegram from K.H. from somewhere out of Bombay, telling Hume *as I see*...'a foolish letter sent against my advice, you must pardon the passion of an old and very, very sick woman.' And then on the following day advised me for the good of the Society to sacrifice my feelings, and since *he* Hume had once offered me his excuses, asked me that I should do the same. I wrote him therefore, another letter, telling him that since K.H. and M. thought I better apologize for some of my rude expressions, I did so. At the same time, having devoted half a page to express sorrow if I had hurt his feelings, I believe I told him worse things on the three other pages than the day before. But now—I will abuse him no more. ...I know *he is doomed* and by his own actions."[16]

Sinnett felt hesitant to speak to Hume about the situation—in part because, to some extent, he shared the latter's point of view, although his loyalty to the Master and his half-acknowledged conviction that the Master was right in his stand weighed heavily in the balance. When next the two Englishmen were together he nerved himself to risk a mild remonstrance.

"I confess I'm puzzled, Hume," he said. "At one time you seem convinced of the value of what the Mahatmas have to teach, and then suddenly you have turned against the whole thing and gone over to the Almora Swami for instruction. Is he so much better than K.H.?"

"For one thing," Hume replied with some satisfaction, "he's willing to concede that a Westerner may have a valid point of view. And I think he isn't any more convinced of the real existence of the Mahatmas than I am."

"But you *know* they exist—or so you told Davidson. You said you had had many conversations with them.[17] How then can you doubt?"

To his surprise Hume looked mildly embarrassed.

"Davidson talks too much," he said. "Anyhow, I'm not certain that they are correct in what they teach.[18] And I could have taught someone in one week all they have given us in a year and a half. They think they know more about me than I know about myself, which is ridiculous. K.H. goes so far as to say that I am 'changeable'! He doesn't even realize how many-sided I am and that he simply sees different sides at different times."[19]

Sinnett reflected that Hume wasn't being very consistent. At one moment he all but denied the existence of the Mahatmas; at the next he apparently allowed their existence but disagreed with their viewpoint, especially since he felt that viewpoint did not do him justice. But, Sinnett told himself, he wasn't Hume's keeper. Besides, the Master *had* warned him about permitting himself to be too influenced by his colleague. He decided that, after all, he was answerable only for his own conviction, which seemed somehow to be at the core of his feelings for the Master, regardless of occasional surface doubts and—he had to admit it—his own sense of frustration that he had not been permitted direct contact with him. He conveniently forgot, as he always did when this thought was strong in him, that the Master had told him several times that he *could* not satisfy his desire so long as no change was made in his way of life.

14

Changing Circumstances

As might have been expected, the emotional stress to which H.P.B. had been subjected took its toll of her physical well being. Never in the best of health, although she had phenomenal endurance and will power, she finally succumbed again and took to her bed. The Mahatma M., in one of his now rare letters to Sinnett, held Hume largely responsible for this crisis[1] and commented that H.P.B. had become so ill that he was "forced to carry her away."[2]

The Master K.H., writing to Sinnett in September 1882, from a lamasery near Darjeeling* which he described as "the object of H.P.B.'s longings," said that probably he would have to "interview in my own skin the Old Lady if M. brings her here. And—he has to bring her—or lose her forever—at least as far as the physical triad is concerned."[3]

Apparently the situation which had earlier prevented her visit to the Masters had moderated, for there appeared to be no resistance to the plan on the part of the Mahachohan.

H.P.B. had known of this heavenly boon in store for her,[4] and when she learned that the time had come for her to go, she was so excited that she rose from her bed for the first time in a week to write to Sinnett. The letter consisted mainly of comments about Hume; she herself did not hold him fully responsible, she said, for she had been ailing for some time. But there was little doubt that his bitter attacks had precipitated the severe illness. Also, the circumstances of being snubbed by some other acquaintances was extremely painful to her. She had, on the previous day, been taken to the doctor, and on the way another carriage had crossed the path of her own. Its occupants—two ladies whom she had met and who would, in

---

* Probably in Sikkim or at the Phari Jong Monastery. (*Guide* 116)

ordinary circumstances, certainly have bowed to her—gave no sign of recognition but "looked very proud and disdainful... Well," she added, "I was fool enough to resent it."[5]

Sinnett had sent her copies of some recent letters from Hume and she had, she said, sent these off "for the delectation of M. and chelas."[6] But, most importantly, pasted onto her letter was a note from the Mahatma K.H. to her in which he said: "I will remain about 23 miles off Darjeeling till Sep. 26th—and if you come you will find me in the old place..."[7]

"Oh, I do hope she can be helped!" said Patience Sinnett when she read this letter. "I almost feel sometimes that I should go to Bombay to be with her when she falls into one of these spells."

"I'm afraid you would be traveling back and forth a great deal of the time, then," her husband said drily. "She always seems to recuperate—at least enough to carry on, and to write pretty vigorous letters of protest about whatever has happened at the time to upset her."

"Well, I can't say I blame her," Patience responded with what, for her, savored of indignation. "I simply don't understand why Allan keeps going out of his way to make things difficult for her. And I don't understand either why the Masters bother with him, when he seems to spend most of his time thinking up nasty things to say about them."

"I admit he's pretty cantankerous," Sinnett conceded. "I think the Master M. has lost patience with him. He seems to think it pointless for K.H. to go on sacrificing himself for such a man."[8]

"Why does he, I wonder?"

"For more than one reason, probably," he said thoughtfully. "Partly, I suppose, because of Hume's literary ability, which K.H. seems to admire. But also—I'm sorry to have to say this—it seems to be because, if the Master rejects him completely, he is likely to turn into an even more active enemy. I can't always understand the Masters' motivations, and I've sometimes doubted K.H.'s assurance that they have a reason for everything they do, but I have to confess it seems to work out that way."

Patience caught her husband's hand in her own; her eyes were shining.

"Percy—if H.P.B. recovers sufficiently, we ought to invite her to stop with us for a while on her way back to Bombay."

"As you wish, my dear," he agreed without much enthusiasm. "Probably we shall have returned to Allahabad by that time."

A chela by the name of Gargya Deva* had been sent to escort H.P.B. to where the Masters were waiting. She left Bombay in the greatest secrecy, even some members of the Society who visited headquarters believing her simply to be out of sight. The authorities had refused to grant her safe passage into either Sikkim or Bhutan, but she would not give up the trip so she was forced to travel without a pass.

"Had I not gone incognito till I reached the hills and turned off the railway to enter Sikkim," she wrote Sinnett later, "I would *have never been allowed to enter it unmolested* and would not have seen M. and K.H. in their bodies both. Lord, I would have been dead by this time."[9]

A further difficulty attended her progress. Word had somehow got around that she was traveling to see the two Mahatmas, and while they were quiet about her identity, groups of Theosophists managed to get on the train with her at various places so that she and Gargya Deva were put to considerable trouble to avoid them. In this she seemed to be aided on several occasions. Once, when she had to change from one railway station to another, the train took off suddenly, leaving many followers and even much of her own luggage behind. The few who managed to climb on in time failed, for one reason or another, to reach Darjeeling with her. Only one of them managed to get across the border into Sikkim and, eventually, to meet his Master.‡

H.P.B. stayed for two days with the Mahatmas and, during that time, she recovered almost miraculously.†

---

* In an article by this chela entitled "Himalayan and Other Mahatmas" published in *The Theosophist* of December 1883, he stated that he had lived with the Mahatmas.

‡ *See* "How a Chela Found His Guru" by S. Ramaswaimer, MTL 321; LMW 2:163

† The method employed by the Mahatma M. to cure H.P.B. comes to light in a letter she wrote the following year to M. Biliere, a friend in Paris: "Last year the doctors condemned me... I went to Sikkim, to the entrance to Tibet, and there my beloved Master repaired kidneys and liver, and in three days' time I was as healthy as ever. They say it was a miracle. He only gave me a potion to drink seven times a day, from a plant in the Himalayas." (*Guide* 152)

"Oh, the blessed, blessed two days," she wrote later to Sinnett from Darjeeling. "It was like old times when the bear‡ paid me a visit. The same kind of wooden hut, a box divided into three compartments for rooms, and standing in the jungle on four pelican's legs; the same yellow chelas gliding noiselessly; the same eternal 'gul-gul-gul' sound of my Boss's inextinguishable chelum pipe; the old familiar sweet voice of your K.H. (whose voice is still sweeter and face still thinner and more transparent) the same *entourage* for furniture—skins, and yak-tail stuffed pillows and dishes for salt, tea, etc."[10]

As soon as her health was sufficiently improved, the Masters sent H.P.B. to Darjeeling. "She is not safe in Sikkim," wrote the Master K.H. to Sinnett. "The Dugpa opposition is tremendous and unless we devote the whole of our time to watching her, the 'Old Lady' would come to grief."[11]

In her letter to Sinnett from Darjeeling, H.P.B. commented that she was being pestered by would-be visitors but that she had refused to see any of them. "I came here for our Brothers and Chelas and the rest may go and be hanged," she said. She had received the invitation to stop with them on her way back to Bombay and assured Sinnett that she meant to accept their kind invitation. "I cannot leave Darjeeling while my Boss is hovering near by," she said. "He goes away in a week or ten days and then I will leave Darjeeling and if you permit me to wait [on] you at your home I will do so with real pleasure." She added at the end: "Boss gives you his love—I saw him last night at the Lama's house."[12]

It was past the middle of October before H.P.B. reached Allahabad, to which the Sinnetts had returned. She was still somewhat weak but seemed completely rejuvenated in spirit by her stay with the two Mahatmas and the later contacts with her own Master. Patience exerted herself to take the tenderest care of her, and even Sinnett—too well bred to be other than polite to her as a guest in this house, although at times with a condescension of which he was quite unaware—felt in greater than usual charity with her. He had been both amused and surprisingly moved by the Master K.H.'s description of her meeting with the two Mahatmas:

‡ The Mahatma M.

"I don't believe I was ever so profoundly touched by anything I witnessed in all my life," said K.H., "as I was with the poor old creature's ecstatic rapture, when meeting us recently both in our natural bodies, one—after three years, the other—nearly two years absence and separation in the flesh. Even our phlegmatic M. was thrown off his balance by such an exhibition of which he was chief hero. He had to use his *power* and plunge her into a profound sleep, otherwise she would have burst some bloodvessel, including kidneys, liver and her 'interiors'—to use our friend Oxley's favorite expression—in her delirious attempts to flatten her nose against his riding mantle besmeared with Sikkim mud. We both laughed; yet could we be otherwise than touched?"[13]

This letter from the Master contained other references to H.P.B. "In your opinion," he wrote, "H.P.B. is, at best, for those who like her despite herself—a quaint, strange woman, a psychological riddle; impulsive and kindhearted, yet not free from the vice of untruth. We, on the other hand, under the garb of eccentricity and folly—we find a profounder wisdom in her *inner* Self than you will ever find yourselves able to perceive. In the superficial details of her homely, hard-working, common-place daily life and affairs, you discern but unpracticality, womanly impulse, often absurdity and folly; we, on the contrary, light daily upon traits in her inner nature the most delicate and refined, and which would cost an uninitiated psychologist years of constant and keen observation, many an hour of close analysis and efforts to draw out . . . and thus learn to know her true *inner* Self."[14]

Sinnett had been reading the letter aloud to Patience, taking advantage of an interlude when H.P.B. was resting in her own room. He paused at this point to say:

"Here it is again—more talk about how different the Old Lady is inwardly from what she is outwardly. It's quite a puzzle to me."

"I suppose so," Patience replied. "And yet you know that is how I have always felt about her—that we simply don't see beyond the surface most of the time."

"I think *you* do," Sinnett said gently, "although I confess I myself am more often than not put off by some of the surface manifestations."

But he was wholly in sympathy with his wife's concern for H.P.B. While she was with them, she was permitted to rise when she chose, and always a servant was there with her morning tea or coffee as soon as a sound was heard from her room. She was not asked to perform any phenomena, and even discussions of serious matters were avoided unless she herself initiated them. The rest and peace which characterized the visit completed the restoration begun during the blissful experience of being again with her Master and the healing he had performed. She was ready again to take up the work to which her life was dedicated.

When she left for Bombay, she was accompanied by several Bengali members and by S. Ramaswamier, the chela who had managed to reach Sikkim with her. The Convention of the Society was held on December 7th, and the rest of the year was devoted to moving the headquarters of the Society from Bombay to the newly purchased property near Madras in South India.

Col. Olcott, in his travels about India, had been constantly on the alert to discover a suitable new site for a permanent headquarters. Several liberal offers of houses, free of rent, had been made in Ceylon, and the Colonel was linked strongly to that island country through the intensive work he had done there. But both he and H.P.B. hesitated to isolate themselves from India, and several other practical considerations made it seem inadvisable to go there. Earlier in 1882, however, they had been invited to look at a property called Huddleston Gardens at Adyar, near Madras, which was available at a surprisingly low price. Once they had seen it, they "knew that our future home was found."* With the help of some interested members, they were able to manage the financing—a debt which, incidentally, was to be fully discharged during the following year.

The transfer to the new headquarters was made on December 17, "the event being fixed in H.P.B.'s memory," wrote Olcott, "by the theft of her handsome Kashmir chudder,† through an outside window of the railway carriage while we were occupied at the other side in giving and receiving compliments and salaams. Her remarks upon the incident, when it was discovered, will not bear repetition."[15]

---

* For a description of Adyar see ODL 2:360-61.

† A woman's shawl

Arrived at Madras, the founders were escorted "in grand style to Adyar, which seemed to smile upon its future masters. The reader can hardly imagine our pleasure in settling into a home of our own, where we should be free from landlords, changes, and the other worries of the condition of tenancy."‡

The Colonel added: "The year 1882 went out with me working at my desk alone."

Other events had taken place during the last few months of 1882. Hume had finally resigned as President of the Simla Eclectic Theosophical Society and Sinnett had been elected to fill the vacancy. This change took place while the Sinnetts were still in Simla, and although they anticipated returning shortly to Allahabad, Sinnett accepted the post; the Mahatma K.H. had made it clear that he wished him to do so,[16] Hume having failed signally to make any significant contribution to the work in that city.[17]

Hume had, as a matter of fact, told Sinnett of his intention to resign and had suggested that the latter accept the office.

"I'm most emphatically not willing to continue," he said. "I think the whole system and policy of the Brothers are completely wrong[18] and I can't pretend any longer to take orders from them."

"I'm not aware that they ever give orders," Sinnett reminded him quietly. "A bit much in the other direction, it seems to me. They leave you wondering sometimes just what *is* the best course of action, and sometimes even whether they really care what you do."

"Well—right. Perhaps I shouldn't have used the word 'orders,' although I always have the feeling that, even if they

‡ A curious entry in the Colonel's diary follows these comments: "The remaining days of December were filled with the petty annoyances of getting servants, overseeing mechanics, making the first necessary repairs, and receiving and unpacking our furniture. The Teacher (M.) came daily to see H.P.B., and I have it recorded that on 29th December, she 'made me promise that if she should die, no one but myself should be allowed to see her face. I am to sew her up in a cloth and have her cremated.' That, you see, was nine years before her corpse was carried to the Woking Crematory, near London; hence the possibility of her sudden death was even then kept in mind." (ODL 2:392) Speculation on what lay behind such a request is almost inevitable—although it *is* sheer speculation to say that perhaps, even then, H.P.B. was being given her choice whether to continue with the work or be released from the physical body which was so burdensome to her, and perhaps she feared that, in a moment of desperation, she might sometime choose the latter. Whatever the reason for her request, it is apparent that the possibility of death was in her mind.

don't let one know what they expect, they seem to disapprove of almost everything."

Sinnett reflected how oddly different people could react to the same situation. He considered that "disapprove" was hardly the right word. The Mahatmas seemed to him able to discern with penetrating insight all those hidden—or not so hidden—motivations which influenced one's actions and to follow, then, whatever course seemed indicated without the emotional reactions to which ordinary people were subject. Such impersonality must have been dearly bought, he told himself. But he did not believe that his friend would ever be able to see this.

Sinnett felt some uneasiness about undertaking the presidency of the Simla Society, since he was uncertain what he could do at a distance. Patience reminded him that he had managed to continue his editorial work for the *Pioneer* at the same distance and that no doubt he could discharge his new duties equally well from the opposite direction.

"It may mean frequent trips to Simla," he said rather dubiously, but she accepted this prospect with her usual equanimity.

He took some heart from the Master's words which had reached him via H.P.B. while she was still in Darjeeling: "Hail and success to the 'new President' at last!"[19]

Further encouragement came in the next letter from the Mahatma.

". . . the disposition and abdication of our great 'I am'," the Master wrote, "is one of the most agreeable events of the season for your humble servant. *Mea culpa!* I exclaim, and willingly place my guilty head under the shower of ashes—from the Simla cigars if you like—for it was my doing! Some good has come of it in the shape of excellent literary work—(though, indeed, I prefer your style)—for the Parent Body, but none whatever for the hapless 'Eclectic.' "[20]

The Master went on to say that he would not like to see Hume sever his connection with the Society altogether, affirming Sinnett's own impression by commenting: " . . . first, for his own intrinsic literary worth, and then—because you would be sure to have an indefatigable though a *secret* enemy, who would pass his time in writing out his ink dry against theosophy, denouncing all and everyone in the Society to all and everyone outside of it, and making himself disagreeable in a thousand ways. As I once said, he may seem to forgive . . . but in reality he neither forgives nor ever forgets."[21]

This, Sinnett himself had been finally convinced, was the truth, although he sometimes had a lingering inclination to agree with his friend in some respects. He had, however, lost sympathy with the latter's inclination to be vitriolic about matters which did not please him, particularly concerning the "dear Old Lady" and "dear Old Olcott," as well as the Brothers and their teachings.

In the letter congratulating Sinnett on his election to the presidency of the Simla Society, the Master K.H. had promised to tell him of a "ludicrous" incident in connection with a communication from C.C. Massey which Sinnett had received and sent on to him. In the letter explaining his own part in the transition the Master fulfilled this promise. One of the most amusing incidents in the *Letters,* it reveals, at the same time, yet another beautiful facet of the Mahatma's character:

. . . Your letter, enclosing that of C.C.M. [Massey] was received by me on the morning following the date you had handed it over to the 'little man.'* I was then in the neighborhood of Pari-Jong, at the gun-pa of a friend, and was very busy with important affairs. When I received intimation of its arrival, I was just crossing the large inner courtyard of the monastery; bent upon listening to the voice of Lama Tündhüb Gyatcho, I had no time to read the contents. So, after mechanically opening the thick packet, I merely glanced at it, and put it, as I thought, into the travelling bag I wear across the shoulder. In reality though, it had dropped; and since I had broken the envelope and emptied it of its contents, the latter were scattered in their fall. There was no one near me at the time, and my attention being wholly absorbed with the conversation, I had already reached the staircase leading to the library door, when I heard the voice of a young *gyloong* calling out from a window, and expostulating with someone at a distance. Turning around I understood the situation at a glance; otherwise your letter would have never been read by me for I saw a venerable old goat in the act of making a morning meal of it. The creature had already devoured part of

* Probably Babajee (sometimes called Dharbagiri Nath), a chela at headquarters. He is elsewhere referred to in the *Letters* in this fashion.

C.C.M.'s letter, and was thoughtfully preparing to take a bite of yours, more delicate and easy for chewing with his old teeth than the tough envelope and paper of your corresponding epistle. To rescue what remained of it took me but one short instant, disgust and opposition of the animal notwithstanding—but there remained mighty little of it! The envelope with your crest on it nearly disappeared, the contents of the letters made illegible—in short I was perplexed at the sight of the disaster. Now you know why I felt embarrassed: *I had no right to restore it, the letters coming* from the "Eclectic" and connected directly with the hapless "Pelings" on all sides. What could I do to restore the missing parts! I had already resolved to humbly crave permission from the Chohan to be allowed an exceptional privilege in this dire necessity, when I saw his holy face before me, with his eye twinkling in quite an unusual manner, and heard his voice: "Why break the rule? I will do it myself." These simple words, *Kam mi ts'har*—I'll do it," contain a world of hope for me. He has restored the missing parts and done it quite neatly too, as you can see, and even transformed a crumpled broken envelope, very much damaged, into a new one—crest and all. Now I know what great power had to be used for such a restoration, and this leads me to hope for a relaxation of severity one of these days. Hence I thanked the goat heartily; and since he does not belong to the ostracised Peling race, to show my gratitude I strengthened what remained of teeth in his mouth, and set the dilapidated remains firmly in their sockets, so that he may chew food harder than English letters for several years to come.[23]

"How I wish the whole world could know about this," said Patience, tears of mixed laughter and pathos streaming down her cheeks. "How much more one can love them in realizing they still have their human side. And their sense of humor!" she added.

"Well, K.H. once complimented you for pointing this out," he reminded her,[24] joining in her irresistible mirth. "I wonder if Hume would appreciate this story."

"Better not test him," she admonished. "He'd merely be set off on another diatribe. How interesting that the Master had no right to correct the situation himself."

"I suppose, from a strictly occult point of view, he had to take the consequences of what certainly seemed a moment of carelessness."

"But he didn't after all! The blessed Mahachohan! I'll revere him forever."

Sinnett, too, took some comfort from the Master's story of the incident. He had been inclined to regard the Mahachohan as an inexorable disciplinarian, whose sternness was never relaxed; now—somewhat surprisingly to himself—he felt a sense of gratitude toward him for helping to extricate the Master K.H. from his dilemma. He had learned much during the past year, he decided, in spite of Hume's contention that the Mahatmas had taught them almost nothing; he had more than enough material for the new book which he was just beginning,* and in spite of minor annoyances and problems, he felt it had been a year of progress.

But 1882 was not yet through with him. Near its close, even Patience's sturdy positiveness received a shock when the proprietors of *The Pioneer* notified Sinnett that his services with that newspaper were to be terminated. Sinnett himself felt no real surprise. Somewhere, from some half-closed corner of his mind, the possibility had more than once leered at him, but he had never given it an opportunity to come out into the daylight and be examined. Now he was forced to do so. When, finally, he looked the fact full in the face, he knew that his preoccupation with Theosophy and the Theosophical Society, while undoubtedly the chief factor in the decision, was not the only one. Almost from the first day of Rattigan's appearance on the scene, there had been between them a half-veiled hostility—or, in the best of terms, a basic lack of confidence.[25] But Rattigan's interest in the paper was the controlling one and his word was final.

To be sure, the arrangement was fair enough: Sinnett was to be paid a full year's salary in advance; and during that time, it was assumed, he would be able to find other lucrative employment.

Once accepted, the development was not too devastating. There would be funds for other ventures. Perhaps he would

---

* *Esoteric Buddhism*, published in June 1883.

return to England. Although he had lived in India for many years, this prospect had a certain attraction. He believed that when Patience recovered from her shock, she would not be reluctant to go "home." And no doubt Denny's health would be benefited. At any rate, he reflected, he would not have to make up his mind in haste. No decision need be made until after the first of the year. Perhaps even the Mahatma might have some suggestion for his future.

15

The Phoenix

"Yes, it would be nice to go home," said Patience, with a faraway expression in her eyes. "But I think of some other possibilities, too."

The Sinnetts were sitting over their after-dinner coffee and now were resuming a conversation which had been suspended until the servants had left the room.

"For instance?" her husband asked.

"Well, I've sometimes thought—perhaps I've never mentioned it because it seemed such a remote possibility—that is you had your own newspaper, you could do something to promote more freedom—political freedom, I mean—in India, something that would help the people in a way that no one is doing now. It's all quite vague in my mind, but the idea nags me, now that you're free to make plans."*

Sinnett was looking at her in astonishment.

"Does it seem preposterous?" she asked, with a tentative smile. "You know, of course, that I'll be happy with whatever decision you make."

"No," he assured her warmly. "It is not preposterous. At least, I don't think it is I'm surprised because I've been half-way toying with some such idea myself, even though I admit the prospect of returning to England—at least while my new book is being published—appeals to me strongly. But I would need a lot more capital than I have for such a project."

"I suppose so," she agreed. "But I'm sure Col. Olcott would help."

He shook his head dubiously.

---

* Nowhere, in accounts of this period, is it indicated that the idea of a new newspaper originated with Mrs. Sinnett. It might have done so, since this would have been entirely consonant with her character. It seems logical, however, that it must have been discussed between the Sinnetts before it took concrete form in his mind.

"I don't see how he could—not with money anyhow. He and H.P.B. are having enough difficulty with expenses just now, as it is. She even sold her jewelry, the Colonel wrote me. I hadn't told you because I didn't want to distress you. He said, too, that his own sister in America, who has several small children and of whom he is very fond, was quite destitute and he didn't see how he could spare even a few rupees to help her. The Old Lady made him do it—and then—quite a wonderful thing—the Mahatma M. contributed something to the fund.[1] One of the difficulties, I understand, is that people don't pay their dues— especially the members in London. I'm a bit ashamed of that. Perhaps I ought to write to some of them. I've already sent Olcott a cheque, of course."

"Oh, I'm glad for that," she said approvingly. "But how dreadful for people not to pay their dues to the Theosophical Society. They wouldn't think of neglecting to pay dues to any other organization they belong to, I'm sure. But, you know, I didn't really mean that anything should be taken from the funds of the Society. It's just that the Colonel always seems so resourceful." She chuckled suddenly. "I'll never forget his description of the cart he built to travel about in Ceylon."*

He too smiled at the recollection.

"Yankee ingenuity, he called it! Unfortunately, building an ingenious mechanical contraption is rather different from launching a new newspaper."

"Yes, I know. I only meant that some of the same ingenuity might be exercised." She was silent for a few moments, sipping her coffee. "I wonder," she said finally, "what the Master would think of such an idea."

---

* This was, said the Colonel, "a two-wheeled traveling cart on springs, which could give ample sleeping accommodations for four people; had lockers projecting from the sides for holding table furniture, tinned provisions, a small library, and my bathing kit; two large ones under the floor for baggage, sacks of vegetables and curry-stuffs; a tight canvas roof on hoop-iron ribs, a chest in front for tools and spare ropes, hooks underneath for water buckets, cattle trough, etc., a secure shelf over the axle for the driver's cooking pots, and rings behind for attaching a led bullock.... I lived in this conveyance for weeks at a stretch. It weighed less than a country cart and was comfortable as need be. By a simple change of longitudinal seat-planks inside, I could, at will, have a writing room, dining room, sleeping room, or an omnibus-like arrangement with two cushioned seats running fore and aft to accommodate eight sitters. It was as much a novelty to the simple country folk as the Buddhist Catechism, and priests and laity used to flock around to see its mechanical wonders." (ODL 3:306)

Sinnett glanced at her sharply and set his own cup and saucer aside.

"I hesitate. . . it seems an imposition. Still, I know he is concerned for the masses of India. Perhaps there is no harm in asking. He can't any more than tell me it's strictly my own business. I'll write to Olcott too. He may have some ideas."

The Mahatma K.H. was far from giving Sinnett such a brusque reply as he had half-expected, although no specific advice was immediately forthcoming.

"Before I give you any definite answer to your business letter," the Mahatma wrote, "I desire to consult our venerable Chohan. We have, as you say, 12 months time before us."[2]

Well, thought Sinnett, the idea wasn't going to be rejected out of hand at any rate; it must be considered of some importance if it was to be presented to such a high authority.

At the moment, the Master continued, he had "a little business on hand, that is very important, as it hinges on to a series of other deliberate untruths, whose real character it is high time to prove. We are called in so many words, or rather five letters, 'liars'. . . and accused of 'base ingratitude.' The language is strong, and willing as we should feel to borrow many a good thing from the English, it is not politeness, I am afraid, that we would feel inclined to learn from the class of gentleman represented by Mr. Hume." He asked Sinnett to search his memory concerning an incident which had taken place at a meeting of the Simla Eclectic Society some time previously.* Those present were Sinnett, "the Hume pair, the Gordon couple, Davison, and H.P.B." The business was, in itself, he said, "of very little importance" and he urged Sinnett not to stop to argue over its "utter unworthiness" but to rely upon the Adepts' "seeing something of the future which remains hidden to you." The incident seemed to hold potentials of future repercussions, not to mention the fact that Djual Khul and H.P.B. had quarreled over their differing recollections as to whether or not the matter had been entered in the minutes by Davison, the then secretary. H.P.B. main-

---

* Probably when H.P.B. and Sinnett were visiting in that city in 1881, while Patience was still in England.

tained that it had; Djual Khul that it had not. "Of course he was right and she was wrong."†

The happening itself involved a letter to Hume from another member "expressing contempt for theosophy and suspicion about the good faith of H.P.B." Hume had sent the letter to K.H. to read, and the latter had returned it to Hume through H.P.B. She gave it back to Hume during the meeting and said that the Mahatma had "given orders through her to the General Council to invite the Babu (the writer of the letter) to resign. Thereupon Mr. Hume proclaimed most emphatically: 'In such case your Koot Hoomi *is no gentleman.* The letter is a private letter and under these circumstances no gentleman would ever think of acting as desired by him.' Now the letter was not a private one, since it was circulated by Mr. Hume among the members. At the time I paid no attention whatever to the fling. Nor had I come to know of it through H.P.B., but through G. Khool who had heard it himself and has an excellent memory."

The Master asked Sinnett to oblige him by "writing for me two lines telling me as *you* remember the event."[3] He commented further that Hume "must be made to realize that were he really as great as he asserts, or even if he were himself quite satisfied with his greatness and the infallibility of his power of memory, whatever even the adepts might think, he would remain indifferent to, at any rate, would not be so vulgarly abusive as he is now. His sensitiveness is in itself evidence of the doubts lurking in his mind as to the validity of the claims he so boastfully puts forth;* hence his irritability, excited by anything and everything that is likely to disturb his self-delusions. I hope you will not refuse a direct and clear answer to my direct and clear question."

No subsequent correspondence seems to deal with this matter, so it may perhaps be assumed that Sinnett's reply settled the issue. Obviously it did not settle Hume, however, for he continued to be obsessed with causing all the difficulties

† Perhaps Djual Khul was present in his subtle body, as he was not among those listed by the Master. Undoubtedly H.P.B. was the only one who knew he was there.

*Hume appeared to be suffering from delusions of grandeur, believing that he was "fast becoming an adept" (ML 333/328), ". . . sees sights and believes in them as revelations." (LBS 35) He also claimed to be a yogi. (ML 334/329) Not long afterward the Mahatma was to state that Hume was "now entirely in the hands of the Brothers of the Shadow." (ML 337/332)

he could for his former colleagues, mainly under the guise of benefiting the Society and "saving" it from some fate which he never clearly specified.

Some days elapsed before Sinnett heard again from the Mahatma, and he was beginning to wonder whether the Mahachohan had flatly vetoed his suggestion regarding to newspaper venture, or even refused K.H. permission to respond to it. However, the first paragraph of the next letter, when it finally came, set his mind at rest: ". . . The Chohan is not to be consulted every day on such 'worldly' matters, and that is my excuse for the unavoidable delay."

The letter set forth, in numbered order and in considerable detail, the Master's notes on the Mahachohan's views.[4] Briefly these were that the establishment of such a journal was desirable and feasible; that the Brothers could help and guide, for ". . . Tho' separated from your world of action we are not entirely severed from it so long as the Theosophical Society exists. Hence, while we cannot inaugurate it publicly and to the knowledge of all theosophists and those concerned, we may, and *will* so far as practicable, aid the enterprise." Some specific suggestions followed:

Capital might be invested so as to assure a modest interest with little or no risk, although for the ordinary speculator there would be some uncertainty in any attempt to found a new journal designed to favor the native interests. To give some special inducements to native capitalists who might be asked to invest, Sinnett himself should take no more salary than he was then receiving from *The Pioneer* until the venture proved itself a success. He should be allowed "the usual and necessary personal expenses of travel when on business for the journal until the capital shall be earning 8 per cent." Of the profits between eight and twelve per cent he should have one quarter share, and of all above twelve persent, one half share. He should have entire control over the journal "with some reassuring provisos that power should not be transferable to a successor without the consent of a majority of the capital represented in the ownership; and that it should cease when it became apparent that the journal was being used against the interests to promote which it was founded."

Without some such reservations, the Master pointed out, deep-seated prejudices and suspicions would cause native capitalists—"especially the rajahs"—to hesitate. "The whole

Anglo-European community," he added, "now suffers in native opinion for the commercial sins of dishonest houses who have heretofore broken faith with the capitalists." At the same time, the provisos should be so framed as to protect Sinnett's own interests. He might offer to have occasional inspection of books and accounts, "since your personal integrity cannot be guaranteed for all your servants. But this is not to diminish your authority over the management of the journal in all departments."

The Master said further that it would be desirable to have the whole capital paid in before the journal was definitely inaugurated, but whatever amount was not immediately needed could be placed at interest, and a Sinking Fund should be created out of the income of the journal itself. Any contracts and copartnership papers might be deposited in confidential hands mutually agreeable and their nature kept secret "until the arrival of a certain specified contingency. This would show good faith on both sides and inspire confidence."

A few days before writing this letter, the Master mentioned, he had overheard Olcott trying to interest several influential theosophists in the proposed new journal. One of them, a chela and the editor of an Indian newspaper, *The Mirror,* had pointed out that probably not one of the native princes who might be induced to invest in the new project would be influenced by patriotic motives. The Master mentioned some of the motivations—all of them heavily weighted with self-interest—which several of them might have in mind. However, he said, with proper agents and discreet negotiations, five lakhs* might be raised.

He suggested that, for the time being, Sinnett should keep his own counsel and not inform the proprietors of *The Pioneer* of his plans. He could remain on that job until November of 1883 in any event, if he wished, and this would give his friends time to manage "the difficult and delicate negotiations" involved in the new venture. He saw many difficulties in the way of success, and he himself was prohibited by the rules of the Order from exercising any occult powers of assistance. Yet he *could* help to some extent and would do so. He advised Sinnett further that he should not promise the proprietors of

* A lakh represents the figure 100,000; in this case, therefore, 500,000 rupees.

The Pioneer not to start another paper. *"They are frightened to death*—I tell you. They might even make it pleasant and profitable to you to continue directing the Pioneer, *with increased editorial powers and salary* for this they could better afford than to have you compete with them with 5 lakhs at your back." For the present, he suggested that Sinnett follow his original program. "You must be complete and sole master of a paper devoted to the interests of my benighted countrymen."

The letter closed with a further reference to Hume, who had been writing vitriolic letters about the Masters, H.P.B., the Theosophical Society, etc., to C.C. Massey and Stainton Moses in London.

"And this," said the Master, "the man who swore his word of honor but the other day that he would *never* injure the Society, whatever may be his opinion of us personnally." Hume had now, said the Master, placed himself under the influence of the dugpas.[5]

Sinnett felt deeply saddened by Hume's behavior. There was now little communication between the two Englishmen. Hume, still involved with his "good old swami,"† made no effort to get in touch with Sinnett, and the latter felt that any remonstrances on his part would be useless and even resented.

The following weeks were largely taken up with consultations and conferences with those who were undertaking to develop effective plans for promotion of the new paper, to be called *The Phoenix.* Sinnett continued to put in his appearances in the offices of *The Pioneer,* greeting his proprietors—on those rare occasions when he came face to face with one of them— with a cool but unfriendly attitude which masked an inner sense of satisfaction. He did not discuss his tentative plans with any of his associates on the journal and went about his work quietly and with what he hoped was no outward change in his demeanor. An occasional upsurge of his desire to return to England still troubled him but he felt now that the Master had expressed approval of and sympathy with the *Phoenix* project, he should not abandon it. At one time he confessed this to the Mahatma and received in reply the comment: "...you are wrong friend, *very* wrong in consenting to stop

† The Swami from Almora, Hume's new "guru."

here ONLY for *my* sake. I, at least, do not feel myself selfish enough to accept the sacrifice."[6]

In the same letter, the Master assured him ("before quitting my novel relation of a business advisor") that ". . . we will help the enterprise from first to last as fully as possible within our rules, but the initiative *must* be taken by your friends and *ought* to be guided and sympathised with by yourself, and I will just tell you why. While the greatest good ought to result from the successful establishment of such a journal, the strict law of justice forbids us to do aught to lessen in the slightest degree the merit to which he who shall make the dream a reality will be entitled."[7]

Unfortunately, the letters which Hume had been writing to members of the British Theosophical Society were having their effect. This, along with other difficulties that had arisen, had brought that group to an extremely low point. In an effort to infuse new life into it, C.C. Massey had proposed that Mrs. Anna Kingsford assume the Presidency, and she had agreed to the arrangement conditionally.[8] There was some delay in consummating the plan, however, and Massey wrote to the Master K.H. asking him to undertake to "inspire" Mrs. Kingsford[9] and thus the members of the London group. The Master refused and wrote to Sinnett: ". . . we demand neither allegiance, recognition (whether public or private) nor will we have anything to do with, or say to the British Branch—*except through you.*"[10] He was concerned because Mrs. Kingsford had claimed that before the appearance of her book, *The Perfect Way,* "no one 'knew what the Oriental school really held about Reincarnation'; and added that 'seeing how much has been told in that book the adepts are hastening to unlock their own treasures.'" Mr. Massey, it seemed, had accepted her claim as literally valid and had "blossomed into an adroit compliment to the lady that would not discredit a plenipotentiary." Massey was quoted as having said, "Probably it is felt (by the Brothers) that a community among whom such a work as 'The Perfect Way' can be produced and find acceptance is ready for the light!" Let this idea gain currency, the Master said, and it would tend to the establishment of a sect with Mrs. Kingsford at its head. She was, said the Master, "a highly estimable authoress" but she was "not exempt from a considerable dose of vanity and despotism, hence—bigotry."

"Thus elevate the misconception into an undue importance; impair thereby her own spiritual condition by feeding the latent sense of Messiahship; and you will have obstructed the cause of free and general independent enquiry which her 'Initiators' as well as we would wish promoted." The Master asked Sinnett to tell Mr. Massey the truth.

A surprising suggestion came toward the end of the letter. It might, after all, be advisable for Sinnett to go to England for a few months[11] and enlist Massey's help in straightening out the tangle: "...explain the true situation and establish the Society *yourself.*" If this was not done, there was every likelihood that the situation, complicated by Hume's continuing letters, would complete the work of destruction and it would be impossible "to undo the mischief."

Sinnett could not deny that the suggestion had tremendous appeal for him. The Master had added the comment that he might devote some of his time in England to further theosophical writing, and Sinnett reflected eagerly that he would surely have time to complete and publish his second book, *Esoteric Buddhism*, which he had already begun.

He thought too, that he detected a gleam of happiness in his wife's eyes when they discussed the possibility. She restrained any expression of delight, however, and asked whether the new venture could proceed without him.

"I can do very little in an overt way anyhow," he said, "since Rattigan is not to know of my part in it, if this can be avoided. I know Olcott is working on it, and others are approaching some of the princes and the wealthy landowners. I'm afraid they haven't had much success so far, but it may take some time to convince those who might be interested that such a paper would ultimately benefit India."

"If they really care about that," said Patience.

"Oh ho! Don't tell me you're becoming a pessimist!" he teased her.

"No—not really," she denied, "but you know as well as I do that personal interests can be terribly powerful where money is involved. I can see so much *good* that you might do with such a paper, but I do wonder..."

She wondered even further when the Mahatma confessed in a subsequent letter (one that was received, as a matter of fact, a month after the Sinnetts had arrived in England) that he had scarcely known "until I had begun to watch the development of this effort to erect a bulwark for Indian interests, how deeply my poor people had sunk. As one who watches the signs of fluttering life beside a dying bed, and counts the feeble breaths to learn if there may still be room for hope, so we Aryan exiles in our snowy retreat have been attentive to this issue. Debarred from using any abnormal powers that might interfere with the nation's *Karma*, yet by all lawful and normal means trying to stimulate the zeal of those who care for our regard, we have seen weeks grow into months without the object having been achieved. . . . I stepped outside the usual limits to aid your particular project from a conviction of its necessity and its potential usefulness. . . . But in this uncongenial experience of meddling in a business affair, I have ventured within the very breath of the world's furnace. I have suffered so much from the enforced insight at short distance into the moral and spiritual condition of my people, and been so shocked by this nearer view of the selfish baseness of human nature (the concomitant, alas, of the passage of humanity through our stage of the evolutionary circuit); I have seen so distinctly the certainty that it cannot be helped—that I shall henceforth abstain from any repetition of the unbearable experiment."[12]

Patience had raised the question of what would be done about Sinnett's Presidency of the Simla Eclectic Society if they should return to England. The Master K.H. solved this problem with the information that Col. and Mrs. Gordon were being transferred from Calcutta to Simla and the suggestion that Col. Gordon be asked to take over the post in an Acting capacity. He would, he said, ask Olcott to send Col. Gordon an official paper to this effect and would give the latter instructions.[13]

"Some are born for diplomacy and intrigue," said the Master. "I rather think that it is not my particular province. Withal, I believe the arrangement calculated to impede Mr. Hume's intrigue and his endeavours to have the Society (Eclectic) dead and buried, thus showing those concerned with it that he was its Creator and Preserver, and that his retirement was its death-knell."[14]

The way seemed at last to be cleared and the decision to return to England became inevitable.

Rattigan was informed of the impending move in a cool, businesslike note and responded in like manner. No doubt, thought Sinnett, remembering the Master's comments, his former employer was glad to have him out of the country; there was less fear of his popularity at a distance of several thousand miles. The balance of Sinnett's promised salary for the year was paid to him, and this, with his personal savings, amounted to a considerable sum which he felt he could put to good use whatever his future might hold.

Sinnett had asked the Mahatma whether March 30 would be a good date on which to sail, and the Master had replied that it was "as good as any other."[15] Later, he suggested April 7, [16] but by that time plans had been made and the Sinnetts were reluctant to change them. Sinnett himself was already halfway to England in imagination; Denny was beside himself with excitement; and Patience found herself looking forward to the move with increasing anticipation.

It was, nevertheless, with deeply mixed emotions that they embarked from Madras on the next to the last day of March 1883. They had visited the new headquarters of the Theosophical Society to bid farewell to H.P.B. and Damodar. Olcott was away on a tour in which he was combining efforts to promote *The Phoenix* with the many remarkable healings which he performed almost daily.*[17]

Patience, suddenly moved almost beyond bearing by a shadow of sadness and resignation in H.P.B.'s expressive eyes, threw her arms about the older woman and almost burst into tears.

"Goodbye, dear friend," she said huskily. "I know it isn't forever. I will surely see you again before too long."

"Here or in England," H.P.B. assured her, returning the warm embrace. "We aren't through with each other yet!"

"For which I am so very thankful." Patience swallowed a huge lump in her throat. "You must take care of your dear self."

Damodar, a trifle shy, yet smiling with good will, said somewhat formal farewells.

"Mind you," said H.P.B., as she and Sinnett shook hands. "I don't know a thing about your blessed paper. Master tells me nothing!"

---

*For accounts of these and other healings done by Col. Olcott, *see* especially the second volume of *Old Diary Leaves*.

Sinnett's mind was already half-committed to another kind of future. But he smiled and said, "Who knows, at this stage, which way the wind will blow?"

"Well I hope it blows to some purpose and gets rid of some of the cobwebs in the minds of half the rich princes of India!" was her emphatic rejoinder. "Now, be sure to write at once when you know something about the fate of your new book."

He promised readily and said that she would be one of the first to receive a copy.

"And I hope you won't be too harsh in your judgment," he added.

"Don't try to be modest with me!" she admonished. "You know very well it will be superb. And besides, you know how grateful the Master K.H. is for all your literary contributions. But don't expect this book to be the popular success *The Occult World* has been. It's pure philosophy and people aren't half as eager to exercise their wits as they are to hear about something strange and unusual. You're not to let that deter you, though."

Later, watching the shores of India recede as the S.S. *Peshawer* moved out to sea, Sinnett was thinking of these words and wondering what, indeed, the future held for him. What did he want it to hold? he asked himself. He hoped it would hold continuing communication with the Master K.H. whether or not he returned to India. He had no real premonition, however, that he was seeing those shores for the last time.

16

A Case of Incomplete Transmission

ol. Olcott returned to Adyar on May 26, 1883, physically very much depleted from the many healings he had been performing. As a matter of fact, he had been "ordered home" and told not to do any more healings until he had further instructions from his Master.[1] He had scarcely arrived at the Society's headquarters when he received a letter from the Mahatma K.H. informing him of this restriction and asking him to tell Mr. Sinnett that he should not be surprised at "checks upon checks" in the matter of the proposed new newspaper. Capitalists were hoarding their money instead of investing it. Since he had been barred from the first from performing "miracles" he saw "delays, disappointments, trials of patience..." He did not yet see complete failure.

There were other matters in the letter which the Master felt Sinnett should know. He suggested that since the English mail was scheduled to leave on the following day it might be well to get off word to Sinnett on the same ship.[2]

Olcott, too severely fatigued to contemplate writing to Sinnett himself, commented to Damodar, who was in the headquarters office with him at the time:

"I think I'll just send this letter to Sinnett. I wonder why the Master didn't write to him directly."

"Perhaps for two reasons, sir," Damodar replied. "The letter contains an order for you to stop doing healings. Possibly less power was required to include the message for Mr. Sinnett in your letter than to reach him in England."

"True, no doubt, Olcott agreed. "And I suppose the Master couldn't write through H.P.B. because of his reference to that letter from Hume that she doesn't know anything about. No telling what emotional eruptions that might have caused. Still, he must have used a considerable amount of power to copy the letter and send the copy on to Sinnett."

177

"One doesn't always know why the blessed Masters do certain things," Damodar said thoughtfully. "But I do not question."

Olcott nodded. "Nor I. I'm sure it was right that Sinnett should know about it."

These comments concerned a long letter from Hume to the Colonel which the latter had placed in the bottom of his trunk to avoid H.P.B.'s discovering it. In it, Hume had indulged in virulent attacks upon practically everyone connected with the Theosophical Society, even characterizing Sinnett as "a credulous imbecile to be led by the nose." In his letter to Olcott, the Master begged the latter's pardon for "the bad taste" which had compelled him to duplicate the letter for Sinnett but said that it was necessary that the latter should be able to "verify my old warning that he (Hume) meant to set all your friends in London against the Society." The diabolical malice which breathed through the letter, said the Master, "comes straight from the *Dugpas* who provoke his vanity and blind his reason." Further, the Mahatma said, Hume was doing all he could to wreck any chances for success of the *Phoenix* venture; he had distinctly injured the project "not only with the Maharajah of Cashmere but with many more in India."

One other statement in the letter was perhaps meant to inform Sinnett that the leadership of the British Theosophical Society was not at once to pass into his hands: "The turn of the Kingsford-Maitland party has come."[3]

Olcott sent the letter on to Sinnett but it was not received in England until after the middle of June. It was less depressing to Sinnett than it might have been had it not been for the fact that *Esoteric Buddhism* had come off the press on June 11 and was already attracting unexpectedly favorable attention. That Sinnett's interpretation of some concepts was later to be called into question by H.P.B. in *The Secret Doctrine*, resulting in a strain on their friendship was something of which he was at this stage wholly unaware.[4] He accepted without rancor—indeed with some gratification—the Master's statement in a letter received in July that "a few undetectable mistakes and omissions notwithstanding, your 'Esoteric Buddhism' is the only right exposition—however incomplete—of our Occult doctrines. You have made no cardinal, fundamental mistakes."[5] Still later, the Master was to speak of "the real vital errors" in the book but to say, at the same time, that "... the outside reader is none the wiser... and no one, so far has noticed."[6]

The Sinnetts had immediately become caught up in the affairs of the London Theosophical Society. Mrs. Kingsford was now serving as its President, and Edward Maitland was Vice-President. Meetings were held mainly at the Arundale home in Elgin Crescent. Mrs. Arundale and her daughter, Miss Francesca Arundale, were deeply interested in Theosophy and gathered about them an intelligent group seriously concerned with study. Sinnett was enormously pleased that interest in the theosophical movement had begun to spread rapidly "in some of the upper levels of Society,"[7] and to meet, at the Arundales', some leading members of the relatively new Society for Psychical Research. He was ambitious that the Theosophical Society should gain recognition among persons of prominence in London; the matter of a proposed newspaper in India designed to benefit the masses of the population there began to fade rapidly from his consciousness. In fact, it took on an aura of unreality.

This somewhat complacent attitude was shattered late in the summer when Patience, who had written to H.P.B. shortly after their arrival in England, received a reply posted at Ootacumund in the Nilgiri Hills. H.P.B. had gone there for a rest and to escape the South India heat. She was staying at "The Retreat," home of General Rhodes E. Morgan and Mrs. Morgan.* She had no good news to tell of the Phoenix project.

"Since your departure I am eternally in hot water for that blessed paper, "she wrote. "K.H. used me... like a post-horse. I stirred up all our 69 Societies in India, and letters sent to your dear *Hub*† will show to him and you that I have been kicking in this atmosphere like 'un diable dans le l'eau benie.'‡ This horrid, dirty agitation kills all. Everyone seems to have lost his head over the Bill and this idol business. I wish to Heavens Ilbert and Ripon and your indigo planters got all drowned in their own dye! Your politics will drive me mad like

---

* Pioneer Theosophists and friends of long standing who were to prove friends indeed at the most serious crisis in H.P.B.'s life.

† Dr. William Hübbe Schleiden of Elberfeld, Germany who was to be the first President of the German Theosophical Society.

‡ "A devil in holy water."

a March hare;# and if the Boss (Sinnett) does not come (back) to India, I will emigrate 'arms et bagages' to Ceylon or Burma—I won't remain here with Hume."

How could she know, she asked, whether "the money would come at all... What can I do when even K.H. seems to give it up in disgust and despair... Ah, if the old Chohan only but permitted our Masters to exercise their powers for one day! But He will never interfere with India's punishment, its Karma, as he says..."

Olcott was in Ceylon, H.P.B. commented, and had "grown a beard to the seventh rib and hair floating in silvery locks like a Patriarch. He is going to London in January, I think... Well, I hope you will not see him, for you will be back here. Oh hopes, sweet and delusive!"[8]

"Oh dear!" Patience said to her husband as she read this aloud, "I do think those hopes are delusive—for if the *Phoenix* is a failure, what have we to go back to India for?"

"I begin to think we shall not go back," he agreed, "even to please the 'Old Lady.'"

Patience was reading on down the page: "Poor Minnie Hume! Do listen, Percy."

The *Phoenix* project was becoming hopelessly involved with a most unstable political situation in India. A thorough study of Indian political history would be necessary for a full understanding of the circumstances which were to have such profound effect upon the plans for the *Phoenix*. Briefly, Lord Ripon, then Viceroy of India, had attempted to institute some reforms to promote local self-government, and Mr. (later Sir) Courtenay Ilbert, Legal Member of Council, had introduced a bill designed to make some changes in the administration of justice. Up to that time no persons other than Europeans or, in more technical language, "European British subjects," could be appointed justices of the peace with jurisdiction over persons of the same category, in districts outside the limits of the Presidency towns. The bill proposed to remove the limitation from the Code of Criminal Procedure "at once and completely" and consequently to confer on many native or Indian-born magistrates authority to deal with Europeans, as with anybody else. The proposal, although in appearance reasonable and fair, roused the most violent opposition among the planters in the indigo and tea districts and among other classes of the non-official European population in all parts of India. They feared, and not altogether without reason, that their safety in up-country places might be endangered in certain contingencies. A strong counter-agitation was started among the educated Indians, the result being an outbreak of bitter racial feeling such as had not been experienced since the days of the Mutiny. The excitement of the public mind became so threatening that the government was obliged to withdraw the Bill, and to be content with a much less drastic amendment to the Code, which reserved to European alleged offenders the right to claim trial by jury. The ill-feeling roused by the unlucky Bill did not die down for a long time. (The *Oxford History of India*, Vincent A. Smith, C.I.E., Oxford at the Clarendon Press, 1920, p 756.)

She read from H.P.B.'s letter:

"'Poor Minnie Scott is getting blind. She is at the. . . paternal residence. Davison is here. Keeps two hotels for his Mother and brother-in-law and gets 800 rupees a month. Hates Hume and keeps letter from him in which he tells of his long conversations in the Museum with K.H. and M. and now tries to show that they do not exist. Davison is disgusted with him and so are all those who know him...!'"

"But here—" Patience looked up with a smile, "here is something to please you. 'My Boss M. says that Mr. Sinnett does "an immense good" in England.'"

"Well," he said, trying not to show his pleasure too obviously, "I try to justify my presence here so far as I can."

Patience gave her delightful chuckle, for she was proud of her husband and of the manner in which the other menbers of the Theosophical Society seemed to look to him and seek his opinion on philosophical matters.

"I think it's due to you that William Crookes* has joined the Society," she reminded him. "That is no small accomplishment."

"It may be that he merely wants to make sure what we are all about, or even to have a chance to look at our papers," he countered. "Not all his brother scientists agree with him about radiant matter, you know, although the Master thinks highly of it and says that he may even discover that there are states of matter higher still.[9] Anyhow," Sinnett crushed out the cigar which he had been enjoying and rose to stand looking thoughtfully out of the window, "I think it's probably high time I began to make some more specific plans here, since it seems obvious that the *Phoenix* project is going to die."

"It does look hopeless," she conceded. "I feel so sorry about all those who have put so much effort into it. And I expecially regret the disappointment that I imagine the Master must feel. I'm sure he has done everything he could for it."

"No question of that, and I am grateful. He'll feel regret because he thought it would help India, but it won't affect him personally."

"He may be disappointed for your sake, too," she reminded him gently. "I believe he wanted to stay in India."

---

* Later Sir William Crookes; knighted in 1884.

"Perhaps. But now I am here, and I must begin to think about what I am going to do."

In pursuance of this objective, Sinnett placed an advertisement in a London journal to the effect that he would consider investing money in some newspaper on which he could serve in an editorial capacity, thus insuring him gainful employment as well as interest on his capital. He received only one reply to this advertisement—from a man named Bottomley—the result of which was eventually to separate him from that capital, although for some time his business ventures were to prosper in a most satisfactory manner. The unfortunate developments took several years to unfold and were not, he considered, due to any dishonesty on the part of his associate.[10]

Active participation in the affairs of the Theosophical Society continued, and occasional letters were received from the Mahatma K.H. One very long one containing much philosophy and dealing with a number of subjects, was designed by the Master to be read to the members of the London Lodge, if Sinnett desired to do so.[11] It covered an effort by the Master to clarify some misunderstandings of the occult teachings on the part of C.C. Massey and others, carried a rather dire warning about the dangers of chelaship to any individual not spiritually prepared for its rigorous requirements, mentioned some aspects of Hindu mythology, pointed out the lack of insight into Buddhism on the part of some prominent Orientalists, presented perhaps the most complete philosophical explanation of the Theosophical Seal to be found anywhere in theosophical literature, and touched upon some abstruse principles of occultism. Sinnett himself came in for some mild criticism:

"You share with all beginners," the Master said, "the tendency to draw too absolutely strong inferences from partly caught hints, and to dogmatize thereupon as though the last word had been spoken. You will correct this in time. You may misunderstand us, are more than likely to do so, for our language must always be more or less that of parable and suggestion where treading upon forbidden ground; we have our own peculiar modes of expression and what lies behind the fence of words is even more important than what you read. But still—TRY."

Further letters received during the late summer dealt with the increasing inevitability of failure in the *Phoenix* matter and with some of the factors involved, showing that the Master had a clearer understanding of the complex political situation in India than might have been expected of one not actively involved in it. It was apparent also that he really was disappointed, since he had seen in the *Phoenix* some genuine possibility for benefit to his countrymen.

At about this time a further development brought acute distress to the Sinnetts and temporarily drove all personal considerations from their minds. The September 1, 1883 issue of *Light*, the English Spiritualist journal, published a letter from a Henry A. Kiddle of America which, by implication, accused the Mahatma K.H. of plagiarism.*

Some Spiritualists were hostile to the Theosophical Society, and particularly to H.P.B., and were eager to cast doubt on the existence of the Mahatmas. Undoubtedly this stemmed from earlier days when H.P.B., in New York, explained the rationale of spiritualistic phenomena and demonstrated that she herself could produce the same manifestations without assistance from disembodied entities. Her explanations had been vehemently rejected by many Spiritualists, who then inevitably parted company from her.

It happened that, in August of 1880, Mr. Kiddle had given an address before an assemblage of Spiritualists at Lake Pleasant, New York. This adress was published in the *Banner ·of Light*, a prominent Spiritualist organ. Sinnett's book, *The Occult World*, published during the summer of 1881, quoted parts of some letters from the Mahatma K.H. Reading this book, Mr. Kiddle came across some sentences resembling what he had said in his Lake Pleasant lecture. He claimed that he had written Mr. Sinnett about this but had never received a reply.

"Perhaps he did write me," Sinnett admitted. "But if so I don't remember. I had so many letters after that book came out—most of them favorable, but a number with one complaint or another, and I got so I paid no attention to them."

C. C. Massey, himself a Spiritualist and a member of the London Theosophical Society, to whom this remark was addressed, agreed.

*For a full and detailed account of what came to be called "The Kiddle Incident" *see* Mary K. Neff's *The "Brothers" of Madame Blavatsky*, pp. 97-115. This includes parallel columns showing the disputed passage in both contexts. Quotations from Spiritualist journals are taken from H.P.B.'s Scrapbooks. A resume of the article is given as Appendix E in the *Guide*.

"I suppose so. No doubt this happens to every author. But this is very damaging, you know."

Sinnett felt that Massey was not reluctant to have suspicion cast upon the Master.

"It's outragious!" he said angrily. "Of course I'll answer this letter."

He did so, commenting that all he could say at the moment was that the passage quoted from his "revered friend" had been introduced with the expression, "Plato was right. . ."[12] and that this seemed to point to some origin for the sentences immediately following which might "have lain behind both the letter and the lecture." He said that it would take some time to get an explanation from India; meanwhile he pointed out that "the path leading to acquaintanceship with the Adepts is always found strewn with provocation to distrust them, for reasons very fully detailed in my books; their policy at present is rather to ward off than to invite European confidence."

Other Theosophists joined the controversy, notably Col. Olcott, who reminded readers that unconscious plagiarism was not at all uncommon. He mentioned several cases of similar coincidences. "I do not undertake to explain the Kiddle mystery at all," he said, "nor do I think it of much consequence. It is highly absurd to think that a mind capable of reducing to expression in a foreign tongue so lofty a scheme of evolution as that in *Esoteric Buddhism* would be driven to fish for ideas in Mr. Kiddle's speeches, or the pages of any Spiritualistic journal."

H.P.B. wrote an agitated letter to Sinnett:

"K.H. plagiarized from Kiddle! Ye gods and little fishes. . . If they knew what it was to dictate *mentally* a *precipitation* as D. Khool says—at 300 miles distance; and had seen as all of us. . . the original fragments on which the precipitation was photographed, from which the young fool of a chela had copied, unable to understand half of the sentences and so skipping them; then they would not be idiotic enough to accuse an Adept. . . of such an absurd action. . . K.H. blows me up for talking too much—says He needs no defence and that I need not trouble myself. But if He were to kill me, I cannot hold my tongue—on general principles and as a sign of loyalty to them . . . Ever since Subba Row brought to me the original scrap of Kashmir paper (given to him by my Boss) on which appeared that whole page from the letter you published. . . I understood what it meant. Why, that letter was but one-third of the letter dictated and never published, for you have not received it..."

At this point several lines of H.P.B.'s writing had apparently been completely erased and the following note appeared in K.H.'s handwriting: "True proof of her discretion! I will tell you all myself as soon as I have an hour's leisure."

Following this came another sentence of H.P.B.'s: "But since they don't want me to speak of this, I better not say a word more lest M. should again pitch into me!"[13]

Even Subba Row who, from the first, had disapproved of the manner in which H.P.B. had made the existence of the Masters a matter of public knowledge, felt constrained to write guardedly of the matter. His letter appeared in *The Theosophist* for December 1883. He pointed out that there was no reference to Plato in Mr. Kiddle's remarks, and that there were certain alterations of the language in the passage "which show that the Mahatma never intended to borrow Mr. Kiddle's ideas and phrases, but that he rather intended to say something against them." Also, he said, the grammatical construction of some of the sentences was incorrect, and it appeared that some words had even been lost.

"Therefore," he added, "from a careful perusal of the passage and its contents, any unbiased reader will come to the conclusion that somebody must have greatly blundered, and will not be surprised to hear that it was unconsciously altered through the carelessness and ignorance of the chela by whose instrumentality it was 'precipitated.'... I now assert that I know for certain *from an inspection of the original precipitation proof,* that such was the case with regard to the passage under discussion. The Mahatma against whom the accusation has been brought will, of course, think it beneath his dignity to offer any explanation in his own defense to Mr. Kiddle or his followers and supporters. But I hope Mr. Sinnett will be so good as to place before the public as soon as possible such explanation or information as he may be permitted by the Mahatma concerned."

It was not until December that Sinnett received from the Mahatma K.H. his explanation of the incident,[14] which confirmed what both H.P.B. and Subba Row had said. However, the Master's account was given under a partial pledge of secrecy.

"My good and faithful friend," he said, "the explanation herein contained would have never been made but that I have of late perceived how troubled you were during your conversations upon the subject of 'plagiarism' with some friends—C.C.M. particularly. Now...to withhold the truth from you would be cruelty; nevertheless to give it out to the world of prejudiced and malignantly disposed Spiritualists would be sheer folly. Therefore we must compromise: I must lay both yourself and Mr. Ward,* who shares my confidence, *under a pledge never to explain without special permission from me the facts* hereinafter stated by me to anyone—not even to M. A. Oxon and C. C. Massey, included for reasons I will mention presently...If pressed by any of them you may simply answer that the 'psychological mystery' was cleared up to yourself and some others...I give you *carte blanche* to say anything you like—even the reason why I rather have the real *facts* withheld from the general public and most of the London Fellows—all except the details you alone with a few others will know. As you will perceive, I do not even bind you to defend my reputation—*unless* you feel yourself satisfied beyond any doubt, and have well understood the explanations yourself."[15]

After some further comments along this line, the Mahatma said: "The solution is so simple, and the circumstances so amusing, that I confess I laughed when my attention was drawn to it, some time since. Nay, it is calculated to make me smile even now, were it not for the knowledge of the pain it gives to some true friends."

He explained that he had framed the letter while on a journey on horseback and had dictated it to a young chela who was "not yet expert at this branch of psychic chemistry." K.H. had been in the saddle for forty-eight hours consecutively and was physically very tired and "half asleep." "Besides this," he added, "I had very important business to attend to psychically, and therefore little remained of me to devote to

---

* Mr. Sam Ward, sometimes called "Uncle Sam" in the *Letters*. He was an American businessman who was in London at the time some of the events described took place. He was an uncle of F. Marion Crawford, who wrote the occult novel *Mr. Isaacs*. He used a monogram on his personal stationery which consisted of a compass with the letters "SW" in the southwest quadrant. Two of these letterheads appear in the Folios in the British Museum, one a bogus spiritualistic note to Sinnett from M., and another used by M. to write Sinnett and warn him of the fraud. References in ML (427/421) indicate that the Mahatma K.H. held Mr. Ward in some affection and regard. He gave away 250 copies of *The Occult World* to friends.

that letter... When I awoke I found it had already been sent on, and as I was not anticipating its publication, I never gave it from that time a thought."

Much earlier in their correspondence the Mahatma had explained that letters precipitated by chelas were always examined "and all mistakes corrected."[16] In this instance, however, the Mahatma said, when the young chela asked him whether he would look the letter over and make corrections, "I answered, imprudently, I confess—'anyhow will do, my boy—it is of no great importance if you skip a few words.'" Half of the letter had therefore been omitted, "and the other half more or less distorted by the 'artist.'"

"Now I had never evoked spiritual Mr. Kiddle's physiognomy," the Master wrote, "never had heard of his existence, was not aware of his name. Having, owing to our correspondence and your Simla surroundings and friends, felt interested in the intellectual progress of the phenomenalists ... I had directed my attention, some two months previous, to the great annual camping movement of the American Spiritualists in various directions, among others to Lake or Mount Pleasant. Some of the curious ideas and sentences representing the general hopes and aspirations of the American Spiritualists remained impressed on my memory, and I remembered only these ideas and detached sentences, quite apart from the personalities of those who harboured or pronounced them. Hence my entire ignorance of the lecturer whom I have innocently defrauded, as it would appear, and who raises the hue and cry. Yet had I dictated my letter in the form it now appears in print, it would certainly look suspicious ... But I did nothing of the kind, as the original impression now before me clearly shows."

The Master then digressed to give Sinnett an explanation of "mental telegraphy"[17] and of how the principles involved in the process had resulted in some words being more sharply photographed in the chela's brain "and thence on the paper before him." He then repeated for Sinnett's benefit "*verbatim* from the restored fragments" the entire passage as he had dictated it, underlining in red (shown in italics in the book) the sentences which had been omitted from the letter as Sinnett had received it.[18]

"This is the true copy of the original document as now restored—the 'Rosetta Stone' of the Kiddle incident," he wrote. "I have done, and you may now, in your turn, do what you please with these facts, except the making use of them in print or even speaking of them to the opponents, save in general terms. You must understand my reasons for this. One does not cease entirely, my dear friend, to be a man nor lose one's dignity for being an *adept*. In the latter capacity, one, no doubt, remains in every case quite indifferent to the opinion of the outside world. The former always draws the line between *ignorant surmise* and—deliberate, *personal insult*. I cannot really be expected to take advantage of the first to be ever hiding the problematic 'adept' behind the skirts of the two supposed 'humourists'; and as *man*, I had too much experience lately in such above said insults with Messrs. S. Moses and C.C. Massey to give them any more opportunities to doubt the word of 'K.H.', or see in him a vulgar defendant, a kind of guilty, tricky Babu before a panel of stern European jurymen and Judge."

Sinnett felt greatly relieved by this letter, although privately he wished profoundly that he had not selected that particular letter to expose to the public in his book. He felt especially frustrated that he was unable to give all the facts to Massey and Moses, whom the Master had specifically excluded from those who might be informed.*

"Say nothing," Patience advised. "It won't be long before there will be another nine days wonder and all this will die a natural death."

She proved to be at least a partial prophet, for if the incident was never entirely forgotten, it faded into the background as other matters demanded their place in the attention of the people concerned. Primarily the harmonious relations between Sinnett and Mrs. Kingsford, which had characterized their early association, began to fray at the edges and the London Theosophical Society entered upon some rather tumultuous days.

---

*In the Fourth English Edition of *The Occult World* (1884), Sinnett mentioned some articles covering the "Kiddle Incident" published in *The Theosophist* for December 1883, and added: "A month or two after the appearance of those fragmentary hints, I received a note from the Mahatma relieving me of all restriction previously imposed on the full letter of explanation he had previously sent me."

17

Historic Journey

"And what are you going to do now?"

H.P.B. turned her luminous eyes from the letter in her hand, dated in October 1883, to the young man who sat beside her, who had given it to her to read.

He replied with quick assurance: "I'm going to join Col. Olcott, of course!"

"So easily you decide!" she exclaimed, her eyes shading to a twinkle. "His trips are always what he calls 'bone-banging' you know. As he says here," she indicated the letter in her hand, "he goes about in every sort of conveyance—bullock carts or anything—no matter how uncomfortable, if it will take him where he wants to go."

"If he can stand it, I should be able to. I'm a good deal younger than he is."

There was an undertone of something in his voice which puzzled H.P.B. Ambition? Self-doubt? She couldn't at the moment pinpoint it, although her intuition told her it was there. Well, he must be given his chance. No one, for want of opportunity, should be made to stand waiting at the door of theosophical enterprise; workers were too sorely needed for that. Besides, he would probably do some good if his enthusiasm could be channeled in the right way, and no doubt her indefatigable colleague could accomplish this better than anyone else could.

"Yes, true," she said, after a moment's silence during which these thoughts flashed through her mind. "You should be able to reach him at Sholapore. He's due there in a few days."

She returned his letter to him and he folded it and put it in his pocket with an air of satisfaction.

"Thank you," he said, "I hoped you would tell me I could go."

The young man was William T. Brown, a Scotsman just graduated in law from Glasgow University, who had arrived at Adyar two days after the Colonel had left for a trip through North India. Brown had joined the Theosophical Society in England. Essentially restless and seeking something, he scarcely knew what, he had caught fire and desired at once to go to India to help with the work there, and perhaps to meet those Personages of whose existence he had received some intimations while still a student.

In the course of a letter to H.P.B. on several matters, Mr. Sinnett had mentioned Brown somewhat slightingly because he had befriended Mrs. Sarah Parker, another member of the London Lodge* whom Sinnett characterized as "rather coarse-fibered."[1] H.P.B. had immediately risen to Mrs. Parker's defense, writing Sinnett that she had known the woman for eight years, that she was "an enthusiast, a lunatic in many things, but no better, more sincere, truthful, honest woman ever breathed in an Irish carcase." Mrs. Parker had, as a matter of fact, practically pauperized herself in an attempt to help some of her Irish countrymen who had fallen on evil times in America, and Brown had tried to help her. "He was kind to her," wrote H.P.B. to Sinnett, "while others were harsh and cold to her in London, yourself to begin with."†[2]

Brown and Mrs. Parker had traveled to Adyar together, he financing her trip in the amount of £60. Upon arriving there, learning that Col. Olcott had departed but two days earlier on a northern tour, Brown had immediately written him offering his services. The letter reached the Colonel at Hyderabad, and he replied in "a kind and most explicit letter," as he recorded in his diary, "warning him of the self-sacrifice he must expect to make; the public ingratitude, individual treacheries, libelous attacks on character, unjust suspicion of motives, bad fare and

---

*The name adopted by the British Theosophical Society under the leadership of Mrs. Anna Kingsford. (LBS 58)

†Close contact with Mrs. Parker changed H.P.B.'s opinion of her and, two months after defending her to Sinnett, she was to write to him in quite different terms about the woman, calling her "an ungrateful, vain, selfish, ridiculous old mare." This was not due to Mrs. Parker's treatment of her personally, but to the woman's treatment of Brown, with whom she (Mrs. Parker) quarreled ceaselessly while he was at Adyar, calling him a "mean, Scotch blackguard" whose money could never repay what she had done for him, etc., etc., and because, when the Masters failed to give Mrs. Parker recognition, she called them "ungrateful curs." (LBS 67)

fatiguing journeys by nights and days in all sorts of conveyances; warning him to return to Europe if he had expected anything else, and leave H.P.B. and myself to continue the work we had begun with our eyes open."[3]

It was this letter which Brown had shared with H.P.B.; he wasn't sure whether this was in the hope that she would encourage him or completely veto his trip. But the moment she had turned those great eyes of hers upon him, he felt convinced that he wanted to meet what seemed an exciting challenge. He telegraphed at once to Olcott that he was coming and, on October 10, joined the Colonel, as H.P.B. had suggested, at Sholapore.

He was to prove useful in several ways. He was able to deliver lectures which seemed well received, and at one time, at the Colonel's direction, he went with another of his traveling companions, L.V.V. Naidu, to Rawalpindi to form a branch of the Theosophical Society.

Before this took place, however, Olcott journeyed to Bombay to meet H.P.B., who had come north from Madras for that purpose; they were expecting to visit a nearby Maharajah who had sent them money for their expenses. The visit was not made, as the Maharajah telegraphed them there that he was unable to receive them.

It was during this time at Bombay that the Colonel received from his Master direct orders to suspend all healing services.[4] In spite of his earlier instructions, he had found it impossible to refuse the many who clamored for his help and, as a result, he had dangerously depleted his own vitality. He himself felt that "the prohibition came none too soon" for he had been noting danger signals and had found that far more time and effort than formerly were required to effect any cures. During the past year he had treated "one way or another some 8,000 patients" and felt that he had about come to "the last 'volt' in his vital battery."[5]

"You had better pay attention to it this time," said H.P.B. emphatically.

"I know," he agreed, "but it is very difficult. There's that invitation from the Maharajah of Kashmir, which I have already accepted. He is not in good health and I'm sure he expects me to cure him."

"Well, you can't. Although," she added thoughtfully, "you might be able to help him. I doubt he can be cured." She put

aside the book she had been reading. "I may as well go back to
Adyar. I'd be about as welcome as the plague if I went along
with you."

Olcott could do nothing but agree with this, since his time
and attention were always fully occupied with lectures and
conferences at every station of the party's tour. He saw her
established in her compartment on the train and waved a
cheerful farewell, hiding the fact that he was deeply touched by
her pathetic and forlorn expression as the train moved away.

Olcott rejoined his party, which now included Damodar "by
command of his Guru." His presence with them was to make
the trip one of the most memorable of all the Colonel's many
travels.*

The first incident occurred at Cawnpore, which the party
reached on the evening of November 3. As they were settling
into their quarters, Damodar moved close to Olcott and, with
his usual deference, said softly:

"Sir, there is a message for you in your writing desk. It
concerns something about which you have been wondering."

Olcott always carried with him a portable writing desk
which he kept locked and the key to which was always in his
pocket.

He glanced keenly at the young man. What was happening?
Had Damodar at last broken through some barrier in his inner
nature? He was aware of the boy's often exaggerated
austerities, but he had come to accept these as part of his
intense and driving temperament. It was always "all or
nothing" with the young Brahmin who had abandoned family
and caste to throw himself into the work of the Theosophical
Society and to fit himself to see the Master in whom he
believed implicitly from earlier visions which had come to him
during a childhood illness. He would do what he would do,
thought the Colonel. He remembered the day Damodar had
learned to swim—an incident characteristic of his unflinching
determination. Olcott had been teaching H.P.B. the art in the
river back of the headquarters building. Damodar who, up to a

---

*For more detailed accounts of the incidents related in this chapter *see* ODL
3:Chapters 2-5. To avoid distraction, specific page numbers are not shown;
also the events are related here in a semi-fictional style, which the writer
believes has not in any way violated the spirit of the historical accounts.
Sources other than the above are indicated.

point, was "one of the greatest cowards in the water" Olcott had ever seen, joined them for his own lesson. He shivered and trembled as he walked into the water and seemed reluctant to get wet all over. Neither Olcott nor H.P.B. was inclined to spare him. "A pretty Adept you'll make if you can't even get your knees wet," Olcott chided him half-sternly. Damodar did not reply, but the next day he came with them again and plunged in and swam across the whole stream, hardly stopping for a breath. He had decided he would swim or die.[6] The incident had greatly increased the older man's respect for him.

Now, Col. Olcott placed his hands on Damodar's shoulders and looked directly into his eyes—handsome eyes they were, alive and expressive. He was about to ask a question, but thought better of it. He simply pressed the thin shoulders lightly and turned to open his desk. The letter was there, in the handwriting of the Master K.H., and it contained the suggestion which the Colonel needed. Later he was to comment that this handwriting had been pronounced by one of H.P.B.'s enemies as "her concoction and nothing more." As she and the Colonel were five days postal distance apart in this instance, he pointed out that the forgery theory could hardly be made to stand.

The following morning, Olcott and Brown went to the Cawnpore post office to collect their mail. Letters were regularly forwarded from Adyar to points along their route and they never missed calling for them at every stop. This morning there was rather a large stack of mail for the Colonel. An envelope postmarked at Capri caught his eye as he looked quickly through the letters.

"Hello," he exclaimed, "here's something from Sam Ward. Nice to hear from one of my own countrymen now and then."

He found, however, when he opened the letter back in their quarters, that the message to him was short. It enclosed a letter for the Mahatma K.H. and asked that Olcott send it on if at all possible. Of course, thought Olcott, Ward wouldn't know he was a thousand miles from headquarters and H.P.B. He puzzled a bit over what to do with the letter. Then he had an inspiration. He called Damodar to him and asked the question he had almost asked the young man on the previous evening.

"You are in touch with the Mahatma K.H. at night, are you not?"

Damodar nodded; his eyes had caught the name on the envelope in the Colonel's hand.

"Yes sir. I have been able to travel to his ashram every night while my body sleeps. Others are usually there."

"I understand. Do you think you could take this letter and ask the Master whether he would be willing to receive it?"

"I shall be glad to try, sir," Damodar said eagerly. "If it is your wish," he added as an afterthought.

"Well, I'd like to oblige a good friend. Thank you very much."

Olcott handed the letter to Damodar, who took it at once to his cot and placed it under his pillow.

They were not to know the result of this experiment until several days later. The Colonel purposely refrained from asking Damodar whether he had delivered the letter, preferring to wait for developments, and Damodar was too shy to offer an explanation until asked.

When the party reached Aligarh on November 12th, the Colonel went as usual to the post office to pick up his mail. In it he found a letter from H.P.B. postmarked at Madras (the postal address for Adyar) on November 5 and stamped as being received at Aligarh on November 10—the two cities being five days' rail journey apart. Olcott wrote in his diary: "Enclosed in her letter was Mr. Ward's identical letter to K.H., which, it will be remembered, I received and handed to Damodar at Cawnpore on the 4th—that is to say the evening before she posted it at Adyar... I submit," he added, "this is about as clear a provable case of instantaneous transportation of a material object between two distant points as can be found on record. Collusion and trickery are barred by the evidence of the postal markings."

But he was curious. How had H.P.B. got hold of Ward's letter?

"Can you remember what happened?" he asked Damodar at the first opportunity.

"Yes, I think so," the young man replied. "I held the letter in my hand as I put my body to sleep. Then immediately, as I always do, I made a dash for the home of the Master in the Himalayas. But when I got there, he himself was away somewhere in his own astral body. I suppose it was by the power of his attraction for me, but I was suddenly swept away —almost as though I had stepped into a deep, strong river current and had lost my footing. The next thing I knew, I was at Adyar, in the presence of both the blessed Master and H.P.B. I told the Master about the letter—and he saw it in my hand, of course—so I gave it to him. He told me to return to my own place, which I did. That is all I remember."

"It's a great deal," said Olcott with much satisfaction. "He has seen the letter then, and I'm sure Ward will be answered in some way."

Undoubtedly he explained to himself, by some occult chemistry or physics, the letter had been "astralized" even as Damodar had been, and thus could be taken along with him.

Meanwhile, at Moradabad, one of the stops between Cawnpore and Aligarh, Damodar had given the Colonel another example of his increasing ability to travel psychically. At this point he went to Adyar, talked with H.P.B., heard the voice of a Master giving a message to Olcott, and asked H.P.B. to telegraph the substance of this message to him to satisfy him of Damodar's veracity. When Damodar reported this to the Colonel, several other persons were present in the room, and Olcott asked them to sign a certificate, which he prepared, giving the facts. The next morning the expected telegram arrived. It corroborated Damodar's account and, again, those present signed a certification of its authenticity.

All this by no means ended the startling events which transpired during the tour of the group through the northern cities of India.

Between Delhi and Meerut, Olcott, Damodar, and Mr. T. Narainswamy, another member of the Theosophical Society who had joined them simply as a companion, were traveling in the same railway carriage. Damodar was drowsing, his body moving uneasily. Suddenly he roused, looking rather startled.

"May I ask what time it is, sir?" he said.

The Colonel consulted his watch.

"Almost six o'clock. Why do you ask?"

"I have just been to Adyar," Damodar replied. "Madame has met with an accident. I don't know whether it is serious, but I think she caught her foot in the carpet and fell rather heavily on her right knee."

Transcribing from his diary some time later, Olcott commented:

"The reader will observe that the young man was but a beginner in occult science and incapable as yet of accurate recollection, in returning to outward consciousness, of his experience on the other planes of being."

However, he wrote a certificate of the occurrence and got Narainswamy to sign it with him, noting the time. At the next station, he got out of the train and telegraphed H.P.B.: "What accident happened at headquarters at about 6 o'clock?"

The train reached Lahore the next morning at nine o'clock. The party was met by a group of Theosophists who escorted them to a camp north of the city, where they had erected six tents and four large open canvas pavilions for use during the Colonel's stay. The escort remained to visit for awhile, and Olcott, always mindful of the necessity of authenticating phenomena, told them of the incident on the train the previous evening and wrote his usual memorandum, which he sent around for all the members of the group to sign.

"I am expecting a telegram from Madame Blavatsky," he told them, "but it hasn't yet arrived."

When most of the group left to take their morning baths, Olcott asked one member to remain with him until the telegram arrived, which it did a short time later. He passed it over to the man without opening it, and asked him to keep it until the others returned. When it was finally opened at noon, nine persons were present in addition to Olcott's party, and all happily attested to the circumstances. The telegram, dated 7:55 a.m. at Adyar, read: "Nearly broke right leg tumbling from Bishop's chair, dragging Coulomb, frightening Morgans. Damodar startled us."

A man in the group spoke up, half-jokingly, half as though to satisfy his own doubts.

"Someone is going to say this was collusion between Damodar and Madame Blavatsky."

Headshakings and doubtful smiles greeted this remark, and Olcott said:

"Do you think it likely that a fat woman of 16-stones' weight is going to give herself a serious injury for the sake of befooling me? If it was a conspiracy, they might better have agreed on something simpler and much less painful."*

*H.P.B.'s injury was indeed painful and she was a long time recovering from it. Writing to Sinnett on another matter on November 17, she interpolated: "I am nearly paralyzed and obliged to use a crutch and be wheeled about the house. Better to die." She closed with, "Yours, legless and snappingly desperate. H.P.B."

This time the heads nodded and pleased smiles broke out. A concerted murmur of "yes, yes" came from the group.

"Besides," Olcott pointed out, "Madame Blavatsky mentioned something in her telegram that I didn't know. Major-General and Mrs. Morgan of Ootacamund are visiting at Adyar. Did you know this, Damodar?"

The young man shook his head. "There were others in the room, I think," he said.

His very uncertainty convinced Col. Olcott even more than an accurate accounting of details would have done. Obviously Damodar's chagrin at H.P.B.'s injury had wiped some of the details from his mind.

The party stayed for three days in Lahore. Olcott and Brown shared a tent separated into two rooms by a screen. On the night of November 19, Olcott was wakened by feeling a hand laid upon him. Much alarmed, since they were outside the protection of the Lahore police, he caught the "interloper" by the upper arms and asked him in Hindustani who he was and what he wanted.

"Do you not know me?" asked a very kind, sweet voice. "Do you not remember me?"

The Master K.H.! The Colonel was so overcome that he wanted to leap out of bed and prostrate himself before his visitor.

"But his hand and voice stayed me," he wrote in his diary, "and after a few sentences had been exchanged, he took my left hand in his, gathered the fingers of his right hand into the palm, and stood quiet beside my cot, from which I could see his divinely benignant face by the light of the lamp that burned on a packing-case at his back."

Presently Olcott felt some soft substance forming in his hand and heard a murmured blessing as the Master touched his forehead. Then he was gone, passing into Brown's part of the tent.

"When I had time to pay attention to myself," wrote Olcott, "I found myself holding in my left hand a folded paper enwrapped in a silken cloth... I found it to be a letter of private counsel, containing prophecies of the death of the two then active opponents of the Society."[7] These prophecies were fulfilled shortly afterward.

The letter referred also to the visit paid by the Mahatma Morya to Olcott when the latter was still living in New York, on which occasion the Mahatma had left his turban as an earnest of his presence in the room. "At New York," the letter said, "you demanded of... an objective proof that his visit to you was not a *Maya*, and he gave it; unasked, I give you the present one; tho' I pass out of your sight, this note will be to you the reminder of our conferences. I now go to young Mr. Brown to try his intuitiveness. Tomorrow night, when the camp is quiet and the worst of the emanations from your audience have passed away, I shall visit you again for a longer conversation, as you must be forewarned against certain things in the future."

The Master left a letter in Brown's hand also. The young man described this later in a pamphlet entitled "My Life."

... I am awakened by the presence of someone in my tent. A voice speaks to me, and I find a letter and silk handkerchief within my hand. I am conscious that the letter and silk handkerchief are not placed in my hand in the customary manner. They grow "out of nothing." I feel a stream of "magnetism" and lo! it is "materialized." I rise to read my letter and examine the handkerchief. My visitor is gone. The handkerchief is a white one of the finest silk, with the initials K.H. marked in blue. The letter is also in blue in a bold hand.

On the next evening, at about ten o'clock, Damodar and Brown sat with Olcott in his tent awaiting the promised visit from the Master. A chela came first and beckoned to Damodar. Soon the Mahatma K.H. appeared. Olcott and Brown remained seated while Damodar conversed with the Master for a few moments, after which he returned to the tent. Olcott wondered whether he was actually to have the promised visit with the Master, but later, while he was writing in his diary, the same chela who had summoned Damodar lifted the portiere and beckoned to him, pointing to the figure of the Master who waited for him "out on the plain in the starlight."

"I went to him," Olcott recorded, "we walked off to a safe place at some distance where intruders need not be expected, and then for about a half-hour he told me what I had to know, and what does not concern third parties, since that chapter of T.S. history was long since closed." He added the words: "The august visitor told me, however, that he had not come to me in his own motion entirely, although glad to come to me in person, but had been sent by the Authority higher than himself, who was satisfied with my fidelity and wished me to never lose confidence. There were no miracles done at the interview, no magic circles traced on the ground, no gum-burning lamps placed around it and burning with stately blue flames; just two men talking together, a meeting, and a parting when the talk was over."

The next day the party broke camp and left Lahore for Jammu, where the Maharajah of Kashmir, whose invitation Olcott had mentioned to H.P.B., had his lower capital. They were first housed in a luxurious rest-house where they were received by "an army of servants." However, learning that a famous European doctor had been sent for by the Maharajah to prescribe for him, and that this doctor would be lodged with their party, and feeling that he could not bear the sight of his "dear dark-complexioned colleagues being scornfully looked down upon, as they would most certainly be," Olcott asked that his party be changed to a smaller bungalow, and the transfer was made.

This bungalow had four intercommunicating rooms. Col. Olcott had one room, Damodar another, Brown another, and Naidu and Narainswamy shared the fourth. This arrangement had some significance for the alarming event which subsequently took place.

In the meantime, Olcott spent considerable time at the palace of the Maharajah, where he found that he was able to provide some relief to the suffering man by performing simple mesmeric passes over his body and by counseling with him in long daily visits. There he met various officials, including the Prime Minister and the Chief Justice. The latter came one evening to the bungalow to chat with Olcott's party and, in the course of a pleasant conversation, mentioned that the Maharajah was so taken with the Colonel that he would give him anything he might ask for. Olcott himself "took this for what it was worth," but after the Chief Justice had gone, Brown, after an awkward moment, surprised him by asking:

"Since the Maharajah is willing to give you anything, do you suppose you could get me an appointment as a Judge?"

For a moment Olcott simply stared at him. When he found his voice all he could say was "What!" Then, recovering himself, he added sharply, "I thought you came here to devote yourself to the unselfish work of helping Theosophy."

"Well, yes," said Brown in some embarrassment, "but one must think of the future, too."

"The future!" The Colonel almost thundered. "I warned you in my letter to expect nothing but a chance for self-sacrifice. Incredibly—and I don't know why—you have just been honored by a visit from a Master, and let me tell you that is something that has never happened to many of our oldest members. And you are ready to leave it all at the first temptation and take a post for which you probably aren't qualified in the least. I'm amazed at you, Brown!"

Now quite chagrined at his temerity the young man did not reply. The Colonel went on: "If the Maharajah has any respect for me it's because he knows I wouldn't take for myself or for any private friend any present or favor whatsoever."

Brown was aware that Olcott had declined to receive personally all the gifts of cash and costly clothing which their host had tried to present to him at the time of his arrival, that the Maharajah had been just as stubborn in his insistence as Olcott had been in his refusal, and that the matter was finally resolved by Olcott's accepting the gifts, including Rs. 500, for the Theosophical Society. He now murmured some assent to the Colonel's remarks and said no more. The incident was closed. But the Colonel commented in his diary: "...his character-gauge had been exposed to me once for all and his subsequent career has corroborated my impressions."*

Then occurred the event which was to provide some of the most anxious hours Olcott had ever known. On the morning of the 25th of November, he awoke to find that Damodar had disappeared, leaving not the slightest clue to where he had gone or when, or whether, he might be expected to return. Olcott searched the four communicating rooms of the bungalow but found they were completely empty; his other companions had gone to the river to bathe.

---

*During 1884, Brown served on the Board of Control and the General Council of the Theosophical Society at Adyar. The next year he left India for America, where he underwent several changes of mind regarding his future. He visited England, saw Sinnett, went to Germany and met with members there, again traveled to the United States, and finally settled in India, where reputedly he turned Catholic, taking the soutane but after a few days again becoming a laic. Olcott reported (ODL 3:326) that he finally became an instructor in a Catholic College in the Madras Presidency. "He married a Eurasian lady who provided a home for the restless man." (*Damodar* 572)

Seeing a servant outside, Olcott called to him from a window. He had some difficulty making himself understood and understanding what the servant said in reply, but finally he grasped that the young man had gone away alone, at daybreak, but had left no message.

Completely puzzled, the Colonel returned to his own room. There, lying on his table, was a note from the Master K.H. telling him not to worry about the lad, who was under his protection, but giving no hint concerning his return. Olcott had heard no one and the circuit of the four rooms had taken very little time; he had no idea how or by whom the note had been placed on his table.

His next action, obeying an unexplainable impulse, was to bring all Damodar's luggage and bedding into his own room and place it under his cot. He then sent a telegram to H.P.B.:

"The Masters have taken Damodar return not promised."[8]

H.P.B. received the telegram at Adyar at 10:15 a.m., but added to the Colonel's words was a message from the Master: "We will send him back. K.H."

Later, Olcott found another note on his table. This was from Damodar, and he embodied its message in another telegram to H.P.B.:

"Damodar left before dawn at about eight o'clock letters from him and Koot Hoomi found on my table—Don't say whether return or not—Damodar bids us farewell conditionally and says brother theosophists should all feel encouraged knowing that he has found the blessed masters and been called by them. The dear boy's recent development astonishing. Hooney* bids me await orders."[9]

That evening, Olcott received an answering wire from H.P.B. She told him that the Master K.H. had promised Damodar's return and added that he must not allow Damodar's luggage, *especially his bedding,* to be touched by anyone else. Was this long distance telepathy or what? the Colonel wondered. For here he was being instructed to do the very thing he had been moved to do immediately after

---

*Undoubtedly meant for Koot Hoomi, misunderstood by the telegraph operator. H.P.B. sent both of these telegrams to Sinnett, along with one sent to her by Brown, presumably telling her of his meeting with the Mahatma for she commented: "Why should Brown be so favoured—is what I cannot understand.He may be a good man but what the devil has *he* done so holy and good!" (LBS 72)

Damodar had disappeared. He still didn't know why he had done it or why it was necessary.

Two days of anxious waiting ensued. On the evening of November 27, Damodar returned.

He was greatly changed. "He left, a delicate-framed, pale student-like young man, frail, timid, deferential," wrote Olcott. "He returned with his olive face bronzed several shades darker, seemingly robust, tough, and wiry, bold and energetic in manner. We could scarcely realize that he was the same person."

Damodar himself described his experience with considerable restraint, although he was allowed to tell of it. He said, in part:

I had the good fortune of being sent for, and permitted to visit a Sacred *Ashram* where I remained for a few days in the blessed company of several of the much doubted Mahatmas of Himavat and Their disciples. There I met not only my own beloved Gurudeva and Col. Olcott's Master, but several others of the Fraternity, including One of the Highest. I regret that the extremely personal nature of my visit to those thrice blessed regions prevents my saying more of it. Suffice it that the place I was permitted to visit is in the Himalayas, not in any fanciful Summer Land, and that I saw Him in my own sthula sarira (physical body) and found my Master identical with the form I had seen in the earlier days of my chelaship.*

Olcott's party was once more complete and he felt as elated as he had earlier been dejected. His affection for his companions—in part stimulated by his contact with the Mahatma K.H. and the boundless love and compassion which had radiated from him—was so genuine and spontaneous that it touched the hearts of all of them. It was a happy group that prepared for the last lap of their journey when the time for their departure from Jammu arrived. The annual Convention of the Theosophical Society was soon to take place, and Olcott knew there was a considerable distance yet to travel to reach Adyar.

The Maharajah was most reluctant to have Olcott leave, but he was grateful for the help he had received, and on the day of their leavetaking Olcott found in his room in the bungalow

---

*First published in *The Theosophist* for December-January 1883-4. Also see *Damodar*, pp. 333-36, and *MTL*, pp. 247-50.

more gifts of beautiful and expensive garments and two huge bags, each containing Rs. 1000. These, with the earlier gift of Rs. 500, brought the total for which Olcott receipted for the Society to Rs. 2,500.

"The treasurer's Report to that year's T.S. Convention," he was later to write, "shows that, of this sum, I gave Rs. 1,500 toward the purchase of the Adyar property, and the remaining Rs. 1,000 to the Current Expense Account."

He bestowed the gifts of clothing on H.P.B. and other friends, keeping for himself only one small scarf with which to protect his throat when on tour.

The journey from Jammu to Adyar was accomplished by elephant travel, train, and bullock carts. It was long and tiring, but had in it something of the nature of a triumphal return. They arrived at Adyar on December 15.

His "Old Chum" for her part, still nursing her injured knee, was nevertheless so happy to have her beloved associates with her again that she was her most charming and ebullient self, listening to their accounts of the happenings of their journey and entertaining them in return with her own stories of the more mundane events at headquarters, every one of which she managed somehow to infuse with significance.

The Convention which followed was a tremendous success, marked by a gift of Rs. 500 from the Mahatma K.H. to help defray expenses. The year closed on a triumphant note.

"The future sparkled with bright promise," wrote Olcott. "But the lower gods were envious, and were already forging the thunderbolt that Mara meant to hurl at us within the next few months. . . ."

18

Crisis in London Lodge

"**K**ingsford must remain president."

This telegram from the Mahatma K.H. was received by Sinnett early in December of 1883.* He was astonished and, quite frankly, disappointed. Never had the Mahatmas interfered in the affairs of the Theosophical Society in any such arbitrary manner. Mrs. Kingsford had been President of the London Lodge for the past year, but this was understood to be a somewhat temporary arrangement and an election was to take place shortly after the first of January. Why, he wondered, did the Master wish her to continue?

Sinnett told himself that he had no desire actually to depose Mrs. Kingsford, but he was aware that the members had been turning to him in increasing numbers as the more authentic source of teachings and he felt that perhaps, as head of the organization, he might be able to undo some of what he felt was the damage done by the present incumbent and her few followers—much fewer in number now than even a short time ago.

As usual, he turned to Patience with his dilemma. The experiences of the past few years had strengthened and sensitized the bond between them; invariably her gentle wisdom soothed his irritation and removed from his mind—or at least softened—the hovering shadows of doubt and disbelief.

"Yes, it is surprising," she agreed, when he showed her the telegram and fretted over what he was to do about it, saying that he could hardly believe the Master meant it. "But of course he meant it. There's something behind it, I'm sure." She chuckled suddenly. "One thing is certain. People who say our dear H.P.B. is writing all these communications from the

*The telegram is in Folio 6 of the *Mahatma Letters* in the British Museum. It is not in the published volume.

Mahatmas couldn't accuse her of sending this telegram. She doesn't have a very high opinion of Mrs. Kingsford."

"Definitely not," he said, remembering several letters from the "Old Lady" in which she had forcibly expressed her views about the English woman. "Calls her the 'Divine Anna'—and even more bizarre names than that. So far as I can tell, she hasn't a good word to say for her. I'm not sure that's right, either. Mrs. Kingsford *is* a brilliant woman."

"And wholly convinced of her own infallibility," Patience added quietly, but without malice. "This doesn't explain the telegram, however. I don't see that you can do anything about it at the moment, except perhaps discuss it with some of the members. Even that might not accomplish much without knowing what's behind the Master's decision."

"I think it would simply stir things up unnecessarily. The members would resent it."

"Why not wait a bit?" she suggested. "Surely the Master will write you. He would hardly leave you up in the air on anything so important."

"He seems to leave me up in the air on a good many things!"

"Now, Percy," she placed her hand on his in gentle reproach. "Sometimes I think you believe he has nothing to do but turn the Brotherhood inside out for your benefit. You know he can't do that."

He smiled and bent to kiss her forehead lightly.

"No wonder he thinks so highly of you," he said more calmly. "No doubt some explanation will be forthcoming."

He folded the telegram and put it in his pocket, later to be deposited with other communications from the Mahatmas.

"Incidentally, Sam Ward is back in town," he said, remembering that Massey had told him of seeing the American.

"That's nice. Do you think you could discuss the telegram with him?"

"I'm not sure. I'll be seeing him soon, no doubt."

It was not the telegram which was the subject of conversation, however, when he spent an evening in the pleasant rooms in Piccadilly maintained by the American as his London residence.

Along with C. C. Massey, Dr. George Wyld, and one or two others in the London Lodge, Sinnett had retained what he liked to think was a scientific interest in spiritualism. William Eglinton was gaining a reputation as a medium and Ward had invited him to hold some séances in his home. It was here that Sinnett met the young medium for the first time; although the latter's sojourn in India had lasted a number of months, Sinnett had never found the opportunity to go to Calcutta where he was staying with Col. and Mrs. Gordon.

As a matter of fact, Eglinton had tried—following his return from India—to abandon the practice of mediumship and get a foothold in the publishing field. This did not prosper and he returned to the one occupation in which he knew he could make a living.[1]

Sinnett had long since overcome the jealousy that had tormented him when it seemed that Eglinton (who, he considered, had done nothing to deserve it) was to be favored by a visit from the Mahatma K.H. in person—something he himself had longed for, and been consistently denied, since he had received the first letter from the Master in the fall of 1880. He had, however, become convinced that, whatever the identity of the visitor Eglinton had seen and talked with on board the S.S. *Vega* in March of 1882, it was not, in physical fact, the Mahatma; the latter himself had hinted that it was simply his *mayava rupa*—an illusory body.[2] Sinnett knew that his revered Teacher had incurred some displeasure from the Mahachohan for permitting Eglinton to believe that he actually had been visited by the Master.[3] He remembered, too, that the Mahatma had commented on Eglinton's inherent good nature "and other good qualities" (along with some serious weaknesses), adding that he was "naturally truthful" when not under control.[4] He had said, too, that it was not "true" Spiritualism" that the Brotherhood opposed but rather "indiscriminate mediumship, physical manifestations, materializations, and trance-possessions especially."[5] Well, Eglinton was a trance-medium and had been since he was a boy.[6] But his séances had attracted considerable attention, and Sinnett had looked forward to attending one of them; underlying his fascination with phenomena, of which he had never cured himself, was a genuine desire to understand what was taking place. So it was with considerable interest that he joined a small party, which included F.W.H. Myers of the Psychical Research Society, C.C. Massey, and Eglinton, for a dinner at Sam Ward's home. Massey left soon after they rose from the table, having another engagement, but the others remained, curious to see what might happen.

What happened was a strange sort of séance.

Eglinton first announced: "We wish to state to prevent any future misunderstanding that whatever phenomena may present themselves to you this evening, we are in no way responsible for them and have no hand in their production."[7]

The others assumed that the "we" referred to Eglinton himself and the guide "Ernest." But who, then, was to produce the phenomena?

Eglinton immediately went into trance. The first message to be received was supposedly from the "Old Lady" and in her handwriting—a very good likeness, as it happened—which appeared on a card under Eglinton's hand. She sent "loving greetings" to a "Lonie" or "Louis" (unidentified), and to C.C. Massey—with whom, as a matter of fact, she was not on speaking terms (or on writing terms, since she was some thousands of miles away) and who had already left the party. This was followed by what purported to be a message from the Mahatma M. from Ladakh, "in a feigned hand,"[8] bidding Sinnett to "prepare for our coming as soon as we have won over Eglinton."

There was little more save a confused vision by "Uncle Sam" Ward of the Mahatma K.H. "descending a hill on horseback,"[*9] and, after a time, the party broke up. Eglinton gave Sinnett the message from the Mahatma, and when Sinnett reached home he placed it with other communications from the Masters.† He was considerably puzzled over its meaning. Neither this nor the supposed message from H.P.B. made any sense to him, but he hoped he would be enlightened; it seemed to him that the Masters (if indeed they had had anything at all to do with this séance), were going out of their way to bewilder him.

Sinnett wrote to H.P.B., telling her about the séance, hoping that perhaps she would be able either to verify or deny the message from herself; he had half suspected her of some trickery in the matter, although he had no idea what she might have hoped to achieve by it. The writing on the card did

---

*He was in Cambodia at the time (ML 432/425).

†This message, which is on a sheet of Sam Ward's stationery, is in Folio 6 of the *Letters* in the British Museum. The writing bears no resemblance to that of the other letters from this Mahatma. It is not included in the published volume.

resemble hers, however, and he wanted to know whether she actually had sent such a message. He mentioned also that Mrs. Kingsford seemed to have an increasing tendency to dominate the London Lodge rather than to work within that group "as the predominant organization."[10] He felt that Mrs. Kingsford herself was not wholly aware of this, but it was beginning to alienate some of the members.

The year ended before he had a response from H.P.B., and this was only a short note. The envelope in which it arrived was a bulky one, however, for enclosed in it were letters from both the Mahatma M. and the Mahatma K.H.

"There's a love chit for you just received," H.P.B. began her note. "I guess my Boss splits himself owing to Eglinton's *haut fait de magie** and explains as promised. Of course you would not believe me—if the card was such a 'good imitation of my handwriting' and I am sure Mr. C. C. M. must have strengthened your belief that it was some new fraud...†

"Well, there's a letter from Mahatma K.H. also."

Then, turning to the affairs of the London Lodge, "All Mr. Massey's doings, was it not he, and *he alone*, who proposed and had her elected as the only possible Saviour of the British Theos. Society? Well, now thank him and keep her to turn all of you into a jelly. Of course she will wag you as her tail more than ever. I know it will end in a scandal. Well Olcott is coming and then you will have *nolens volens* to accept the decision of the 'nominal' President. My Boss gave him instructions and hurries him on. Yours—but not Mrs. Kingsford's. H.P.B."[11]

These remarks were not particularly instructive, Sinnett felt, although he couldn't but agree that, if something was not done, Mrs. Kingsford would soon be "wagging" the London Lodge rather than serving as its inspired leader.

He was extremely surprised to have a letter from the Mahatma M. and he was further astonished to see that it was written on a sheet of Sam Ward's distinctive stationery.[12]

"My humble pranams Sahib," the Mahatma wrote. "Your memory is not good."

---

*Great feat of magic.

†In addition to H.P.B.'s comments in this letter, she referred again to the matter more than a year later. "... Was not that my *identical* handwriting on that card? And yet you know it was not done by me. Alexis Coulomb's handwriting is naturally like mine." (LBS 115)

He reminded the Englishman that the Master K.H. had warned him to be prepared, in London, for false messages purporting to come from the Mahatmas through mediums and had assured him that they would not be authentic unless preceded by three passwords which the Master had communicated to him.[13]

"True," thought Sinnett, "there was certainly nothing to indicate that these messages were genuine. There was only that rather silly speech by Eglinton."

The Master M.'s attention was attracted to the séance, he said, when the "spooks" began to forge H.P.B.'s handwriting, and then to give a message supposed to come from him. He was not in Ladakh as indicated but in Lhassa, "smoking your pipe."* When he became aware of what was going on, he put aside his pipe and watched—and then, apparently in instantaneous astral travel, he himself was in the room with the group at the séance, invisible to all except the "spooks" who did not mind him. He helped himself to a sheet of Mr. Ward's stationery, "just to show you I watched." The whole thing was a hoax from beginning to end.

But, the Mahatma advised, "...you must not be too hard upon the wretched young fellow. He was utterly *irresponsible* on that night...he is really honest in his way and to be pitied." He suggested that perhaps K.H. might prevail upon Sam Ward to find Eglinton some kind of job to relieve him of the necessity of earning his living as a medium, or, as the Mahatma M. expressed it, "...to save the poor wretch from the two elementaries—which have fastened on him like two barnacles and thus save him from a life of infamy which kills him." The young man was "not guilty of any *conscious*, deliberate jugglery that night," the Master added. "He got a passionate desire to join the L.L. [London Lodge] and as the wish is father to the deed—his astral ticks fabricated the letter of *mine* through means of their own. Had he done it himself he would have remembered it was not my handwriting as he is familiar with it through Gordons...At any rate, ask him for the card of Upasika [H.P.B.] with her alleged writing on it. It is a good thing to keep and show occasionally to the Masseys of

---

*On his trip to London in 1881, Sinnett had brought back a gift of a pipe for the Mahatma M. (ML 374/367).

the L.L. who believe pure lies and will suspect fraud where none is meant."

Near the close of this letter, the Master M. said, ". . . though I am the first to advise Mrs. K's re-election—nevertheless, I would sooner trust W.E.'s (Eglinton's) clairvoyance than Mrs. K's or rather her *rendering* of her visions."

Sinnett shook his head as he handed Patience the letter to read.

"This whole business is a gigantic puzzle," he said. "Why should the Master M. want Mrs. Kingsford to continue as President when he has such a lack of confidence in her? Especially when it seems she is doing everything she can to discount the existence of the Brotherhood and to gain adherents for her own ideas."

"But they never care about that, you know," she reminded him. "Surely this must have some bearing on that mysterious telegram. What does the Master K.H. say in his letter?"

He opened the other enclosure. This letter began by reminding him of a statement he had made at one time to H.P.B. to the effect that he would follow the Master's advice in almost anything that might be asked of him. "Well—the time has come to prove your willingness. And since, in this particular case, I myself am simply carrying out the wishes of my Chohan, I hope you will not experience too much difficulty in sharing my fate by doing—as I do."

The fact was that the Mahachohan wished Mrs. Kingsford to remain President of the London Lodge. ". . . her anti-vivisection struggles and her strict vegetarian diet have won entirely over to her side our stern Master. He cares less than we do for any outward—or even inward—expression or feeling of disrespect in the Mahatmas." He added that Mrs. Kingsford was "very young, and her personal vanity and other womanly shortcomings are to be laid at the door of Mr. Maitland and the Greek chorus of her admirers."[14]

The Master K.H. enclosed in his letter another missive to be delivered, sealed, to one of the Councilors or Vice-Presidents of the Lodge; C.C. Massey was suggested, as he was a friend of both Sinnett and Mrs. Kingsford. But Sinnett could use his own judgment. All he was asked to do personally was to insist that this communication be read before a general meeting composed of as many theosophists as could be gathered together, and that this be done "at the earliest opportunity."

The letter, the Master said, "contains and carries within its folds and characters *a certain occult influence* that ought to reach as many Theosophists as possible." Sinnett himself was to read it first.

It began rather whimsically: "Friends and Opponents." He had just ordered two telegrams sent, the Master said, one to Mrs. Kingsford and one to Mr. Sinnett, to notify both of them that Mrs. Kingsford should continue as President of the London Lodge.* This was at the "express wish of the Chohan Himself" and was not in any sense a matter of personal feeling. It rested entirely "on the advisability of having at the head of the Society, in a place like London, a person well suited to the standard and aspiration of the (so far) ignorant (of esoteric truths) and therefore malicious public." Nor was it of the slightest consequence whether she entertained "feelings of reverence or disrespect toward the humble and unknown individuals at the head of the Tibetan Good Law—or the writer of the present, or any of the Brothers—but rather a question whether the said lady is fitted for the purpose we have all at heart, namely the dissemination of Truth through Esoteric doctrines, conveyed by whatever religious channel, and the effacement of crass materialism and blind prejudice and skepticism."

Sinnett was reading the letter aloud, and here he paused to say, "This strikes me as rather inconsistent. So often the Mahatmas talk about the necessity for skepticism—and now K.H. is saying we need to efface it."

She smiled at him affectionately.

"You know, dear," she said, "that wonderful keen mind of yours is always snipping away at things before you know what they *are*."

He looked startled.

"So? In what way? I know I'm always being told I'm too matter of fact."

She was thoughtful for a moment. When she spoke it was tentatively.

"I didn't mean precisely that. Although, if it's true, it's a good thing. So many are likely to go off into all kinds of wild suppositions, and we need a balance. But, no, what I meant

*The telegram to Mrs. Kingsford is, of course, not available. Obviously it contained the same message as that sent to Sinnett.

was—well, you know you have so often thought that it would be possible for the Masters—or H.P.B. even—to perform some kind of phenomenon that would convince the skeptics once and for all. I remember that was your idea when you made your first suggestion to the Master, way back in the beginning. But it never works that way. Skepticism isn't cured by anything that happens outside ourselves." She paused reflectively, while he hung on her words; he had always trusted her intuition more than he had his own logic, and he felt she was about to say something important. "As soon as the circumstances change and the evidence disappears, the disease returns," she went on. "No, I think the Master means something else. The only way to efface skepticism is to *know*—to know directly—without any need for dramatic outer evidence. Then prejudice and skepticism simply become irrelevant."

He had been listening intently, and now he sighed slightly.

"Well, Patty, I wish I could see that as clearly as you do. I didn't let my mind snip at what you were saying, you may be sure, but I have to confess I'm not entirely clear about what you mean. I'm afraid K.H. was right when he said I needed to develop my intuition."

She smiled. "What more does he say?" she asked.

He resumed reading.

As Mrs. Kingsford had rightly observed, the letter went on, the Western public should understand the Theosophical Society to be "'a Philosophical School constituted on the ancient Hermetic basis'—that public never having heard of the Tibetan and entertaining very perverted notions of the Esoteric Buddhist System."

The Hermetic Philosophy, the Master observed, "suits every creed and philosophy and clashes with none. It is the boundless ocean of Truth, the central point whither flows and wherein meet every river—whether its source be East, West, North, or South." The only object to be striven for, said the Master, "is the amelioration of the condition of Man by the spread of truth suited to the various stages of his development and that of the country he inhabits and belongs to. Truth has no ear-mark and does not suffer from the name under which it is promulgated."

The Mahatma pointed out that both Mrs. Kingsford and Mr. Sinnett were needed and appreciated by "our revered Chohan" because they were two poles calculated to keep the whole body in "magnetic harmony." Mrs. Kingsford was well suited to lead the movement for the coming year, since she was capable of presenting the esoteric concepts in a manner comprehensible to Westerners.

"But the services of Mr. Sinnett in the good cause are great indeed—far greater, so far, than of any Western Theosophist—therefore a new arrangement is found advisable."

This new arrangement was that those who wished to "follow absolutely the teachings of the School to which we of the Tibetan Brotherhood belong, should be formed under Mr. Sinnett's direction and *within* the 'London Lodge T.S.'" Mrs. Kingsford who was to remain President, would head the group who wished to pursue a more western approach to the study.

Sinnett was not surprised at this suggestion, since he himself had mentioned to the Master the desirability of some such plan and the latter had indicated his approval.[15]

The letter went on: "It is necessary for the parallel progress of the groups under Mrs. K. and Mr. S. that neither should interfere with the beliefs and rights of the other."

The Master then suggested the appointment of "*fourteen* Councillors—one half openly inclining toward Christian Esotericism as represented by Mrs. K., and the other half following Buddhist Esotericism as represented by Mr. S., all important business to be transacted by a majority of votes."[16]

When this letter was read to the assembled members of the London Lodge, it was far from having a unifying effect. The "magnetic harmony" which the Master had suggested would be created by the presence of the "two poles"—Mrs. Kingsford and Mr. Sinnett—failed to manifest itself and the poles moved farther apart than ever. The arguments seemed to go on endlessly, and finally it was suggested that the issues could not be settled immediately and that further thought had to be given by all to the implications of the Mahatma's letter.

Sinnett himself did not approve the appointment of fourteen councilors, seeing in such an arrangement many potentials for mischief. He wrote the Mahatma K.H. to this effect.

Dissension and disagreement continued, and before any resolution of the difficulty could be reached a further telegram was received from the Master K.H.: "Postpone election letter follows."

What now, indeed? It was a time of severe testing for Sinnett. Did not the Masters know what they wanted?

Perhaps it was the Mahachohan again. Could that venerable Being, however high and holy he might be, stationed as he was amidst the "eternal snows" of far-off Tibet, know what was desirable and necessary for a sophisticated group of intellectuals in a modern metropolis such as London? But the direction was clear: postpone the election. That Sinnett was willing enough to do.

The situation was further complicated by the fact that, in December of 1883, Mrs. Kingsford and Mr. Maitland had issued a circular letter entitled "A Letter Addressed to the Fellows of the London Lodge of the Theosophical Society by the President and Vice-President of the Lodge" which embodied a severe criticism of the teachings contained in Sinnett's new book, *Esoteric Buddhism.* Sinnett had tried to be objective about this even though he considered it mistaken as well as gratuitous. Toward the end of January 1884, T. Subba Row, in collaboration with "another still greater scholar"[17] issued in pamphlet form a "Reply" to the circular.* He sent this to H.P.B. with a covering letter requesting her to forward it on to the London Lodge. She did so in a letter to Sinnett dated January 25, 1884,[18] enclosing with it "by order of my Boss" two letters from Mrs. Kingsford to her which she asked Sinnett to "fondly read and preserve for Olcott when he comes—he will be with you about March 15th or 16th." Mohini was to accompany him.†

Subba Row had shown to her a letter from the Mahatma M. which, among other things, contained what she called "some funny news." "It appears that you go against my Boss's advice that there should be 14 councillors in your Lodge—7 for you and 7 for Kingsford, for it is *his* dodge. He writes the particulars now for Subba Row's information in writing the pamphlet and his words are: 'I thought my Peling friend, Sinnett Sahib, more perspicacious—tell him I have advised only 7 councillors on the side of the yellow haired woman because I knew that it was *four too many.* She is needed in the Society but not as the head of it, if it can be helped.'"

---

*The full text of this "Reply" is to be found in *Esoteric Writings* of T. Subba Row, TPH, Adyar, 1931. It has to do with technical points and is quite lengthy and involved.

†Mohini Mohun Chatterjee, a chela of K.H. The purpose of his visit was to help in giving the European members a better understanding of Eastern doctrines.

"Now what does all this mean?" asked H.P.B. "Do *they* or do they not want Mrs. K?...(I) gave it up long ago. They tell me nothing and—I ask nothing."

So the "Old Lady" too was bewildered over developments, Sinnett thought wryly. Perhaps he too would have to "give it up."

H.P.B. went on in her letter: she was mortally ill and the Mahatma M. had ordered Olcott to take her to Southern France "to some secluded village, on the seashore or in the Alps for a long and entire rest of three months at least." She did not want to go, she said, but upon the urging of members, she had agreed to do so. "I consented on the following condition," she said, "*I must not, shall not, and will not go to London.*" She thought she would go to Marseilles and Paris, and then "right to some secluded spot in the Mountains, where I can catch hold of my Boss's astral coattails whenever I choose."

So, she would be coming to Europe with Olcott and Mohini after all! Sinnett was not pleased at this development; in his view it was ripe with seeds of trouble. He had been sufficiently concerned over what Olcott might do to disturb an already delicate situation. But this! Despite her statement that she would not come to London, he was not at all sure that she would be able to resist.

19

A Surprise Appearance

The train bearing the Paris passengers to London on April 5, 1884 pulled slowly into Victoria Station and the platform was soon filled with the happy chatter of arrivals and those who had come to meet them.

"Like little islands," thought Patience Sinnett as she watched. "Every little group absorbed in itself and unaware of anyone else. And why should they be, when it comes to that? ...Oh!" she said suddenly, aloud. "There they are! Oh dear, they don't see us!" She stood on tiptoe and waved.

"Oh yes, I see them." Sinnett was tall enough that his wave attracted the attention of a rather stocky middle-aged man with a long beard who, with an impressive-looking young Indian, was about to be carried off with the crowd in another direction.

"Goodness!" observed Patience, "the Colonel's beard *has* grown, hasn't it? And how dignified Mohini looks—and so young, too."

"Yes, quite handsome," Sinnett replied. "Welcome, Olcott," he said cordially as the two men came together and shook hands. "I hope you had a pleasant trip over."

"Splendid!" Olcott turned to greet Patience, who extended both hands and was smiling her warmest smile. "My dear Mrs. Sinnett, how good of you to come along to meet us."

He turned to his companion. "This is Mohini—I think you haven't met him."

"*Namaskar,*" murmured the young man, an engaging smile lighting up his rather somber face, his hands together in the traditional Indian salutation, and bowing to Patience a little more deeply perhaps than to her husband. She returned the greeting gracefully. Sinnett nodded and smiled but without adopting what was still to him a foreign gesture.

"We're so happy to see both of you," said Patience. "We've been in our own home now for some time, so we hope we can make you comfortable."

After staying with Patience's mother and in other more or less temporary quarters ever since their return to England, the Sinnetts had finally found what they were looking for in a house at 7 Ladbroke Gardens,[1] and Patience had been indulging her housewifely instincts by making it attractive and comfortable. She was thankful that they were well settled so that they need not be lacking in hospitality.

"How did you leave Madame?" asked Sinnett with interest. He was still hoping that she would live up to her resolve not to come to London.

"Fairly well, I think, although she has her bad days. We've been besieged by visitors. And I must say we've had a lot of attention in the Paris press. *Le Rapel* gave us three columns.[2] Judge was there from New York, incidentally. He's on his way to India."

"Oh, so?" Sinnett responded. "I hope to meet him some day. Was the publicity favorable?"

"Yes, quite, although I must say it inclined to the sensational—as seems to be the habit with newspapers."

Sinnett mentally added: "Or wherever the 'Old Lady' is." Aloud he said only, "Rather their stock in trade, of course."

He had brought along a servant to look after the visitors' luggage, and the Sinnetts and their guests were soon comfortably settled in the carriage, moving away from the station as fast as the traffic would allow. Mohini seemed rather quiet and shy, but they were to learn that he was indeed an extremely brilliant individual with a profound grasp of theosophical and Vedic teachings, an excellent command of English, an attorney by profession, and an able advocate of his own convictions when he chose to defend them.

It was not until they were settled down after dinner that evening that Sinnett and Olcott were able to discuss the affairs of the London Lodge. Mohini took no part in the discussion, although he listened attentively and appeared to absorb all that was said.

"I've been curious about the results of the circular you sent to all of us from Nice," Sinnett said in an exploratory opening. "If I have a right to know, of course," he added quickly.

The "circular" had gone to every member of the London Lodge asking for a confidential opinion of the situation in that organization, to be sent to the Colonel at his Paris address.

"Certainly you have," Olcott assured him. "And I may tell you that, with very few exceptions, the members lean to the teachings you are giving and prefer you to Mrs. Kingsford."

"Yes, I am aware of that. I've been asked to accept the presidency at our election—it's almost on us, as you know—which we postponed from an earlier date at the direction of the Mahachohan. I have since had a letter from the Master K.H. dictated to one of his chelas and meant for the Lodge. It explains that the Mahachohan wanted to avoid the appearance of precipitancy in the matter and give us time to consider further."[3]

The letter had been read to the members, as the Master K.H. had suggested in a postscript. "I would have you prevent, if possible, another 'coup de theatre,'" the Master said. "However natural such sensational surprises may be in politics when parties are composed of devotees whose souls rejoice in party intrigue, they are very painful to witness in an association of persons who profess to give themselves up to the most solemn questions affecting human interest. Let meaner natures wrangle if they will; the wise compound their differences in a mutually forebearing spirit."

The letter itself explained that the postponement of the election was "absolutely necessary." It referred to the circular issued by Mrs. Kingsford and Mr. Maitland and said that this had greatly altered the case. "Always on the strength of the principle of impartial justice involved, we find ourselves obliged not to ratify literally our decision as to her re-election but to add to it certain clauses and make it henceforth impossible for the President and members to misconceive our mutual position."

It was far from the thought of the Mahatmas, the letter said, "to erect a new hierarchy for the future oppression of a priest-ridden world. As it was our wish *then* to signify to you that one could be both an active and useful member of the Society without inscribing himself our follower or co-religionist, so is it *now*. But it is just because the principle has to work both ways, that. . . we feel, and would have it known, that we have no right to influence the free will of the members in this or any other matter. Such interference would be in flagrant contradiction to the basic law of esotericism that personal psychic growth accompanies, *pari passu*, the development of individual effort, and is the evidence of acquired personal merit."

Referring to a statement made by Mrs. Kingsford in one of her letters to H.P.B.,[4] the Master continued, "Were I to have acceded to the lady's desire to appoint her as the 'Apostle of Eastern and Western Esotericism' and try to force her election on even *one* unwilling member, and taking advantage of Mr. Sinnett's never wavering warm regard for myself, influence his future attitude toward herself and the movement, I would then indeed deserve to be taunted as 'the oracle of the Theosophists!'"

Sinnett shared these and other comments in the letter with Olcott, who nodded his head in agreement.

"I'm sure the Masters are concerned that the situation be resolved as wisely as possible," he said. "I have had two communications from the Master K.H. myself—one on board ship and one on the way up here on the train. The first one rather took me to task for being too impulsive and not paying enough attention to my first impressions. The Master said one thing about H.P.B. that I echo and applaud—that one of the most valuable effects of her mission is that it drives people to self-study and destroys any blind servility to persons. If only some of her fanatical followers could realize that! She has her failings, as we all know—and who does not?—but she is great enough, and we owe her enough, without trying to make her into an infallible goddess!"[5]

"I confess I am one who rather suffers from her idiosyncrasies." Sinnett smiled wryly. "But I also agree with what you say."

He did not ask about the second letter from the Mahatma K.H. but the Colonel obliged without a request.

"I had brought along the responses to my circular to the members," he said, "to read on the way here from Paris. I was going through them on the train. I had just come across a statement in Bertram Keightley's letter—he said he had entire confidence that the Masters would 'order all things well'— when a letter came fluttering down from the roof of the railway carriage, right over Mohini's head.[6] The Master said that those who have been so puzzled over the policy of the Masters with respect to the London Lodge would understand its necessity better when they became more acquainted with the occult art of drawing out the hidden capacities and propensities of beginners in occult study. It was necessary to bring the whole thing to the surface."

"That is the kind of remark that made Hume furious," Sinnett commented. He himself felt some of the irritation which invariably characterized his own reaction to what he considered rather devious and unfair means of making people reveal the less desirable traits in themselves. "I confess I myself resist it somewhat," he added honestly. "But I do not intend to permit my name to be advanced for President. I'm convinced it isn't desirable for Mrs. Kingsford to continue, so I am going to nominate Finch.'"[7]

Col. Olcott gave him a keen glance.

"I don't know Finch very well. Has he something special to recommend him?"

"G.B. Finch? Yes, I think so. He is a barrister—he was Senior Wrangler at Cambridge. He has deep and sympathetic interest in Theosophy and is always present at our meetings. I don't think he should be President indefinitely, but right now he seems to me the best choice."

"What do you think of chartering a separate branch for Mrs. Kingsford?" asked Olcott.

"That might be feasible. I had suggested to the Master K.H. some time ago that we have a sort of society within the society—that is, that those who wanted to study the Eastern teachings could form a separate group, but integrated within the larger group. The Master seemed to think well of the idea[8] but it didn't quite come out that way in his letter proposing a new arrangement for the London Lodge."

"So I understand. Nevertheless, I think I'll make this proposal to Mrs. Kingsford and see if we can't arrive at some more harmonious situation. Obviously, things can't go on as they are."

"True, I fear. Even though K.H. assured me that all this dissension is better than what he called 'the old paralytic calm.'[9] He commented that an outbreak of fever in the human body is evidence that nature is trying to expel the seeds of disease. Perhaps we've been getting rid of some of these. We can only hope so."

"Well, we've had problems in the Society before, Sinnett. I've come to the conclusion that is our fate."

"Our karma, rather," Sinnett answered shortly. "We make our own."

Olcott sighed but his eyes twinkled.

"And I fear the Society has made a lot of it. All the more reason why we should try to resolve our difficulties in a spirit of good will. I will call on Mrs. Kingsford tomorrow."

"Please understand that my personal disagreements with her don't affect my respect for her unusual abilities—her intelligence, her talents as an organizer, her force of character—for she is a strong person, you know."

"Unquestionably," the Colonel agreed. "But we learn one thing, at least—or try to—and that is that we should tend to be a little more objective about our relationships than we have been in the past."

"We've inaugurated one most useful practice since we came to this house," said Sinnett, wanting to give Olcott as total a picture of their theosophical activities as possible. "Every Tuesday afternoon we have an 'at home' and our drawing room is always filled with theosophical friends and the visitors who have become interested in our ideas. It seems to have been a successful activity. Of course you will see most of the members of the Lodge at our election meeting. That will be held in Finch's chambers, by the way."[10]

"I hope to meet Mrs. Arundale and Miss Arundale," Olcott commented. "They seem to be most devoted members."

"Indeed they are. And they are looking forward to having you spend some time in their home, incidentally."

Sinnett was glad that the Colonel had introduced these names; he remembered the Master K.H.'s comments in one of his more recent letters to the effect that it would not be politic to have Olcott remain exclusively as the Sinnett's guest during his stay in London, but that he should divide his time between their home and those of other members who might care to invite him.[11]

"Fine," said Olcott, falling in with the idea at once. "In fact, I think it would be wise for me to get better acquainted with all the members so that I can have a clearer understanding of their viewpoints."

The two men talked on for some time, going over the more intricate details of the difficulties which had beset the London Lodge during Mrs. Kingsford's regime. Mohini had remained attentive but silent. Asked now if he had any comments, he shook his head and replied, "I will wait. I do not yet know these people."

Patience joined them for a brief chat, and tea was served. Not long afterward, because it had been a long and tiring day for the travelers, it was decided that they would retire and continue their discussions on another day.

"I'll talk to Massey and Mrs. Kingsford tomorrow," Olcott said as they parted. "I must know what they have to say."

"Of course," agreed Sinnett, wondering a little how susceptible Olcott would be to Mrs. Kingsford's charms if she chose to exercise them.

Olcott did not, as a matter of fact, feel drawn to Mrs. Kingsford, "...although," he was to write later, "it did not take many minutes for me to gauge her intellectual power and the breadth of her culture. There was something uncanny to me in her views about human affection. She said she had never felt love for a human being; that people had told her, before her child was born, to wait its appearance and she would feel the great gush of mother-love and the fountains of her affection would be unsealed; she had waited, the child had been shown her, but her only feeling was the wish that they should take it away out of her sight! Yet she lavished excessive love on a guinea-pig and, in his *Life of Anna Kingsford*, Mr. Maitland's splendid pen has made us all see, as in a mental Kinematograph, his great colleague carrying her little beast around her with her in her travels, lavishing on it her caresses, and keeping the anniversary of its death as one does that of a near relative."[12]

Olcott was accustomed to dealing with all sorts of individuals, however, and he did not permit himself to be put off by his somewhat chilling impression of her. He had already discussed with Massey the idea of chartering a separate branch of the Society to be called the "Hermetic Lodge, T.S.," with Mrs. Kingsford at its head, and that gentleman had agreed that this might be in the interests of all concerned. The Colonel had known and liked Massey from the very inception of the Theosophical Society, and he refused to be antagonized by the latter's expressed skepticism about the Mahatmas; he believed the lawyer's doubts to be honest ones.

The Colonel had listened sympathetically to the complaints against Mrs. Kingsford from other members of the London

Lodge. It was generally customary, these members commented, for Mr. Sinnett to address the lodge at their regular meetings. His talks were appreciated by all. But before Mrs. Kingsford would permit any questions or discussions of his comments, she insisted on restating his whole address in her own terms and from her own point of view, which quite often did not agree with his and which therefore tended more to confuse the members than to enlighten them. This practice had the further disadvantage of creating boredom and impatience. Moreover, Mrs. Kingsford frequently came very close to unwarranted criticism of Sinnett's presentations and even of the Masters who were his source of information.[13]

Olcott did not mention these complaints to Mrs. Kingsford, feeling that if she would accept his suggestion, the situation would be remedied. As it turned out, she was quite agreeable to the idea of having her own lodge, and the Colonel left her in a mood of optimism.

On the evening of the election, the Sinnetts had as an extra guest a young curate from outside of London, Charles W. Leadbeater, who had recently joined the Theosophical Society and who, since he lived fifty miles away, had a standing invitation to dine and stay overnight with the Sinnetts when he was able to get into town for meetings. Olcott liked him at once. Theosophy was quite new to the young clergyman, but he had absorbed quickly such information as he had been able to glean, and so the dinner table conversation was lively and stimulating.

In years to come, Mr. Leadbeater was to record the experiences of this period, and his description of the events of that election meeting deserves repetition. He pointed out that it had been the almost unanimous desire of the members that Sinnett should accept the Presidency, but that he was unwilling to do so, not wishing to carry any personal differences with Mrs. Kingsford into the politics of the Lodge. Consequently, when, as the meeting progressed, Mr. Maitland proposed the reappointment of Mrs. Kingsford (the separate branch apparently having been forgotten for the moment), "he found only one or two members to support him, at which Dr. Kingsford showed most undignified annoyance." Sinnett then proposed Mr. G. B. Finch, at whose chambers the meeting was being held, and he was "at once elected by an overwhelming majority."

Olcott was presiding, but had some difficulty in dealing with Mrs. Kingsford, who persisted in interrupting repeatedly on one point or another. The meeting seemed doomed to drag on interminably and everyone was getting bored and restive.

Benches had been hired for the occasion and were extended in the long room almost back to the door at its end. Leadbeater and a friend were seated just opposite the door, with only a few members in their immediate neighborhood. Being at some distance from the chair, they were not paying very close attention, although they were aware that both Olcott and Mohini were "trying their best to extract something sensible and useful from a very wearisome and unprofitable discussion." Suddenly the door opened and "a stout lady in black came quickly in and seated herself at the outer end of our bench."

Mr. Leadbeater described the subsequent events:

She sat listening to the wrangling on the platform for a few minutes, and then began to exhibit distinct signs of impatience. As there seemed to be no improvement in sight, she then jumped up from her seat, shouted in a tone of military command the one word "Mohini!" and then walked straight out of the door into the passage. The stately and dignified Mohini came rushing down that long room at his highest speed, and as soon as he reached the passage threw himself incontinently flat on his face on the floor at the feet of the lady in black. Many people arose in confusion, not knowing what was happening; but a moment later Mr. Sinnett himself also came running to the door, went out and exchanged a few words, and then, re-entering the room, he stood up on the end of our bench and spoke in a ringing voice the fateful words: "Let me introduce to the London Lodge as a whole—Madame Blavatsky!"

The scene was indescribable; the members, wildly delighted and yet half-awed at the same time, clustered round our great Founder, some kissing her hand, several kneeling before her, and two or three weeping hysterically. After a few minutes, however, she shook them off impatiently, and was led up to the platform by Colonel Olcott, and after answering a few questions she demanded from him an explanation of the unsatisfactory character of the meeting upon which she had descended so abruptly. The Colonel and Mr. Sinnett explained as well as they could; but she summarily ordered them to close the meeting, and called upon the officials to meet her at once in conference. The members departed in a condition of wild excitement and the officials waited upon Madame Blavatsky in one of the adjacent living rooms.

Now, as I had been invited to spend the night at Mr. Sinnett's, I, though a new and insignificant member, had to stay behind along with the greater people; and so it happened that I was a witness of the very remarkable scene which followed. Madame Blavatsky demanded a full account of the condition of the Lodge, and of the differences between Mr. Sinnett and Dr. Kingsford; and having received it, she proceeded to rate both of them exactly as if they had been a pair of naughty schoolboys, and finally actually made them both shake hands before us all as a token that their differences were amicably settled! . . .

Madame Blavatsky and Colonel Olcott both accompanied our party to Mr. Sinnett's house and stayed there until a late hour, Madame Blavatsky expressing vigourous condemnation of the inefficiency of the officials in not managing the meeting better. I was of course presented to her, and Mr. Sinnett took occasion to tell her of my letter to the spiritualistic journal *Light* on the subject of the spirit Ernest's disavowal of our Masters. When she heard that little story she looked at me searchingly and remarked,

"I don't think much of the clergy, for I find most of them hypocritical, bigoted and stupid; but that was a brave action, and I thank you for it. You have made a good beginning; perhaps you may do something yet."

. . . I wish I could convey to my readers some adequate conception of what she was to me and to all of us who were so highly favoured as to come into close touch with her—of the truly tremendous impression that she made upon us, of the deep affection and the intense enthusiasm which she evoked.[14]

H.P.B. explained to the Sinnetts that she had suddenly decided to come to London because she felt she simply had to be present at the election.

"And if I hadn't, would it ever have ended?" she asked.

"Probably we would have been still sitting there," Patience said with her pleasant chuckle.

H.P.B. remained with the Sinnetts for a week before returning to Paris, Olcott and Mohini having moved to the home of the Arundales. Throngs of visitors filled the Sinnett home during that time, but there were no further startling developments.

When they had seen H.P.B. off on the train that was to carry her to the channel crossing and had waved farewell to her from the platform, Patience observed:

"I really believe she didn't want to go."

"She will be back," her husband replied somewhat grimly. "And I am not too happy about that. Meanwhile, my dear, you look tired out. I think we should go somewhere for a little holiday."

Suiting the deed to the thought, they left soon for a few weeks in Hastings, where Patience had no responsibilities of hospitality or of housekeeping, and she returned quite refreshed.

The "Hermetic Lodge T.S." became an established fact on the 9th of April. Unfortunately, it did not prove to be a resolution of the problem. The members wanted to get the benefit of the studies in both Lodges, and "the effect was to keep up the excitement."[15] The Colonel was finally obliged to issue a new rule to the effect that "multiple membership would not be allowed; no person could be an active member of more than one branch simultaneously; and where double membership existed, choice should be made in which group the individual preferred to remain."

The effect of this was to threaten the disruption of the Hermetic Lodge. After consultations with Massey, Olcott suggested that Mrs. Kingsford should return her charter and form her friends into an independent society, thus making it feasible for members to belong to both groups if they wished to do so. This plan was eventually effected and the former Hermetic Lodge T.S. became the "Hermetic Society" with Mrs. Kingsford as President and Mr. Maitland as Vice-President. Their first meeting was held on May 9th, and Olcott "made a friendly address of good wishes and sympathy for the new society."[16]

Col. Olcott was being somewhat lionized in these days. Interest in Theosophy was spreading throughout London's social circles; the Colonel met Sir Edwin Arnold, who invited him to lunch and gave him some pages from the original manuscript of *The Light of Asia.* * He discussed Theosophy with the poet Robert Browning; Earl Russell invited him to Oxford for a night, and Lord Burthwick carried him off to his place in Scotland for a fortnight. "At one table I met an officer of the Queen's Household and a famous General; at another, one of the greatest of modern painters," reported Olcott.[17] "Everywhere the theme of talk was Theosophy; the tide was rising. The ebb was to follow, but as yet no one foresaw it in Europe, for it was to begin in Madras..."

*Now in the Archives at the International Headquarters of the Theosophical Society, Adyar, Madras, India.

20

The Coulomb "Revenge"

Before leaving Adyar on the European trip, Col. Olcott had appointed a committee, which he named the Board of Control, with Dr. Franz Hartmann as Chairman, to manage the affairs of headquarters during his and H.P.B.'s absence. Although the physician was relatively new in the Theosophical Society, Olcott had considerable confidence in him. He was a naturalized American citizen of Bavarian birth, deeply interested in philosophy, widely traveled, and a student of comparative religions, including those of the American Indians. Other members of the Board of Control were Damodar, Subba Row, St. George Lane-Fox—an electrical engineer recently arrived from England—and W. T. Brown, the young Scotsman who had accompanied Olcott on his recent trip in northern India. The Colonel was pondering whether he should expand the committee further still, when Emma Coulomb came into his room after a brief knock. He had answered with a preoccupied "Come in" and he now turned to her in some impatience.

"Yes, Mrs. Coulomb?"

She was smiling her most ingratiating smile.

"Mr. Olcott," she said, "I hope you won't mind if I come to you with a suggestion."

As a matter of fact, he did mind, for he was not pleased at being interrupted; there were many decisions to make and many arrangements to complete before he and H.P.B. could get away. Further, he didn't particularly like the woman. He regarded her as a gossip and a tale-bearer who was constantly pontificating on religious matters of which her ignorance was pronounced. But he realized that his long absences had given him little opportunity to observe her. He knew that H.P.B. disliked and distrusted her, but he had never had an explanation of this attitude from his colleague and he had more or less judged it to be one of her idiosyncrasies. So far as he was aware, Mme. Coulomb was a hard worker and discharged her housekeeping duties faithfully; she had been in complete charge of these functions since the departure of Rosa Bates while they were still located in Bombay. She made at least a show of being devoted to H.P.B., and occasionally he had felt a little sorry for her when he thought his "chum" was being unnecessarily short with her over some trifling matter. Remembering this now, he was moved by his innate fairness to forget his impatience. He sat back from his desk.

"Of course not," he assured her. "What's on your mind?"

"It's about this Board of Control, Mr. Olcott. I wonder why you didn't put my husband on it."

"Coulomb?" Olcott raised his eyebrows in surprise. "I hadn't thought of it. Why do you think he should be on it?"

"Well, you see," her eyes were shaded so that he could not be sure of her emotion although he took it to be one of slight embarrassment, "I think he is going to be hurt if you ignore him. He's been with you now for three years, and he has worked hard. He has the welfare of the Society at heart, and—well, you see, Mr. Olcott, my husband is a proud man, and it is just going to crush him if you treat him like he doesn't matter."

Olcott thought this a bit extravagant, but he had nothing against Alexis Coulomb. The man seemed capable. He was extremely handy with tools of all kinds, and in a place the size of Adyar there was constant need for someone with knowledge of carpentry and other maintenance skills. He was also a clever draftsman, with a flair for copying the handwriting of other people—his own being not unlike that of H.P.B.'s as a matter of fact.[1] So far he had used this talent only as a kind of game* and it never crossed the Colonel's mind that it might later be employed for a more deadly purpose. He considered Coulomb a

---

*In a letter written to Sinnett some time later, H.P.B. commented: "We all know how Damodar was once deceived by an order written *in my handwriting* to go upstairs and seek for me in my bedroom in Bombay, when I was in Allahabad. It was a trick of M. Coulomb, who thought it good fun to deceive him, 'a chela,'—and had prepared a semblance of myself lying on my bed, and having startled Damodar—laughed at him for three days. Unfortunately that bit of a note was not preserved. It was not intended for any phenomenon but simply 'a good farce' by Coulomb, who indulged in many." (LBS 115)

quiet, well-behaved person, seemingly perfectly honest. He was later to write in his diary: "If I had even an inkling of her (Mme. Coulomb's) real character, instead of making her husband...a Committee man, I should have had our servants chase them out of our compound with bamboo switches."[2]

On that day in February 1884, however, Olcott had no suspicion that the Coulombs would indeed prove treacherous. Mme. Coulomb reminded him again that he had known her husband for several years and added that some other members of the Board of Control were relatively new in the Theosophical Society and could not possibly be as familiar as he was with the requirements of headquarters.

Olcott disliked being pushed into making a decision without the opportunity to consider it from all angles, but he was eager to end the interview and he could foresee no developments which might cause him to regret such a move as Mme. Coulomb was suggesting.

"Very well," he said finally. "Tell your husband I will place him on the Board and will send him a written statement to that effect. Now, if you will excuse me..."

Turning again to his desk, he missed the light of triumph which flared briefly in his visitor's eyes. But she could not entirely keep the feeling from her voice as she expressed her thanks and left the room. That undertone struck a note of uneasiness in him but he dismissed it at once, since he felt he had weightier matters to consider.

Olcott was not then aware that Mrs. Coulomb had tried numerous times to get money from wealthy visitors at Adyar. In particular she had approached a well-to-do nobleman, Prince Hurrisinghi, member of the Theosophical Society, for a "loan" of 2,000 rupees, with which she anticipated that she and her husband would start a hotel business—something that had always fascinated them. The Prince was considerably embarrassed, not knowing precisely what position she occupied in the household. He half-promised, "probably hoping that the matter would be forgotten, at least until such time as he could find out more about what was behind the request."[3]

Mme. Coulomb blamed H.P.B. for her failures in this respect, even those of which H.P.B. was unaware. "She cursed everybody in general and Madame Blavatsky especially,"

wrote Dr. Franz Hartmann,* "and told me under the seal of
secrecy that Madame Blavatsky was indebted to her for
money lent to her in Egypt; but when cross-questioned afterwards she denied the statement and declared herself to be
indebted to Madame Blavatsky. Madame Blavatsky was
naturally annoyed by these proceedings; but a few tears shed
by Madame Coulomb with the assistance of a handkerchief, set
the matter all right."[4]

Dr. Hartmann considered Mme. Coulomb rather an ob-
noxious person, a mischief-maker who went around eaves-
dropping, looking through keyholes, and generally appearing
when she was not wanted. "She had a real flair for prying into
other peoples' affairs," he commented.[5]

H.P.B. and Col. Olcott, engrossed with plans for their
departure, paid no attention to small domestic annoyances, for
at this time no suspicion of a conspiracy disturbed them.

Shortly after arriving at Adyar, Dr. Hartmann had offered
his services to the Masters in a note which he gave to Olcott,
who placed it in the Shrine."‡ A reply received from the
Mahatma M. two weeks later informed the doctor that he (the
Master) had inspired Olcott with the idea of suggesting that
Hartmann come to Adyar. He advised the doctor to remain
and take part in the work of the Society.†

Just before the departure of the travelers, Hartmann received another letter from the Mahatma M. which indicated
the latter's foreknowledge of the crisis which was to take place.
This letter came to him in a remarkable manner.

He had sought out H.P.B. to ask her about a matter over
which he had been puzzling.

"Why don't you ask the Master?" she said, after she had
listened to his rather hesitant presentation of his problem. "I

---

*Dr. Franz Hartmann wrote a *Report of Observations Made During a Nine-
Months Stay at the Headquarters of the Theosophical Society,* published
October 4, 1884, by Graves, Cookson & Co., Madras. It contains a valuable
record of this period.

‡A portable cabinet which had been constructed in the "Occult Room" next
door to H.P.B.'s room for the purpose of sending and receiving correspondence with the Masters. It could be taken apart to enable H.P.B. to pack it in
her trunk while she was traveling in the hills during the hot season at
Adyar. (*Damodar* 531)

†From the English rendering of the German text published in Lotusblüthen
LXV, 142-3. The original English text has not been published. (*Damodar*
601)

think you would get an answer." She was silent for a few moments and then added, "Do you not feel his presence? I do, and I am sure he is writing something."

Dr. Hartmann was certain that he too felt the influence of the Master; he could almost see his face. He was about to say something to this effect when Mme. Coulomb came into the room.

He didn't like the way the woman suddenly appeared whenever and wherever she pleased and regardless of what private conversation she might be interrupting. He wondered whether she had been listening but decided that probably she had not or she would have stayed out of sight to hear his reply to H.P.B. She seemed rather in a hurry.

"Madame," she said, "I need the pincers and I can't put my hands on them. Do you have them by any chance?"

"I?" queried H.P.B. in surprise. "What would I be doing with pincers?"

Dr. Hartmann was about to let Mme. Coulomb deal with her own frustration when he was suddenly moved to say:

"I have some in my desk. I'll get them for you."

Wondering a little why he bothered, he went to his room and opened the drawer of his desk. The pincers, along with a few other articles, lay there. He had removed his papers from that drawer on the previous evening so that nothing even resembling a letter was among the items. He picked up the pincers and was about to close the drawer when suddenly a large envelope appeared before his eyes. It was addressed to him in the well-known handwriting of the Master, and the seal bore the Master's initials in Tibetan characters.

Hurriedly he opened the envelope and scanned the contents. It was a long, very kind letter dealing with the matters he had just been discussing with H.P.B.

"Now, if I know anything at all," he wrote later, "I know that my drawer contained no such letter when I opened it, and that there was nobody visible in my room at the time. The letter...must have been written, sealed and put into the drawer in less than four minutes, while it took exactly forty minutes to copy it the next day...."[6]*

*For excerpts from this letter see *Damodar* 602. Nowhere is the letter given in full; apparently it contained direct personal advice to Dr. Hartmann. There was in the same envelope a photograph, cabinet-size, of the Master's face, with a dedication to Hartmann on the back of it.

Dr. Hartmann returned to H.P.B.'s room and delivered the pincers to Mme. Coulomb. She murmured something that might have been "Thank you" and went on about her work. He showed the envelope to H.P.B. and explained where he had found it.

"I haven't yet read it thoroughly," he said, "but I note the Master mentions 'a variety of unexpected emergencies' which he says he foresees. I'm inclined to wish you and Col. Olcott weren't going away."

"There are always unexpected emergencies, I have found. If we could foresee them they wouldn't be emergencies. Still," she looked thoughtful, "if my Boss mentioned them I'm sure they will not be unimportant... Well, I know that Olcott and I are both grateful to you for taking on so much responsibility while we are away."

"With inspiration such as I find in this letter," he replied, "I should be a coward not to try, at least."

"You must feel free to use my rooms and my desk—and my library, of course—whenever you wish," H.P.B. said kindly.

"That is indeed generous of you," he replied. "I expect I shall take advantage of the offer."

He was to remember this later when the time came to test that offer.

Hartmann and a few others, including Mme. Coulomb, went with the travelers—Col. Olcott, H.P.B., Mohini Chatterji, and the faithful servant Babula—to Bombay to see them off and to wish them *bon voyage.* The Doctor wondered why Mme. Coulomb was permitted to go, but understood that she had pleaded for H.P.B.'s permission; he supposed it took more energy to refuse than to say yes, and H.P.B. seemed rather weary and nervous as they left Adyar. En route to Bombay they stopped for a short visit with Prince Hurrishinghi, and here, it developed, Mme. Coulomb found opportunity to remind the prince of his "promise." But this time H.P.B. heard of it and "unceremoniously put a stop to the whole matter."[7]

Mme. Coulomb managed with great difficulty to hide her fury over this development as they continued on their journey but it nevertheless seethed beneath the surface. When finally she bade farewell to H.P.B., however, she was profuse in her protestations of friendship and loyalty.

"I shall guard your things with my life," she said, dabbing her eyes with a handkerchief and sniffling realistically. "I don't know how I shall endure your absence for so long a time."

"You will manage," H.P.B. assured her rather shortly. She gave the woman a keen glance. "You have the Board of Control to fall back upon if any difficulties arise."

As usual, Mme. Coulomb lowered her eyes—a trick she had when she did not wish others to discover her real feelings. Her hands trembled but she did not speak until H.P.B. had turned away and only Babula remained near her, holding tightly to some of the innumerable items which his mistress insisted on taking with her whenever she traveled. Then Mme. Coulomb turned on the unsuspecting servant and said in a low voice which shook with anger:

"Let her make no mistake! I'll have my revenge on her for preventing me from getting my two thousand rupees!"

Babula considered this to be merely Mme. Coulomb's customary spitefulness and did not trouble to repeat it to his mistress until some time later, when the "revenge" was under way.

Before returning to Adyar with the rest of the group, Mme. Coulomb left them to visit with some clergymen whose names she did not reveal.[8] It was known, however, that as early as 1881, while the headquarters of the Theosophical Society was still in Bombay, she had tried to sell some "secrets" to a clergyman there but had been repulsed.[9] Whether this was her object at this time, no one knew, for she kept her own council.

Back at Adyar, Alexis Coulomb assumed possession of H.P.B.'s rooms, where he remained for hours at a time with the door locked, engaged in some mysterious occupation which he did not explain until Dr. Hartmann questioned him. The rain had done some damage to one of the walls, he said, and he had been busy repairing it. Mme. Coulomb had the keys to the room and only she, in addition to her husband, was admitted at any time.

On a day when Dr. Hartmann called a meeting of the Board of Control, it seemed advisable to find a place where they could be entirely free of interruption or disturbance of any kind. Remembering H.P.B.'s offer, he proposed that the Board should convene in her quarters. But to this M. Coulomb made the immediate objection.

"I have Madame's orders," he said stiffly. "I am not to permit *anyone* to go upstairs until she returns."

The Doctor looked at him in astonishment.

"But she expressly offered the use of her rooms and her library at any time I might wish," he protested. "She made the same offer to Subba Row and others, I understand."

Coulomb was adamant.

"I cannot and I will not admit anyone to Madame's rooms without her express instruction to me."

"But that will take months to get—unless we telegraph," Hartmann argued, "and it's too absurd for that."

"It is her order," insisted M. Coulomb. "And I do not disobey it."

Dr. Hartmann did not believe the man but there was nothing he could do at the moment, since he had no way of gaining access to the upstairs. The Board of Control had perforce to meet elsewhere.[10] Coulomb sat stiffly throughout the session, listening but making no contribution to the discussion.

Dr. Hartmann wrote at once to H.P.B. but it was three months before her explanation reached him. It came in a letter addressed to Mr. Lane-Fox answering some of that gentleman's questions:

"She (Mme. Coulomb)" wrote H.P.B., "swore to me that she would take care of my rooms, only asking me to let it be known that *she alone* had the right over all and would have and keep the key. Having told Dr. Hartmann that he was welcome to my books and my desk in my absence, she made a vow when alone with me, and declared that if I allowed one single person to have access to my rooms, she would answer for nothing—that the 'shrine' would be desecrated, etc."

H.P.B. enclosed in the envelope a blackmailing letter which she had received from Mme. Coulomb in which the latter warned her to "beware of the consequences of a rupture."[11]

"This shows," wrote Dr. Hartmann in his *Report,* "how Madame Coulomb gained possession of the upper story. It was necessary for the Coulombs to remain in that possession, as without it their plot could not be carried to a successful conclusion."

Writing of these circumstances, a later historian commented:

Alexis Coulomb evidently soon began to make various holes, sliding panels and trap doors in the wall between H.P.B.'s bedroom and the so-called "Occult Room" in which the portable Shrine was hanging. The latter had been used as a kind of "astral post office" containing two pictures of the Masters. He soon found that the undertaking was more difficult than he had imagined. Exhaustive examinations later on proved that his panels and trap doors never worked smoothly and that had they been in actual use, they would probably have been detected forthwith.

Had Madame Coulomb been able to hold her tongue, however, chances are that her husband would have been able to construct a more convincing set of contrivances and thus make Madame Blavatsky and her colleagues look worse in the eyes of the world than they did. As good luck would have it, one day, she taunted Damodar and told him that Mme. Blavatsky had ordered her husband to construct trap doors.[12]

This was a mistake. Damodar promptly issued an affidavit:

"On the evening of March 7th, 1884, I asked Mr. Coulomb for the use of Madame Blavatsky's rooms, but he said he could not grant my request as Madame Blavatsky was very strict about her rooms, books, etc., and that he would have to be responsible for them.

"Madame Coulomb repeatedly said that she had a grievance against Madame Blavatsky and was determined to get her 'revenge...' She said that she did not feel in sympathy with the society and that her conscience revolted against it. A few days after that she said that she would burst up the society."[13]

There ensued a critical and confusing period during which other affidavits were received from various members. The Board of Control, exclusive of M. Coulomb, made plans to "impeach the Coulombs because of many charges of 'gross misconduct'—lying about the Society, slandering its officers, wasting the Society's money, etc."[14]

Then came a surprising letter from the Mahatma K.H. addressed to Dr. Hartmann and advising kindness toward Mme. Coulomb, saying that she was "irresponsible" but suggesting that she be left in charge of the household duties except that the Board of Control should see that no unnecessary expenditures were incurred. "A good deal of reform is necessary and can be made rather with the help than the antagonism of Mme. C." the letter said.[15]

At first, in view of the known perfidy of Mme. Coulomb, Dr. Hartmann was inclined to doubt the authenticity of this letter.

But it came in an unquestionable manner. The Board of Control was, in fact, engaged in drawing up the charges against the Coulombs when "the astral body of a Chela appeared and handed the...letter to Damodar."[16] It was in the handwriting of the Mahatma K.H., enclosed in a Chinese envelope, and addressed to Dr. Hartmann.[17]

"It was well that we obeyed the instructions," Hartmann was to write later. "An explosion produced at that time would have been premature, and transatlantic telegrams might have seriously interfered with Col. Olcott's work in Europe."[18]

The letter did not, however, stop the efforts of the Board of Control to remove the Coulombs from Adyar. Dr. Hartmann offered them a fourth interest in some silver mines which he owned in Colorado in the United States, and Mr. Lane-Fox was willing to lend them the money to get themselves there.[19] They seemed delighted with the suggestion but did nothing to put it into effect.

In late March, Damodar and Mr. Lane-Fox planned to go to Ootacamund, and Mme. Coulomb asked that she might accompany them. Probably in some relief at getting her away from Adyar for a time, her request was approved and she was given money to buy some new clothes. While at Ootacamund, she became very pious, attended church often, and made frequent visits to her "spiritual advisers." She urged all those with whom she came in contact to sever their connections with the Theosophical Society, saying that it was "all humbug, the phenomena were not genuine, and she could reveal a great deal if she chose to do so."[20]

In London, Col. Olcott received from Mme. Coulomb a letter purporting to be directed to her by Dr. Hartmann charging H.P.B. with lying and Col. Olcott with being "no better than he should be." On the back of this letter, in the handwriting of the Mahatma M. was a short note: "A clumsy forgery, but good enough to show how much an enterprising enemy can do in this direction...M"[21] Later, Dr. Hartmann, when he saw the letter, admitted that the handwriting somewhat resembled his own but called it "stupid" and "a forgery."[22]

Near the end of April Dr. Hartmann received a letter from a friend in Europe and found, on the inside, in the handwriting of the Mahatma M.: "The matter is serious. I will send you a letter through Damodar. Study it carefully. M."

Damodar was still in Ootacamund, but a few days later the promised letter came from him. The Mahatma M. wrote:

"April 26, 1884.—For some time already the woman has opened communication—a regular diplomatic *pourparler* with the enemies of the cause, certain padres.—She hopes for more than 2,000 Rupees from them, if she helps them ruining or at least injuring the Society by injuring the reputation of the founders. Hence hints as to 'trap doors' and tricks. Moreover when *needed* trapdoors *will be found,* as they have been forthcoming for some time. They are sole masters of the top storey. They have full entrance to and control the premises.

"'Monsieur' is clever and cunning at every handicraft, good mechanic and carpenter and good at walls likewise. *Take note of this ye Theosophists.* They hate you with all the hatred of failure against success; the Society, Henry, H.P.B., theosophists, and aye the very name Theosophy. The _____ are ready to lay out a good sum for the ruin of the Society they hate. Moreover the J_____ in India are in direct understanding with those of London and Paris.

"Keep all said above in strictest confidence, if you would be strongest. Let her not suspect you know it, but if you would have my advice be prudent. Yet act without delay.—M."[23]

A letter came to Mme. Coulomb (with a copy to Damodar) from Col. Olcott in Paris, telling her he had received information about the falsehoods she had been circulating concerning "trap doors and other apparatus for trick manifestations" and that she had openly expressed her hostility toward the Theosophical Society. He was "saddened" by these disclosures, he said, but assured her that "the theosophical movement does not rest at all for its permanency upon phenomena, and even if you could prove that every supposed phenomena ever witnessed by me or anyone else was false, it would not alter my opinion one iota as to the benefit to be derived by the world from the Society's work . . ." He pointed out that phenomena occurred even when H.P.B. was not present—when she was far away, as a matter of fact. "I must tell you candidly," he said, "that I do *not* think it right or fair that you should either help to injure the Society by unsettling people's minds about H.P.B. or myself, or any one else working with us, or by hinting that there was any political design hidden under the surface, when you know or ought to know that it as false as false can be."* There was more to this letter, all couched in the Colonel's usual forthright manner.[24]

For some reason Damodar did not at once share with other members of the Board of Control his copy of this letter—a fact which caused Dr. Hartmann considerable irritation when he discovered it.[25]

The party returned from Ootacamund and the question of whether the Coulombs would go to America again arose. M. Coulomb said yes; Mme. Coulomb said no. She wasn't satisfied with the financial arrangements, hoping that the individuals with whom she was negotiating for the sale of her "secrets" might be more generous. Further, she still cherished hopes of revenge. The result was that she and her husband had a violent quarrel, which did nothing to lighten the atmosphere at Adyar or to resolve the problem of their departure. When asked about their plans, they announced coolly that they would not leave until Madame Blavatsky had returned.

This contingency was an unfortunate one, for a letter came from H.P.B. saying that she would not return to Adyar as long as the Coulombs were there.[26]

A meeting of the General Council of the Theosophical Society was therefore called, and ten charges were brought against Mme. Coulomb, although she was tried on only three:

1. Four affidavits stated that Mme. Coulomb had told members that the object of the Society was to overthrow British rule in India.
2. Nine affidavits stated that she had said that the objects of the Society were against true religion.
3. Ten affidavits gave evidence that she claimed that the phenomena were either frauds or the work of the devil.

Mme. Coulomb neither admitted nor denied the charges, but the evidence was so conclusive that she was unanimously ordered expelled from the Society. The husband was asked to resign, but as he could not make up his mind he was also expelled.[27] However, he reiterated that they would not leave before H.P.B. returned and declared their intention to move upstairs and live in her rooms.

Telegrams were immediately dispatched to H.P.B. and Olcott asking that M. Coulomb be released from his "duty" to

---

*Mme. Coulomb had revived the old accusation that H.P.B. was a Russian spy and that the Theosophical Society was a subversive organization.

maintain the sanctity of H.P.B.'s quarters. The response was, of course, prompt and positive. The entrance to the rooms had been put under guard to prevent the Coulomb's from taking possession, and Mr. Coulomb finally capitulated and surrendered the keys. He insisted, however, that this be done in the presence of witnesses. Mme. Coulomb added what she no doubt thought was leverage by demanding Rs. 3000 for her "silence"—a demand which was completely ignored.*

A committee composed of Dr. Hartmann and several others, including Subba Row, Damodar, and W. T. Brown, went to H.P.B.'s rooms to examine them. They found that M. Coulomb had indeed done some work there but that it was incomplete. There was, however, no communication between the shrine and the other room. M. Coulomb confessed to having made all the holes and sliding panels which were discovered but claimed that this was at the command of Madame Blavatsky—an illogical statement on the face of it, the Committee felt, for why should H.P.B. suddenly need these devices when she had been performing phenomena for years without them? It was decided to leave them intact, however.

"It was evident," said Dr. Hartmann in his Report, "that with very little labour these traps could have been finished and made to look very suspicious, and we have reason to believe that it was M. Coulomb's intention to finish them before Madame Blavatsky's return from Europe."[28] Perhaps then, with H.P.B. helpless in the face of the "evidence," Mme. Coulomb would have her full "revenge."

A few days after this inspection, M. Coulomb requested a private interview with Dr. Hartmann. It turned out to be anything but private, as his wife stood near the door and listened to the whole conversation; and when M. Coulomb informed the Doctor that 10,000 rupees had been placed at his disposal if he would ruin the Theosophical Society, she called out to him in French, "Do not commit yourself!"[29]

M. Coulomb was immediately disabused of any hope he might have cherished that the Theosophical Society would be willing to purchase his "silence" with a like sum.

---

*The following statement is found in *Damodar* 587: "It is significant that with all these 'disclosures' and implied threats not one word was mentioned in regard to any letters between Madame Blavatsky and Madame Coulomb which three months later were to open the lid to Pandora's box."

On the 25th day of May the Coulombs finally left Adyar "and were received in the home of their new friends in Madras. Their plans having miscarried so far, they now set about to remedy their failures and achieve their ends through new methods."[30]

Note: The reader will understand that it is impossible to include in a book of this kind all the references to and accounts of what has come to be called "The Coulomb Conspiracy." Descriptions vary slightly in minor details but all basically agree on what took place. By far the most succinct and explicit account of these happenings and the investigation by Richard Hodgson of the Society for Psychical Research which followed, is found in the small book, *Obituary: The "Hodgson Report" on Madame Blavatsky* by Adlai E. Waterman, Adyar: Theosophical Publishing House, 1963. This powerful little book contains a photographic copy of Richard Hodgson's Plan of the then second floor of the headquarters building at Adyar, showing the rooms of H.P. Blavatsky and the arrangement of the Occult Room where the controversial Shrine was located. Other valuable accounts will be found in *Old Diary Leaves* by Henry Steel Olcott, Volume 3; *Damodar and the Pioneers of the Theosophical Movement* by Sven Eek; *A Short History of the Theosophical Society* by Josephine Ransom; Howard Murphet's two biographies, *Hammer on the Mountain* (Olcott) and *When Daylight Comes* (H.P.B.), and other works having to do with the history of the Theosophical Society.

Coming Events Cast Shadows

"I tell you, we have got them thinking!" said Col. Olcott glee-fully, as he, with Sinnett and Mohini, left the rooms of the of the Society for Psychical Research where they had just met with a special Committee of Investigation.* "Mohini, you did yourself proud. I was pleased with your comments."

"Thank you, sir," responded the younger man. "The questions were not always easy to answer."

The interview had been concerned with the receipt of letters from the Mahatmas, the precipitation of handwriting, phe-nomena connected with the shrine room at Adyar, the Adepts' telepathic powers, and other happenings in which the three had been involved and which were not explainable in terms of ordinary experience.

"They were generally open-minded," added Sinnett. "Except Podmore, of course."

The Committee had consisted of Messrs. F.W.H. Myers, Edmund Gurney, Herbert Stack, Frank Podmore, all members of the Society for Psychical Research, and its President, Prof. Sidgwick.[1] The aim was to explore and, if possible, assess the validity of the paranormal phenomena connected with H.P. Blavatsky, the Theosophical Society, and the Mahatmas. Podmore was the only one who seemed determined to deny that there could possibly be any validity in these manifes-tations. Abnormality had to be assumed, he conceded, but one must assume abnormal dishonesty on the part of the persons

---

*It is not entirely clear from the source material whether these three gentle-men were interviewed by the SPR separately or in a group. But all were interviewed. For the purposes of this story it is expedient to handle the matter as though it were a single occasion.

involved rather than abnormal psychic powers.[2] This attitude seemed to Sinnett unscientific and he said so.

"He scarcely listens to the evidence," offered Mohini. "It seems he has already decided that it can't be so."

"Nevertheless," said Olcott soberly, "we told the truth. In every instance. I could not detect in any of the evidence we gave the slightest tendency to embellish or distort the truth. Podmore to the contrary!"

"They had to admit that some things simply couldn't be explained away," Sinnett pointed out, and Mohini added with a smile, "Much as they seemed to want to."

And indeed when the Society for Psychical Research issued a "preliminary and provisional report" on this early evidence, it was with the admission that there was a *prima facie* case for some part at least of the claims made and that these could not be ignored.[3] The report was circulated only among members of the Society for Psychical Research, and no firm conclusions were ventured.

The meeting with the Committee of Investigation took place on May 11, 1884, only a few days before the Coulombs, in India, finally left Adyar to go to the home of one of the missionaries in Madras. The disagreeable events transpiring at the Theosophical Society headquarters, however, had seemed more in the nature of annoyances than of grave concern to Olcott, and even to H.P.B., who was enjoying great popularity in Paris. It was not believed that the Coulombs could actually do serious or permanent harm to the Society; this in spite of the fact that the Mahatma K.H., in the letter to Olcott which had dropped over Mohini's head when the two of them were en route to London, had warned him not to be surprised at any news coming from Adyar. Nor should he be discouraged, the Master had added. "You have harboured a traitor and an enemy under your roof for years," he said, "and the missionary party are more than ready to avail of any help she may be induced to give. A regular conspiracy is on foot."[4]

But even this ominous note was all but lost in the enthusiasm and high hopes engendered by the success of the Theosophical Society in Europe. The work in Paris was going well; a German branch of the Society was beginning to seem more than a possibility, with the wealthy Gebhard family of

Elberfeld as its nucleus;* and, in London, where Sinnett's
Esoteric Buddhism had been such an unexpected success,
Theosophy was more and more popular with the intelligentsia.
The Sinnetts still held their regular "at home" on Tuesday
afternoons, and their drawing room was "always crowded with
Theosophical friends and visitors whom they brought."[5] Many
of these visitors they were never to see again or, at most, only
a few times. A number were to continue and commit their
interest to the new movement in which they found such inspiration and such liberating ideas. Three in particular were to
play a prominent part in the future of Theosophy in Europe.
These included Countess Constance Wachtmeister, English-
born wife of a Swedish diplomat, who had met H.P.B. in Paris,
who was herself clairvoyant and clairaudient, and who later
was to be a source of great strength and encouragement to
H.P.B. throughout the writing of *The Secret Doctrine.* The
other two were Mr. Bertram Keightley and his nephew Dr.
Archibald Keightley, who were to be instrumental in launching
the first edition of H.P.B.'s greatest work. The excitement and
interest were intense and the clouds of disaster beginning to
loom on the horizon were as yet unrecognized.

About this time a young American widow, Mrs. Laura Holloway, came to London, "determined to find out the truth"
about the Mahatmas. She herself had some clairvoyance; she
had read *The Occult World* and *Esoteric Buddhism* and had
resolved that she herself would become a chela or "upset the
whole imposture" if it turned out to be such.[6] She stayed for
about a week with the Arundales before accepting the
invitation of the Sinnetts to make an extended visit with them,
Olcott having moved to the Arundales in the meantime.
Sinnett was much impressed with Mrs. Holloway, believing
her to be "a wonderfully gifted psychic."[7] Mr. W. Q. Judge,
who knew the lady, had written to Olcott from Paris that she
was possibly ". . . a magnificent coadjutor, *if not* a successor
to H.P.B. and one who has trained abilities of the kind that
make H.P.B. so remarkable." He commented also that when

---

*The Gebhards and Sinnetts had been friends for some time. Mrs. Mary
Gebhard had personally traveled to London to meet them in August 1883,
after reading *Esoteric Buddhism,* and the Sinnetts had later paid the
Gebhards a somewhat lengthy visit. (*Autobiography* 37-8).

this possibility was mentioned to H.P.B. she exclaimed: "Oh my God, if I shall only find in her a successor, how gladly will I peg out."[*8]

It was, however, Mrs. Holloway who later was to be the unintentional cause of strained relations between Sinnett and the Arundales. While this was not an immediate development, it coincided with other events which transpired during that fateful summer, when an irreparable *faux pas* by Col. Olcott, together with repercussions from Mme. Coulomb's machinations in India, brought the prestige of the Theosophical Society, and particularly that of H.P.B., crashing about the heads of the faithful on both sides of the world.

In late June, H.P.B. returned to London from Paris as a guest of the Arundales. When she and Mrs. Holloway met, they seemed at once to be friendly. Although Mrs. Holloway's psychic faculties were as yet undeveloped, she understood and appreciated something of the enormous capacities of the older woman, and the latter was in turn unfailingly kind and helpful to her. No ripple disturbed the smooth-flowing current of theosophical progress.

On June 30, a group which included the Sinnetts, Olcott, Mrs. Holloway, the Arundales, Mohini, H.P.B. and some others, attended a gathering of the Society for Psychical Research. They were looking forward pleasantly to an interesting evening, and, as the meeting progressed, this anticipation seemed wholly justified. Only Patience felt some uneasiness but told herself that she was probably only borrowing trouble.

For a time it seemed she might be right. The program moved smoothly and held the attention of the audience. It was not until well along in the evening that both she and her husband became aware that H.P.B. was watching Olcott with a shade of anxiety in her eyes. What this meant Sinnett himself had no idea, although he was aware that the speaker—later he could not even remember who this was—had made some comments to which Olcott, with his boundless enthusiasm for his own convictions, might well take exception. Almost, H.P.B.

---

[*]The Master K.H., however, wrote of Mrs. Holloway in this respect: "Her clairvoyance is a fact, her selection and chelaship, another. However well fitted psychically and physiologically to answer such selection, unless possessed of spiritual, as well as of physical unselfishness, a chela whether selected or not, must perish as a chela in the long run." (ML 359/353)

seemed to be holding the Colonel in his seat by the very force of her will. But eventually this proved unequal to whatever it was in him that forced him suddenly to his feet. He had not been invited to speak; he had not asked to be recognized; he simply burst forth into what was probably the most inexcusable extemporaneous speech he had ever made in his life. He pulled from his pocket a ridiculous Indian toy which he had carried about with him of late. It was a tin figure of the Buddha mounted on wheels, which could be moved about in a way which was supposed to represent ideas connected with the Buddhist faith. It was at best a childish thing; at worst, foolish and vulgar.

For some reason Patience had anticipated that he might do something indiscreet in connection with this toy, since he was so fascinated with it, and she had gone that afternoon to the Arundales to warn H.P.B. of the possibility and suggest that she ask Olcott to leave it at home. But several other guests were present and she had no opportunity to speak to H.P.B. about it.[9] She tried to assure herself that he himself would see the bad taste of exhibiting it and would restrain his enthusiasm. This had proved a futile hope.

Everyone in the room was shocked; everyone was embarrassed for the speaker. But these reactions were mild compared to the feeling of the members of his own group. Sinnett had always deplored what he considered a lack of refinement and good taste in the American, although he tried to remember the fine and noble qualities which were also a part of the other man's character. At this moment his mind went back to the excruciating embarrassment he had felt when, on an occasion in his own home with friends gathered in elegant evening dress, Olcott had suddenly appeared in an Indian dhoti.* Neither the dhoti nor the shirt he wore with it was wholly fresh. The man seemed to have no sense of the fitness of things, Sinnett told himself now. Patience was embarrassed and her heart ached for both the Colonel and H.P.B. The others were suffering their own individual humiliations. But H.P.B. seemed frozen, her face a dead white, her eyes closed, her hands clutching each other until the knuckles lost all color.

"Let us go," she said finally in a low voice to Sinnett. But he shook his head.

*A loose garment worn below the waist by men in India.

"Too conspicuous," he answered, his own horror subsiding slightly as he felt his wife's hand slide into his and her fingers press his own. He returned the pressure and gave her a warm smile of gratitude.

When, at the close of the meeting, they finally did leave, it was in utter silence, without stopping to greet or to exchange comments with others as they would normally have done. The only words said during the whole miserable ride to the Sinnett's home were H.P.B.'s, "I am coming home with you," and Patience's response, "Of course you are." The Colonel looked completely dejected and offered no comment either in defense of or in apology for himself. Sinnett was hoping there would be some opportunity to point out tactfully to Col. Olcott that such antics were hardly looked upon with favor in the London circles in which he was now moving.

As it turned out there was little need for him to mention the fiasco to the American. H.P.B. herself took care of that. She restrained herself while in the carriage, but they were barely inside the Sinnetts' house before she unleashed her fury on her colleague. She was still livid and her voice shook as she turned on him.

"Well, Olcott, if you ever made an ass of yourself you did it tonight! What in God's name did you hope to accomplish by all that unmitigated nonsense? You've alienated the most powerful friends we had in London. You've set their teeth on edge! You've turned them all against us! God knows what will be the results of this night's work!"

There was much more. Once started, she seemed unable to stop; her denunciations grew so loud and piercing that Sinnett almost feared she would disturb the neighbors. She had known, she said, that Olcott was about to commit some assinine indiscretion and she had tried to prevent it. But all in vain. He was determined to be bombastic; he was determined to disgrace them all; he was determined to make the Masters ridiculous in the eyes of all those unbelievers!

Everyone in the room sat silent and appalled, with the exception of Olcott himself who kept moving about, "making futile remarks from time to time," saying he knew he had made a mistake but was willing to make up for it. At that, H.P.B. suggested that he leave the Theosophical Society, since he had so disgraced it. This was the deadliest thing she could have said. Olcott stared at her for a moment as though she had struck a knife into his heart. He held up his hand and his voice trembled as he replied:

"I don't care what you say. I am in the Society and I shall remain and work for it until the Master turns me out. Do you want me to commit suicide?"

H.P.B. seemed struggling for breath. Then, in a half-strangled voice, she said, "No. What's done is done."

No one else spoke. Finally H.P.B. added heavily:

"I'm as much of an ass as you are to let myself go like that. I wouldn't have had this happen for all the wealth in India. But whatever it means, we'll have to face the consequences."

She turned to the others, her face still strained and pale.

"It is for the cause I suffer," she muttered. "It is not for myself."*

As might have been expected it was the calm, soft voice of Patience Sinnett which brought some sanity back into the situation. She moved to touch Olcott's shoulder briefly in reassurance and then she took one of H.P.B.'s hands in her own.

"You must stay the night, dear Old Lady," she said, using the term by which they had all come to speak of and to Madame Blavatsky.[10] "You must surely be very tired."

"Yes," agreed H.P.B. "I *am* tired. But so is everyone else, I imagine. No, I must go on. I have imposed on all of you enough for one evening."

Sinnett made no protest. He did not know whether he was the more disgusted with her or with Olcott, and at the moment he wished profoundly that he was rid of both of them. He had never wanted H.P.B. to come to London in the first place. He was glad, now, that he had not dismissed the carriage for he wanted to see them gone. As he escorted them to the door he could not speak. They turned to thank him and to say good-night, but, seeing that he himself was barely able to control his anger, they went on silently and, as silently, returned to their lodgings at the Arundale's.

For once, Sinnett did not even want to discuss the situation with Patience. He was to write later that, in his opinion, all the tragic happenings which ensued during the rest of the year and beyond—H.P.B.'s disgrace and the near-collapse of the entire

*For Sinnett's account of this scene, on which the fictionalized version is based, *see* his *Autobiography* 42-3. See also *Guest* 51-2.

Theosophical Society—were "all the fruits of that miserable evening."[11]

This was undoubtedly too severe a judgment, for it failed to take into consideration the Coulombs and their machinations in India. But the incident obviously weighed heavily in subsequent decisions of the Society for Psychical Research. It continued to weigh heavily in Sinnett's mind also, and he found himself struggling with resentment and suspicion such as he had never before had to face. He hoped he could hide these feelings from Patience, but she was too perceptive to remain unaware that something was troubling him deeply and that even his attitude toward the Masters seemed to have undergone a subtle change. This distressed her also; she suffered intensely from what occasionally amounted to childish pettishness on the part of her husband. Wisely, she held her peace, hoping that he would eventually overcome the difficulty and even be able to talk it out with her. His feeling for the Old Lady seemed to be one of scarcely veiled hostility, and he did not even attempt to hide his outrage with Olcott.

A diversion of interest was provided by what appeared to be a burgeoning of Mrs. Holloway's psychic faculties. Vivid flashes which she claimed were pictures of the Mahatmas were impressed upon her frequently; she occasionally gave Sinnett messages which she said came from the Master K.H.; and on one occasion he was convinced that the Master actually possessed her and spoke to him directly.[12]

A slight strain had developed in the relations between Sinnett and the Arundales, due to some remark he had made which Mrs. Holloway had passed on and which his friends had interpreted as disloyal to the Masters.[13] In the hope that it might ease the situation, Sinnett wrote to the Master K.H. and, among other things, asked permission to tell Miss Arundale about the "direct" communication through Mrs. Holloway.

The answer came in a long and rather severe letter; the denial that Mrs. Holloway had been used as a medium was unequivocal.[14]

"You ask me if you can tell Miss Arundale what *I* told you thro' Mrs. Holloway," the Master wrote. "You are quite at liberty to explain to her the situation, and thereby justify in her eyes your *seeming* disloyalty and rebellion against us, as she thinks. You can do so the more since I have never bound you to anything thro' Mrs. H.; never communicated with you or any one else thro' her—nor have any of my, or M.'s chelas, to my knowledge...She is an excellent but quite undeveloped clairvoyante. Had she not been imprudently meddled with, and had you followed the old woman's and Mohini's advice indeed, by this time I might have spoken with you through her—and such *was* our intention."[15]

Sinnett simply did not believe this, so convinced was he of the validity of the session with Mrs. Holloway. Why should the Master take a stand that was patently false and totally inconsistent, he asked himself. Then the dark suspicions that had lately been tormenting him but which he had denied full recognition burst through his restraint. The Old Lady! She must have fabricated the whole letter—or dictated it to some chela or other. For it had come through her.

He went back to the beginning to scan the letter, seeing it this time through the eyes of his doubts rather than with his usual eagerness to learn and take to heart whatever the Master might say. For some reason he clung to his suspicions; they gave support to his belief in his own rightness. Several times he almost lost them, for the letter was so sincere, so characteristic of the Master's style and concern for underlying motivations that he had to keep reminding himself that the statement about Mrs. Holloway *had* to be wrong and that therefore the whole letter was suspect. Certainly the Master— if the letter *was* from the Master—made no effort to spare his feelings. But then, he never had. Still, that wasn't strictly true. He had been frank on many occasions, but he had always been kind. Well, this letter too was kind, Sinnett had to admit, even though he was not entirely willing to accept all that it said.

He tried to remember what he had written in his letter to the Master. Perhaps he had been too critical, too vehement. But he was sure he had said only what he was convinced was right.

"...It pained me for you," wrote the Mahatma, "whose heart I read so well—every protest and doubt of your purely intellectual nature, of your cold Western reason—notwithstanding. But my first duty is to *my* Master. And duty, let me tell you, is for us stronger than any friendship or even love;... Unfortunately, however great your purely *human* intellect, your spiritual intuitions are dim and hazy, having been never developed. Hence, whenever you find yourself confronted by an apparent contradiction, by a difficulty, a kind of *incon-*

sistency of occult nature...forthwith your doubts are aroused, your suspicions bud out—and one finds that they have made a mock of your better nature, which is finally crushed down by all these deceptive appearances of outward things!"

Well, thought Sinnett, there *was* a kind of inconsistency in occultism. One constantly ran into annoying paradoxes which served to unsettle one's convictions and complicate one's understanding. He wished he could appreciate paradoxes as Patience did, for instance; she seemed to resolve them instantly and without having to confront the agonizing doubts which they raised in his own mind.

"You were told," went on the Master, "that the path to Occult Sciences has to be trodden laboriously and crossed at the danger of life; that every new step in it leading to the final goal, is surrounded by pit-falls and cruel thorns; that the pilgrim who ventures upon it is made first to confront and *conquer* the thousand and one furies who keep watch over its adamantine gates and entrance—furies called Doubt, Skepticism, Scorn, Ridicule, Envy and finally Temptation...and that he who would see *beyond* had first to destroy this living wall; that he must be possessed of a heart and soul clad in steel, and of an iron, never failing determination, and yet be meek and gentle, humble and have shut out from his heart every human passion that leads to evil. Are you all this? Have you ever begun a course of training which would lead to it? No; you know it as I do."

The Master then reviewed some of the steps of their association and mentioned the failure of the *Phoenix* attempt and the part that karma had played in that.

"...you do know that there was a time when you felt the profoundest contempt for us all, of the *dark* races; and had regarded the Hindus as an *inferior* race. I will say no more. If you have an intuition, you will work out *cause* and *effect* and perhaps realize whence the failure...You know that even to write to you occasionally has been permitted only as a special favour after the Phoenix failure.

"You also resent the apparent absurdity of entrusting H.S.O. with a mission *you* find him unfit for, in London at any rate—socially and intellectually. Well—some day perchance, you may also learn that you were equally wrong in this, as in many other things...

" . . . you have treated both H.S.O. and H.P.B. in a very *cruel* way . . . You feel profoundly hurt at what you choose to call an evident and growing 'unfriendliness, the change of tone,' and so on. *You are mistaken from first to last.* There was neither 'unfriendliness' nor any change of feeling. You simply mistook M.'s natural *brusqueness* whenever he speaks or writes seriously."

This last, Sinnett knew, had to do with a letter received some time earlier from the Mahatma M. in which he had pointed out that Mohini had not been well-cared for in London; that while he was in the Sinnett's home, he had been assigned to a room without a fireplace and as a consequence had suffered greatly from the cold.[16]

There was further reference to this fact in the letter from the Master K.H.:

"He (Mohini) never uttered one word of complaint, and I had to protect him from a serious illness to give him my time and attention. . . *Hence* M.'s tone that you complain of. . . ."

The denial that the Master had used Mrs. Holloway to speak directly to Sinnett came in one of the later paragraphs. There were a few other stern reminders of the true nature of the situation, among them some comments on the insidious nature of suspicion.

"With this last remark we may," wrote the Master, "let this matter drop forever. You have brought suffering upon yourself, upon your lady and many others—which was quite useless and might have been avoided had you only abstained from creating yourself most of the causes. . . the strange idea that we are quite unable to see for ourselves; that our only data is that which we find in our chelas' minds; hence—that we are not the 'powerful beings' you have represented us, seems to haunt you with every day more. Hume has begun in the same way. I would gladly help you and protect you from his fate, but unless you shake off yourself the ghastly influence that is upon you I can do very little. . . ."

At the end of the letter, the Master asked Sinnett to attend and to speak at a meeting to be held at Prince's Hall, a farewell *conversazione* in honor of H.P.B. and Col. Olcott while both were still in England. "This I ask you to do *for my sake* and also for your own," the letter said.

Sinnett did not want to attend or to participate in the affair, but he knew that H.P.B. was eager to have him do so. As he read these words, all the suspicions which the letter had to some extent allayed rose up in him again in bitterness. He believed that, even if part of the letter was genuine, the Old Lady must have inserted these words to compel his submission.* He was to write later, "...I was somehow drawn into the conversazione and I am not surprised to find in my diary a remark to the effect that I did not speak up to my usual level."[17]

Right now, however, so insistent were his doubts that he scarcely saw the closing words of the letter: "So far my friendship for you remains the same as ever—for we never were yet ungrateful for services rendered."

Sinnett could not forbear a sharp letter to H.P.B. This brought an immediate reply.

"It is very strange that you should be ready to *deceive yourself* so willingly," she wrote. "I have seen last night whom I had to see, and getting the explanation I wanted I am now settled on points I was not only doubtful about but positively averse to accepting. And the words in the first line are words I am bound to respeat to you as a warning, and because I regard you, after all, as one of my best *personal* friends. Now you *have* and *are* deceiving, in vulgar parlance, *bamboozling* yourself...
The *letter is from Him,* whether written through a chela or not; and—perplexing as it may seem to you, contradictory and 'absurd,' it is the full expression of his feelings and *he maintains* what he said in it. For me it is surpassingly strange that you should accept as His only that which dovetails with your own feelings, and reject all that contradicts your own notions of the fitness of things. Olcott has behaved like an ass, utterly devoid of tact; he confesses it, and is ready to confess it and say *mea culpa* before all the Theosophists—and it is more than any Englishman would be willing to do. This is perhaps

---

*In connection with this suspicion, a statement by the Mahatma K.H. in a letter to Mrs. Laura Holloway (LMW 1:149-50) is of interest. Referring to H.P.B., the Master said: "You do not realize that when speaking of, or as from us, she dares not mix up her own personal opinions with those she tells you are ours. None of us would dare to do so, for we have a code that is not to be transgressed." Mrs. Holloway was for a while a personal chela of the Master K.H. "She had unusual psychic gifts which at one time seemed capable of being sufficiently developed to make her a mediator such as Damodar and H.P.B. had become." She failed her probation. Some years later, she wrote a series of articles which contained letters from the Master K.H. These have been reprinted in LMW. (*Damodar* fn. 515)

why, with all his lack of tact, and his frequent freaks that justly shock your susceptibilities and mine too, heaven knows! going as he does against every conventionality—he is still so liked by the Masters, who care not for the flowers of European civilization. Had I known last night what I have learnt since— i.e., that you imagine, or rather force yourself to imagine that the Mahamta's letter is not wholly orthodox and was written by a chela to please me, or something of the sort, I would not have rushed to you as the only plank of salvation...If you—the most devoted, the best of all Theosophists—are all ready to fall a victim to your own preconceptions and believe in new gods of your own fancy, dethroning the old ones—then, notwithstanding all and everything Theosophy has come too early in this country."[18]

There was a reference to the London Lodge and a statement that she would "retire from it altogether unless we agree to disagree no more."

At the moment, Sinnett cared little whether the disagreement continued. He still wanted to believe in the authenticity of the "direct" communication from the Master through Mrs. Holloway; from the inception of his association with that august Personage Sinnett had longed for some contact more intimate than correspondence. The Master had repeatedly said, in effect, "Not yet..." But Sinnett felt that by this time his continued unstinting efforts on behalf of Theosophy surely merited some special recognition. He spent a great deal of time silently mulling over the situation without coming to any conclusion which fully satisfied him. To add to his anxiety there had recently been one or two rather annoying developments in connection with his business affairs; these had generally prospered during the past year, but the immediate prospect was beginning to seem somewhat clouded.

"I think you need to get away," Patience said to him one morning when he had been particularly uncommunicative. "These past few months have been a very great strain on all of us."

He glanced at her quickly, rather startled. He had been so immersed in his own misery that he had failed to take into consideration that she must be suffering from its repercussions; and this notwithstanding the Master's comment that he had caused her pain.

"Yes, Patty," he said and, to her delight, his smile seemed natural and affectionate. "You are right as always. I've got one or two business matters to take care of but they shouldn't detain me long. Where would you like to go?"

She pondered for a moment.

"Well," she said, "the Old Lady and Mrs. Holloway are going to Elberfeld to visit the Gebhards. We haven't been invited to accompany them, and perhaps it is just as well right now. I'll let you decide."

A grateful smile, which warmed and healed her, spread over his face.

"I've been thinking about writing another book," he said, "something different—perhaps an occult novel.* I might be able to start on it if we can get free from so many distractions. Does Switzerland appeal to you?"

By the happy shine in her eyes he knew he had hit upon the right choice.

* It was during this trip that Sinnett began the novel *Karma*. (*Autobiography* 45)

22

The Shadows Descend

On July 27, 1884 the "Theosophische Gesellschaft Germania" was formed at Elberfeld, Germany, at the home of Gustav and Mary Gebhard and their family. Col. Olcott had journeyed to Elberfeld to inaugurate the new branch, and William Hübbe-Schleiden, eminent Doctor of Jurisprudence and Political Economy, came from Hamburg for the occasion. Dr. Hübbe-Schleiden was elected President, Mrs. Gebhard Vice-President, Mr. Gebhard Treasurer, and their son Frank Gebhard, Secretary.[1]

"This was the beginning of the movement in the most intellectual country in Europe," Olcott was to write. He felt that Germany had lost much of its earlier spirituality and he hoped that the influence of Theosophy might bring about some renascence of that quality. In the interest of this development, he and Dr. Hübbe-Schleiden left Elberfeld on August 1st and traveled about the country for a fortnight, meeting with influential people and presenting theosophical ideas. Olcott returned to the Gebhards in time to welcome H.P.B., her aunt Mme. Fadeyev (who had joined her in Paris), Mrs. Holloway, Mohini, Bertram Keightley, and Mrs. and Miss Arundale, who arrived in a group from London on August 17.*

"What a glorious reunion!" cried Olcott as he greeted them. The outpouring of his abundant good will gave a lift to their spirits, which were slightly dampened with the physical fatigue of their journey. "Now we'll have some good times indeed!"

---

*Mr. Sinnett blamed H.P.B. for the fact that he and Mrs. Sinnett had not been invited to be part of this group, a circumstance, he felt, of some embarrassment to Mrs. Gebhard. (*Autobiography* 44-5) They were to go to Elberfeld later on, however, after some of the others had gone but while H.P.B. was still there. (*Autobiography* 47)

This proved to be a true prophecy. "The Gebhard mansion could contain us all," he wrote, "and the next five days passed away like a bright dream."[2]

There was a great deal of coming and going of prominent and interesting persons. H.P.B. "sparkled like champagne with her witty talk" and the pleasant companionship and brilliant conversations set the tone for a memorable period. Among the visitors was "the talented Russian Solovioff, whose book, appearing long after H.P.B.'s death which made it possible for him to tell his falsehoods about her, shows him to be as heartless and contemptible, though fifty times more talented than the Coulombs."[†3]

The Russian's later attack on his countrywoman could never have been anticipated from his demeanor at Elberfeld, however, and he was always a welcome and fascinating member of any group.

In the course of these altogether delightful and happy days, several letters appeared phenomenally under circumstances "which all agreed could not have given any opportunity for collusion by H.P.B. with any member of the party."[4]

Another exciting event was the arrival of Herr Hermann Schmiechen who came to take advantage of H.P.B.'s presence to make some slight alterations in the portraits of the Mahatmas M. and K.H. which he had painted earlier in London.[*] Before he left, he added a portrait of H.P.B. to the collection.

It was during this time at Elberfeld that the Colonel completely recovered the vitality which had been so depleted by the healings he had done during the past two years. There were, in the compound of the villa, some "majestic old pine

---

† "In 1895, four years after H.P.B.'s death, V. S. Solovyoff wrote a series of articles in a Russian paper about H.P.B. The SPR, not content with the wrong it had already done her, caused these articles to be translated, abridged, and made into a book by Walter Leaf, D. Litt., which was published on its behalf. The book was called *A Modern Priestess of Isis* ... Solovyoff's work was full of innuendos, and he betrayed H.P.B. and her family without scruple." (SH 214-15)

* In ODL 1:370-73, Olcott relates that, when living in New York, he became the possessor of a profile drawing of the Mahatma M. While this was a true likeness, it did not, in his opinion, "show the soul splendor that lights up an adept's countenance." (ODL 3:155) In London, during that summer of 1884, he had spoken to some artist friends, each of whom consented to attempt a portrait which the Colonel hoped would do greater justice to the original. To

trees, under whose shade it was pleasant to lie and look out upon the lake." Olcott suddenly remembered that he had been told of a certain Adept in Tibet who was in the habit of lying with his back against the trunk of a pine tree and thus absorbing some of its healing aura. He adopted the practice with the amazing result that within a few days he was completely cured.[5]

He was to have need of his restored strength.

Like an approaching storm which may send out in advance small disturbances and tiny eddying whirlwinds, the tempest that was about to beat upon the heads of the Theosophists announced itself in a letter from Damodar received on September 10.

The missionaries, said the young man, were "hatching a plot, evidently with the help of Mme. Coulomb." The woman was "going about here and there, breathing vengeance against H.P.B. and the Society."[6] The immediate future was dark and foreboding.

There had, of course, been a few earlier indications of what was happening at Adyar, but none of these had had the impact on the triumphant Theosophists in Europe now created by this pessimistic letter from Damodar. Further, it had been a long time on its way from Madras to London and thence to Elberfeld in Germany, and who knew what might have transpired in the meantime? They were soon to learn.

The September issue of *The Christian College Magazine*, published in Madras, carried an article which embodied letters purporting to have been received by Mme. Coulomb from H.P.B. from various parts of India. The Calcutta correspondent of the London *Times* got hold of the story and cabled it to

---

each in turn he lent a photographic copy of the crayon sketch of the Master's profile. The results were "instructive" but not satisfying. Then Herman Schmiechen, a German artist living in London, joined the Theosophical Society and, to the Colonel's delight, at once agreed to an "inspirational" test. He began work on the 19th of June and finished on the 9th of July. Olcott visited his studio several times alone and once with H.P.B., and both were delighted with "the gradual development of the mental image which had been vividly impressed upon his brain, and which resulted in as perfect a portrait of my Guru as he could have painted from life." (ODL 3:156) The portrait was the face in full front view and the artist had "poured into the eyes such a flood of life and sense of the indwelling soul as to fairly startle the spectator. It was as clear a work of genius and proof of the fact of thought transference as I can imagine." (ibid) Following the completion of this portrait, the artist painted one of the Mahatma K.H.

his newspaper. It was published, along with the alleged letters, in the September 20 issue of that prestigious journal.[7]

"If the extracts had been genuine," wrote a later commentator, "they would have proved that Madame Blavatsky, co-Founder and Corresponding Secretary of the Society, had been for years producing bogus phenomena. The conclusion to be drawn from the article was that the Mahatmas were H.P.B.'s own invention, and that she had fooled everyone, including her partner, ex-sleuth and lawyer Colonel Olcott. The only ones not hoodwinked were the self-confessed unscrupulous Coulombs" who admitted to being H.P.B.'s confederates.*

Col. Olcott wrote: "Only by the reaction was it now seen how widespread the interest in our views had become, and it is doubtful if any Society had ever before had to sustain so terrible an attack. It almost seemed as if the very reactive bitterness of public denunciations of Mme. Blavatsky was the strongest proof of the deep impression which her revelations of the existence of the Eastern School of Adepts, their individual characters and spiritual attainments, and the part they play in the progress of our race, had made on the public mind."[8]

H.P.B. herself was crushed and refused to see or talk with anyone for several days. The spirits of the whole party at Elberfeld were severely depressed, but for the time being all were too stunned to take any action.

Col. Olcott was the first to come to a decision. He returned to London preparatory to embarking for India where he knew he was more sorely needed at the moment than he could possibly be in Europe. A few days after he had gone, the Sinnetts arrived at Elberfeld. A series of telegrams had passed between Mrs. Gebhard and Sinnett while he and Patience were still in Switzerland—Mrs. Gebhard urging them to come and Sinnett showing considerable reluctance, since he still harbored some resentment against H.P.B. in the belief that she had prevented their being invited earlier.[9] It was his wife's cheerful positiveness which finally convinced him that the decent thing to do was to accept Mrs. Gebhard's invitation, especially as one of her telegrams declared that the Mahatma wished them to come.[10]

Nevertheless, relations between Sinnett and H.P.B. were strained. He was not able to forget his resentment and sus-

*Howard Murphet: *When Daylight Comes,* 163

picion immediately, and she—although she had finally emerged from her seclusion—seemed hardly herself; her usual sparkle and vivacity were completely gone. She was facing her own decisions.

This resulted, first, in her resignation as Corresponding Secretary of the Theosophical Society. She wrote about this to Francesca Arundale, who had returned to London: "I have disconnected myself with it publicly; for I think that so long as I am in and at the head of the Society I will be the target shot at, and that the Society will be affected by it . . . My heart—if I have any left—is broken by this step."*[11]

One morning, a day or so after the Sinnett's arrival, as the group drifted into the morning room after breakfast, H.P.B. announced:

"I must return to London. And I must get back to Adyar. Something has got to be done, and Olcott will need me there. I can't just sit here and let that woman and the missionaries destroy the Society."

Her decision was, of course, not unexpected, and all present encouraged her.

"I will go with you," said Mrs. Holloway. It's time Mohini and I got on with our book anyhow."†

Sinnett was certain that Mrs. Gebhard was relieved to see them go, as he himself was. Whether or not this was true, their hostess's courtesy never failed, and when the two women departed on October 5, with Rudolph Gebhard accompanying them, it was with her warm invitation to return.

Patience, too, said an affectionate farewell to her old friend.

"For," she said to her husband afterward, "whatever she has done—and I can't believe she is guilty of the deceit you suspect her of—she has been kindness itself to me and I love her dearly. I can't bear to see her suffer so."

---

*H.P.B. was persuaded by friends to withdraw this resignation. It was merely a postponement, however; her official resignation from the post came several months later.

†Mrs. Holloway and Mohini collaborated in writing *Man: Fragment of Forgotten History,* which was published during the following year, 1885. This work, "though excellent in part, was marred by her alleged inspiration and dictation by 'Student,' a character created by her imagination." (*Damodar* 628)

The tragedy in the older woman's face had torn her sensitive heart and she longed to give some comfort when, alas, there seemed none to give beyond the assurance of her friendship.

While still in Elberfeld, Sinnett received a letter from the Mahatma K.H. It was both a message of encouragement and one designed to straighten out his thinking on some matters in which he had been mistaken.[12] There are some indications that Mrs. Holloway was the intermediary in this instance.

"It was not best that you should come to Elberfeld sooner," the Master said. "It is best that you should have come now. For you are better able now to bear the strain of the present situation. The air is full of the pestilence of treachery; unmerited opprobrium is showering upon the Society and falsehood and forgery have been used to overthrow it. Ecclesiastical England and official Anglo India have secretly joined hands to have their worst suspicions *verified* if possible and at the first plausible pretext to crush the movement. Every infamous device is to be employed in the future as it has in the present to discredit *us* as its promoters, and yourselves as its supporters. For the opposition represents enormous vested interests . . ."

"We are in for some unpleasantness," Sinnett commented as he handed the letter to Patience. "And I suspect that is far too mild a term."

"Oh, Percy, I'm so sorry!" she responded. "You have been so faithful!"

Her eyes fell on the beginning of the letter.

"Why, the Master's very first words praise you!"

"Yes," he admitted, "and I thank him for that. I haven't felt altogether pleased with myself lately. But that isn't all, by any means."

She read on, the emotions inspired by the letter reflecting themselves in her sensitive face. Finally she gave a little sigh and raised her eyes.

"I suppose somehow one always must pay the penalty for devotion to an ideal," she murmured.

For the Master's words were formidable:

" . . . Among the 'shining marks' at which the conspirators aim, you stand. Tenford greater pains than heretofore will be taken to cover you with ridicule for your *credulity,* your belief in me—especially, and to refute your arguments in support of the esoteric teaching. They may try to shake still more than they already have your confidence with pretended letters alleged to have come from H.P.B.'s laboratory, and others, or with forged documents showing and confessing fraud and planning to repeat it. It has ever been thus. Those who have watched mankind through the centuries of this cycle, have constantly seen the details of this death-struggle between Truth and Error repeating themselves. Some of you Theosophists are now only wounded in your 'honour' or your purses, but those who held the lamp in preceding generations paid the penalty of their lives for their knowledge."[13]

Patience read this passage aloud and added, "Will blind Justice ever balance the scales, do you think?"

"I suppose we must believe so," he replied heavily. "If by justice we mean karma, we have to admit that it never stops any evil from running its full course.

"Yet every evil carries the seeds of its own destruction," Patience said thoughtfully. "One thing I have noticed, again and again, is that even those circumstances which we consider evil seem often to be used in such a way that ultimately they produce their opposite. I wonder if the same thing can be said of good."

He looked startled and replied: "I'm sure it can. We have an example in this whole missionary business. Basically, they want to convert Hindus to what they consider the one true religion. And they are quick to defend that religion against anything they think is a threat to its existence. One can see their reasoning and even their good intentions—or what they believe are good intentions—but one can see too how that very belief, pushed beyond reason, becomes bigotry, which begets terrible evil."

"The spirit of the Inquisition isn't entirely dead, it seems," Patience commented.

She went back to the letter, which carried a reminder that the Master had warned Olcott as early as April "of what was ready to burst at Adyar."

"All will come right in time," the Master said, "only you, the great and prominent heads of the movement be steadfast, wary and united."

This was followed by an explanation of the situation which had earlier been a source of some perplexity and—he had to confess it—lingering resentment on Sinnett's part; he had, as a matter of fact, attributed it to what he considered H.P.B.'s jealousy of Mrs. Holloway, and it had not helped to rid him of the suspicions which he seemed all too ready to harbor against the Old Lady in these days. The Master had seen fit to remove Mrs. Holloway from the Sinnetts' home to that of the Arundales. To have permitted her to remain, the Master now explained, "would have been to her an irreparable psychic loss." He had consented "at her own passionate prayer" to interfere in the matter. Her mind was "being rapidly unsettled and made useless as an occult instrument."

The explanation of this situation was startling: "Your house, good friend, has a colony of Elementals quartered in it, and to a sensitive like her it was as dangerous an atmosphere to exist in as would be a fever cemetery to one subject to morbific physical influences." Sinnett should be "more than ordinarily careful" when he returned not to admit known mediumistic sensitives to his home. There were some suggestions for ridding the house of these influences, such as burning wood fires, writing Damodar to send incense, and so on. "But the best of all means to drive out unwelcome guests of this sort is to live purely in deed and thought. The talismans you have had given you will also powerfully aid you *if you keep your confidence in them and in us unbroken.*"*

Other statements in the letter stood out so much that Patience read them aloud.

". . . if you remain true to, and stand faithfully by, the T.S. you may count upon our aid and so may all others to the full extent that they shall deserve it."

"There is a hero-worshipping tendency clearly showing itself, and you, my friend, are not quite free from it yourself. I am fully aware of the change that has lately come over you but this does not change the main question. If you would go on with your occult studies and literary work—then learn to be loyal to the idea, rather than to my poor self."

". . . even an adept when acting in his body is not beyond mistakes due to human carelessness."

The Master said he could now send occasional letters and instructions with any certainty only through Damodar. "But before I can do even so much the Soc. especially the Hqrs. will have to pass thro' the coming crisis. If you still care to renew

*All the Sinnetts had lockets containing locks of the Master's hair.

the occult teachings save first our post-office. H.P.B. I say
again is not to be approached any longer without her full
consent. She has earned so much and has to be left alone. She is
permitted to retire for three reasons (1) to disconnect the T.S.
from *her* phenomena, now tried to be represented all
fraudulent; (2) to help it by removing the chief cause of the
hatred against it; (3) to try and restore the health of the body,
so it may be used for some years longer."

The letter ended: "Blessings upon you and your ever loyal
lady."

Patience could not help a flush of pleasure at this thoughtfulness.

"Though I must be careful," she said, "to remember what he
says about hero-worship. It's frightfully easy, isn't it, to foster
that attitude."

"Well, my dear," he replied, "I have yet to see a word of
criticism of you in any letter from him—from M. either. Would
that we could all be like you!"

"Oh no!" she cried in shocked protest. "Think how dull that
would be! All rubber stamps off of one mold. No, Percy, I
believe that with all our different temperaments—and even our
failings—we're all used in some way."

"Perhaps we have to believe that if we are to carry on," he
replied.

The Sinnetts did not prolong their visit at Elberfeld but
returned to London on October 9th. On that day the London
Times published a letter from H.P.B. denouncing the "alleged
private letters of herself to Mme. Coulomb as forgeries."[14]

"Sentences here and there I recognize," she said, "taken
from old notes of mine on different matters, but they are
mingled with interpolations that entirely pervert their
meaning."[15]

Her letter was followed by one from St. George Lane-Fox,
who had just returned to London from Madras. As a member
of the Theosophical Society's Board of Control during the
absence of Olcott and H.P.B., he emphatically denounced the
Coulombs, stating that they had been "constructing all sorts
of trap-doors and sliding panels in the private rooms of
Madame Blavatsky who had very indiscreetly given over these
rooms to their charge. As to the letters purporting to have
been written by Madame Blavatsky...I, in common with all
who are acquainted with the circumstances of the case, have no

doubt whatever that, whoever wrote them, they are not written by Madame Blavatsky.''[16]

The theosophical movement in London still carried some momentum from the popularity it had gained during the earlier months of the year; the seriousness of the situation seemed not yet to have penetrated deeply into the consciousness of the members or of the interested public.[17]

Col. Olcott wrote: "Before her departure from Europe, H.P.B. received the most gratifying proofs of the unshaken confidence of our European colleagues in her integrity; the London Lodge and the German and French Branches unanimously adopted resolutions of a complimentary character and the first two cabled their decisions to Adyar. Meanwhile letters and telegrams poured into Headquarters from the Indian Branches, and the reports from our colleagues of the Board of Control—all of which are now lying on my table as I write—became bright and reassuring; we felt that the storm had passed without doing us such grievous damage after all."[18]

This might indeed have been the case had it not been for the fact that the Society for Psychical Research decided that it was time to send an investigator to the headquarters of the Theosophical Society to observe and report on the situation there.

Olcott left London in October and arrived in Bombay in the 10th of November. He was accompanied by Rudolph Gebhard who planned to attend the convention of the Society to be held in late December.

H.P.B. followed Olcott very shortly but was to be slower in reaching India, for she went by way of Egypt. She too had company, for two prominent members of the Theosophical Society in London sailed with her. Mr. A. J. Cooper-Oakley, a Cambridge graduate and student of Indian philosophy and Sanskrit literature, was giving up a promising academic career to devote his energies and time to Theosophy. His wife Isabel, also highly educated, was an independent thinker and deeply interested in the esoteric and the mystical. She too was launching on a life's work for Theosophy. Both had remained loyal to the Society and to H.P.B. and were determined to do what they could to bring about justice in the appalling situation which had developed. Mr. Cooper-Oakley himself planned to spend some time in Egypt looking up the antecedents of the Coulombs.[19] Mrs. Cooper-Oakley was concerned at the moment with support and comfort for H.P.B. who was making a valiant effort to control her intensely emotional nature but who seemed more than likely at any moment to collapse.

The party was joined at Port Said by C.W. Leadbeater, who had made his own decision to surrender all his old ties and spend the rest of his life in service to his Master. He had been unable to sail from England with them because his decision was a last-minute one and he had had to clear away a number of matters before leaving. He remained unconvinced by the accusations against H.P.B., for he himself had received what to him was indisputable evidence of the existence of the Brotherhood which she had introduced to the West.

The information uncovered in Cairo about the Coulombs was indeed sensational. It came from reputable witnesses, including some members of M. Coulomb's own family, and showed that Miss Emma Cutting "had been employed for a short time as governess in the family of S...Pasha but was expelled from his household upon the discovery that she was endeavoring to instil vicious ideas into the minds of her charges; that she pretended to be able to see clairvoyantly buried treasures; that several were induced to dig where she told them, but discovered nothing save once, when they found some doubloons—which a little girl had seen her place in the hole the night before...[and that] the Coulombs were outlaws who had fled the country to escape arrest for fraudulent bankruptcy.[20] Further the Vice-Chancellor of the Russian Legation at Cairo assured Leadbeater in a conversation with him that he knew Mme. Blavatsky intimately, that he had seen her daily during her former stay there, esteemed her highly and had never, until that moment, heard the slightest reflection on her moral character.[21]

Leadbeater wrote all this in a letter from Cairo to the *Indian Mirror,* and his letter was published in the December 16th issue of that journal.[22] The *Indian Chronicle* carried a favorable commentary on the Theosophical Society and its founders, saying that "instead of being made the butt of ridicule and its leaders the subject of persecution, it [the Theosophical Society], ought to be patiently nourished." The Christian scoffers, the article continued, "are perhaps not aware that the existence of the Mahatmas...is universally believed throughout India, and it is preposterous to suppose that the Padris of Madras will do any serious harm to that belief."[23]

Several other newspapers supported this position. "In trying to discredit the existence of such men (Mahatmas), the Missionaries, as the tone of the whole Indian Press showed, were slapping the faces of, and offering deadly insult to, the whole Indian people," wrote Col. Olcott of the general reaction in that country.[24] Apparently the journals that had earlier denounced H.P.B. were silent.

The arrival of Madame Blavatsky and her party in Madras was in the nature of a triumph, Olcott reported. They were met at the pier by a large committee, garlanded, and escorted in procession to a local hall, "where an assemblage that crowded the place to suffocation was waiting. They rose to their feet and gave vent to their feelings in a roar of cheers and vivas, as she slowly walked through the press to the platform, her hand nervously gripping my arm, her mouth set like iron, her eyes full of glad light and almost swimming with tears of joy."[25]

A resolution bearing some 500 signatures was read "amid great excitement. When the outburst of cheering at the end had somewhat subsided, H.P.B. made her first and, so far as I know, only speech from a public platform. She said that 'of all the letters published, not a single one, as it stood, had been written by her. She would deny them all *in toto*... she would be the greatest fool in the world to commit herself so that she might be fairly accused of such vile, disgusting things... As for her accusers, she and Olcott had treated them with all possible kindness, and what should she say of their going over to the enemy's camp, when her back was turned, and selling her like Judas Iscariot? She had not done anything against India of which she should be ashamed, and she was determined to work for India while there was health in her.' (Report in the *Madras Mail*)"[26]

When they were once more back at Headquarters, H.P.B. turned over to Olcott all the written statements which she and her party had collected in Cairo.

"Of course I am going to prosecute the Coulombs," she announced excitedly. "This is legal proof that they are outlaws."

The Colonel's heart sank as he studied the papers. They contained extremely damaging evidence, it was true, but he knew at once they were in no form for production in court. They were the work of amateurs; any attempt to use them in a legal suit could have embarrassing and fatal results. He tried to tell her this.

"Take me to a judge," she demanded, "or to a barrister or solicitor. I don't care who it is—but someone who will listen to me and begin some action to punish those vile people for what they have done!"

He was alarmed at her pale face, her trembling hands, the almost uncontrolled urgency in her voice.

"Now wait a minute, Mulligan," he said in as soothing tones as he could command. "You know you are inclined to do things when you're upset that you regret later. These papers are damning but they don't have anything to do with the present situation and might be more than useless. We could make a worse mess of things if we tried to use them."

"Just take me to a judge," H.P.B. reiterated, her voice growing louder and more insistent. "I'll file an affidavit and get something started on this. I am not going to sit back and take it."

"No, I will not!" he said finally and positively, and her eyes widened as she stared at him; she was unaccustomed to having him deliberately go against her.

"You are beside yourself now, and I don't blame you," he went on. "But there are many things to be considered. You and I are in a sense not independent individuals but simply meshed into the Theosophical Society. The Convention opens in a few days. I propose that we lay the case before the members and get a special committee of our own best lawyers to decide what we ought to do. We could ruin everything if we jump into such a battle on our own."

"I'll go by myself then," she cried, breathing heavily. "I'm going to get this stain wiped off my character if it's the last thing I do!"

"It might well be," he responded, controlling his own rising anger with difficulty. He knew he was right. He suffered with her but he could not permit her to follow a course which was so fraught with possibilities for disaster. "If you do that, I shall resign my office of President and let the Convention decide between us. I know too much about legal practice to do any such foolish thing as you are contemplating."

For a long moment she struggled with herself, clasping and unclasping her hands in an agitated fashion. He could see that he had baffled her. She well knew that in matters of this kind his knowledge was far superior to hers. In anything concerning occultism, the Masters, and all those deep truths of nature into which she had delved for so long, she might be head and shoulders above him. But in dealing with the hard facts of the world she must in the long run bow to him. Finally, with a deep sigh, she gave a slight defeated gesture with her hands and said:

"Very well. Let it be as you say."[27]

The warm and loving greetings H.P.B. received from the delegates to the Convention as they arrived did a great deal to soothe her feelings and reassure her, so that she was almost calm as Olcott rose to give his Presidential Address in the opening session.

The Colonel dealt first with other matters of moment to the Society but finally came to the subject which was actually uppermost in the minds of all of them.*

It was quite natural, he pointed out, that Madame Blavatsky wished to go to court over the serious charges which had been made against her. The curious thing was that, not only some of her friends, but "all of her enemies" urged such a course. "Her assailants especially," he said, "display a very eager and unanimous, not to say suspicious, anxiety for her to do so." The vast majority of members had expressed objection to such action, however. "Their opinion is that, do what our counsel may, it will be impossible to avoid having the trial of Madame Blavatsky's reputation turned into a trial of the truth of the Esoteric Philosophy and of the existence of the Mahatmas and, as those subjects are the most sacred, not only to Hindus but to occultists of all religions . . . the prospect is shocking to their feelings."

These members felt, Olcott went on to say, that in view of the prejudice against the Society by the Anglo-Indians as a class and the certain hostility of the Madras courts, the greatest latitude would be given to opposing counsel "to ask the most insulting questions and goad to desperation our witnesses, especially Madame Blavatsky, whose extreme nervousness and excitability all know. This strictly within the limits of legal practice and without our having any redress."

*For full details *see* ODL 3:190-95

He had represented to Madame Blavatsky, he said, that it was her duty to be governed by the decision of the General Council of the Society. Finally, he had insisted that the whole matter be unreservedly laid before a special Committee of the best lawyers and judicial officers from among the delegates; this committee should be required to examine "the persons and papers" and submit their recommendation for the decision of the Convention before its final adjournment.

The recommendation of the committee subsequently appointed was that "Madame Blavatsky would not prosecute her defamers in a Court of Law." The resolution was signed by fourteen of the most prominent members of the Theosophical Society then resident in India and present at the Convention. It was unanimously adopted.

A figure becoming familiar at Adyar at the time—to all appearances quite friendly—was Mr. Richard Hodgson, sent by the London Society for Psychical Research to conduct an investigation into the bona fides of the Theosophical Society, its leaders, and the mysterious personages claimed to be its inspirers.

23

The Storm Breaks

Richard Hodgson did not remain long at Adyar. He seemed at first friendly enough; he was interested in examining the evidence but gave no indication of hostility. H.P.B. was courteous but far from effusive. There was an element of distrust in her feeling toward him. Indeed, even in London she had had a premonition that some further efforts would be made to discredit the Theosophical Society, and especially herself, and had so expressed herself to Mr. W. T. Stead* at a reception held by the Sinnetts.[1] On another occasion, she had been even more specific in a comment to Mrs. Holloway: "Hodson will be the man the S.P.R. will select to go to India."† She now felt certain that the present circumstances confirmed her intuitions. Her usual sparkle was missing and she could not dissemble. Hodgson's request that she perform some major phenomenon which would be convincing to him was flatly refused—a fact which did nothing to endear her to him or to allay his suspicions.

"It seems to me, old chum," said Olcott to her one day during Hodgson's stay at Adyar, "that you are being short-sighted. He's asking for some display of your powers. Why not give it?"

An angry flush spread over her features.

"When I have performed phenomena," she said, her voice trembling a little, "either on my own or with Master's help, it

---

*Editor of the *Review of Reviews* who was later to persuade Annie Besant to review *The Secret Doctrine*, with the result that she made the acquaintance of H.P.B. and joined the Theosophical Society. She became its second president.

†In Mrs. Holloway's account of this incident she said the remark made little impression on her at the moment because she didn't know what it meant, but "Nothing could be gained by asking her (H.P.B.) for an explanation, for in the time that I knew her I never heard her fully satisfy the curiosity of anyone." (*Damodar* 625-6)

has been for people who were genuinely interested—people who weren't standing back scoffing at the idea of the Mahatmas and the reverence one ought to feel for them. God knows I've done enough to break that down in making them known in the West. I'll never forgive myself for that, and I couldn't bring myself to degrade them just to satisfy Hodgson. He knows absolutely nothing about occultism—and I'm sure his motive is to tear down, to destroy the whole fabric if he can."

"Why should he want to do that?" asked Olcott. "I rather like the young man."

"Yes, I admit he is personable. And I don't say he isn't sincere—at least now. But he has a personal motivation in this, you know. He has his reputation as an investigator to build. You know something of the pressures of that profession, Olcott. He may not be as incorruptible as you were."*

"Well, thank you," he replied, smiling. "You don't often give me compliments."

She sighed slightly, failing to see any humor in the situation.

"I know you well, Moloney," she replied. "But so far as Hodgson is concerned, let him find out what he will. I have nothing to hide."

He echoed her sigh, wishing that she hadn't chosen this time to be stubborn and difficult.

"Well, I'll do what I can to show him our bona fides," he said.

Olcott deeply wanted the Society for Psychical Research to become a true ally of the Theosophical Society and he could see no reason, if the truth could be proved, why this should not be. He made available to Hodgson "all the relevant documents—including diaries" and did what he could to persuade the Indian members at headquarters to cooperate with the investigator.[2]

In this he was less than successful. Damodar and Subba Row particularly made Hodgson's task more difficult. Damodar seemed possessed to try to mislead him, and Subba

---

*A reference to Olcott's special assignments during the Civil War to investigate and help clean up corruption in the War and Navy Departments and, later, his appointment by Edwin M. Stanton, Secretary of War, as special investigator into the assassination of President Lincoln. (*Hammer* 16-21)

Row simply refused to talk or to cooperate in any way. Both found Hodgson's questions and cross-examinations degrading and his rather facetious comments about the Masters blasphemous; they were, in fact, incensed by this latter attitude and therefore deliberately contributed to his confusion.†[3] As a result, he found such "testimony" as they were willing to give more frustrating than helpful.

It may have been as a result of the resentment occasioned by this situation that Hodgson later evidenced "a singular desire to implicate Damodar as a confederate of Madame Coulomb in what he imagined were fraudulent performances of Shrine phenomena." Not only did he falsely allege that the discovery of the trick shrine apparatus had been an "exposure" by the Coulombs, but he claimed that Damodar was a party to the deception and "—in a wild moment of imprudent zeal, emphasizing his certainty by *dual* exclamation points— ridiculed as incredible the idea that 'Mr. Damodar, highly-developed Chela of Mahatma Koot Hoomi, remained entirely ignorant!!' of M. Coulomb's 'hole in the wall immediately behind the Shrine.'"[4]

Mme. Coulomb herself, however, burst this bubble, which was interesting in view of the fact that Hodgson came to regard her as the best authority on the whole situation. She "candidly relates that, far from knowing Damodar to be such a conspirator, she and her husband were fearful lest Damodar expose the 'trap doors' should they be revealed to him; and her husband adds that 'it was only on the morning of the 16th May that I confessed to Mr. Damodar the existence of the trap doors . . . and this confidentially.'"[5]

This confession resulted in a notice from Subba Row, as Vakil of the High Court of Madras, dated that very day, in which he informed Mme. Coulomb that they had committed an offense punishable under the Indian Penal Code, and he called upon them to give a "satisfactory explanation of your conduct with respect to the allegations aforesaid within 24 hours from the receipt of this notice." In case they failed to do this, both criminal and civil proceedings would be taken against them. As a result of some further actions by Damodar, the Coulombs

---

†"Damodar's Teacher Koot Hoomi blamed him and Subba Row for two-thirds of the delusions under which Hodgson laboured, and which were the cause of endless trouble to H.P. Blavatsky and the Society, and whose effects are discernible to this day." (*Damodar* 669) *See also* LBS 222.

received notice on the following day from the Board of Control to leave the premises of the Theosophical Society.

"Not only did Hodgson...falsely and brazenly misrepresent the real course of events, the relation of the witnesses, and especially the testimony of Mme. Coulomb herself, *but he* COMPLETELY SUPPRESSED *these explanations and citations GIVEN BY HIS OWN CHIEF WITNESS—factual explanations that proved his allegations against Damodar to be fundamentally and particularly false and extraordinarily deceitful.*"[6]

"There is now every evidential reason," says the same author elsewhere, "for substantiating Mahatma K.H.'s observation that it was "...the personal disappointment (Hodgson) felt, which made him turn in a fury against the alleged authors of the 'gigantic swindle.'"[7]

Hodgson's attempt to implicate Damodar in the alleged fraud had not yet fully flowered, however, when Olcott, in his efforts to enlighten the investigator, took him to the second floor and to the room where the Shrine had once been located. That it was no longer there provided an awkward moment for the colonel. Hodgson asked why it had been removed and whether H.P.B.'s servant Babula was responsible.

"No indeed," Olcott replied. "It happened last September, while Babula was still in Europe with Madame Blavatsky and long before there was any knowledge that an investigation was to be held. A group of loyal members felt that the Shrine had been desecrated by the Coulombs and they simply took it out and burned it."

Hodgson looked skeptical.

"Very convenient," he murmured.

It had not occurred to Olcott that he would not be believed. He himself had thought the action overzealous and ill-advised but he understood its motivation.

"I'm sorry," he said now. "It happens to be a fact—although I must confess that I was not here and so must simply repeat what I have been told."

Hodgson did not reply but it was apparent that he found in this circumstance increased food for his suspicions,[8] already well nourished by the uncooperative attitude of Damodar and Subba Row. He was later, in his *Report,* to speak well of Olcott's cooperation but to characterize him as a "dupe" of H.P. Blavatsky.[9]

Hodgson cut his stay at Adyar shorter than he had original-ly intended and went to Madras to consult with the Coulombs. Olcott himself was undisturbed by this development, for he felt certain that Hodgson would soon discover obvious holes in that couple's evidence.

Results did not bear out the Colonel's optimism. However unbiased Hodgson may have been at the outset of the investi-gation, circumstances seemed to conspire to weigh heavily against the genuineness of the whole theosophical effort.

"A continuous round of dinner parties did not tend to clear his views," wrote Isabel Cooper-Oakley, "for he had inces-santly poured into his ears a stream of calumny against her (H.P.B.) . . . From hearing everyone say Madame Blavatsky was an imposter he began to believe it: after a few interviews with Madame Coulomb and the missionaries, we saw that his views were turning against the minority (the Theosophists) . . . He omitted some very valuable evidence of phenomena given to him by Mr. Oakley and myself."[10]

At one of the dinner parties to which Mrs. Cooper-Oakley alluded, and at which she and her husband were present, Hodgson spoke of H.P.B. as a "Russian spy" in a manner which assumed agreement by all his listeners.[11] But even Mr. Hume, who was also present at the dinner and who had long since ceased to have any feeling of friendliness for H.P.B. laughed at this statement and reminded Hodgson that he was not in England.

"If there is anybody in the world," he added facetiously, "who doesn't have the right temperament to be a spy, it is certainly Madame Blavatsky! Can't you imagine how she could tangle up a whole network of espionage by going into one of her tantrums!"

There was general chuckling at this, for indeed it seemed obvious. Someone commented that if Hodgson's accusation was true, then indeed the Russian government was hard pressed for agents to do its undercover work. The Cooper-Oakleys too were amused but both spoke vigorously in H.P.B.'s defense.

"Why," said Mrs. Cooper-Oakley, "she has practically alienated some members of her own family, and some of her friends, by her criticism of the methods of the Russian government. This I know to be a fact.[12] You can't seriously entertain such an idea about her, Mr. Hodgson."

Mr. Hodgson did, however, appear to "seriously entertain" this idea and to continue to do so.

"Of course she would make such statements," he said now complacently. "How else could she hope to set suspicions at rest?"

The idea was so far-fetched that several persons at the table almost gasped.

"In fact," Hodgson added gratuitously, "I'm inclined to believe that she is a consummate fraud and perhaps even capable of any crime."[13]

When news of these statements reached H.P.B. she demanded that Hodgson show her the originals of the so-called incriminating letters she was supposed to have written to Mme. Coulomb. She well knew they contained forged interpolations. She had, of course, seen some of the published versions in which the false parts were so cleverly interwoven with things she *had* said—or might have said—in letters to Mme. Coulomb that even she found the effect confusing. "I could *not* have said that," she had told herself more than once as she had read the letters in the London *Times*. She felt now that if she could see the originals which she understood Mme. Coulomb had turned over to Hodgson—although he had never admitted it—she would be able easily to identify those portions that were spurious. Her request, however, was denied, as were subsequent ones to the same effect.[14]

Nor was Col. Olcott permitted to see the original letters. Even if he had believed them to be genuine—and he knew they were not—he could not have conceived that "one of the most brilliant women of her time" would have put herself so completely in the power of so treacherous a person as Mme. Coulomb by such self-incriminating actions.[15] "I can and do say for the hundredth time," he wrote later, "that I have had numberless proofs of H.P.B.'s occult powers, of the clear altruism of her motives, and the moral purity of her life."[16]

H.P.B. had her own theories, not only about the forged sections of the letters but also about Hodgson's reason for refusing to let her and Olcott see them. In a letter to Sinnett written during the following summer she said:

"I have seen Coulomb copying one of such scraps of mine, at his table, at a scene shown to me by Master in the Astral light. Shall my statement be believed, do you think?... The

Coulombs and Patterson* were afraid to let me see these letters and *handle* them, *for they believe and know what Masters can do; they fear the powers of those whom they pretend to have been invented by me.* Otherwise why should they have extracted from Hodgson the promise not to allow the few letters he got from them into my hands? Ask him, ascertain why he has never shown them to me? Why he never told me even that he got them? This is a serious fact, more serious than it appears on the surface. . .

"I know how it was done," she said in the same letter, referring to the forged interpolations in the Coulomb collection, "but since I cannot prove it any more than I can show how my handwriting appeared on my own visiting card at Eglinton's seance.† at 'Uncle Sam's'—what's the use in saying it? Was not that *my identical* handwriting on that card? And yet you know it was not done by me." M. Coulomb, who could imitate her handwriting almost perfectly, she said, had four years in which to study and perfect himself, so that he could copy "every scrap and note of mine to Mme. Coulomb on identical paper and make any interpolations he liked."[17]

She recalled to Sinnett that while she was in Europe during the summer of 1884, Subba Row had written her that Mme. Coulomb was spreading innuendoes about her "fraudulent" phenomena and had asked whether she had ever written the woman any compromising letters. She had answered him (she gave the date as May 1884) that she had *"never written her anything that I should fear to see published;* that she lied and could do what she pleased."[18]

All this was of little use now, however, when Hodgson seemed bent on accepting the statements of the Coulombs and missionaries rather than permitting H.P.B. to see the letters and make her own statements. He did go so far as to submit the letters to two handwriting "experts" who, "after changing their minds pronounced them geniune."‡ Later, they were

*Editor of *The Christian College Magazine* in which the letters were published.

†*See* Chapter 18 for the account of this seance.

‡Col. Olcott, in ODL 3:105-6, pointed out that one of Hodgson's so-called experts had made himself notorious in Europe by declaring certain letters genuine when subsequently the guilty person killed himself in prison after confessing to the forgeries. The German official who disagreed with Hodgson's experts was the chief calligraphist of the High Court of Berlin.

pronounced not genuine by a German expert who saw "not the remotest similarity between H.P.B.'s writing and that of the Mahatma Letters."[19] Hodgson decided in favor of the Coulombs and considered all evidence worthless except that provided by the two conspirators.

While all this was going on in Madras, and H.P.B. was fretting helplessly at Adyar, Olcott received an invitation from King Theebaw III of Burma to visit in his country. The King was much impressed with the work done for Buddhism in Ceylon and wished to discuss possibilities for Burma. As there seemed nothing he could do at the moment in connection with the S.P.R investigation, Olcott decided to accept the invitation. Before he left Adyar, he received a visit from Djual Khul "who talked with me about sundry persons and things. Mr. Leadbeater... sleeping on another *charpai* in the same room, heard the two voices and saw a column of light by my bedside, but could not distinguish the form of my visitor."[20]

The next night the Mahatma M. visited H.P.B. and gave her a new plan for *The Secret Doctrine* which radically changed the program earlier devised for that work; "the gradual building up of the present grand work was the result."[21]

On January 9, Olcott left for Rangoon, taking C. W. Leadbeater with him to help with his general work. They were well received in Burma and Olcott felt that they were able to accomplish something for the cause of Buddhism. His own stay, however, was of short duration. At 1:27 on the morning of January 28, he received a telegram from Damodar: "Return at once, Upasika dangerously ill.[22]

Leaving Leadbeater behind in Rangoon to proceed with the work they had begun, Olcott sailed at once for Madras. It seemed an interminable journey, wondering as he did at almost every moment whether his "old chum" would survive until he arrived. He reminded himself of her numerous critical illnesses, some of which had ended miraculously with a visit from her Master but from all of which she had recovered, and he hoped this would be another such instance.

He arrived at Madras on February 5 and "found H.P.B. in a state between life and death, with congestion of the kidneys, rheumatic gout, and an alarming loss of vitality. Added to this, an enfeebled action of the heart had brought her to a crisis where her life trembled in the balance.[23]

When the Colonel came to her bedside, she called his name weakly; and as he bent over her she put her arms about his shoulders and wept on his breast like a weary, heartsick child. His ready sympathy flowed out to her.

"I was unspeakably glad to be there to, at least, bid her farewell and assure her of my steadfastness," he wrote. If she should go, he felt, his loss would be greater than if she had been his wife or sweetheart or sister, for he would be faced with the necessity of carrying alone "the immense burden of the responsibility with which the Holy Ones have charged us."[24]

Dr. Franz Hartmann and Dr. Mary Scharlieb were attending H.P.B. and considered it a miracle that she still lived, but her Master "had worked the wonder by coming one night when they were waiting for her last gasp, laying his hand on her, and snatching her back from death.[25]

H.P.B.'s health remained in a precarious state for several days, but gradually she grew stronger so that she and Olcott were able to discuss the developments that had taken place during his absence. There had been little change so far as Adyar was concerned, and no encouragement had come either from Hodgson or from friends who had reported to H.P.B. when anything of moment occurred.

"Hodgson has gone to Bombay to visit the 'Crow's Nest,'"* H.P.B. told Olcott with a slightly wry smile.

"Rather useless, I should think," he replied. "What could he hope to find there after all this time?"

"It may not be altogether useless for him. He will go around questioning all the members there, and how in heaven's name they will remember anything accurately after four years is beyond me. Especially when there wasn't any special reason to fix details in their minds. Hodgson won't have much difficulty in cross-examining them into all kinds of inconsistencies."†

The Colonel nodded agreement.

"I'm afraid the cause has sustained a terrible blow," he said sadly. "We still have many friends, but we've lost many too. Well—friends or no friends we must go on."

---

*The headquarters of the Theosophical Society during most of the four years it was located in Bombay before moving to Adyar in December 1882.

†This was precisely what happened, and Hodgson made much of it in his *Report*, inferring that the evidence was thus proved totally unreliable. (*Hammer* 201)

"Yes," she responded, her eyes suddenly bright with unshed tears. "It is the cause that matters. What hurts is that we ourselves have done it so much damage."

He stiffened slightly, knowing that never had he deliberately done anything to harm the work to which he had given his life. Then he remembered that the Master K.H. himself had commented on the many mistakes he had made through excessive zeal; he knew this to be his greatest failing and he felt suddenly humbled.

"We have made many mistakes," he admitted. "But perhaps there is one thing in our favor. We're willing to try to set things right whenever we can. I hardly suppose the Masters expected us to be perfect."

She could not forbear a rueful smile at this.

"It's a good thing they didn't." Then she was serious again.

"There is still work to do, Olcott. The outline of the *Secret Doctrine* that the Boss gave me just before you left is going to change everything. It's a good change, I know. It isn't going to be just a rewriting of *Isis,* but something quite different. I'm eager to get at it—if only this old body will hold together long enough."

The increased sympathy and rapport which had grown out of their misfortunes suffered a shock during the next few days. Mr. Lane-Fox had recently returned from London, and he and Dr. Hartmann, with a few other "newcomers," had conceived the idea that Olcott had outlived his usefulness as President of the Theosophical Society. They proposed to put him aside and transfer the governing powers to a committee composed mostly of themselves. They had managed, before his return from Burma, to get H.P.B. to sign the necessary papers, although she was in fact too ill to know what she was doing.

When confronted with this development, Olcott went at once to her with the papers which Mr. Lane-Fox had delivered to him. He was very angry and deeply hurt.

"Is this your sense of justice, Mulligan?" he demanded, his face flushed and his voice shaking with emotion. "I'm not boasting, but I *have* built up the Society from that tiny beginning almost ten years ago. Do you think I should simply be turned out without even a 'character reference'?" For it seemed to him that this was indeed the case.

Her astonishment was quite obviously genuine.

"What is it, Olcott? What have I done now?"

"What have you done! If you had signed my death warrant it couldn't be any worse!"

He thrust the papers into her hands. She looked at them in a rather bewildered fashion.

"What are these?" she asked.

He calmed himself enough to explain what they contained and called her attention to the fact that her signature was there among the others.

"I guess I did sign something," she said. "Yes, I remember vaguely. I thought I was dying, and they told me this would be best for the Society. But I never thought it meant that you were to be put out. Never, Olcott! I thought it meant that there would be help in carrying on the work."

It was at this moment that a note appeared on the table beside H.P.B. Olcott stared almost in unbelief, but he picked it up and handed it to her. She opened it, read it, and gave it back to him. It was from the Mahatma M.—the Master of both of them—and it told H.P.B. that she might assure both Subba Row and Damodar that even if she should die the link between the Masters and the Theosophical Society would remain unbroken.[26]

"They have been worried about that," she explained briefly.

All his agitation dissolved. His old chum had not betrayed him after all; he was now sure of this. She had been led by her very anxiety for the work to which they were both dedicated to agree to anything that seemed to her to assure that it would go on. He put the note in her hand, folded her fingers over it, and silently left the room.

He had no intention of stepping down to leave the affairs of the Society in the hands of those he felt had insufficient experience. He didn't question their interest and even their commitment, but he knew what he knew. And he did not think his Master was yet ready for him to abandon ship. If he should ever receive a command from that source he would obey it instantly.

When he and H.P.B. were able to discuss the matter again quite calmly, she told him to tear up the papers, that she altogether repudiated such ingratitude. But he did not destroy them, thinking that it would be well to retain them as a matter of record. The others did not press him and what proved to be a rather minor crisis passed without serious repercussions.

H.P.B. was getting about again and had almost recovered when a telegram came from Leadbeater urging Olcott to return to Rangoon, "as there was a very promising opening for the T.S."[27] H.P.B. agreed to his going, although she wept when they parted. "I should have, too," he wrote, "if I had thought it was for the last time, but my mind was now completely reassured on that point. The recollection that she would not be permitted to die before her work was accomplished and somebody was ready to fill the gap she would leave, came back to me. I had forgotten that in my momentary grief at the thought of parting from her."[28]

His confidence in her indestructibility received another shock very shortly. He had been in Burma for less than a month when a wire came from Adyar saying that H.P.B. had suffered a serious relapse and it was essential that he return. He was unable to get passage on that day, and the following day brought a second message. He finally sailed for Madras on March 11th; he was surprised to find an old acquaintance in Captain Allen, who commanded the *Himalaya* and who had served in the same capacity on the ship in which he and H.P.B. had returned from Colombo to Bombay after their 1880 visit in Ceylon.[29] Interesting conversations with this gentleman helped to occupy his mind and thus, to some extent, to allay his anxiety.

When Olcott reached Adyar he found the atmosphere there heavy and even somehow menacing. H.P.B. was again struggling for life, suffering frequent heart palpitations and at times "as vehement as an enmeshed lioness,"[30] a state which certainly was not conducive to her recovery.

To add to their problems, Damodar had finally and permanently left for Tibet to join his Master and they were now without the help of his indefatigable efforts. Olcott had known that Damodar had long been awaiting permission from his Guru to take this step and he was happy that it had at last come. But this did not lighten the atmosphere or ease the pain of the personal loss that the young man's departure meant to him. Only four persons besides himself knew at the time the reason for Damodar's sudden absence; these included H.P.B., Subba Row, Maji (a woman yogi who lived in Benares), and one other whose name is not given but who was "equally well known on both sides of the mountains, and makes frequent religious journeys between India and Tibet."[31]*

Olcott learned for the first time of Hodgson's dinner table remark that H.P.B. was a Russian spy, and he went at once to Madras in company with Mr. Cooper-Oakley, to call upon the investigator.

"Both of us gave our views so clearly," he wrote, "that we came away with the impression that Mr. Hodgson thought the charge as puerile and unfounded as we did. Yet he stuck to it and put the cruel slander into his report to his employers in the S.P.R. Since then I have had no respect for him, for it was a stab in the back to a helpless old woman, who had never done him the least harm."[32]

On March 28, Olcott wrote in his diary: "A day of disagreeable experiences. H.P.B. wild and violent; news of a further step in the plot of the Missionaries against us; threatened suit against General Morgan by the Coulombs. A bizarre rumor, and improbable."

All this was obviously more than H.P.B. was going to be able to stand. "Her face turned purple with the blood that had rushed to her head; her eyes took on a stony, dead appearance and protruded from her head in a frightening manner. She walked the floor in the most extreme agitation until the others expected to see her drop dead at any moment."

"This has got to stop," said Dr. Scharlieb. "She can't go on like this."

---

*Many tales were circulated that Damodar had died on his way to Tibet. For a detailed discussion of this subject see *Damodar* pp. 10-22. The Supplement to *The Theosophist* for July 1886 contains an official notice refuting these rumors:
"To refute the anxiety of a great many friends who have been anxious to learn the fate of our brother Damodar K. Mavalankar, and to dispel the rumors of his death which came by way of Sikkim and Darjeeling, we are very happy to state that we have positive news as late as the 7th of June that he has safely reached his destination, is alive, and under the guardianship of the friends whom he sought. The date of his return, however, is yet uncertain and will probably remain so for a long time to come." This was signed by H.S. Olcott and T. Subba Row. *See also* LMW, First Series, Letter #29, from the Mahatma K.H. to Olcott, received in June of 1886, in which the Master mentions the trials Damodar has had to undergo and comments: "The mental and physical suffering was too much for his weak frame, which has been quite prostrated, but he will recover in course of time." More than four years after Damodar's disappearance, H.P.B. wrote in a letter to her old friend N. D. Khandalavala: "Damodar is not dead and Olcott knows it as well as I do. I had a letter from him not more than 3 months ago." H.P.B.'s letter is dated November 21, 1889, published in *The Theosophist* for August 1932, p. 623.

"What do you suggest?" asked Olcott, feeling almost as though some heavy object had hit him in the solar plexus; for he knew that, in one way or another, he was going to lose his chum.

"I suggest we send her away," said the doctor. "Surely there is some quiet spot in Europe where she can be protected from all this terrible suspense and anxiety."

Dr. Hartmann agreed with her. The difficulty was in persuading H.P.B. herself. At first she denounced everyone, convinced that they had all turned against her and were trying to get rid of her. It was Dr. Scharlieb who finally made her see reason. The Colonel was later to pay tribute to this kindly woman physician by saying that to some extent the theosophical world owed her the subsequent appearance of those later writings of H. P. Blavatsky's which are the crowning achievements of her life; if Dr. Scharlieb had not persuaded her to leave the situation which was daily tearing her to pieces she could hardly have survived to produce those impressive contributions to theosophical literature.

H.P.B. finally agreed, officially resigned her post as Corresponding Secretary, and gave Babula orders to pack her trunk.

Olcott and Dr. Hartmann personally went to Madras the following day and purchased passage for her on the S.S. *Tibre*, which was bound for Naples. Dr. Hartmann agreed, at Olcott's request, to accompany her, since she was in no fit condition to travel without medical supervision. Even so, when she went aboard she was so helpless that "Dr. Mary Scharlieb's husband, one of the Presidency Magistrates, procured the use of a hospital chair, and she, sitting in it, was lifted from the boat on board by a hoisting tackle."[34]

The *Tibre* sailed on March 31, and H.P.B. looked her last upon the country which she loved so deeply, in which she had known such triumph and such disaster, such happiness and such devastating sorrow.* In addition to Dr. Hartmann, she was accompanied by Miss Mary Flynn, at whose parents' home in Madras she had sometimes been a guest and who

---

*Later, at one of the Annual Conventions, as she was unanimously and enthusiastically invited to return if her physician would consent, and although she could never do that, she resumed her old official status. (ODL 3:255)

agreed to stay with her as long as needed, and the young chela Babajee, who had been on the headquarters staff for some time and who, according to a diary entry of Col. Olcott's, was making the journey at the direction of his Guru.

The group remaining at Adyar felt deeply sad to see her go, and the atmosphere for several days was heavy with the awareness of her absence and with the knowledge that the serious problems they all had to face were by no means resolved. Olcott's belief that the rumor concerning the suit against General Morgan was "bizarre" and "improbable" proved to be overoptimistic, for it developed that this actually had been the case. In an article in defense of H.P.B., General Morgan had described Mme. Coulomb as a "forger" and a "purloiner of letters" and this had been seized upon by the missionaries as a likely cause for bringing suit against him. Proof that this was only a ruse to get H.P.B. on the witness stand and thus, relying on her emotional and excitable nature, involve her in some kind of self-incrimination, lay in the fact that when it was learned she had departed for Europe, the action was withdrawn.

Richard Hodgson returned to London in April to present his Report to the Society for Psychical Research. At a subsequent General Meeting of that organization on June 24, with F.W.H. Myers in the Chair, Prof. Sidgwick read the conclusion expressed by the Committee appointed to investigate phenomena connected with the Theosophical Society. It contained the following verdict on H. P. Blavatsky:

"For our own part we regard her neither as the mouthpiece of hidden seers, nor as a mere vulgar adventuress; we think she has achieved a title to permanent remembrance as one of this most accomplished, ingenious, and interesting imposters in history."*

---

*Following the publication, in the July 19, 1968 issue of TIME Magazine, of an article on H.P.B. in the section on "Religion," in which the Report of the S.P.R. was mentioned, the then Hon. Secretary of that Society wrote to TIME as follows:

"We would like to make a correction to the article on Religion published in the issue of 'Time' dated July 19th, 1968. In this feature, under Theosophy, it is stated in connection with Madame Blavatsky quote Controversial wherever she went, she was accused in 1885 by the Society for Psychical Research in London of fraud, forgery and even of spying for the Czar unquote. We would point out that, as stated in all copies of the Proceedings of the Society, 'Responsibility for both the facts and the reasonings in papers published in the Proceedings rests entirely with their authors.'

"Comments on Madame Blavatsky were contained in a report by Richard Hodgson in Part IX of Proceedings dated December 1885 and any accusations therein contained are the responsibility of the author and not this organization. /s/ John Cutten, Esq., Hon. Secretary."

A copy of this letter to TIME was sent to the National President of the Theosophical Society in America.

24

Reflections

Patience Sinnett lingered over her morning coffee. She was alone for the moment; her husband had gone off early on some errand connected with one of his various business enterprises, and Denny, eager to be about his own pursuits, had asked to be excused. A servant had removed the remains of the meal but, at her request, had left the coffee pot with the cup and saucer.

On the table before Patience lay a letter to her husband from the Mahatma K.H. It was the first to be received in many months, and it was the last letter to come from the Mahatma in the long series that had begun in 1880 and had continued almost uninterruptedly through the intervening five years. Although Patience did not then give thought to the fact that the letters might be ending, this one struck a retrospective mood in her. How many letters had there been? she wondered. Percy had a whole box of them. They had come in many ways—phenomenally in some instances, through the regular post in others; they had come not only through the principal intermediary, the Old Lady, but also through Olcott, Damodar, Mohini and, in at least one instance, she believed, through Laura Holloway—now returned to America leaving few to regret her departure. The last letter from the Master—received in November of 1884 had made it clear that the gifted psychic had failed to meet the rigorous tests which apparently no one who ventured the hazards of chelaship could escape. Indeed, the Master had said in that letter (Patience could still see the words in the much-loved handwriting): "... *nothing* short of full confidence in us, in our good motives if not in our wisdom, in our foresight, if not omniscience—which is not to be found on this earth—can help one to cross over from one's land of dream and fiction to our Truth land, the region of stern reality and fact."[1]

Later in the same letter were further words applicable not just to a charming although vain and ambitious woman, but to every aspirant: "Self-personality, vanity and conceit harboured in the higher principles are enormously more dangerous than the same defects inherent only in the lower physical nature of man. They are the breakers against which the cause of chelaship, in its probationary stage, is sure to be dashed unless the would-be disciple carries with him the white shield of perfect confidence and trust in those he would seek out through mount and vale to guide him safely toward the light of Knowledge."[2]

Patience could not forbear a sigh. How many more letters would there be? H.P.B. was surely unable now to carry on the work; Damodar had gone to Tibet; Mohini had been too much influenced by Mrs. Holloway—and was now too much influenced by that strange little man, Babajee—to be altogether reliable. Would they find some other channel through which to maintain even such distant association with those exalted Beings who had so revolutionized their lives? There had been a few hopeful signs through one or two persons they had met in their travels, but these had so far resulted in disappointments. Still, one never knew!

Her eyes fell again on the letter before her. The "centennial attempt* to open the eyes of the blind" had nearly failed, the Master said. There was "but one chance of salvation *for those* who still believe: to rally together and face the storm bravely."[3]

This, Patience knew, had reference to the already sharp and painful repercussions from Richard Hodgson's investigations in India. He had sent sheaves of papers on ahead and had now himself returned to London, determined it seemed—from word that had already filtered out of the S.P.R. deliberations—to destroy the Theosophical Society and particularly that strange, enigmatic woman who had for so long been its guiding spirit.

Patience pushed her cup and saucer aside and rested her chin on her folded hands. She realized that she had not really come to grips with the horror which must now fill all the

---

*Reference to the tradition that, during the last quarter of a century, special efforts made by the Occult Hierarchy to release into the world influences designed to promote the spiritual evolution of humanity.

waking hours of their old friend. How could one endure such an uninterrupted ordeal and remain on this side of that delicate line which separated sanity from madness? Was it true what Subba Row had said? Just a day or so ago, Francesca Arundale had passed on to them a letter from the Old Lady, written from Torre del Greco, near Naples, where she was staying temporarily following her arrival in Europe. In it she related how Subba Row had characterized her to the Cooper-Oakleys as "a shell deserted and abandoned by the Masters" and how he had replied, when she took him to task for such a statement: "You have been guilty of the most terrible of crimes. You have given out secrets of Occultism—the most sacred and the most hidden. Rather *that you should be sacrificed* than that which was never meant for European minds. People had *too much faith in you.* It was time to throw doubt into their minds. Otherwise they would have pumped *out of you all that you know.*" H.P.B. had asked Miss Arundale to let Mr. Sinnett see the letter.[4]

But Subba Row, Patience reminded herself now, had never been willing to share the knowledge of the East with Westerners whom he so distrusted and, in most instances, even disliked. Why should the West be denied these deeper insights into the secrets of life and nature? she asked herself. Were they considered too dangerous to impart to persons steeped in another kind of culture? She had observed, however, that it was not only Western chelas who failed. There were several in Subba Row's native India who had not succeeded in controlling that "self-personality" which the Master had several times mentioned as the undoing of so many aspirants. Few there were like Damodar, whose passionate devotion to his Master, to the Old Lady and Olcott, and to the Theosophical Society itself, eclipsed every other consideration and had finally led him to undertake a journey of unthinkable difficulties and dangers in order to reach the feet of that Master who had become the focus of his life.

Her husband, Patience knew, had never become a real chela, in spite of the enormous privilege of correspondence with two Masters that had been his. At best he could be considered but a "lay chela" and sometimes even that status seemed to be in question. She recalled a letter in which the Master had chided him for delivering something in the nature of an ultimatum concerning the Old Lady, and had added that "... with such feelings smouldering in your heart, you could not be even a 'lay chela.'"⁴ Well, it was undoubtedly better so. She knew his pride and those obscure resistances in him of which he himself seemed unaware. At the same time, she knew that, without him, Theosophy would have had small chance of survival in England. For the London Lodge had been dying, and Anna Kingsford had almost assured its demise.

Her eyes fell again on the letter. "Could your L.L. understand," she read, "or so much as suspect, that the present crisis that is shaking the T.S. to its foundations is a question of perdition or salvation to thousands; a question of progress of the human race or its retrogression, of its glory or dishonour, and for the majority of this race—of being or not being, of annihilation, in fact—perchance many of you would look into the very root of evil, and instead of being guided by false appearances and scientific decisions, you would set to work and save the situation by disclosing the dishonourable doings of your missionary world."⁵

Strong words, dear Master Koot Hoomi, she thought. At the same time she felt helpless in the grip of forces that seemed to strangle decency, that seemed to be drawing an ominous cloak of darkness over the few sparks of enlightenment that had for a time glowed so brilliantly. Perhaps the Theosophists had not tended those sparks as assiduously as they might have. Yet, in spite of the fact that her husband had to support his family and himself, and in spite of the inevitable mistakes that he and all others had made, she knew that keeping alive those sparks had been his principal preoccupation and that even when he had faltered he had never completely abandoned that task.

She half-smiled as she noticed the inevitable postscript to the Master's letter. It was not so labeled, but it was an addition to the letter following the first set of initials. In it the Master spoke of the frightful tests that neophytes in more ancient times had been forced to undergo—tests which made use of all kinds of machinery and chemicals and physical means to try their "constancy, courage and presence of mind."

"But in these days," the Master said, "the vulgarization of science has rendered such trifling tests obsolete. The aspirant is now assailed entirely on the psychological side of his nature . . . to develop every germ good and bad in him in his temperament. The rule is inflexible and not one escapes whether he but writes us a letter, or in the privacy of his own heart's thought formulates a strong desire for occult communication and knowledge. As the shower cannot fructify the rock, so the occult teaching has no effect upon the unreceptive mind; and as the water develops the heat of caustic lime, so does the teaching bring into fierce action every unsuspected potentiality latent in him. . . . Try and remedy the evil done. Every step made by one in our direction will force us to make one toward him. . . . Once more, accept my blessing and parting greeting *if* they have to be my last."[6]

That they were to be the last save for a six-word note to be received several months later ("Courage, patience and hope, my brother."[7]) did not at the moment seem conceivable. Although there was no immediate prospect of a new intermediary —and it would have to be someone with the necessary auric forces—surely the Old Lady would one day be able again to function in that capacity. She had recovered from so many blows that would have completely finished one of lesser determination. Of course, no one could deny that she brought many of her difficulties on herself by her fiery, excitable nature, her inclination to act impulsively, and her inability to "let things be" once they seemed tending toward an equable solution. But Patience felt sure she would rally from the present prostrating blows. She had herself addressed a letter to Torre del Greco assuring H.P.B. of her love for and faith in her. That, she told herself, was the very least she could do.

She was roused from her reflections by the sound of a door closing and her husband's voice: "Patty, where are you?"

"Here," she answered, glad that he had returned and hoping his mission had been successful.

He came to her side and kissed her on the forehead, patting her shoulder in his familiar and comfortable gesture of affection. .

"Any coffee left?" he asked.

She lifted the pot experimentally.

"Yes, but it can't be very hot. Shall I have some made?"

He shook his head.

"It's not that important. Just give me a drop."

She rang for another cup and saucer, poured some tepid coffee for him, and sat quietly until the servant had left the room.

"Was your errand worthwhile?" she asked, when they were alone.

291

"Yes, I think so. We have been very fortunate. There are a few things that concern me, but—well, never mind now. I'm sure there's no dishonesty involved."

He picked up the letter from the Master K.H. and glanced through the pages; he had already read it once.

"This leaves you feeling sad, Patty?" he asked, with a keen glance at her.

"I confess it does, a bit," she answered, smiling somewhat ruefully. "That sentence about the Old Lady especially—near the beginning."

He read aloud: "...dozens of events of a far more distressing character, each of them calculated to crush the hapless woman chosen as victim, are ripe and ready to burst over her head, wounding as badly the Society.' Yes, it does seem ominous."

"What can we do to help, Percy? It may be something that she has to go through, but that's no reason why we should leave her without whatever support we can give her. We know very well, for instance, that the Shrine wasn't a 'trick cabinet' as Mr. Hodgson claims."

They had of course heard of many strange happenings in connection with that controversial piece of furniture, and both were now remembering their own experience during the last few days in India. This had happened while they were stopping at Adyar just before embarking on their journey to England. Sinnett had begun writing *Esoteric Buddhism* and, as questions occurred to him, he set them down on paper. One morning, when Patience came to him about something or other, he gave the questions to her and asked her to pass them on to H.P.B. with the request that she transmit them at her convenience. Patience took them upstairs at once and found H.P.B. in her room. When the latter saw what was on the sheet which Patience gave to her, she said, "Put it in the Shrine, my dear." This Patience did and then went to sit with H.P.B. on the opposite side of the room. They visited for perhaps ten minutes when the Old Lady suddenly became alert.

"You have an answer. I am sure. Mrs. Sinnett."

Patience herself went to the Shrine and found there a short note in the handwriting of the Master K.H. promising to answer the questions on the next day, which he did. The sheet of questions had disappeared. Patience happened to know that the Coulombs, who were now making claims to being H.P.B.'s accomplices, were occupied elsewhere about the headquarters. The incident was a simple one but convincing beyond any doubt.[8]

"You know," Sinnett said now, "it has been rather understood between the Old Lady and me that I would some day write her memoirs—probably after her death. But there hasn't been any definite plan. Perhaps there's no reason to wait until she is gone. It might be a help to her now—especially if more untoward events are to 'burst over her head' as K.H. says."[9]

His wife's eyes were shining.

"What a splendid idea, Percy! And quite like you to think of defending her even though you *have* been rather put out with her lately."

"Well, she's about the most difficult person I know," he said grimly. "But that doesn't alter the fact that, in my opinion, Hodgson and the S.P.R. are being grossly unfair to her. In fact, I think they're being stupid. It's absurd to be intimating —well, more than intimating, in fact—that the Old Lady is an adventuress who concocted the whole theosophical enterprise for her own personal advantage."[10]

"But it hasn't been to her advantage," Patience said quickly. "Good gracious! It's brought her more suffering than anything else—criticism and persecution, and now—disaster. She's not even had so much as a farthing out of it, if it comes to that. She's earned her living by writing. What possible motive could she have for fraud? It seems to me that the question of motivation is something that Hodgson is determined not to examine, with all his poking around."

"I doubt he would understand her motivation. Sometimes I'm confused about it myself. She does something wonderful and then, so far as I am concerned, she undoes ninety percent of it. I've told her so more than once."[11]

"I know," Patience agreed. "She has an unbelievably complex nature and I doubt that anyone fully understands her. But you know that we finally came to see beyond all these strange, and sometimes even unpleasant, surface things to something that must be an inner nature of rare beauty and strength. I'm convinced that whatever she has done—even things that might horrify and disgust us in anyone else—she hasn't done for herself or for any personal gratification, but simply for what she keeps calling 'the Cause.' Even when, in our view, she has gone a bit far to convince someone. But still, I don't doubt for a moment that if she thought it would in any way save the Masters from calumny, she wouldn't hesitate to deny them in toto.* She *is* unpredictable."

"I have to agree with you, my dear. I sometimes wish she were less so—that she were wiser and less fanatically devoted, but I suppose K.H. would tell me I am just seeing things from my arrogant English point of view."

She laughed slightly and put out her hand to touch his.

"Perhaps you are, Percy. And perhaps I am too. But I believe—in fact I don't know how else it could be—that the Masters have to use us in whatever way they can, in spite of all the flaws and weaknesses that keep us from being perfect instruments. You remember that in one of the letters—oh, a long time ago, when you were in Simla with the Humes and I was still in England—the Master told you they had searched the world over to find someone who was both willing and capable of undertaking such a work. It had to be someone whose loyalty was absolutely unquestioned and, at the same time, who had those powers that could be developed as the Old Lady's have been."

He nodded, frowning in some distaste at his last sip of cold coffee.

"He said too, as I recall, that her condition had some connection with the training she had undergone in Tibet—that she had in a sense to leave part of herself there, or something of the kind, to form a link and to make sure that she would never divulge certain things. I've never really understood about that, and I remember Hume went up into the boughs over it. But I don't doubt there is something to it."[12]

"It would be a strange thing not to be a—a whole person, which I suppose is what the Master was saying," Patience offered.

"Well, whatever she had to leave behind, it must have been something that acted as a check on her emotional nature. She certainly hasn't got that anywhere about her. At the same

---

*H.P.B. later claimed that she would indeed do this if necessary. "What saved the situation in the *Report*," she wrote to Sinnett, "was that the Masters are *absolutely denied.* Had Hodgson attempted to throw deception and the idea that *They* were helping, or encouraging or even countenancing a deception by *Their* silence—I would have already come forward and proclaimed myself before the whole world all that was said of me and *disappeared for ever.* This I swear 'BY MASTER'S BLESSING OR CURSE.' I will not see THEM desecrated."

time," he added, almost in apology, "no one can deny that at times she is the most delightful, lovable person one could imagine."

Patience smiled in agreement.

"Think more about writing her memoirs, Percy," she urged. "I believe that would please her, and it might counteract some of Hodgson's nonsense."

"How would you like to visit her when we take our trip to the Continent this year?" he asked.

As always, when she was pleased, her eyes sparkled in a most appealing manner.

"Oh, *could* we?"

"I don't see why not. I could begin to put together the information needed for the memoirs. It seems a sensible idea to me. Of course, we don't know where she will be. She indicated her stay near Naples is only temporary."

This question was settled when the morning post brought Patience an answer to her letter to the Old Lady. It was to be Wurzburg in Germany, H.P.B. said.[13] She liked the place and, besides, it was near Heidleberg and Nuremberg, where one of the Masters had lived at one time.* Elberfeld, too, was relatively close. She had received some money from Russia for her writings, and almost a thousand rupees from India, so she would be able to make the move and live in some "nice set of rooms" where she would write for the rest of her "(un)natural life." She expected her aunt, Mme. Fadeyev, to visit her there and would be happy also to see the Sinnetts if they really cared to come. She thanked Patience for her faith and sympathy but added: "Do not fight for me, my kind, dear Mrs. Sinnett, do not defend me . . . You will hurt yourself and perhaps the *Cause* and do *me* no good. The mud has entered too deeply into the hapless individual known as H.P.B., the chemicals used for the dye of slander were, or rather are, too strong, and death itself, I am afraid, shall never wash away in the eyes of those who do not know me, the dirt that has been thrown at, and has struck on the personality of the 'dear old lady.'"

Some lines further on were the words: "Of *course*, you all who believe in, and respect the Masters cannot without losing every belief in Them, think *me* guilty. . . . One capable of believing that such pure and holy hands can touch and handle

---

*Undoubtedly the Mahatma Koot Hoomi during his education in Europe.

with no sense of squeamishness such a *filthy* instrument as I am now represented to be—are natural born fools....Had I written *even one* of those idiotic and at bottom infamous interpolations now made to appear in the...letters; had I been guilty *once only* of a deliberate, purposely concocted fraud, especially when those deceived were my best, my *truest* friends—no 'love' for such as I! At best—*pity* or eternal contempt."[14]

"Why *must* she use such extravagant phrases?" muttered Sinnett, as Patience paused here because of her own emotion.

Surprisingly, she chuckled.

"That, my dear, *is* your English stiffness! She is Russian, remember, and she has Dulgorukov blood in her veins. That, I understand, has more fire than water in it."

"Perhaps so," he said somewhat grudgingly. "I must confess it seems to me a disagreeable heritage."

"She doesn't offer to serve again as our post office," Patience ventured.

"No, and I don't believe the Master intends it. He has said it will not be done without her consent, and she seems now to have other plans. I hope those mean that she is going to continue with *The Secret Doctrine*. But I don't—I can't—believe that he will simply permit all intercourse between us to be just sharply cut off."

"It may depend on what he is permitted by *his* superiors to do," she reminded him. "He has always labored under restrictions in that respect, you know."

"Regretfully so, from my point of view. But I suppose my point of view is one of ignorance from *his* point of view! Well, whatever happens, I must do what I can to help the Society through this crisis. There is still work to do in the London Lodge."

Although Sinnett, much later, became convinced that the link with the Mahatma K.H. *had* been renewed, he was not to receive another letter from him with the exception of the very short one toward the end of 1885 bidding him have "courage, patience and hope."

To his surprise, however, he received a note from the Mahatma M. during the early fall. Sinnett had been losing patience with the two chelas, Mohini and Babajee, and had not hesitated to make them aware of it. Babajee, it had developed, was an epileptic* and subject to occasional outbursts of erratic and even wild behavior which included bitter denunciations of his benefactress, H.P.B.—a situation which did nothing to help her through the ordeals she was undergoing. Mohini, bound by certain ties of nationality to the younger chela, was inclined to sympathize with him and take his part in several controversies which arose. Further, Mohini had met with so much adulation that it was beginning to go to his head and he was showing evidences of rather poor judgment in his relations with some of the members of the Theosophical Society.† Quite unwillingly, Sinnett had been drawn through correspondence with H.P.B. into some of the developments connected with these situations and was feeling anything but charitable toward the two young Indians. The Master M. rather chided him for this.

"Are you not man of the world enough to bear the small defects of young disciples?" he asked. "In their way they also help—and greatly. In you is also concealed a power to help from your side, for the poor Society will even yet need all it can get. It is good that you have seen the work of a noble woman, who has left all for the cause. Other ways and times will appear for your help, for you are a single witness and well knowing the facts that will be challenged by traitors.

"We cannot alter Karma my 'good friend' or we might lift the present cloud from your path. But we do all that is possible in such material matters. No darkness can stay for ever. Have hope and faith and we may disperse it. There are not many left true to the 'original program.' And you have been taught much and have much that is, and will be, useful."

"'The original program,'" murmured Patience as she finished reading the letter. Tears suddenly pressed her eyelids and she spoke with an uprush of passionate gratitude.

"Do you realize what a tremendous privilege you have had, dear?" she asked, her voice trembling. "Way back in those early days—in Allahabad and Simla and through all the years in between—your constant efforts have helped on the greatest cause in the world! Yes," she laughed shakily, "I know I'm using the Old Lady's word, and I mean it. It *is* a great cause. It's real! If it weren't so it would have perished long ago! The world will still try to kill it—but it can't because it *is* real."

*See letter from Olcott to Countess Wachtmeistr, LBS 331.

†See short biography of Mohini in *Damodar* 638-39.

She reached out and touched his arm as he watched her in growing amazement. She so seldom departed from that unshakable serenity which was her greatest charm and a bulwark of his life. But this too was beautiful, he thought now—beautiful with the vitality of her conviction. He put his hand over hers but could find no words to say what he was thinking; he simply waited with a kind of expectancy which had nothing to do with wanting her to say any specific thing but was more an openness to whatever she might say.

"Oh, dearest Percy, don't you *see*?" she went on urgently. "You've played so great a part! There wouldn't *be* any Theosophical Society in England if it weren't for you. And all this time you've had the guidance and help and—yes, I'm sure, the respect and affection of these compassionate men.... Yes, men," she repeated as his eyebrows rose slightly, "but Masters too because they have mastered their manhood, because they have mastered the secrets of life. They *cannot* have forgotten. They will not forget. Don't ask me how I know this—I just know it. I'm so proud of you, Percy—so terribly proud of you!"

He put his arms about her and held her close for a long moment while her tears found unrestrained release on his shoulder. She has not thought of herself, he realized. She is closer to them than I am! In his heart was an immense tenderness and thankfulness for her, a quite unexpected surge of determination and dedication, and—something new and wholly outside his previous experience—a profound and pure humility.

Epilogue

The devastating final *Report* of the Society for Psychical Research was published in December of 1885. Writing to Sinnett from Wurzburg on the first day of January 1886, in what she entitled "New Year's Reflections," H.P.B. said that a copy had been brought to her by a friend while she and the Countess Constance Wachtmeister* were at tea on the 31st of December. "I read it," she added, "accepting the whole as my Karmic New Year's present—or perhaps as the *coup de grace* of 1885—the most delightful year of the short Theosophical Society's life."†

She found in the *Report* "positively nothing *new* as concerns my humble self," she said. "A good deal concerning yourself and others." She enumerated several items which were "quite new features." One of these was the fact that Babula—her long-time faithful servant—was "quite the hero in this voluminous Report" which asserted that "all my Master's letters have been written by him." Another was that it appeared that Sinnett himself was "also a *semi-confederate* if not a whole one"—he having made "about 60 alterations" in the letters from the Mahatma K.H., after having said that he "had not changed a word."[1]

---

*H.P.B. and the Countess had met in 1884 in both Paris and London. The Countess joined H.P.B. at Wurzburg in late 1885 and remained with her through most of the writing of *The Secret Doctrine*. She herself wrote a most valuable account of that period entitled *Reminiscences of H.P. Blavatsky and The Secret Doctrine*, first published in 1893 and republished in 1976 as a Quest Book by the Theosophical Publishing House, Wheaton, Illinois. (See also *Damodar* 563-65) A number of letters from Countess Wachtmeister to Sinnett are found in LBS.

†The blow suffered by the Theosophical Society at the hands of Richard Hodgson was indeed a grievous one. The Society survived, recovered its vitality, and now has branches in more than 60 countries throughout the world.

"There are dozens of phenomena *that cannot be explained,*" H.P.B. went on. "Some of the most important have taken place in *your house* when I was not there. They were very awkward; and so long as *your trustworthiness* could not be impeached, no great triumph could be achieved by Myers, Hodgson & Co. It was *absolutely necessary* that *you should be shown untrustworthy.* You are in, and they got you. They never could, had you refused point blank to let them have the Mahatma's letters. Your Karma, dear friend."[2]

Sinnett felt that the most constructive thing he could do to help the Old Lady would be to complete the memoirs, for which he had been assembling information for several months. He and Patience had visited H.P.B. in Wurzburg, where he had spent many hours trying to straighten out the often confused accounts of times and places and events which tumbled higglety-pigglety out of Madame Blavatsky's memory. She continued to send, in her letters, bits of information as she recalled them, and he was sometimes almost at his wits' end trying to fit these into a coherent account of her extraordinary career.[3] Ultimately, however, the book was published under the title, *Incidents in the Life of Madame Blavatsky,* chosen because H.P.B.'s "many travels and occult experiences did not lend themselves to accurate reports except in general outlines."[4]

In the book Sinnett commented:

For a whole fortnight (after receipt of the *Report)* the tumult of Madame Blavatsky's emotions rendered any further progress with her work impossible. Her volcanic temperament renders her in all emergencies a very bad exponent of her own case, whatever that may be. The letters, memoranda and protests on which she wasted her energies during this miserable fortnight were few, if any, of a kind that would help a cold and unsympathetic public to understand the truth of things . . . few but her most intimate friends would correctly appreciate their fire and fury. Her language, when she is in fits of excitement, would lead a stranger to suppose her thirsting for revenge, beside herself with passion, ready to exact savage vengeance on her enemies if she had the power. It is only those who know her as intimately as half-a-dozen of her closest friends may, who are quite aware through all this effervescence of feeling that if her enemies were really put suddenly in her power, her rage against them would collapse like a broken soap bubble. Sinnett quoted also from a letter addressed to him by the Countess Wachtmeister in which she pointed out that she had spent several months with H.P.B., had "shared her room and been with her morning, noon and night. I have had access to all her boxes and drawers," the Countess said, "have read the letters which she received and those which she wrote, and I now openly and honestly declare that I am ashamed of myself for having ever suspected her, for I believe her to be an honest and true woman, faithful to death to her Masters, and to the cause for which she has sacrificed position, fortune and health. There is no doubt in my mind that she made these sacrifices, for I have seen the proofs of them, some of which consisted of documents whose genuineness is above all suspicion."

It was indeed important, Sinnett knew, to have close association with H.P.B. in order to form any judgment whatever about her. And even then, one was constantly being surprised, and sometimes even shocked. "Nobody would arrive at sound conclusions about her by collecting evidence about her," he wrote much later. "Only by the extreme intimacy with her that my wife and I acquired during her frequent and protracted visits to us at Allahabad and Simla, and afterwards by painful experiences of her behaviour in London in 1884 and 5, could we have reached that understanding of her complex nature which made us remain her champions through the S.P.R. attack."[5]

In addition to the book about H.P.B., Sinnett wrote and published a pamphlet entitled *The "Occult World" Phenomena and the Society for Psychical Research.* This was in two parts, the first constituting a powerful defense of H.P.B., and the second taking up, point by point, the accusations against himself in the S.P.R. *Report;* the absurdity of its assumptions was cogently and convincingly argued. He included, at the end of the pamphlet, a "Protest" by H.P.B. in which she pointed out that she was without legal recourse, since "my vindication would involve the examination into psychic mysteries which cannot be dealt fairly with in a court of law; and again, because there are questions which I am solemnly pledged never to answer, but which legal investigation of these slanders would inevitably bring to the front, while my silence and refusal to answer...would be misconstrued into 'contempt of court.'"

When H.P.B. was finally able to resume work on *The Secret Doctrine* she found it almost impossible to command the necessary concentration. At one time the Countess, entering the room where she was writing, "found the floor strewn with sheets of discarded manuscript." H.P.B. confessed that she had tried twelve times to write one page correctly but each time the Master had told her it was wrong. "I think I shall go mad," she said, "but leave me alone, I will not pause until I have conquered it, even if I have to go on all night."

The Countess brought her a cup of coffee which somewhat refreshed her. An hour later she had completed the page.[6]

H.P.B.'s traveling library was "extremely limited," the Countess commented in her *Reminiscences,* while her manuscripts overflowed with "references, quotations, allusions, from a mass of rare and recondite works, on subjects of the most varied kind." In every instance, H.P.B. tried to verify the references shown in the "astral counterparts" she had copied, since what she saw was so often as in a mirror with the images reversed. Usually it was possible to make verification. Occasionally, slight errors were detected but there were no major discrepancies. If she needed definite information on any subject "that information was sure to reach her in one way or another, either in communication from a friend far away, in a newspaper or a magazine, or in the course of our casual reading of books. This happened with a frequency and relevance that took it quite out of the region of mere coincidence."[7]

Gradually, however, much of the furor occasioned by the *Report* began to die down. H.P.B. gained greater command of herself and was able to continue with her writing. The Countess returned to her home in Sweden for a time, and H.P.B. moved to Ostend in Belgium to be with her sister and niece who were staying there. The Countess ultimately rejoined her in that city.

A short time later, H.P.B. became so ill that two physicians asserted that she could not live through another twenty-four hours. Countess Wachtmeister herself, to her dismay, could "begin to detect the peculiar faint odor of death which sometimes precedes dissolution."[8]

The Countess sat with her through the night, watching as she became weaker and weaker. Her own fatigue finally overcame her and she drifted into unconsciousness. When she roused herself the sun was beaming its promise of yet another day. Fearful that H.P.B. might have slipped from her body, she glanced quickly at the bed. The Old Lady was looking at her, quite alert, and with a slight twinkle in her eyes.

"Master has been here," she said, her voice quite strong and clear. "He gave me my choice, that I might die and be free if I would, or I might live and finish *The Secret Doctrine*. He told me how great would be my sufferings and what a terrible time I would have before me in England (for I am to go there); but when I thought of those students to whom I shall be permitted to teach a few things, and of the Theosophical Society in general, to which I have already given my heart's blood, I accepted the sacrifice, and now to make it complete, fetch me some coffee and something to eat, and give me my tobacco box."[9]

H.P.B. was to live to complete *The Secret Doctrine* and several other works. She was to go to England as her Master had foretold, and there she was to write and teach until her death on May 8, 1891.* The period was not without vicissitudes but nothing worse could happen to her than the agonies she had endured as a result of the S.P.R. *Report*. She inaugurated a new magazine, which she called *Lucifer*, and established an Esoteric Section of the Theosophical Society.†

Both of these latter moves met with some opposition from her colleague in India, Col. Olcott. He disapproved of the magazine because he felt it would constitute a "rival" to *The Theosophist*, which still carried her name on its title page. But he realized that "she had to have a magazine in which she could say what she pleased."[10] He disagreed with the establishment of an Esoteric Section because he feared an "empire within an empire." The personal intervention of his Master made him change his stand on this matter and, on a visit to England in 1888, he issued "an order in Council," dated 9th October, 1888, forming an Esoteric Section, with Madame Blavatsky as its responsible head.[11]

For the most part, the Colonel himself continued with his travels and lectures, exerting his considerable organizational skills in building up the Society which had suffered such severe

---

*For a detailed description of H.P.B.'s activities during her London residence, *see* Part III of her biography, *When Daylight Comes*, by Howard Murphet.

†Now known as the Esoteric School of Theosophy, administratively separate from the Theosophical Society.

damage during the years 1884-86. In addition, he achieved so much for the cause of Buddhism in Ceylon that that country (now Sri Lanka) continues to honor him on suitable occasions.

It is recorded that during Col. Olcott's last days, when he was ill with a failing heart, he was several times visited astrally by the Mahatmas M. and K.H. Others who were with him saw the figures on two occasions. Olcott's conversations with the Masters concerned the future of the Theosophical Society, his permanent concern until the moment of his death. This occurred at the age of 75, at 7:17 a.m. on the 17th of February 1907. It is perhaps coincidental that he had always been especially interested in—and influenced by—the number 7.*

The two chelas, Mohini and Babajee, who did some good work but also caused some serious difficulties in Europe, both returned to India. Mohini resigned from the Theosophical Society in 1887 and went back to his former home in Calcutta, where he resumed his practice of law.[12] Of Babajee the Master K.H. wrote: "The little Man has failed." Babajee was given money for his passage to India and "died in obscurity after a few years."[13]

A. O. Hume withdrew entirely from the activities of the Theosophical Society and eventually left it altogether. He was instrumental in helping to found the Indian National Congress and served as its General Secretary from 1884 to 1891. He returned to England in 1894. There is no evidence that he and Sinnett were ever again associated.

Although the prestige of the Theosophical Society in London had been "severely shaken," the Sinnetts continued to keep it alive by making their home the center of its activity. Their association with the main work of the Society, however, began to diminish when H.P.B. was brought to London and "a new era dawned for the Theosophical Movement in England."[14]

The idea of having Madame Blavatsky in England originated with Bertram and Archibald Keightley and a few other members of the London Lodge who had remained loyal to her personally. Sinnett did not welcome the idea. Although he was to admit later that "the ultimate results as regards the pro-

---

*For an account of the last days of Col. Olcott *see* Chapter 24 of his biography, *Hammer on the Mountain*, by Howard Murphet.

gress of the movement were important and beneficial," he was so "impressed by the disasters that had ensued from her return in 1884" that he "shrank from the possibility that her presence might give rise in some way to further trouble."[15] The Keightleys had consulted him but were not turned from their purpose by his disapproval. Thus began Sinnett's alienation from his former colleagues. He was not part of the Blavatsky Lodge, which was later formed around the dynamic person of H.P.B., and therefore became isolated from the mainstream of theosophical activities in England, which took on quite a different character from that of former days.

"A new Theosophical era had been inaugurated," he wrote, "in which great progress was made, and in which storms raged from time to time in a way that was not unusual in connection with activities revolving around H.P.B." He and Patience called several times on their old friend, and although their relations remained friendly, they lacked the sustaining element of mutual efforts and goals.[16]

Sinnett was "rather detached in sympathy" from all the enthusiasm by which H.P.B. was surrounded and was largely absorbed in another activity which had begun in the spring of 1888.[17] At that time, he and Patience had been invited by some friends "to meet a lady who was, I was told, desirous of making my acquaintance."[18] Sinnett was never to reveal this lady's name, since at that time—and through her later marriage—she was connected with a family "some representatives of which may still be living when these lines are given to the world."[19] He called her, simply, Mary.*

Mary had considerable psychic powers and Sinnett became convinced that, through her, he was again in "definite communication with the Master."[20] Through this new contact he "gathered a great deal of miscellaneous occult information."[21] The development was kept "profoundly secret from our theosophical friends generally—in accordance with the Master's wish."[22]

"We had been told," Sinnett wrote, "that if she (H.P.B.) came to know of our private privilege her occult powers would enable her to interfere in a way which would imperil its con-

---

*In his *Autobiography* (p. 66) Sinnett recorded that on one occasion, when Mary dropped in at his home on a friendly call at a time when C. W. Leadbeater was present, the latter, with some excitement, "recognized in her aura" that she was one "very advanced in occultism."

tinuance."[23] However, it developed in the course of the association that Mary wanted very much to meet Madame Blavatsky, and permission was finally given. "...the Old Lady took no notice of Mary and was quite unsuspicious of her characteristics."[24]

The reasonably amicable differences which had developed between the Sinnetts and H.P.B. sharpened into something less friendly when *The Secret Doctrine* was published in 1888 and Sinnett found, in its early pages, what he felt was an attack on *Esoteric Buddhism*. He was convinced that this section had been added following H.P.B.'s return to London and that it had been inspired by the "impassioned devotees who surrounded her."[25]

A further unhappy development sharpened the schism. This took place after Sinnett became a partner in the publishing business of G. W. Redway, who later was engaged to print H.P.B.'s magazine *Lucifer*. When she and the Keightleys brought action against Redway for allegedly having over-charged the magazine thirty pounds, Sinnett was inevitably drawn into the suit. The court's decision was in Redway's favor, and this did not improve Sinnett's relations with H.P.B. and the members of the Blavatsky Lodge.[26]

In 1890 the financial ruin which eventually overtook Sinnett after a period of comfortable affluence began to bring about drastic changes in his circumstances. The Sinnetts moved from their Ladbroke Gardens residence to Lienster Gardens and, still later, to a cheaper house in a less desirable neighborhood on Westbourne Terrace Road.[27] They continued nevertheless to hold their Tuesday afternoon gatherings and evening meetings with the "most faithful members of the London Lodge. These meetings were generally well attended, "sometimes as many as sixty" being present. Occasionally Mrs. Annie Besant lectured;* more often this duty fell on Sinnett himself. He shared what he was convinced was the

---

*After reading and reviewing *The Secret Doctrine*, Annie Besant "enthu-siastically joined the Blavatsky household." (*Damodar* 281) In her *Auto-biography* (pp. 443-4) Annie Besant tells of her meeting with H.P.B. She had gone to see her to ask about Theosophy. H.P.B. looked at her "piercingly" and asked her if she had read the Report of the S.P.R. Mrs. Besant said she had not, that she had never heard of it so far as she knew. H.P.B. told her to read it and then come back if she wished. Mrs. Besant borrowed a copy and read it. She wrote: "Quickly I saw how slender was the foundation on which the imposing structure was built, the continued assumptions on which

teaching that had been "coming from the Master via the private channel of communication that had been available for the previous five years."[28]

These activities were carried on during the "long and miserable struggle" of a financial nightmare.† Sinnett was still struggling at the turn of the century but, eventually, with the help of friends, he managed to recover some measure of economic stability, although he never again reached the comfortable circumstances which he had once enjoyed. The whole experience, he said he learned later, was not karmic in nature but was one of several "satanic plots" designed to destroy the Sinnetts' faith in and loyalty to the Master.[29] If, indeed, this was the case, none of them succeeded.

In 1908, as a result of differences with the then President of the Theosophical Society, Annie Besant, the London Lodge, by a "practically unanimous vote" detached itself from the Society. Sinnett was not wholly in sympathy with the move, but in view of the strong feelings of the other members, decided it was useless to attempt opposition. It seemed to him absurd that he should disconnect himself from an organization which he had been so instrumental in establishing—at least so far as the West was concerned, and in which, at different times, he had served for approximately fifteen years as Vice-President. The Elusinian Society ("in touch with Theosophy if not with the Theosophical Society") was formed, with almost the entire former London Lodge as its body of membership.[30]

In 1911, however, Sinnett began to see that this "anomalous arrangement" might as well come to an end. "I remained all the time in touch with the Masters," he wrote, "through a very efficient channel of communication."*[31] Convinced that it was the Master's wish that he again become active in the Theosophical Society, he composed his own differences with Mrs.

conclusions were based, the incredible character of the allegations, and—most damning fact of all—the foul source from which the evidence was derived...I laughed aloud at the absurdity and flung the Report aside." She returned to H.P.B. and asked her to "give me the honor of proclaiming you my teacher in the face of the world."

†The account of this period is given in some detail in Sinnett's *Autobiography* pp. 54-8.

*So far as is known, no correspondence exists to substantiate Sinnett's belief that he had been in touch with the Master following the cessation of letters with which this book is concerned. In his *Autobiography* he mentions other persons who followed Mary in maintaining what he confidently believed was

Besant and was able finally to get the London Lodge reconstituted under a special charter issued by the governing body at Adyar. He served again as Vice-President of the Society from 1911 to 1921.

The year 1908 had, however, been a year of tremendous personal loss and sorrow for Sinnett. On May 11 of that year, Denny Sinnett died of tuberculosis after a short adult life of almost unmitigated failure. His parents had done everything in their power to establish him in gainful occupation on several occasions, but—perhaps due in part to his always delicate health—he was never able to cope successfully with the demands of life.

On the 9th of November in the same year, Sinnett suffered the greatest and most devastating loss of his career when Patience Sinnett died after a lingering illness with cancer. He learned afterward, he recorded, that this manner of death resulted from her own decision to make the sacrifice to a greater end.† At the close of his book, *The Early Days of Theosophy in Europe,* he paid her the following tribute:

> ...in bringing to a close this sketchy review of mistakes and successes, the story will introduce the reader to one person at all events quite unknown to the theosophical world at large whose important share in the early work seems to me, looking back, unblemished by mistake—my wife...I—and perhaps hardly anyone else still living—can appreciate the value of her influence while our house was the centre around which all theosophical activities of the period revolved. And that influence was so effective, as I seem to see now, because it was untainted by the faintest desire for recognition. There was no self-regarding germ in my wife's nature on which evil influences could play to bring about misdirected action, while if there were germs of the right

authentic communication. On pages 89-91, he tells of a friend named Robert King who was apparently to serve in this capacity for the remainder of Sinnett's life. While Robert King brought these communications through while in trance (except on one occasion when he was in full consciousness) Sinnett commented: "He has been emphatically warned never to allow himself to be thus controlled except during these sittings with me and appreciates the dignity of our joint undertaking to the full. He has been repeatedly commended by the Masters for keeping his body in a state in which it can be used in this way." (p. 91)

†Sinnett describes this period of his wife's illness and death, and her subsequent spiritual state, in his *Autobiography,* pp. 84-88, and in an addendum entitled "At a Later Date," p. 8.

kind in people with whom she might be dealing, these were nourished or brought out by her influence in a remarkable manner. As an underlying attitude which conduced to the results I refer to, she was the most absolutely truthful person I had ever known, incapable of deception in any form...

Sinnett's last years were clouded by sadness and recurring poverty, but he was never swayed from his loyalty to the Master, and he continued his theosophical activities to the very end. Financial help from friends and many testimonials of appreciation with monetary content enabled him to carry on. During the last days, Annie Besant herself took the initiative of raising a fund to assist him. "Five thousand pounds were turned over to him but he did not live long to enjoy his surcease from want. He passed away on 27 June 1921, at the age of 81."[32]

Writing in the eightieth year of his life, Sinnett made some comments which might well constitute a kind of perpetual epilogue to the story of any period in the history of the Theosophical Society. He spoke of those exalted Beings who were the real Founders of the Theosophical Society and of how the "blundering human agencies over and over again threatened to wreck the whole undertaking." He wrote of how, after what appeared to be the certain disintegration of the Society, a few strong adherents, "resolute in their own knowledge of the truth, strong in their cognizance of the great powers at the back of the movement" became the nucleus of gradually renewed growth.

"The marvelous vitality of the stupendous philosophic system on which the movement was based asserted itself," he affirmed. "The apprehension of Theosophy as the only satisfactory interpretation of nature and of human life, spread far and wide... the readers of its literature, the students of its teaching gathered round the small nucleus... and re-established the Theosophical Society as a powerful organization...

"Ignoring defects and blunders and personal shortcomings among its proud representatives, the ever increasing volume of thought and sympathy evoked by the literature of Theosophy has clustered round the original society, utterly indifferent to the question of whether this or that individual writer or leader was entitled personally to respect...

"I have often argued that societies and mere physical plane forms like those we inhabit, are destined to perish...But events have shown that however true that theory may be in the long run, it cannot yet be practically applied to the Theosophical Society."[32]

If Alfred Percy Sinnett himself needed an epitaph he might be considered to have written it in the above words. For they seem to strike the keynote of his career from the day he broke through the ice of Anglo-Indian prejudice and hostility to extend hospitality to two theosophical pioneers and thus to change his life and theirs—and undoubtedly the lives of countless others—and to achieve the priceless boon of those communications known as "The Mahatma Letters."

References

(For greater ease of reference, only the abbreviations are used, eliminating the necessity for "ibids" and "op cits.")

(*See* List of Abbreviations, p. xix)

Prologue
1. ODL 1:483
2. ODL 2:1-2
3. ODL 2:3
4. ODL 2:4
5. ODL 2:vii-viii
6. ODL 2:9-12
7. ODL 2:16-17
8. ODL 2:13-14

1
1. ODL 1:457-8
2. ODL 2:449
3. *Hammer* 105
4. ODL 1:453
5. ODL 2:20
6. ODL 2:16
7. ODL 2:20
8. ODL 2:29
9. ODL 3:114

2
1. ODL 2:207
2. ODL 2:297
3. *Daylight* 169
4. SH 209; *The Theosophist,* Aug. 1931, pp. 656-7
5. SH 141
6. ODL 2:225
7. ODL 2:225
8. ML 451/443; LBS 79
9. ODL 1:457
10. ODL 2:226
11. ODL 2:227
12. ODL 2:227
13. OW 33
14. OW 35

15. OW 47
16. OW 82
17. *Autobiography* 28
18. ML 352/346
19. Cf. *Guide* xvii-xviii

3
1. ODL 2:247
2. ML 4
3. ML 2
4. ML 3-4
5. ML 3
6. ML 5
7. OW 70-2
8. ML 2

4
1. OW 89
2. ML 6
3. ML 6
4. ML 12
5. OW 100
6. OW 97-101
7. ML 10
8. OW 101
9. OW 102

5
1. ML 488/481
2. OW 70-2
3. OW 96
4. OW 104
5. ML 12-13; OW 107
6. OW 194
7. ML 11-17

8. ML 14
9. ML 16
10. ODL 2:252-3
11. LBS 6-7
12. ODL 2:266
13. ODL 2:267
14. ML 11
15. ML 443/436
16. OW 122-23
17. ML 434/427
18. ML 31
19. ML 366/359
20. ODL 2:285
21. ODL 2:287

6
1. ML 34
2. LBS 91
3. ML 488/480
4. ML 488/480
5. ODL 2:293-4
6. ODL 2:294
7. LBS 363
8. ML 444/436
9. ML 33
10. ML 27
11. ML 26-7
12. CW 4:223
13. ODL 1:134
14. LBS 69
15. ML 430/424
16. ODL 1:300-01
17. ML 38-9
18. *Autobiography* 31
19. OW 155
20. OW 156
21. ML 38
22. ML 51

7
1 ML 452/445
2 ML 280/276
3 ML 283/278
4 ML 285/281
5 ML 286/282
6 LBS 18
7 LBS 15; *see also* ML 315/311
8 LBS 16
9 LBS 40
10 LBS 34
11 LBS 20
12 LBS 20
13 LBS 20-21
14 ML 315/311
15 LBS 15-16 & 18
16 *The Theosophist,* October 1881, Supplement
17 ML 206/204
18 ML 207/205
19 ML 206-7/204
20 ML 220/218
21 ML 220/218
22 ML 221/218
23 ML 220/218
24 ML 204/202
25 ML 221/219
26 ML 221-2/219
27 ML 203/201
28 ML 204/202
29 ODL 2:vii
30 ODL 1:263
31 ML 44
32 LBS 305-310
33 LMW 1:2-10
34 LMW 1:2

8
1 OW 158
2 ML 440/433
3 OW 158
4 ML 250/247
5 OW 158-9
6 ML 374/367
7 LBS 365
8 ML 375/369
9 ML 219/217
10 ML 219/217
11 ML 219/217
12 ML 219/217
13 ML 219/217

14 ML 222/220
15 ML 223/221
16 ML 227/224
17 LBS 10; ML 248/245
18 LBS 9
19 LBS 5
20 ML 461/454
21 LBS 10
22 LBS 12
23 LBS 11
24 ML 254/251
25 ML 255/251
26 ML 251-2/248
27 ML 254/251
28 ML 253/249
29 ML 256/253
30 ODL 2:326

9
1 ML 248/245
2 ML 260-61/257
3 ODL 2:327
4 ODL 2:327-8
5 ODL 2:329
6 ODL 2:329-39
7 ODL 2:329
8 ODL 2:328
9 ML 250/247
10 ML 70
11 ML 70
12 ML 264/260
13 ML 266/262
14 ML 338/333
15 ML 267-8/263-4

10
1 ODL 2:334
2 SH 165
3 OW 162
4 ML 279/274
5 OW 168; ML 410/404
6 ML 448/481
7 OW 167-69
8 ML 452/444
9 ML 274/270
10 ML 275/271
11 ODL 2:338
12 ML 464/457
13 ML 275/271
14 LBS 26

15 ML 453-54/ 446-47
16 ML 419/413
17 ML 276/272
18 ML 279/275
19 ML 279/275
20 ML 246/243
21 ML 246/243

11
1 *Damodar,* 186
2 *Guide* 111, 229
3 *The Theosophist* April 1882 See also *Damodar* 188
4 ML 412/405
5 ML 411/405
6 ML 113/110
7 OW 172-74
8 ML 284/280
9 OW 175-76
10 ML 112-13/ 109-10
11 LBS 361
12 ML 430/423
13 ML 430/424
14 *Damodar* 200-01

12
1 ML 115/112
2 ML 70
3 ML 60
4 ML 84/82
5 ML 457/450
6 ML 457/450
7 ML 235/232
8 ML 299/294
9 ML 460/453
10 ML 458/451
11 ML 458/451
12 ML 99/97
13 ML 116/112
14 ML 116/112
15 ML 116/112
16 LBS 28-9
17 ML 236/233
18 ML 297/292
19 ML 235/232
20 ML 297/292
21 ML 448/441
22 ML 448/441

23 ML 230/227 &
    295/291
24 ML 237/234
25 ML 238/235
26 ML 448/441
27 ML 228/225
28 ML 294/290
29 ML 295/290
30 ML 296/291
31 ML 297/293
32 ML 298/294
33 ML 299/294
34 ML 301/296
35 ML 302/297
36 ML 302/297
37 LMW 2:140
38 LMW 2:145

13
1   ML 291/286 &
    LBS 44
2   *The Theosophist,*
    August 1882
3   ML 292/288
4   LBS 29
5   LBS 31
6   LBS 304
7   LBS 304
8   LBS 82
9   *Guide* 217
10 ML 292/288
11 ML 289-90/285
12 ML 288-9/284
13 ML 293/288-9
14 LMW 1:66-74
15 LMW I;72
16 LBS 34-5
17 LBS 44
18 LBS 304
19 LBS 304-5

14
1   ML 269/265
2   ML 270/266
3   ML 190/188
4   LBS 37
5   LBS 37
7   LBS 34
8   ML 270/266
9   LBS 38

10 LBS 38
11 ML 445-6/438
12 LBS 39
13 ML 314/309
14 ML 314/309
15 ODL 2:391-2
16 ML 293/288
17 LMW 1:69-70
18 ML 319/314
19 ML 446/439
20 ML 302/298
21 ML 303/298
22 ML 446-439
23 ML 320-21/31?
24 ML 116/112
25 *Damodar* 276

15
1   ML 202/199
2   ML 441/434
3   ML 442/435
4   ML 378-381/
    372-375
5   ML 381/375
6   ML 382/376
7   ML 382/376
8   LBS 22
9   ML 328/323
10 ML 328/323
11 ML 336/330
12 ML 383-4/377-8
13 ML 377/371
14 ML 377/371
15 ML 377/371
16 ML 337/331
17 *Guide* 177-8

16
1   ML 371/364
2   ML 371/364
3   ML 371/365
4   *Damodar* 276
5   ML 392/386
6   ML 357/351
7   *Damodar* 277
8   LBS 43
9   ML 341/335
10 *Damodar* 277
11 ML 338/333
12 ML 24
13 LBS 66-7

14 ML 422/415
15 ML 420/413
16 ML 19
17 ML 422-3/416-7
18 ML 425-6/418-9

17
1   LBS 55
2   LBS 56
3   ODL 3:20
4   ODL 3:21
5   ODL 3:22
6   ODL 2:396-7
7   LMW 1:40
8   ML 456/449
9   ML 456/449

18
1   *Damodar* 200
2   ML 430/423
3   ML 113/110
4   ML 122/119
5   ML 113/110
6   *Damodar* 200
7   ML 431/425
8   ML 431/424
9   ML 432/425
10 *Autobiography*
    40
11 LBS 21-2
12 ML 431/425
13 ML 419/413
14 ML 403/396
15 ML 429/422
16 ML 402/396
17 ML 409/402
18 LBS 73

19
1   *Autobiography*
    40
2   ODL 3:86
3   ML 406/399
4   LBS 37
5   ODL 3:91-2
6   ODL 3:90 &
    LMW 1:42
7   *Autobiography*
    41
8   ML 429/422
9   ML 397/391
10 *Autobiography*
    41

11 ML 397/391
12 ODL 3:93
13 *Theosophy* 33
14 *Theosophy* 36-9
15 ODL 3:96
16 ODL 3:96-7
17 ODL 3:97-8

20
1 SH 210
2 ODL 3:74
3 *Damodar* 58
4 "Report" 30-1
5 "Report" 30
6 "Report" 30
7 *Damodar* 581
8 "Report" 31
9 *Damodar* 580
10 "Report" 32
11 *Damodar* 582
12 *Damodar* 582-3
13 *Damodar* 583
14 "Report" 32
15 *Damodar* 583-4
16 "Report" 33
17 *Damodar* 584
18 "Report" fn. 33
19 *Damodar* 584
20 *Damodar* 584
21 "Report" 34
22 "Report" 34
23 *Damodar* 585
24 "Report"
25 *Damodar* 585-6
26 *Damodar* 586
27 *Damodar* 586
28 "Report" 43
29 "Report" 47
30 *Damodar* 588

21
1 *Damodar* 614
2 ODL 3:108
3 SH 212
4 LMW 1:43
5 *Autobiography* 42
6 ML 360/354
7 *Autobiography* 42

8 *Damodar* 627-8
9 *Early Days* 59
10 *Autobiography* 43
11 *Autobiography* 43
12 *Autobiography* 42; *Early Days* 61
13 ML 355/350; *Autobiography* 42
14 ML 351/345
15 ML 355/350
16 ML 349-40/344
17 *Autobiography* 45
18 ML 460/453

22
1 ODL 3:166
2 ODL 3:173
3 ODL 3:178
4 SH 203
5 ODL 3:175
6 ODL 3:179
7 ODL 3:181
8 ODL 3:181
9 *Autobiography* 46
10 *Autobiography* 46
11 *Daylight* 165
12 ML 322/317
13 ML 322/317
14 ODL 3:182
15 *Daylight* 165
16 *Daylight* 165
17 *Autobiography* 47-8
18 ODL 3:183
19 *Daylight* 168
20 ODL 3:187
21 ODL 3:188
22 ODL 3:187
23 ODl 3:185
24 ODL 3:186
25 ODL 3:186
26 ODL 3:186-7
27 ODL 3:189-90

23
1 LBS 77

2 *Hammer* 200
3 *Daylight* 170; LBS 122
4 *Damodar* 617
5 *Damodar* 617-18
6 *Damodar* 618-19
7 ML 362/356: *Damodar* 616
8 *Hammer* 200
9 *Hamm34 202*
10 *Daylight* 171
11 LBS 94
12 Cf. *Autobiography* 53
13 *Daylight* 172
14 *Daylight* 171
15 ODL 3:188
16 ODL 3:188
17 LBS 115
18 LBS 115
19 SH 213
20 ODL 3:199
21 ODL 3:200
22 ODL 3:205-6
23 ODL 3:207
24 ODL 3:207
25 ODL 3:207
26 ODL 3:208-9
27 ODL 3:209
28 ODL 3:209
29 ODL 3:214
30 ODL 3:217
31 ODL 3:259
32 ODL 3:220
33 ODL 3:222
34 ODL 3:222-25

24
1 ML 358/352
2 ML 359/353
3 ML 362/356
4 LBS 95-6
5 ML 365-359
6 ML 366/360
7 ML 488/481
8 *Autobiography* 36
9 *Early Days* 83-4
10 *Early Days* 84
11 *Early Days* 72
12 *Early Days* 71-2

13 LBS 105
14 LBS 102, 105

Epilogue
1 LBS 135
2 LBS 136
3 *Early Days* 84
4 *Damodar* 279
5 *Early Days* 69
6 *Reminiscences* 25
7 *Reminiscences* 24-7
8 *Reminiscences* 60

9 *Reminiscences* 61-2
10 ODL 3:437
11 ODL 4:64-5
12 *Damodar* 639
13 *Damodar* 539
14 *Early Days* 87
15 *Early Days* 87
16 *Early Days* 88-9
17 *Autobiography* 54, 51
18 *Autobiography* 51
19 *Autobiography* 51
20 *Autobiography* 53

21 *Autobiography* 59
22 *Autobiography* 54
23 *Early Days* 93
24 *Autobiography* 60
25 *Early Days* 92-3
26 *Damodar* 281
27 *Early Days* 113
28 *Early Days* 97, 112
29 *Autobiography* 59
30 *Early Days* 116
31 *Early Days* 117
32 *Damodar* 284

Appendix

Chronology — *The Mahatma Letters*

(Many dates are approximate or estimated. In most instances the date given is the date of receipt of the letter. Occasionally an incorrect date of receipt has been noted on the letter; in such instances the date has been determined by the context.)

Chr. No.	ML No.	Page 2nd ed.	Page 3rd ed.	Date
				1880
1	1	1	1	Oct. 17
2	2	6	6	Oct. 19
3A	3A	10	10	Oct. 20
3B	3B	10	10	Oct. 20
3C	3C	11	11	Oct. 20
4	143	488	481	Oct. 27
5	4	11	11	Nov. 3
6	126	454	447	Nov. 3
		(This is a postscript to ML-4)		
7	106	443	436	Nov.
8	99	435	428	Nov. 20
9	98	434	427	Nov.
10	5	17	17	Nov. 26
11	28	207	205	Fall
12	6	22	22	Dec. 10
13	7	25	25	Jan. 3, 1881
14A	142A	486	479	Feb.
14B	142B	488	481	Feb.
15	8	26	26	Feb. 20
16	107	444	436	Mar. 1
17	31	240	237	Mar. 26
18	9	38	38	July 5
19	121	452	445	July 11
20	49	280	276	Aug. 5
21	27	204	202	Fall
22	26	203	201	Fall
23	104	440	433	Oct.
24	71	374	367	Fall
25	73	375	368	Oct.
26	102	439	432	Oct.
27	101	439	431	Oct.
28	74	375	369	Oct.
29	29	217	215	Oct.
30	36	248	244	Oct. 23
31	134	461	453	Nov. 4
32	40	254	251	Nov.

Chr. No.	ML No.	Page 2nd ed.	Page 3rd ed.	Date
33	114	449	442	Nov.
34	38	250	247	Dec. 10
35	39	253	249	Dec.
36	41	256	252	Dec.
37	37	248	245	Jan. 1882
38	90	412	406	Jan.
39	115	449	442	Jan.
40	108	444	437	Jan.
41	109	444	437	Jan.
42	43	258	255	Jan.
43	42	257	253	Jan.
44	13	70	70	Jan.
45	44	263	259	Feb.
46	12	66	66	Feb.
47	45	264	260	Feb.
48	47	271	267	Mar. 3
49	48	273	269	Mar. 3
50	88	410	404	Mar. 11
51	120	452	444	Mar.
52	144	488	481	Mar. 14
53	136	464	457	Mar.
54	35	246	242	Mar. 18
55	89	410	404	Mar. 24
56	100	438	431	Mar.
57	122	452	445	Apr.
58	130	457	450	May
59	132	459	452	June
60	76	376	369	June
61	17	117	113	June
62	18	119	115	June
63	95	429	423	June
64	131	458	451	June
65	11	59	59	June
66	14	78	77	July
67	15	88	87	July
68	16	99	97	July
69	69	373	366	July
70A	20A	123	120	July
70B	20B	125	121	July
70C	20C	127	123	July
71	19	122	119	Aug. 12
72	127	455	447	Aug. 13
73	113	448	441	Aug.
74	30	228	225	Aug.
75	53	294	290	Aug.
76	21	134	131	Aug.
77	50	286	282	Aug.
78	51	287	283	Aug.
79	116	450	443	Aug.
80	118	450	443	Fall
81	52	288	284	Fall

Chr. No.	ML No.	Page 2nd ed.	Page 3rd ed.	Date
82	32	242	239	Fall
83	125	453	446	Fall
84	111	446	439	Sept.
85A	24A	178	175	Sept.
85B	24B	180	177	Sept.
86	112	447	440	Sept.
87	34	245	242	Fall
88	10	52	52	Fall
89	46	268	264	Fall
90	22	137	133	Oct.
91	110	445	437	Oct.
92	54	302	298	Oct.
92A	23A	144	141	Oct.
93B	23B	149	145	Oct.
94	117	450	443	Oct.
95	72	374	368	Nov.
96	92	419	413	Nov.
97	70	373	367	Dec.
98	105	441	434	Dec.
99	78	378	372	Dec.
100	79	382	376	Dec.
101	57	327	322	Jan. 6, 1883
102	56	325	320	Jan.
103A	91A	415	409	Jan.
103B	91B	416	409	Jan.
104	80	383	377	Jan. or Feb.
105	25	191	188	Feb. 2
106	103	440	432	Feb.
107	77	377	371	Mar.
108	58	336	331	Mar.
109	119	451	444	Mar.
110	67	371	364	Mar.
111	59	338	333	July
112	81	383	377	July
113	82	387	381	Aug.
114	83	393	387	Sept.
115	128	456	449	Nov.
116	129	456	449	Nov.
117	93	420	413	Dec.
118	96	431	424	Dec.
119	86	403	376	Jan. 1884
120	85	398	391	Jan.
121	84	397	391	Jan.
122	87	406	399	Jan.
123	68	372	366	Feb.
124	94	429	422	Feb.
125	61	349	344	Apr.
126	62	351	345	July
127	133	460	453	July
128	63	356	350	Summer
129	60	349	343	Sept.

130	55	322	317	Oct.
131	66	366	360	Oct.
132	135	464	457	Oct.
133	137	467	459	Nov.
134	64	358	352	Nov.
135	138	468	460	Mar. 1885
136	65	362	356	Mar. or April
137	97	433	426	Fall
138	145	488	481	Fall
139	140	478	470	Jan. 1886
140	141	482	474	Mar.
141	139	475	468	Mar.

Letters for which dates cannot be determined

A	33	244	241
B	75	375	369
C	124	453	446
D	123	453	446

Cross Reference

ML	Chron.	Page 2nd ed.	3rd ed.
1	1	1	1
2	2	6	6
3A	3A	10	10
3B	3B	10	10
3C	3C	11	11
4	5	11	11
5	10	17	17
6	12	22	22
7	13	25	25
8	15	26	26
9	18	38	38
10	88	52	52
11	65	59	59
12	46	66	66
13	44	70	70
14	66	77	78
15	67	88	87
16	68	99	97
17	61	117	113
18	62	119	115
19	71	122	119
20A	70A	123	120

ML	Chron.	Page 2nd ed.	3rd ed.
20B	70B	125	121
20C	70C	127	123
21	76	134	131
22	90	137	133
23A	93A	144	141
23B	93B	149	145
24A	85A	178	175
24B	85B	180	177
25	105	191	188
26	22	203	201
27	21	204	202
28	11	207	205
29	29	217	215
30	74	228	225
31	17	240	237
32	82	242	239
33	A	244	241
34	87	245	242
35	54	246	242
36	30	248	244
37	37	248	245
38	34	250	247
39	35	253	249
40	32	254	251
41	36	256	252
42	43	257	253
43	42	258	255
44	45	263	259
45	47	264	260
46	89	268	264
47	48	271	267
48	49	273	269
49	20	280	276
50	77	286	282
51	78	287	283
52	81	288	284
53	75	294	290
54	92	302	298
55	130	322	317
56	102	325	320
57	101	327	322
58	108	336	331
59	111	338	333
60	129	349	343
61	125	349	344
62	126	351	345
63	128	356	350
64	134	358	352
65	136	362	356
66	131	366	360

ML	Chron.	Page 2nd ed.	3rd ed.
67	110	371	364
68	123	372	366
69	69	373	366
70	97	373	367
71	24	374	367
72	95	374	368
73	25	375	368
74	28	375	369
75	B	375	369
76	60	376	369
77	107	377	371
78	99	378	372
79	100	382	376
80	104	383	377
81	112	383	377
82	113	387	381
83	114	393	387
84	121	397	391
85	120	398	391
86	119	403	396
87	122	406	399
88	50	410	404
89	55	410	404
90	38	412	406
91A	103A	415	409
91B	103B	416	409
92	96	419	413
93	117	420	413
94	124	429	422
95	63	429	423
96	118	431	424
97	137	433	426
98	9	434	427
99	8	435	428
100	56	438	431
101	27	439	431
102	26	432	439
103	106	440	432
104	23	440	433
105	98	441	434
106	7	443	436
107	16	444	436
108	40	444	437
109	41	444	437
110	91	445	437
111	84	446	439
112	86	447	440
113	73	448	441
114	33	449	442
115	39	449	442

ML	Chron.	Page 2nd ed.	3rd ed.
116	79	450	443
117	94	450	443
118	80	450	443
119	109	451	444
120	51	452	444
121	19	452	445
122	57	452	445
123	C	453	446
124	D	453	446
125	83	453	446
126	6	454	447
127	72	455	447
128	115	456	449
129	116	456	449
130	58	457	450
131	64	458	451
132	59	459	452
133	127	460	453
134	31	461	454
135	132	464	457
136	53	464	457
137	133	467	459
138	135	468	460
139	141	475	468
140	139	478	470
141	140	482	474
142A	14A	486	479
142B	14B	488	481
143	4	488	481
144	52	488	481
145	138	488	481

The complete text of The Mahatma Letters to A.P. Sinnett *is available in a clothbound edition as is* A Readers Guide to the Mahatma Letters. *These books are invaluable to anyone interested in learning more about the unique and controversial correspondence between A.P. Sinnett and the Mahatmas during the late nineteenth century.*

Available from:
Quest Books
306 West Geneva Road
Wheaton, Illinois 60187